Operational Risk

Operational Risk

Modeling Analytics

Harry H. Panjer

A JOHN WILEY & SONS, INC., PUBLICATION

Library of Congress Cataloging-in-Publication Data:

Panjer, Harry H.
    Operational risk : modeling analytics / Harry H. Panjer.
        p. cm.
    Includes bibliographical references and index.
    ISBN-13 978-0-471-76089-4
    ISBN-10 0-471-76089-7
    1. Risk management.   I. Title.

    HD61.P36 2006
    658.15'5—dc22   2006044261

Printed in the United States of America.

10 9 8 7 6 5 4 3 2

Contents

Preface

This book is is designed for the risk analyst who wishes to better understand the mathematical models and methods used in the management of operational risk in the banking and insurance sectors. Many of the techniques in this book are more generally applicable to a wide range of risks. However, each sector has its unique characteristics, its own data sources, and its own risk migation and management strategies. Other major risk classes in the banking sector include credit risk and market risk. In addition to these, the insurance sector also assumes the risk in the insurance contracts that it sells. The product risk in the insurance sector may dominate all other risk classes.

This book is organized around the principle that much the analysis of operational risk consists of the collection of data and the building of mathematical models to describe risk. I have not assumed that the reader has any substantial knowledge of operational risk terminology or of mathematical statistics. However, the book is more challenging technically than some other books on the topic of operational risk but less challenging than others that focus on risk mathematics. This is intentional. The purpose of the book is to provide detailed analytical tools for the practicing risk analyst as well as serving as a text for a university course.

This book could serve as a text at the senior undergraduate or first-year graduate level for a course of one semester for students with a reasonable background in statistics, because many sections of the book can be covered rapidly. Without a moderate background in statistics, students will require two semesters to cover the material in this book. For chapters involving numerical computations, there are many exercises for students to practice and reinforce concepts in the text.

Many of the concepts in this book have been developed in the insurance field, where the modeling and management of risk is a core activity. This book is built on previous books by this author along with co-authors, in particular *Loss Distributions* [53], *Insurance Risk Models* [93], and two editions of *Loss Models: From Data to Decisions* [69].

H. H. PANJER

Acknowledgments

I thoroughly enjoyed writing this book. I was very much inspired by the dramatic level of growth of interest in modeling and managing operational risk in the banking and insurance sectors. In particular, many emerging methods and models that have appeared in the operational risk literature are directly related to the content of the book, *Loss Models: From Data to Decisions* [69], which I coauthored with Stuart Klugman and Gordon Willmot. That book was focused on applications in the insurance sector. They have been very generous in allowing to use large parts of that book in modified form in the present book.

I am also indebted to two students, Yixi Shi and Shuyin Mai who assisted in numerous technical aspects of producing this book. And finally, thanks to my wife Joanne Coyle, who tolerated my many weekends and evenings at the office.

H.H.P.

Part I

Introduction to operational risk modeling

1

Operational risk

Anything that can go wrong will go wrong.

—Murphy

1.1   INTRODUCTION

Operational risk has only in recent years been identified as something that should be actively measured and managed by a company in order to meet its objectives for stakeholders, including shareholders, customers, and management. These objectives include future survival of the company, avoidance of downgrades by rating agencies and remaining solvent for many years to come. Operational risk is becoming a major part of corporate governance of companies, especially in the financial services industry. This industry includes both banks and insurance companies, although they have somewhat different historical cultures in most countries. More recently in other fields such as energy, where trading and hedging activity mirrors similar activity in the financial services industry, operational risk is being recognized as a vital part of a broader enterprise risk management framework.

   The definition of operational risk has not yet been universally agreed upon. In very general terms, operational risk refers to "risk" associated with the "operations" of an organization. "Risk" is not defined very specifically, nor is "operations." Generally, the term "risk" refers to the possibility of things going wrong, or the chances of things going wrong, or the possible consequences of things that can go wrong. "Operations" refers to the various functions of the organization (usually a company such as a bank or insurance company) in conducting its business. It does not refer specifically to the products or services provided by the company. In banking, operational risk does not include the risk of losing money as a result of normal banking activities such as investing, trading, or lending except to the extent that operational activities affect those normal activities. An example of such an operational risk in banking is fraudulent activity, such as unauthorized lending where a loan officer ignores rules, or rogue trading in which a trader is involved in trading activity beyond limits of authorization. The well-known classic example of a rogue trader is Nick Leeson, whose activities resulted in the failure of Barings Bank, leading to its takeover by the ING financial services conglomerate.

operational risk is generic in nature. The operational risk concept applies to organizations of all types. However, the specifics of operational risk will vary from company to company depending on the individual characteristics of the company. For example, a manufacturer will be exposed to somewhat different operational risks than a bank or an insurance company, but many are the same. The risk of shutdown of the operations of a company because of IT failure, flooding, or an earthquake exists for any company. While the principles of operational risk modeling and management apply to all types of organization, in this book we will look at operational risk from the vantage point of a financial institution, such as a bank or insurance company.

Measurement and modeling of risk associated with operations for the financial sector began in the banking industry. Operational risk is one of several categories of risk used in enterprise risk management (ERM). ERM involves all types of risk faced by a company. Operational risk is one part only.

Many financial institutions have incorporated ERM into a new governance paradigm in which risk exposure is better understood and managed. The responsibility for the risk management function in a company often falls under the title of chief risk officer (CRO), a title first held by James Lam in the 1990s [72]. The CRO is responsible for the entire ERM process of the company in all its business units. Within the ERM process are processes for each risk category. Within the operational risk category, the responsibilities include:

> Developing operational risk policies and internal standards
> Controlling the operational risk self-assessment in each business unit
> Describing and modeling all internal processes
> Testing all processes for possible weaknesses
> Developing operational risk technology
> Developing key risk indicators
> Planning the management of major business disruptions
> Evaluating the risk associated with outsourcing operations
> Maintaining a database of operational risk incidents
> Developing metrics for operational risk exposure
> Developing metrics for effectiveness of risk controls
> Modeling losses using frequency and severity

    Modeling potential losses using statistical tools

    Calculating economic capital required to support operational risk

This book is primarily concerned with the last three items in this list.

In the banking sector, risks are generally described to be part of market risk, credit risk, or operational risk. In carrying out normal banking activities associated with investment in bonds issued by other companies, a loss in value due to overall interest rate changes in the market place is considered market risk, a loss in value due to a downgrade or bankruptcy of the issuer is a credit risk, but a loss due to an execution error, such as an error in timing or delivery of a trade, by the bank is an operational error.

At the time of writing this book, market and credit risk are much more well developed than operational risk. One of the reasons for this is the general dearth of publicly available operational risk data. This is in direct contrast to market risk and credit risk, for which data are widely available, particularly for the shares and bonds (and the related derivative products) of publicly traded companies. In the very recent past, the situation has changed as a result of gathering and sharing of historical data on operational risk losses. At the time of writing of this book, many organizations are building historical databases on past operational events in addition to building systems for the reporting and recording of new operational risk events as they occur. One major challenge, which is addressed later in this book, is how to combine data from several companies or the industry as a whole in building a model for a single company. This problem is sometimes called "scaling" because different companies are of different sizes and are therefore subject to risks of different sizes.

Although operational risk was originally defined to capture all sources of risk other than market and credit risk, several more specific definitions of operational risk have become well-known. In a paper published in 1998, the Basel Committee [9] on Banking Supervision (BCBS) identified the most important aspects of operational risk as relating to breakdowns in internal control and corporate governance. Effective internal controls should result in minimizing internal errors, fraud by staff, and failures to execute obligations in a timely manner. Failure of corporate governance can lead to poor internal controls.

The British Bankers Association [18] defined risk as the "risk associated with human error, inadequate procedures and control, fraudulent criminal activities; the risks caused by technological shortcomings, system breakdowns; all risks which are not "banking" and arise from business decisions as competitive action, pricing, etc.; legal risk and risk to business relationships, failure to meet regulatory requirements or an adverse impact on the bank's reputation; "external factors" including natural disasters, terrorist attacks and fraudulent activity, etc."

This all-encompassing definition was narrowed somewhat in the definition provided by the Basel Committee. In its consultative document on a capital adequacy framework [10] and its subsequent document on operational risk

[11], the BCBS defined operational risk as "the risk of losses resulting from inadequate or failed internal processes, people and systems or from external events." It includes strategic, reputational risk and systemic risks.

In its monograph dealing with capital requirements for insurance companies, the International Actuarial Association (IAA) [60] adopted the Basel Committee definition. It further noted that the definition is intended to include legal risks but exclude strategic, reputational risk and systemic risks. There remains some controversy over these items. Is a strategic decision that is later found to be in error really an operational risk? Is a loss in reputation an operational risk or simply the result of an operational risk event?

Operational risk in the banking sector is believed to represent about 30% of the total risk assumed by a bank. This contrasts with 60% for credit risk , 5% for market risks, and 5% for remaining miscellaneous risks. It is likely that the operational risk is proportionately smaller in the insurance sector. There have been some well-known significant operational losses in the insurance sector. The "misselling" of pension annuity products in the UK in the 1990s was a direct result of a lack of controls on the way in which the products were represented to potential customers.

It should be noted that losses from both internal and external events are included in the definition of operational risk. Internal events are events that result from the failure of some process or system operated by the organization. External events are those whose occurrence cannot be controlled by the company. The company can only mitigate the impact of these external events. It cannot prevent an earthquake, but it can ensure that its main computers are in an earthquake-proof building. In contrast, the occurrence of internal events is directly under the control of the company. Its risk management strategies can address both minimizing the occurrence of the event and mitigating the impact of the event when it occurs.

1.1.1 Basel II - General

The Basel Committee (in its "Basel II" framework) has been working on developing a framework for the determination of minimum capital requirements for banks. Included in the minimum capital requirement to be implemented in 2006 or later is a capital charge for operational risk. The minimum capital requirement falls under Pillar I of a three-pillar concept. The remaining two pillars relate to the supervisory process and market conduct. In this book, we shall focus on this first pillar only by addressing the question of how to probabilistically model losses arising from operational risk events. However, it is useful to understand the entire Basel II framework.

Pillar I: Minimum capital requirements There are three fundamental elements in the minimum capital requirement for regulatory purposes: the definition of regulatory capital, risk-weighted assets, and the minimum ratio of capital to risk-weighted assets. Risks are categorized into five categories:

1. credit risk
2. market risk
3. operational risk
4. liquidity risk
5. legal risk

Explicit and separate minimum capital requirements for operational risk have been added to the Basel II framework. Specifically for operational risk, there is a range of options for determining minimum regulatory capital requirements including building internal models of the company's operational risk profile. However, such minimum capital requirements will need to be supported by a robust implementation of the second and third pillars.

Pillar II: Supervisory review process   The second pillar focuses on the prudential supervision by regulatory authorities of banks' capital adequacy as well as the banks' internal risk management systems. There are four key principles under Pillar II:

1. Banks should have a process for assessing their overall capital adequacy in relation to their risk profile and a strategy for maintaining their capital levels. This requires: i) strong board and management oversight; ii) sound capital assessment; iii) a comprehensive system for assessment of risks; iv) ongoing monitoring and reporting; and v) internal control review.
2. Supervisors should review and evaluate banks' internal capital adequacy assessments and strategies, as well as their ability to monitor and ensure their compliance with regulatory capital ratios. Supervisors should be able to take action when they are not satisfied with the results of this process.
3. Supervisors should expect banks to operate above the minimum capital ratios and should have the ability to require banks to hold capital in excess of the minimum.
4. Supervisors should seek to intervene at an early stage to prevent capital from falling below the minimum levels required to support the risk characteristics of a particular bank and should require rapid remedial action if capital is not maintained or restored.

For operational risk, this means that banks must monitor all operational risk events and have internal control processes in place that are transparent to banking supervisors. This will assist both banks and supervisors to understand past and potential future areas of losses from operational risk events. This better understanding of operational risk should have a direct effect on the operational risk by identifying areas where the bank can reduce both the frequency and the severity of those events.

Pillar III: Market discipline   The objective of Pillar III is to encourage market discipline by developing a set of disclosure requirements that will allow market participants to assess key pieces of information on the scope of application, capital, risk exposures, risk assessment processes, and hence the capital adequacy of the institution. These are especially useful when banks are given the authority to use bank-specific internal models in assessing their own risk profiles.

1.1.2   Basel II - Operational risk

Under Basel II, banks will be allowed to chose from three approaches: the basic indicator approach, the standardized approach, and the advanced measurement approach (AMA). Banks are encouraged to move along the spectrum of methods as they develop the capabilities to do more advanced modeling. Under the basic indicator approach for operational risk, banks are required to hold a flat percentage (15%) of positive gross income over the past three years. Under the standardized approach, banks' activities are divided into eight business lines: i) corporate finance, ii) trading and sales, iii) retail banking, iv) commercial banking, v) payment and settlement, vi) agency services, vii) asset management, and viii) retail brokerage. A flat percentage, ranging from 12% to 18%, is applied to the three-year average positive gross income for each business line. The minimum capital is the sum over all business lines. Both the basic indicator approach and the standardized approach are relatively crude methods that do not in any way allow banks to take credit for doing a good job in mitigating operational risk.

Under the AMA, banks are allowed to develop sophisticated internal models of the actual risks of the company including the interactions between them and any risk mitigation strategies used by the company. However, the bank is required to make significant investment in the management of operational risk. Specifically, i) a bank's board of directors and senior management must be actively involved in the oversight of the operational risk framework, ii) its operational risk management system must be conceptually sound and must be implemented with integrity, and iii) it must devote sufficient resources to the use of the AMA in the major business lines as well as in the control and audit areas.

Before full implementation, banks will be required to demonstrate that their systems are credible and appropriate by reasonably estimating unexpected losses based on the combined use of internal and relevant external loss data, scenario analysis and bank-specific environment and internal control factors. Furthermore, the bank must have an independent operational risk management function that is responsible for designing and implementing the bank's risk operational management framework. The bank's internal operational risk management system must be closely integrated into the day-to-day risk management processes of the bank. There must be regular reporting of operational risk exposures and loss experience to business unit management, senior management, and the board of directors. The bank's operational risk management system must be well documented and reviewed regularly by internal or external auditors.

On the quantitative requirements for using the AMA approach, the Basel Committee [12] states:

> *Given the continuing evolution of analytical approaches for operational risk, the Committee is not specifying the approach or distributional assumptions used to generate the operational risk measure for regulatory capital purposes. However, a bank must be able to demonstrate that its approach captures potentially severe "tail" loss events. Whatever approach is used, a bank must demonstrate that its operational risk measure meets a soundness standard comparable to that of the internal ratings-based approach for credit risk, (i.e. comparable to a one-year holding period and a 99.9th percentile confidence interval).*
>
> *The Committee recognises that the AMA soundness standard provides significant flexibility to banks in the development of an operational risk measurement and management system. However, in the development of these systems, banks must have and maintain rigorous procedures for operational risk model development and independent model validation. Prior to implementation, the Committee will review evolving industry practices regarding credible and consistent estimates of potential operational losses. It will also review accumulated data, and the level of capital requirements estimated by the AMA, and may refine its proposals if appropriate.*

This book will focus on probabilistic models and statistical tools that can be used for building the internal models of operational risk that can be used under the AMA by a bank or an insurance company.

In the same document, the Basel Committee goes on to state:

> *A bank's risk measurement system must be sufficiently "granular" to capture the major drivers of operational risk affecting the shape of the tail of the loss estimates.*

This means that any model acceptable for the AMA must be very detailed and be sensitive to the possibility of extreme events. The shape of the tail of a loss distribution determines the likelihood of large losses. These need to be well understood because a single large loss can have a significant impact on a company. The issue of different tails of distributions is addressed throughout this book.

Continuing in the same document, the Committee states:

> *Risk measures for different operational risk estimates must be added for purposes of calculating the regulatory minimum capital requirement. However, the bank may be permitted to use internally determined correlations in operational risk losses across individual operational risk estimates, provided it can demonstrate to the satisfaction of the national supervisor that its systems for determining correlations are sound, implemented with integrity, and take into account the uncertainty surrounding any such correlation estimates (particularly in periods of stress). The*

> *bank must validate its correlation assumptions using appropriate quantitative and qualitative techniques.*

This means that it is important to understand that there may be a possibility of diversification between operational risks. However, it is recognized that this may not be possible "in periods of stress," that is, in periods where everything seems to be going wrong. This idea can be captured through tail correlation, which is covered later in this book.

The Basel Committee document goes on to discuss data requirements for an internal risk measurement system. Internal loss data are crucial for the credible modeling of an organization's operational risk profile.

> *Banks must track internal loss data according to the criteria set out in this section. The tracking of internal loss event data is an essential prerequisite to the development and functioning of a credible operational risk measurement system. Internal loss data is crucial for tying a bank's risk estimates to its actual loss experience. This can be achieved in a number of ways, including using internal loss data as the foundation of empirical risk estimates, as a means of validating the inputs and outputs of the bank's risk measurement system, or as the link between loss experience and risk management and control decisions.*
>
> *Internal loss data is most relevant when it is clearly linked to a bank's current business activities, technological processes and risk management procedures. Therefore, a bank must have documented procedures for assessing the on-going relevance of historical loss data, including those situations in which judgement overrides, scaling, or other adjustments may be used, to what extent they may be used and who is authorised to make such decisions.*
>
> *Internally generated operational risk measures used for regulatory capital purposes must be based on a minimum five-year observation period of internal loss data, whether the internal loss data is used directly to build the loss measure or to validate it. When the bank first moves to the AMA, a three-year historical data window is acceptable ....*

Thus building a loss data history is imperative to moving to an AMA for modeling risk capital. A bank's internal loss collection processes must meet the certain standards established by the Committee. The Committee is also very explicit about what data should be collected:

> *A bank's internal loss data must be comprehensive in that it captures all material activities and exposures from all appropriate subsystems and geographic locations. A bank must be able to justify that any excluded activities or exposures, both individually and in combination, would not have a material impact on the overall risk estimates. A bank must have an appropriate de minimis gross loss threshold for internal loss data collection, for example 10,000 Euros. The appropriate threshold may vary somewhat between banks, and within a bank across business lines and/or event types. However, particular thresholds should be broadly consistent with those used by peer banks.*

The concept of a threshold becomes very important in the statistical analysis of operational risk losses. In statistical terms, ignoring small losses is called truncation of the data, in particular left truncation. It is important to know the truncation threshold for each recorded loss, because the threshold could be changed over time, or it could be different for different types of losses. It is particularly important when combining data from different banks into a single industry database or when combining external data with a bank's own data. The statistical issue of truncation will be dealt with thoroughly in this book. External data can be combined with bank data in a rigorous systematic way.

> *A bank's operational risk measurement system must use relevant external data (either public data and/or pooled industry data), especially when there is reason to believe that the bank is exposed to infrequent, yet potentially severe, losses. These external data should include data on actual loss amounts, information on the scale of business operations where the event occurred, information on the causes and circumstances of the loss events, or other information that would help in assessing the relevance of the loss event for other banks. A bank must have a systematic process for determining the situations for which external data must be used and the methodologies used to incorporate the data (e.g. scaling, qualitative adjustments, or informing the development of improved scenario analysis). The conditions and practices for external data use must be regularly reviewed, documented, and subject to periodic independent review.*

1.2   OPERATIONAL RISK IN INSURANCE

On the insurance side of the financial services industry, the development of capital requirements for operational risk has significantly lagged the developments in the banking sector. Insurers deal with risk and the management of risk on a day-to-day basis. However, this risk is primarily the risk inherent in the insurance contracts assumed by the insurer. In the jargon of risk management this type of risk is "business risk." As a business that is less transaction-oriented and less trading-oriented than banks, insurance companies have paid less attention to operational risk. But this is changing. At the global level, the International Association of Insurance Supervisors (IAIS) is in the process of developing a parallel but somewhat similar framework for the overall regulation of insurance. Its early work suggests three blocks of issues and a set of eight principles or "cornerstones" that will result in guidance to insurance companies. The three blocks of issues roughly parallel the three pillars of Basel II. The fifth principle dealing with absorption of losses states, "Capital requirements are needed to absorb losses that can occur from technical and other risks." The discussion of this principle refers directly to operational risk. The International Actuarial Association (IAA) book [60] reflects early work conducted by the IAA as a contribution to the IAIS effort in developing the regulatory framework.

Within Europe, the European Commission has initiated a "Solvency II" project for insurance regulation that also parallels Basel II but is applicable to European insurers. What we refer to as operational risks are somewhat covered by the term "risks that are difficult to quantify or to measure a priori." These include failings of management, major business decision risk, and failings in underwriting and claims handling. This list is rather short and misses some other key operational risks associated with failings in other operational areas such as sales. Furthermore, risk of external events has not been considered. At the time of writing this book, because of the dearth of available data and other difficulties in definition and measurement, operational risk is to be treated within the second pillar (governance process and controls) under Solvency II. However, as databases are developed, it is expected that Pillar I-type measurement and modeling will become the norm. Some insurance-related organizations are building data bases that make use of data coming directly from insured losses covering events that might be considered operational risks. The IAA book [60] recommends that operational risk should ultimately be handled with a Basel II approach under the first pillar. However, it would be reasonable to use a second pillar approach until insurance regulators, the industry, and the actuarial profession develop definitions and methods of measurement necessary for a first pillar approach.

Some recent external operational risk events in the US have pointed North American insurers in the direction of more active risk management (second pillar). The concentration of insurance brokerage employees in the World Trade Center on September 11, 2001 identified a personnel concentration risk to insurers. Extensive power blackouts in 2003 tested companies' computer systems and business continuity plans. The SARS epidemic in 2004 tested the abilities of banks and insurers in Hong Kong to continue operations as the movement of employees was severely restricted.

In this book, we will not try to define the various types of operational risk events that must be considered. This needs to be done at some point by every company, by industry groups, and by regulators. However those events are defined, in this book we will focus on modeling the chances that the event will occur and the consequences of the occurrence of the event.

1.3 THE ANALYSIS OF OPERATIONAL RISK

Various definitions of operational risk refer to events. The only events that are interesting to us from the point of view of operational risk are those that result in a loss. Inconsequential events are of no interest and as such are not treated as events for the purpose of the analysis of risk. As will be pointed out later in this and later chapters, the definition of an event is critical to any analysis because the definition affects how we count the events.

In order to measure the impact of operational risk, it seems natural to consider both how many events might occur and the potential impact of each of those events. This approach to analysis is called a frequency/severity approach. This approach is commonly used in studies of losses in the insurance industry. The approach requires the risk analyst to separate the "count" or frequency of losses from the "impact" or severity of the losses. This is especially natural when the severity (per loss) does not depend on the number of losses, as is commonly assumed in modeling most risks. Consider, for example, errors made by automatic banking machines in dispensing money. An operational error can occur if the machine dispenses two bills that stick together as one bill. The number of errors increases as the number of machines increase, but the loss per loss event is unaffected.

Also for many types of losses, the severity or size of individual losses may be expected to increase over time as a result of normal inflationary growth. Similarly, expected frequency also increases as the number of exposure units (customers, employees, transactions, etc.) increases.

Risk managers use a variety of tools to assess and manage risk exposure. Frequency and severity are usually separately addressed in risk management strategies. Process control of internal processes can be used to minimize the frequency of risks associated with internal procedures. The development of internal policy and procedure manuals assists in defining what is acceptable activity and, more importantly, what is not acceptable activity. Process control systems, such as "six sigma" methodologies, can be employed to study and improve the performance of high-frequency transactions. Risk managers can also employ methods to control the severity of operational loss. For example, most organizations purchase directors and officers liability insurance coverage to protect against actions taken against directors and officers. Similarly, the company may purchase business interruption insurance to protect it against loss as a result of external events such as power grid failure (as occurred in the US and Canada in 2003), terrorist attack (as occurred in the US in 2001), or a hurricane (as occurs frequently in the US). Insurance usually carries with it a deductible so that a portion of the risk is still retained (or self-insured) by the company.

Risk managers will measure all risks consistently but may add special procedures for very large risks, often called "jumbo" risks. This reflects the different approaches to risks with different frequency/severity profiles. Risks can be classified according to whether the frequency is high or low and whether the severity is high or low. Here the terms "high" and "low" are used in a purely relative sense, that is, relative to other risks or, perhaps, relative to the size of the company. In general, we shall refer to the spectrum running from high-frequency-low-severity (HFLS) to low-frequency-high-severity (LFHS). It is not necessary to discuss high-frequency-high-severity risk because a history of this type of risk will certainly put a company out of business! Similarly, low-frequency-low-severity risk has little potential impact.

Model-based frequency/severity modeling is a main focus of this book. Because senior management (and regulators, rating agencies, and shareholders) are interested in the potential overall impact, frequency and severity modeling are combined in the development of "aggregate" loss models. Frequency and severity modeling is done the same way for both LFHS and HFLS situations, at least in principle. However, LFHS will often attract additional analysis, that is, there will be serious analysis of the single possible big events that can bring down (or at least impair) the company. The next section discusses the model-based approach to operation risk management. Later, Chapter 7 will deal with possible extreme losses.

Model-based approaches to operational risk require significant amounts of data in order to calibrate the models to provide realistic outcomes. In the banking sector, a number of databases have been developed to help understand the frequency and severity of various types of operational risk. On the insurance side, at the time of preparation of this book, some organizations have begun to build databases. However it will be some time before their databases are broadly usable for calibrating models.

The remainder of this book is premised on the assumption that data will be available for the risk analyst. The tools in this book come mainly from the insurance industry, where actuaries have been involved in modeling the risk assumed by insurers in the insurance contracts that they sell.

1.4   THE MODEL-BASED APPROACH

The model-based approach involves the building of a mathematical model that can be used to describe, forecast, or predict operational loss costs or to determine the amount of capital necessary to absorb operational losses with a high probability. The results of the model can be used to better understand the company's exposure to operational risk, and the potential impact on the company of various possible mitigation and management strategies.

A model is a simplified mathematical description that is constructed based on the knowledge and experience of the risk analyst combined with data from the past. The data guide the analyst in selecting the form of the model as well as in calibrating the parameters in the model.

Any model provides a balance between simplicity and conformity to the available data. Simplicity is measured in terms of such things as the number of unknown parameters; the fewer the simpler. Conformity to data (or "fit") is measured in terms of the discrepancy between the data and the model or, equivalently, how well the model fits the data.

There are many models and many models with the same level of complexity; for example, the same number of parameters. Model selection requires consideration of both the mathematical form of the model and the number of parameters in the model. Model selection is based on an appropriate balance between the two criteria, namely, fit and simplicity. Appropriateness may depend on the specific purpose of the model.

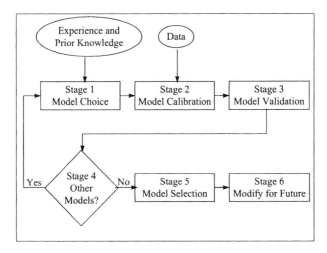

Fig. 1.1 The modeling process

1.4.1 The modeling process

The modeling process is illustrated in Figure 1.1, which describes six stages.

Stage 1 One or more models are selected based on the risk analyst's prior knowledge and experience and possibly on the nature and form of available data. In studies of the size of operational risk losses, a set of statistical distributions, such as lognormal, gamma, or Weibull, may be chosen.

Stage 2 The model is calibrated based on available data. In studies of operational losses, the data may be information about each of a set of actual losses. The model is calibrated by estimation of parameters based on the available data.

Stage 3 The calibrated model is validated to determine whether it conforms adequately to the data. Various diagnostic tests can be used. These may be well-known statistical tests, such as the chi-square goodness-of-fit test or the Kolmogorov–Smirnov test, or may be more qualitative in nature. The choice of test may relate directly to the ultimate purpose of the modeling exercise.

Stage 4 This stage is particularly useful if Stage 3 revealed that all models are inadequate. It is also possible that more than one valid model will be under consideration at this stage.

Stage 5 All valid models considered in Stages 1–4 are compared, using some criteria to select between them. This may be done by using the test results previously obtained or may be done by using other criteria. Once the best model is selected, the others may be retained for later model sensitivity analysis.

Stage 6 Finally, the model is adapted for application to the future if the data were from the past and the model is to be used for the future. This could involve adjustment of parameters to reflect anticipated inflation or change in exposure from the time the data were collected to the period of time to which the model will be applied.

As new data are collected or the environment changes, the six stages will need to be repeated to improve the model. In practice, this should be a continuous process.

1.5 ORGANIZATION OF THIS BOOK

This book takes the reader through the tools used in modeling process beginning with organization of the remainder of this book is as follows:

1. Review of probability—Almost by definition, uncertain events imply probability models. Chapter 2 reviews random variables and some of the basic calculations that may be done with such models.

2. Probabilistic measurement of risk—Probability models provide a probabilistic description of risk. Risk measures are functions of probability models. They summarize in one number (or very few numbers) the degree of risk exposure. Chapter 3 provides a technical description of the state of the art in risk measurement analytics.

3. Understanding probability distributions—In order to select a probability model, the risk analyst should possess a reasonably large collection of such models. In addition, to make a good a priori model choice, characteristics of these models should be available. In Chapters 4 and 5, a variety of distributional models are introduced and their characteristics explored. This includes both continuous and discrete distributions. The range of distributions in these chapters is much greater than in most standard books on statistical methods.

4. Aggregate losses—To this point the models are either for the amount of a single loss or for the number of payments. What is of primary interest to the decision-maker, when modeling operational losses, is the total possible amount of losses. A model that combines the probabilities concerning the possible number of losses and the possible amounts of each loss is called an aggregate loss model. Calculations for such models are covered in Chapter 6.

5. Extreme value theory—In studying operational risk, special attention must be paid to high-impact extreme, but rare, events. This is the subject of Chapter 7.

6. Copula methods—Dependencies among risks must be understood so that appropriate credit can be given for diversification when risks may exhibit correlation of some type. Chapter 8 introduces many relevant copula models.

7. Review of mathematical statistics—Techniques of mathematical statistics are needed to calibrate models and make formal choices among models based on available data. While Chapter 9 is not a replacement for a thorough treatment of mathematical statistics, it reviews the essential items needed later in this book. The reader with a good background can skim this chapter quickly.

8. Calibrating parametric models—Chapters 10 and 11 provide methods for parameter estimation for the continuous and discrete models introduced earlier. Model selection is covered in Chapter 12.

9. Chapter 13 applies special statistical methods for the study of very large possible losses, the jumbo risks that require deeper individual study.

10. Finally, in Chapter 14, we consider estimation methods for multivariate models, in particular the estimation and selection of copulas.

    This book provides many tools necessary for carrying out the modeling of operational risk for an organization. However, we do not attempt to discuss building an operational risk management program for an organization, a program that would include process controls and other aspects of risk management. As such, our scope is relatively narrow. Within this narrow scope, the treatment of topics is quite comprehensive and from a practical perspective. We have not incorporated some topics that are, at this stage, more interesting to the theoretician than the practicing risk analyst.

2

Basic probability concepts

Whenever you set out to do something, something else must be done first.

—Murphy

2.1   INTRODUCTION

An operational risk model is a set of mathematical functions that represents uncertain future losses. The uncertainty may be with respect to any or all of occurrence (*Is there a loss?*), timing (*When does the loss event occur?*), and severity (*What is the size of the loss when the event occurs?*). Because the most useful means of representing uncertainty is through probability, we concentrate on probability models. In this first part of the book, the following aspects of operational risk probability models will be covered:

1. Definition of random variable, important functions, and some examples

2. Basic calculations from probability models

3. Specific probability distributions and their properties

4. More advanced calculations using loss models

Before we begin, we need to be clear about a few basic definitions used in probability. **Phenomena** are occurrences that can be observed. An **experiment** is an observation of a given phenomenon under specified conditions.

The result of an experiment is called an **outcome**; an **event** is a set of one or more possible outcomes. **Probability** is a measure of the likelihood of the occurrence of an event. It is measured on a scale of increasing likelihood from 0 (impossible) to 1 (certain). A **random variable** is a function that assigns a numerical value to every possible outcome.

The following list contains a number of random variables encountered in operational risk work:

1. The percentage of the dollar value of a transaction lost as a result of an error (**Model 1**)

2. The number of dollars lost as a result of a fraudulent transaction (**Model 2**)

3. The number of fraudulent transactions in one year (**Model 3**)

4. The total dollars lost as a result of fraudulent transactions in one year (**Model 4**)

Because all of these phenomena can be expressed as random variables, the machinery of probability and mathematical statistics is at our disposal both to create and to analyze models for them. Key probability concepts will be illustrated with the above four models. Later, two additional models will be introduced.

2.2 DISTRIBUTION FUNCTIONS AND RELATED CONCEPTS

Definition 2.1 *The* ***cumulative distribution function*** *(also called the* ***distribution function*** *and usually denoted* $F_X(x)$ *or* $F(x)$*)*[1] *of a random variable* X *is the probability that* X *is less than or equal to a given number* x. *That is,* $F_X(x) = \Pr(X \leq x)$.

The abbreviation **cdf** is often used for the distribution function.
The distribution function must satisfy the following requirements[2]:

- $0 \leq F(x) \leq 1$ for all x.

- $F(x)$ is nondecreasing.

---

[1] When denoting functions associated with random variables, it is common to identify the random variable through a subscript on the function. Here, subscripts will be used only when needed to distinguish one random variable from another. In addition, for the six models to be introduced shortly, rather than writing the distribution function for random variable 2 as $F_{X_2}(x)$, it will simply be denoted $F_2(x)$.

[2] The first point follows from the last three.

- $F(x)$ is right-continuous.[3]

- $\lim_{x \to -\infty} F(x) = 0.$

- $\lim_{x \to \infty} F(x) = 1.$

It is possible for the distribution function to have jump, that is, to be discontinuous at some points. When it jumps, the value of the distribution function at the point of the jump is assigned to the top of the jump as a result of the right-continuity requirement.

Here are possible distribution functions for each of the four models.

Model 1

$$F_1(x) = \Pr(X \leq x) = \begin{cases} 0, & x < 0, \\ 0.01x, & 0 \leq x < 100, \\ 1, & x \geq 100. \end{cases}$$

This random variable could serve as a model for the percentage loss for an operational risk event. In the above model (the uniform distribution) all loss percentages are equally likely to occur. □

Model 2

$$F_2(x) = \Pr(X \leq x) = \begin{cases} 0, & x < 0, \\ 1 - \left(\dfrac{2000}{x + 2000} \right)^3, & x \geq 0. \end{cases}$$

This random variable could serve as a model for the actual loss in a single transaction as measured in dollars (or other currency). In the above model (a Pareto distribution), there is no upper limit on the loss. □

Graphs of the distribution function for Models 1 and 2 appear in Figures 2.1 and 2.2. (Graphs for the other models are requested in Exercise 2.2).

Model 3

$$F_3(x) = \Pr(X \leq x) = \begin{cases} 0, & x < 0, \\ 0.5, & 0 \leq x < 1, \\ 0.75, & 1 \leq x < 2, \\ 0.87, & 2 \leq x < 3, \\ 0.95, & 3 \leq x < 4, \\ 1, & x \geq 4. \end{cases}$$

---

[3] Right-continuous means that at any point x_0 the limiting value of $F(x)$ as x approaches x_0 from the right is equal to $F(x_0)$. This need not be true as x approaches x_0 from the left.

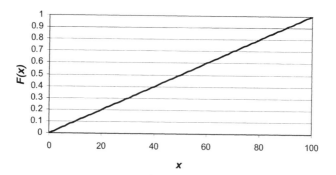

Fig. 2.1   Distribution function for Model 1

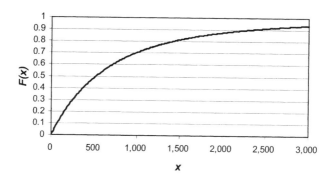

Fig. 2.2   Distribution function for Model 2

This random variable could serve as a model for the number of losses on one type of risk in one year. Probability is concentrated at the five points (0, 1, 2, 3, 4), and the probability at each is given by the size of the jump in the distribution function. While the above model places a maximum on the number of losses, models with no limit (such as the Poisson distribution) could also be used. Distributions whose distribution functions look like step functions (as the above one does) are called discrete distributions (see below).   □

Model 4

$$F_4(x) = \Pr(X \le x) = \begin{cases} 0, & x < 0, \\ 1 - 0.3e^{-0.00001x}, & x \ge 0. \end{cases}$$

This random variable could serve as a model for the total losses from a single risk over a one-year period. Most of the probability is at zero because there is a 70% chance of no loss. The remaining 0.3 of probability is distributed over positive values. It should be noted that this type of random variable can be used for the sum of random variables (representing losses) of the Model 2 type where the number of such random variables in the sum is itself a random variable (representing number of losses) of the Model 3 type. This can be represented as

$$X = X_1 + X_2 + ... + X_N$$

where N is the (random) number of losses. When $N = 0$, there are no losses and $X = 0$. □

Definition 2.2 *The **support** of a random variable is the set of numbers that are possible values of the random variable.*

Definition 2.3 *A random variable is of the **discrete** type if the support contains at most a countable number of values. It is of the **continuous** type if the distribution function is continuous and is differentiable everywhere with the possible exception of a countable number of values. It is of the **mixed** type if it is not discrete and is continuous everywhere with the exception of at least one value and at most a countable number of values.*

The distribution function for a discrete variable looks like a step function. It has constant value except at the jump points. The jumps are the values with positive probability. A distribution of the mixed type will have at least one jump. Requiring continuous variables to be differentiable allows the variable to have a density function (defined later) at almost all values.

Example 2.4 *For each of the four models, determine the support and indicate which type of random variable it is.*

The distribution function for Model 1 is continuous and differentiable except at 0 and 100 and therefore is a continuous distribution. The support is values from 0 to 100 with it not being clear whether 0 or 100 are included. The distribution function for Model 2 is continuous and differentiable except at 0 and therefore is a continuous distribution. The support is all positive numbers and perhaps 0. The random variable for Model 3 places probability only at 0, 1, 2, 3, and 4 (the support) and thus is discrete. The distribution function for Model 4 is continuous except at 0, where it jumps. It is a mixed distribution with support on nonnegative numbers. □

These four models illustrate the most commonly encountered forms of the distribution function. For the remainder of this text, values of functions like the distribution function will be presented only for values in the range of the support of the random variable.

Definition 2.5 *The **survival function** (also called the **decumulative distribution function** and usually denoted $\overline{F}(x)$ or $S(x)$) for a random variable X is the probability that X is greater than a given number. That is, $\Pr(X > x) = 1 - F(x) = \overline{F}(x) = S(x)$.*

As a result, from the properties of the cumulative distribution function, the survival function has the following properties:

- $0 \leq \overline{F}(x) \leq 1$ for all x.

- $\overline{F}(x)$ is nonincreasing.

- $\overline{F}(x)$ is right-continuous.

- $\lim_{x \to -\infty} \overline{F}(x) = 1$.

- $\lim_{x \to \infty} \overline{F}(x) = 0$.

It is possible for the survival function to jump (down). When it jumps, the value is assigned to the bottom of the jump as a result of the right continuity.

Because the survival function is the complement of the distribution function, knowledge of one implies knowledge of the other. In practice, when the random variable is measuring time, the survival function is usually presented because it represents the proportion of "survivors." When it is measuring losses, the distribution function is usually presented. However, there is nothing lost by not following this convention.

Example 2.6 *The survival functions for the four models:*

$$\overline{F}_1(x) = 1 - 0.01x, \ 0 \leq x < 100,$$

$$\overline{F}_2(x) = \left(\frac{2,000}{x + 2,000}\right)^3, \ x \geq 0,$$

$$\overline{F}_3(x) = \begin{cases} 0.5, & 0 \leq x < 1, \\ 0.25, & 1 \leq x < 2, \\ 0.13, & 2 \leq x < 3, \\ 0.05, & 3 \leq x < 4, \\ 0, & x \geq 4. \end{cases}$$

$$\overline{F}_4(x) = 0.3e^{-0.00001x}, \ x \geq 0.$$

□

Graphs of the survival functions for Models 1 and 2 appear in Figures 2.3 and 2.4.

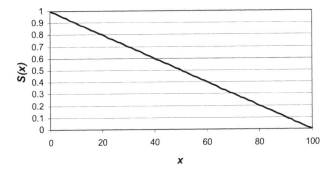

Fig. 2.3 Survival function for Model 1

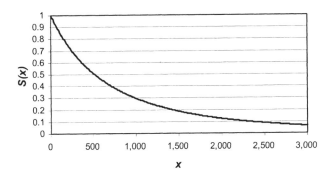

Fig. 2.4 Survival function for Model 2

Either the distribution or the survival function can be used to determine probabilities. Let $F(b-) = \lim_{x \nearrow b} F(x)$ and let $\overline{F}(b-) = \lim_{x \nearrow b} \overline{F}(x)$ be defined as the limits as x approaches b from below. Then we have $\Pr(a < X \le b) = F(b) - F(a) = \overline{F}(a) - \overline{F}(b)$ and $\Pr(X = b) = F(b) - F(b-) = \overline{F}(b-) - \overline{F}(b)$. When the distribution function is continuous at x, $\Pr(X = x) = 0$; otherwise the probability is the size of the jump. The next two functions are more directly related to the probabilities. The first is for distributions of the continuous type, the second for discrete distributions.

Definition 2.7 *The **probability density function** (also called the **density function** and usually denoted $f_X(x)$ or $f(x)$) is the first derivative (i.e., the slope) of the distribution function or, equivalently, the negative of the derivative of the survival function. That is, $f(x) = F'(x) = -\overline{F}'(x)$. The density function is defined only at those points where the derivative exists.*

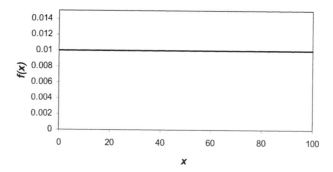

Fig. 2.5   Density function for Model 1

The abbreviation **pdf** is often used for the probability density function. Although the probability density function does not directly provide probabilities, it does provide relevant information. Values of the random variable in regions with higher density values are more likely to occur than those in regions with lower values. Probabilities for intervals and the distribution and survival functions can be recovered by integration for distributions of the continuous type. That is, when the density function is defined over the relevant interval, $\Pr(a < X \le b) = \int_a^b f(x)dx$, $F(b) = \int_{-\infty}^b f(x)dx$, and $\overline{F}(b) = \int_b^\infty f(x)dx$.

Example 2.8 *The density function of the four models are*

$$f_1(x) = 0.01, \quad 0 < x < 100,$$
$$f_2(x) = \frac{3(2,000)^3}{(x + 2,000)^4}, \quad x > 0,$$
$$f_3(x) \text{ is not defined},$$
$$f_4(x) = 0.000003e^{-0.00001x}, \quad x > 0.$$

It should be noted that in Model 3, we could also interpret the pdf as being zero at all points except 0, 1, 2, 3 and 4. Model 4 is a mixed distribution; there is also discrete probability at 0.   □

Graphs of the density functions for Models 1 and 2 appear in Figures 2.5 and 2.6.

Definition 2.9 *The **probability function** (also called the **probability mass function**, usually denoted $p_X(x)$ or $p(x)$) describes the probability at a distinct point x. The formal definition is $p_X(x) = \Pr(X = x)$.*

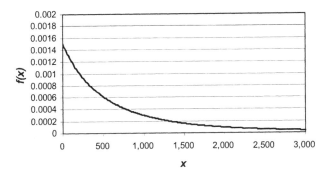

Fig. 2.6 Density function for Model 2

For discrete random variables, the distribution and survival functions can be recovered as $F(x) = \sum_{y \leq x} p(y)$ and $\overline{F}(x) = \sum_{y > x} p(y)$.

Example 2.10 *For the four models,*

$$p_1(x) \text{ is not defined,}$$

$$p_2(x) \text{ is not defined,}$$

$$p_3(x) = \begin{cases} 0.50, & x = 0, \\ 0.25, & x = 1, \\ 0.12, & x = 2, \\ 0.08, & x = 3, \\ 0.05, & x = 4, \end{cases}$$

$$p_4(0) = 0.7.$$

It is again noted that the distribution in Model 4 is mixed, so the above describes only the discrete portion of that distribution. For Model 4 we would present the complete probability (density) function as

$$f_4(x) = \begin{cases} 0.7, & x = 0, \\ 0.000003e^{-0.00001x}, & x > 0. \end{cases}$$

When the density function is assigned a value at a specific point, as opposed to being defined on an interval, it is understood to be a discrete probability mass. □

Definition 2.11 *The **hazard rate** (or **failure rate**, usually denoted $h_X(x)$ or $h(x)$) is the ratio of the probability density function to the survival function* at all points where the probability density function is defined. That is, $h(x) = f(x)/\overline{F}(x)$.

In actuarial or demographic applications, the hazard rate is often called the force of mortality. When called the force of mortality, the hazard rate is often denoted $\mu(x)$, and when called the failure rate, it is often denoted $\lambda(x)$. In this book we will always use $h(x)$ to denote the hazard rate. Regardless of notation, it may be interpreted as the probability density at x conditional on knowing that the argument will be at least x. From the simple relationship between distribution and survival functions, we also have $h(x) = -\overline{F}'(x)/\overline{F}(x) = -d\ln \overline{F}(x)/dx$. For any interval $(0, b)$ where the hazard rate exists, the survival function can be recovered from the expression $\overline{F}(b) = e^{-\int_0^b h(x)dx}$.

Example 2.12 *For the four models,*

$$h_1(x) = \frac{0.01}{1 - 0.01x}, \quad 0 < x < 100,$$

$$h_2(x) = \frac{3}{x + 2,000}, \quad x > 0,$$

$$h_3(x) = \text{undefined},$$

$$h_4(x) = 0.00001, \quad x > 0.$$

Once again, note that for the mixed distribution the hazard rate is only defined over the continuous part of the support of the distribution.   □

Graphs of the hazard rate functions for Models 1 and 2 appear in Figures 2.7 and 2.8.

The following model illustrates a situation in which there is a point where the density and hazard rate functions are not defined.

Model 5 An alternative to the simple distribution in Model 1 is given below.

$$\overline{F}_5(x) = \begin{cases} 1 - 0.01x, & 0 \le x < 50, \\ 1.5 - 0.02x, & 50 \le x < 75. \end{cases}$$

It is piecewise linear and the derivative at $x = 50$ is not defined . Therefore, neither the density function nor the hazard rate function is defined at $x = 50$ because the slopes to the left and right of $x = 50$ have different values. Unlike the mixed model of Model 4, there is no discrete probability mass at this point. Because the probability of the occurrence of $x = 50$ is zero, the density or hazard rate at $x = 50$ could be arbitrarily defined with no effect on subsequent

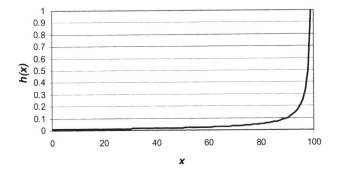

Fig. 2.7   Hazard rate function for Model 1

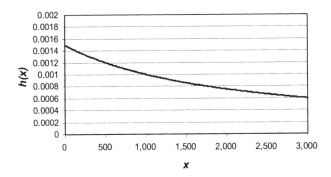

Fig. 2.8   Hazard rate function for Model 2

calculations. In this book, such values will be arbitrarily defined so that the function is right continuous.[4]   □

A variety of commonly used continuous distributions are presented in Chapter 4, and many discrete distributions are presented in Chapter 5. An interesting characteristic of a random variable is the value that is most likely to occur.

---

[4]By arbitrarily defining the value of the density or hazard rate function at such a point, it is clear that using either of them to obtain the survival function will work. If there is discrete probability at this point (in which case these functions are left undefined), then the density and hazard functions are not sufficient to completely describe the probability distribution.

Definition 2.13 *The **mode** of a random variable (or equivalently of a distribution) is the most likely value of the random variable. For a discrete variable it is the value with the largest probability. For a continuous variable it is the value for which the density function is largest.*

Example 2.14 *Determine the mode for Models 1-5.*

Model 1: The density function is constant. All values from 0 to 100 could be the mode, or equivalently, it could be said that there is no (single) mode.

Model 2: The density function is strictly decreasing and so the mode is at 0.

Model 3: The probability is largest at 0, so the mode is at 0.

Model 4: As a mixed distribution, it is not possible to define a mode for Model 4.

Model 5: The density function is constant over two intervals, with higher values from 50 to 75. The values between 50 and 75 are all modes, or equivalently, it could be said that there is no single mode.   □

2.3 MOMENTS

The moments of a distribution are characteristics that can be used in describing a distribution.

Definition 2.15 *The **kth raw moment** of a distribution is the expected (average) value of the kth power of the random variable, provided it exists. It is denoted by $\mathrm{E}(X^k)$ or by μ'_k. The first raw moment is called the **mean** and is usually denoted by μ.*

For random variables that take on only nonnegative values (i.e., $\Pr(X \geq 0) = 1$), k may be any real number. When presenting formulas for calculating this quantity, a distinction between continuous and discrete variables must be made. The formula for the kth raw moment is

$$\mu'_k = \mathrm{E}(X^k) = \int_{-\infty}^{\infty} x^k f(x)dx \text{ if the random variable is of the continuous type}$$

$$= \sum_j x_j^k p(x_j) \text{ if the random variable is of the discrete type,}$$

$$(2.1)$$

where the sum is to be taken over all possible values of x_j. For mixed models, evaluate the formula by integrating with respect to its density function wherever the random variable is continuous and by summing with respect to its probability function wherever the random variable is discrete and adding the results. Finally, it should be noted that it is possible that the integral or sum will not converge to a finite value, in which case the moment is said not to exist.

Example 2.16 *Determine the first two raw moments for each of the five models.*

The subscripts on the random variable X indicate which model is being used.

$$E(X_1) = \int_0^{100} x(0.01)dx = 50,$$

$$E(X_1^2) = \int_0^{100} x^2(0.01)dx = 3{,}333.33,$$

$$E(X_2) = \int_0^{\infty} x \frac{3(2{,}000)^3}{(x+2{,}000)^4}dx = 1{,}000,$$

$$E(X_2^2) = \int_0^{\infty} x^2 \frac{3(2{,}000)^3}{(x+2{,}000)^4}dx = 4{,}000{,}000,$$

$$E(X_3) = 0(0.5) + 1(0.25) + 2(0.12) + 3(0.08) + 4(0.05) = 0.93,$$

$$E(X_3^2) = 0(0.5) + 1(0.25) + 4(0.12) + 9(0.08) + 16(0.05) = 2.25,$$

$$E(X_4) = 0(0.7) + \int_0^{\infty} x(0.000003)e^{-0.00001x}dx = 30{,}000,$$

$$E(X_4^2) = 0^2(0.7) + \int_0^{\infty} x^2(0.000003)e^{-0.00001x}dx = 6{,}000{,}000{,}000,$$

$$E(X_5) = \int_0^{50} x(0.01)dx + \int_{50}^{75} x(0.02)dx = 43.75,$$

$$E(X_5^2) = \int_0^{50} x^2(0.01)dx + \int_{50}^{75} x^2(0.02)dx = 2{,}395.83.$$

$\square$

Before proceeding further, an additional model will be introduced. This one looks similar to Model 3, but with one key difference. It is discrete, but with the added requirement that all of the probabilities must be integral multiples of some number. In addition, the model must be related to sample data in a particular way.

Definition 2.17 *The **empirical model** is a discrete distribution based on a sample of size n that assigns probability $1/n$ to each data point.*

Model 6 Consider a sample of size 8 in which the observed data points were 3, 5, 6, 6, 6, 7, 7, and 10. The empirical model then has probability function

$$p_6(x) = \begin{cases} 0.125, & x = 3, \\ 0.125, & x = 5, \\ 0.375, & x = 6, \\ 0.25, & x = 7, \\ 0.125, & x = 10. \end{cases}$$

□

Alert readers will note that many discrete models with finite support look like empirical models. Model 3 could have been the empirical model for a sample of size 100 that contained 50 zeros, 25 ones, 12 twos, 8 threes, and 5 fours. Regardless, we will use the term empirical model only when it is based on an actual sample. The two moments for Model 6 are

$$E(X_6) = 6.25, \quad E(X_6^2) = 42.5$$

using the same approach as in Model 3. It should be noted that the mean of this random variable is equal to the sample arithmetic average (also called the sample mean).

Definition 2.18 *The* **kth central moment** *of a random variable is the expected value of the kth power of the deviation of the variable from its mean. It is denoted by* $E[(X - \mu)^k]$ *or by* μ_k. *The second central moment is usually called the* **variance** *and often denoted* σ^2, *and its square root,* σ, *is called the* **standard deviation**. *The ratio of the standard deviation to the mean is called the* **coefficient of variation**. *The ratio of the third central moment to the cube of the standard deviation,* $\gamma_1 = \mu_3/\sigma^3$, *is called the* **skewness**. *The ratio of the fourth central moment to the fourth power of the standard deviation,* $\gamma_2 = \mu_4/\sigma^4$, *is called the* **kurtosis**.[5]

For distributions of continuous and discrete types, formulas for calculating central moments are

$$\mu_k = E[(X - \mu)^k]$$
$$= \int_{-\infty}^{\infty} (x - \mu)^k f(x)dx \text{ if the random variable is continuous}$$
$$= \sum_j (x_j - \mu)^k p(x_j) \text{ if the random variable is discrete.} \quad (2.2)$$

In reality, the integral need be taken only over those x values where $f(x)$ is positive because regions where $f(x) = 0$ do not contribute to the value of the integral. The standard deviation is a measure of how much the probability

---

[5] It would be more accurate to call these items the "coefficient of skewness" and "coefficient of kurtosis" because there are other quantities that also measure asymmetry and flatness. The simpler expressions will be used in this text.

is spread out over the random variable's possible values. It is measured in the same units as the random variable itself. The coefficient of variation measures the spread relative to the mean. The skewness is a measure of asymmetry. A symmetric distribution has a skewness of zero, while a positive skewness indicates that probabilities to the right tend to be assigned to values further from the mean than those to the left. The kurtosis measures flatness of the distribution relative to a normal distribution (which has a kurtosis of 3). Kurtosis values above 3 indicate that (keeping the standard deviation constant), relative to a normal distribution, more probability tends to be at points away from the mean than at points near the mean. The coefficients of variation, skewness, and kurtosis are all dimensionless quantities.

There is a link between raw and central moments. The following equation indicates the connection between second moments. The development uses the continuous version from equations (2.1) and (2.2), but the result applies to all random variables.

$$\mu_2 = \int_{-\infty}^{\infty} (x-\mu)^2 f(x)dx = \int_{-\infty}^{\infty} (x^2 - 2x\mu + \mu^2)f(x)dx$$
$$= E(X^2) - 2\mu E(X) + \mu^2 = \mu_2' - \mu^2. \tag{2.3}$$

Example 2.19 *The density function of the gamma distribution with pdf*

$$f(x) = \frac{(x/\theta)^\alpha e^{-x/\theta}}{x\Gamma(\alpha)}, \quad x > 0$$

appears to be positively skewed (see Figure 2.9). Demonstrate that this is true and illustrate with graphs.

The first three raw moments of the gamma distribution can be calculated as $\alpha\theta$, $\alpha(\alpha+1)\theta^2$, and $\alpha(\alpha+1)(\alpha+2)\theta^3$. From formula (2.3) the variance is $\alpha\theta^2$, and from the solution to Exercise 2.5 the third central moment is $2\alpha\theta^3$. Therefore, the skewness is $2\alpha^{-1/2}$. Because α must be positive, the skewness is always positive. Also, as α decreases, the skewness increases.

Consider the following two gamma distributions. One has parameters $\alpha = 0.5$ and $\theta = 100$, while the other has $\alpha = 5$ and $\theta = 10$. These have the same mean, but their skewness coefficients are 2.83 and 0.89, respectively. Figure 2.9 demonstrates the difference. □

Note that when calculating the standard deviation for Model 6 in Exercise 2.6 the result is the sample standard deviation using n as opposed to the more commonly used $n-1$ in the denominator. Finally, it should be noted that when calculating moments it is possible that the integral or sum will not exist (as is the case for the third and fourth moments for Model 2). For the models we typically encounter, the integrand and summand are nonnegative and so failure to exist implies that the required limit that gives the integral or sum is infinity. See Example 4.14 for an illustration.

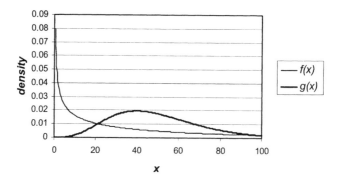

Fig. 2.9 Densities of $f(x) \sim \text{gamma}(0.5, 100)$ and $g(x) \sim \text{gamma}(5, 10)$

Definition 2.20 *For a given value of a threshold d with $\Pr(X > d) > 0$, the* **excess loss variable** *is $Y = X - d$ given that $X > d$. Its expected value,*

$$e_X(d) = e(d) = \mathrm{E}(Y) = \mathrm{E}(X - d|X > d),$$

is called the **mean excess loss function**. *Other names for this expectation, which are used in other contexts, are* **mean residual life function** *and* **expectation of life**.

The conditional random variable $X - d|X > d$ is a **left-truncated and shifted random variable**. It is left-truncated because values below d are not considered; i.e., they are ignored. It is shifted because d is subtracted from the remaining values. When X is a payment variable, as in the insurance context, the mean excess loss is the expected amount paid given that there is a positive payment in excess of a deductible of d. In the demographic context, X is interpreted as the age at death; and, the mean excess loss (expectation of life) is the expected remaining lifetime given that the person is alive at age d. The kth moment of the excess loss variable is determined from

$$e_X^k(d) = \frac{\int_d^\infty (x - d)^k f(x)dx}{1 - F(d)} \quad \text{if the variable is of the continuous type}$$

$$= \frac{\sum_{x_j > d}(x_j - d)^k p(x_j)}{1 - F(d)} \quad \text{if the variable is of the discrete type.} \quad (2.4)$$

Here, $e_X^k(d)$ is defined only if the integral or sum converges. There is a particularly convenient formula for calculating the first moment. The development is given below for the continuous version, but the result holds for all random variables. The second line is based on an integration by parts where the antiderivative of $f(x)$ is taken as $-\overline{F}(x)$.

$$
\begin{aligned}
e_X(d) &= \frac{\int_d^\infty (x-d)f(x)dx}{1-F(d)} \\
&= \frac{-(x-d)\overline{F}(x)\big|_d^\infty + \int_d^\infty \overline{F}(x)dx}{\overline{F}(d)} \\
&= \frac{\int_d^\infty \overline{F}(x)dx}{\overline{F}(d)}.
\end{aligned}
\tag{2.5}
$$

Definition 2.21 *The **left-censored and shifted random variable** is*

$$
Y = (X-d)_+ = \begin{cases} 0, & X < d, \\ X-d, & X \geq d. \end{cases}
$$

The random variable is left-censored because values below d are not ignored but are, in effect, set equal to 0. There is no standard name or symbol for the moments of this variable. For events such as losses that are measured in a monetary unit, the distinction between the excess loss variable and the left-censored and shifted variable is important. In the excess loss situation, any losses below the threshold d are not recorded in any way. In the operational risk context, if small losses below some threshold d are not recorded at all, the distribution is left-truncated. If the number of such small (and treated as zero) losses is recorded, the loss amount random variable is left-censored. The moments can be calculated from

$$
\begin{aligned}
\mathrm{E}[(X-d)_+^k] &= \int_d^\infty (x-d)^k f(x)dx \text{ if the variable is of the continuous type,} \\
&= \sum_{x_j > d} (x_j - d)^k p(x_j) \text{ if the variable is of the discrete type.}
\end{aligned}
\tag{2.6}
$$

Example 2.22 *Construct graphs to illustrate the difference between the excess loss random variable and the left-censored and shifted random variable.*

The two graphs in Figures 2.10 and 2.11 plot the modified variable Y as a function of the unmodified variable X. The only difference is that for X values below 100 the variable is undefined while for the left-censored and shifted variable it is set equal to zero. □

The next definition provides a complementary function to the excess loss.

Definition 2.23 *The **limited loss random variable** is*

$$
Y = X \wedge u = \begin{cases} X, & X < u, \\ u, & X \geq u. \end{cases}
$$

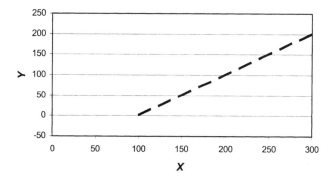

Fig. 2.10   Excess loss variable

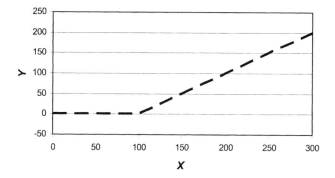

Fig. 2.11   Left censored and shifted variable

*Its expected value, $E[X \wedge u]$, is called the **limited expected value**.*

This variable could also be called the **right-censored random variable**. It is right-censored because values above u are set equal to u. In the operational risk context a limit to a loss can occur if losses in excess of that amount are insured so that the excess of a loss over the limit u is covered by an insurance contract. The company experiencing the operational risk loss can lose at most u.

Note that $(X - d)_+ + (X \wedge d) = X$. An insurance analogy is useful here. Buying one insurance contract with a limit of d and another with a deductible of d is equivalent to buying full coverage. This is illustrated in Figure 2.12. Buying only the insurance contract with a deductible d is equivalent to self-insuring losses up to d.

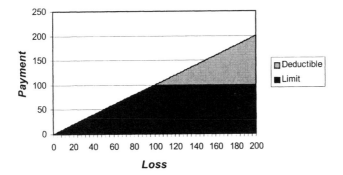

Fig. 2.12 Limit of 100 plus deductible of 100 equals full coverage

Simple formulas for the kth moment of the limited loss variable are

$$\mathrm{E}[(X \wedge u)^k] = \int_{-\infty}^{u} x^k f(x)dx + u^k[1 - F(u)]$$

if the random variable is continuous

$$= \sum_{x_j \leq u} x_j^k p(x_j) + u^k[1 - F(u)]$$

if the random variable is discrete.   (2.7)

Another interesting formula is derived as follows:

$$\mathrm{E}[(X \wedge u)^k] = \int_{-\infty}^{0} x^k f(x)dx + \int_{0}^{u} x^k f(x)dx + u^k[1 - F(u)]$$

$$= x^k F(x)\big|_{-\infty}^{0} - \int_{-\infty}^{0} kx^{k-1} F(x)dx$$

$$- x^k \overline{F}(x)\big|_{0}^{u} + \int_{0}^{u} kx^{k-1}\overline{F}(x)dx + u^k \overline{F}(u)$$

$$= - \int_{-\infty}^{0} kx^{k-1} F(x)dx + \int_{0}^{u} kx^{k-1}\overline{F}(x)dx,$$ (2.8)

where the second line uses integration by parts. For $k = 1$, we have

$$\mathrm{E}(X \wedge u) = - \int_{-\infty}^{0} F(x)dx + \int_{0}^{u} \overline{F}(x)dx.$$

If the loss distribution has only nonnegative support, then the first term in the right-hand side of the above two expressions vanishes. The kth limited moment of many common continuous distributions is presented in Chapter

4. Exercise 2.12 asks you to develop a relationship between the three first moments introduced previously.

2.4 QUANTILES OF A DISTRIBUTION

One other value of interest that may be derived from the distribution function is the quantile function. It is the value of the random variable corresponding to a particular value of the distribution function. It can be thought of as the inverse of the distribution function. A percentile is a quantile that is expressed in percentage terms.

Definition 2.24 *The* **100pth percentile** *(or* **quantile**) *of a random variable* X *is any value* x_p *such that* $F(x_p-) \leq p \leq F(x_p)$. *The 50th percentile,* $x_{0.5}$ *is called the* **median**.

If the distribution function has a value of p for exactly one x value, then the percentile is uniquely defined. In addition, if the distribution function jumps from a value below p to a value above p, then the percentile is at the location of the jump. The only time the percentile is not uniquely defined is when the distribution function is constant at a value of p over a range of values. In that case, any value in that range can be used as the percentile.

Example 2.25 *Determine the 50th and 80th percentiles for Models 1 and 3.*

For Model 1, the pth percentile can be obtained from $p = F(x_p) = 0.01x_p$ and so $x_p = 100p$, and in particular, the requested percentiles are 50 and 80 (see Figure 2.13). For Model 3 the distribution function equals 0.5 for all $0 \leq x < 1$ and so all such values can be the 50th percentile. For the 80th percentile, note that at $x = 2$ the distribution function jumps from 0.75 to 0.87 and so $x_{0.8} = 2$ (see Figure 2.14).   □

2.5 GENERATING FUNCTIONS

Sums of random variables are important in operational risk. Consider the operational risk losses arising from k units in the company. The total operational risk losses over all k units is the sum of the losses for the individual units. Thus it is useful to be able to determine properties of $S_k = X_1 + \cdots + X_k$. The first result is a version of the central limit theorem.

Theorem 2.26 *For a random variable S_k as defined above, $\mathrm{E}(S_k) = \mathrm{E}(X_1) + \cdots + \mathrm{E}(X_k)$. Also, if $X_1, \ldots, X_k$ are mutually independent, $\mathrm{Var}(S_k) = \mathrm{Var}(X_1) + \cdots + \mathrm{Var}(X_k)$. If the random variables $X_1, X_2, \ldots, X_k$ are mutually indepen-*

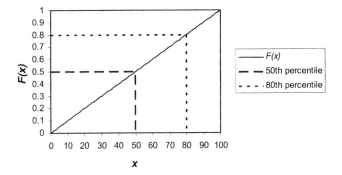

Fig. 2.13   Percentiles for Model 1

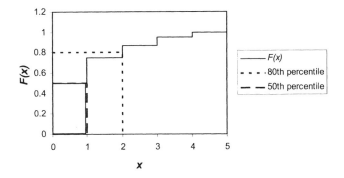

Fig. 2.14   Percentiles for Model 3

dent and their first two moments meet certain regularity conditions, the stan-dardized sum $[S_k - E(S_k)]/\sqrt{\text{Var}(S_k)}$ has a limiting normal distribution with mean 0 and variance 1 as k becomes infinitely large.

Obtaining the exact distribution of S_k may be very difficult. We can rely on the central limit theorem to give us a normal approximation for large values of k. The quality of the approximation depends in the size of k and on the shape of the distributions of the random variables $X_1, X_2, \ldots, X_k$.

Definition 2.27 *For a random variable X, the **moment generating function** (mgf) is $M_X(t) = E(e^{tX})$ for all t for which the expected value exists. The **probability generating function** (pgf) is $P_X(z) = E(z^X)$ for all z for which the expectation exists.*

Note that $M_X(t) = P_X(e^t)$ and $P_X(z) = M_X(\ln z)$. Often the mgf is used for continuous random variables and the pgf for discrete random variables. For us, the value of these functions is not so much that they generate moments or probabilities but that there is a one-to-one correspondence between a random variable's distribution function and its mgf and pgf (i.e., two random variables with different distribution functions cannot have the same mgf or pgf). The following result aids in working with sums of random variables.

Theorem 2.28 *Let $S_k = X_1 + \cdots + X_k$, where the random variables in the sum are mutually independent. Then the exact distribution of the sum is given by the mgf and pgf as $M_{S_k}(t) = \prod_{j=1}^{k} M_{X_j}(t)$ and $P_{S_k}(z) = \prod_{j=1}^{k} P_{X_j}(z)$ provided all the component mgfs and pgfs exist.*

Proof: We use the fact that the expected product of independent random variables is the product of the individual expectations. Then,

$$M_{S_k}(t) = \mathrm{E}(e^{tS_k}) = \mathrm{E}[e^{t(X_1 + \cdots + X_k)}]$$

$$= \prod_{j=1}^{k} \mathrm{E}(e^{tX_j}) = \prod_{j=1}^{k} M_{X_j}(t).$$

A similar argument can be used for the pgf. □

Example 2.29 *Show that the sum of independent gamma random variables, each with the same value of θ, has a gamma distribution.*

The moment generating function of a gamma variable is

$$\mathrm{E}(e^{tX}) = \frac{\int_0^\infty e^{tx} x^{\alpha-1} e^{-x/\theta} dx}{\Gamma(\alpha)\theta^\alpha}$$

$$= \frac{\int_0^\infty x^{\alpha-1} e^{-x(-t+1/\theta)} dx}{\Gamma(\alpha)\theta^\alpha}$$

$$= \frac{\int_0^\infty y^{\alpha-1}(-t+1/\theta)^{-\alpha} e^{-y} dy}{\Gamma(\alpha)\theta^\alpha}$$

$$= \frac{\Gamma(\alpha)(-t+1/\theta)^{-\alpha}}{\Gamma(\alpha)\theta^\alpha} = \left(\frac{1}{1-\theta t}\right)^\alpha, \quad t < 1/\theta.$$

Now let X_j have a gamma distribution with parameters α_j and θ. Then the moment generating function of the sum is

$$M_{S_k}(t) = \prod_{j=1}^{k} \left(\frac{1}{1-\theta t}\right)^{\alpha_j} = \left(\frac{1}{1-\theta t}\right)^{\alpha_1 + \cdots + \alpha_k}$$

which is the moment generating function of a gamma distribution with parameters $\alpha_1 + \cdots + \alpha_k$ and θ. □

Example 2.30 *Obtain the mgf and pgf for the Poisson distribution with pf*

$$p(x) = \Pr\left(X = x\right) = \frac{\lambda^x e^{-\lambda}}{x!}, \quad x = 0, 1, 2, \dots \; .$$

The pgf is

$$P_X(z) = \sum_{x=0}^{\infty} z^x \frac{\lambda^x e^{-\lambda}}{x!} = e^{-\lambda} \sum_{x=0}^{\infty} \frac{(z\lambda)^x}{x!} = e^{-\lambda} e^{z\lambda} = e^{\lambda(z-1)}.$$

Then the mgf is $M_X(t) = P_X(e^t) = \exp[\lambda(e^t - 1)]$. □

2.6 EXERCISES

2.1 Determine the distribution, density, and hazard rate functions for Model 5.

2.2 Construct graphs of the distribution function for Models 3–5. Also graph the density or probability function as appropriate and the hazard rate function, where it exists.

2.3 A random variable X has density function $f(x) = 4x(1 + x^2)^{-3}$, $x > 0$. Determine the mode of X.

2.4 A nonnegative random variable has a hazard rate function of $h(x) = A + e^{2x}$, $x \geq 0$. You are also given $\overline{F}(0.4) = 0.5$. Determine the value of A.

2.5 Develop formulas similar to (2.3) for μ_3 and μ_4.

2.6 Calculate the standard deviation, skewness, and kurtosis for each of the six models.

2.7 A random variable has a mean and a coefficient of variation of 2. The third raw moment is 136. Determine the skewness.

2.8 Determine the skewness of a gamma distribution that has a coefficient of variation of 1.

2.9 Determine the mean excess loss function for Models 1–4. Compare the functions for Models 1, 2, and 4.

2.10 For two random variables, X and Y, $e_Y(30) = e_X(30) + 4$. Let X have a uniform distribution on the interval from 0 to 100 and let Y have a uniform distribution on the interval from 0 to w. Determine w.

2.11 A random variable has density function $f(x) = \lambda^{-1}e^{-x/\lambda}$, $x, \lambda > 0$. Determine $e(\lambda)$, the mean excess loss function evaluated at $x = \lambda$.

2.12 Show that the following relationships holds:

$$E(X) = E(X \wedge d) + \overline{F}(d)e(d) \qquad (2.9)$$
$$= E(X \wedge d) + E\left[(X - d)_+\right].$$

2.13 Determine the limited expected value function for Models 1–4. Do this using both (2.7) and (2.9). For Models 1 and 2 also obtain the function using (2.8).

2.14 Define a right-truncated variable and provide a formula for its kth moment.

2.15 The distribution of individual losses has pdf

$$f(x) = 2.5x^{-3.5}, \ x \geq 1.$$

Determine the coefficient of variation.

2.16 Possible loss sizes are for $100, $200, $300, $400, or $500. The probabilities for these values are 0.05, 0.20, 0.50, 0.20, and 0.05, respectively. Determine the skewness and kurtosis for this distribution.

2.17 Losses follow a Pareto distribution with $\alpha > 1$ and θ unspecified. Determine the ratio of the mean excess loss function at $x = 2\theta$ to the mean excess loss function at $x = \theta$.

2.18 The cdf of a random variable is $F(x) = 1 - x^{-2}$, $x \geq 1$. Determine the mean, median, and mode of this random variable.

2.19 Determine the 50th and 80th percentiles for Models 2, 4, 5, and 6.

2.20 Losses have a Pareto distribution with parameters α and θ. The 10th percentile is $\theta - k$. The 90th percentile is $5\theta - 3k$. Determine the value of α.

2.21 Losses have a Weibull distribution with cdf

$$F(x) = 1 - e^{-(x/\theta)^{\tau}}, \ x > 0.$$

The 25th percentile is 1,000 and the 75th percentile is 100,000. Determine the value of τ.

2.22 Consider 16 independent risks, each with a gamma distribution with parameters $\alpha = 1$ and $\theta = 250$. Give an expression using the incomplete gamma function for the probability that the sum of the losses exceeds 6,000. Then approximate this probability using the central limit theorem.

2.23 The sizes of individual operational risk losses have the Pareto distribution with parameters $\alpha = 8/3$, and $\theta = 8,000$. Use the central limit theorem to approximate the probability that the sum of 100 independent losses will exceed 600,000.

2.24 The sizes of individual operational risk losses have the gamma distribution with parameters $\alpha = 5$ and $\theta = 1,000$. Use the central limit theorem to approximate the probability that the sum of 100 independent losses exceeds 525,000.

2.25 A sample of 1,000 operational risk losses produced an average loss of $1,300 and a standard deviation of $400. It is expected that 2,500 such losses will occur next year. Use the central limit theorem to estimate the probability that total losses will exceed the expected amount by more than 1%.

3

Measures of risk

It is impossible to make everything foolproof, because fools are so ingenious.

—Murphy

3.1 INTRODUCTION

Probability-based models provide a description of risk exposure. The level of exposure to risk is often described by one number, or at least a small set of numbers. These numbers are necessarily functions of the model and are often called "key risk indicators." Such key risk indicators indicate to risk managers the degree to which the company is subject to particular aspects of risk. In particular, Value-at-Risk (VaR) is a quantile of the distribution of aggregate risks. Risk managers often look at "the chance of an adverse outcome." This can be expressed through the VaR at a particular probability level. VaR can also be used in the determination of the amount of capital required to withstand such adverse outcomes. Investors, regulators, and rating agencies are particularly interested to the company's ability to withstand such events.

VaR suffers from some undesirable properties. A more informative and more useful measure of risk is Tail-Value-at-Risk (TVaR). It has arisen independently in a variety of areas and has been given different names including Conditional-Value-at-Risk (CVaR), Conditional Tail Expectation (CTE) and Expected Shortfall (ES). In this book we first focus on developing the underlying probability model, and then apply a measure of risk to the probability model to provide the risk manager with useful information in a very simple format.

The subject of the determination of risk capital has been of active interest to researchers, of interest to regulators of financial institutions, and of direct interest to commercial vendors of financial products and services. At the international level, the actuarial and accounting professions and insurance regulators through the International Accounting Standards Board, the International Actuarial Association, and the International Association of Insurance Supervisors are all active in developing a framework for accounting and capital requirements for insurance companies. Similarly, the Basel Committee and the Bank of International Settlements have been developing capital standards for use by banks.

3.2 RISK MEASURES

Value-at-Risk (VaR) has become the standard risk measure used to evaluate exposure to risk. In general terms, the VaR is the amount of capital required to ensure, with a high degree of certainty, that the enterprise doesn't become technically insolvent. The degree of certainty chosen is arbitrary. In practice, it can be a high number such as 99.95% for the entire enterprise, or it can be much lower, such as 95%, for a single unit or risk class within the enterprise. This lower percentage may reflect the inter-unit or inter-risk type diversification that exists.

The promotion of concepts such as VaR has prompted the study of risk measures by numerous authors (e.g., Wang [122], [123]). Specific desirable properties of risk measures were proposed as axioms in connection with risk pricing by Wang, Young, and Panjer [125] and more generally in risk measurement by Artzner et al. [6].

We consider a random variable X_j representing the possible losses (in our case losses associated arising from operational risk) for a business unit or particular class of risk. Then the total or aggregate losses for n units or risk types is simply the sum of the losses for all units

$$X = X_1 + X_2 + \ldots + X_n.$$

The study of risk measures has been focused on ensuring consistency between the way risk is measured at the level of individual units and the way risk is measured after the units are combined. The concept of "coherence" of risk measures was introduced by Artzner et al [6]. This paper is considered to be the groundbreaking paper in the area of risk measurement.

The probability distribution of the total operational losses X depends not only on the distributions of the operational losses for the individual business units but also on the interrelationships between them. Correlation is one such measure of interrelationship. The usual definition of correlation (as defined in statistics) is a simple linear relationship between two random variables. This linear relationship may not be adequate to capture other (nonlinear) aspects of the relationship between the variables. Linear correlation does perform perfectly for describing interrelationships in the case where the operational losses from the individual business units form a multivariate normal distribution. Although the normal assumption is used extensively in connection with the modeling of changes in the logarithm of prices in the stock markets, it may not be entirely appropriate for modeling many processes including operational loss processes. For financial models and applications, where much of the theory is based on Brownian motion or related processes resulting in normal distributions, the normal distribution model serves as a benchmark and provides insight into key relationships. From the insurance field, it is well known that skewed distributions provide better descriptions of losses than symmetric distributions.

There are two broad approaches to the application of risk measurement to the determination of capital needs for complex organizations such as insurance companies and banks. One approach is to develop a mathematical model for each of the risk exposures separately and assign a capital requirement to each exposure based on the study of that risk exposure. This is often called the risk-based capital (RBC) approach in insurance and the Basel approach in banking. The total capital requirement is the (possibly adjusted) sum of the capital requirements for each risk exposure. Some offset may be possible because of the recognition that there may be a diversification or hedging effect of risks that are not perfectly correlated. The second approach uses an integrated model of the entire organization (the internal model approach). In this approach, a mathematical model is developed to describe the entire organization. The model incorporates all interactions between business units and risk types in the company. All interrelationships between variables are built into the model directly. Hence, correlations are captured in the model structure. In this approach, the total capital requirement for all types of risks can be calculated at the highest level in the organization. When this is the case, an allocation of the total capital back to the units is necessary for a variety of business management or solvency management reasons. The first approach to capital determination is often referred to as a "bottom-up" approach, while the second is referred to as a "top-down" approach.

A risk measure is a mapping from the random variable representing the loss associated with the risks to the real line (the set of all real numbers). A risk measure gives a single number that is intended to quantify the risk exposure. For example, the standard deviation, or a multiple of the standard deviation of a distribution, is a measure of risk because it provides a measure of uncertainty. It is clearly appropriate when using the normal distribution. One of the other most commonly used risk measures in the fields of finance and statistics is the quantile of the distribution or the Value-at-Risk (VaR). VaR is the size of loss for which there is a small (e.g. 1%) probability of exceedence. VaR is the most commonly used method for describing risk because it is easily communicated. For example an event at the 1% per year level is often described as the "one in a hundred year" event. However, for some time it has been recognized that VaR suffers from major problems. This will be discussed further after the introduction of coherent risk measures.

Throughout this book, the risk measures are denoted by the function $\rho(X)$. It is convenient to think of $\rho(X)$ as the amount of assets required for the risk X. We consider the set of all random variables X, Y such that both cX and $X + Y$ are also in the set. This is not very restrictive, but it does eliminate risks that are measured as percentages as with Model 1 of the Chapter 2. Nonnegative loss random variables that are expressed in dollar terms and that have no upper limit satisfy the above requirements.

Definition 3.1 *A **coherent risk measure** $\rho(X)$ is defined as one that has the following four properties for any two bounded loss random variables X and Y:*

1. *Subadditivity:* $\rho(X + Y) \leq \rho(X) + \rho(Y)$.
2. *Monotonicity: If $X \leq Y$ for all possible outcomes, then $\rho(X) \leq \rho(Y)$.*
3. *Positive homogeneity: For any positive constant c, $\rho(cX) = c\rho(X)$.*
4. *Translation invariance: For any positive constant c, $\rho(X+c) = \rho(X)+c$.*

Subadditivity means that the risk measure (and hence the capital required to support it) for two risks combined will not be greater than for the risks treated separately. This reflects the fact that there should be some diversification benefit from combining risks. This is necessary at the corporate level, because otherwise companies would find it to be an advantage to disaggregate into smaller companies. There has been some debate about the appropriateness of the subadditivity requirement. In particular, the merger of several small companies into a larger one exposes each of the small companies to the reputational risk of the others. We will continue to require subadditivity as it reflects the possibility of diversification.

Monotonicity means that if one risk always has greater losses than another risk under all circumstances, the risk measure (and hence the capital required to support it) should always be greater. This requirement should be self-evident from an economic viewpoint.

Translation invariance means that there is no additional risk (and hence capital required to support it) for an additional risk for which there is no additional uncertainty. In particular, by making X identically zero, the assets required for a certain outcome is exactly the value of that outcome. Also, when a company meets the capital requirement by setting up additional risk-free capital, the act of injecting the additional capital does not, in itself, trigger a further injection (or reduction) of capital.

Positive homogeneity means that the risk measure (and hence the capital required to support it) is independent of the currency in which the risk is measured. Equivalently, it means that, for example, doubling the exposure to a particular risk requires double the capital. This is sensible because doubling the position provides no diversification.

Risk measures satisfying these four criteria are deemed to be coherent. There are many such risk measures.

Example 3.2 (Standard deviation principle) *The standard deviation is a measure of uncertainty of a distribution. Consider a loss distribution with mean μ and standard deviation σ. The quantity $\mu + k\sigma$, where k is the same fixed constant for all distributions, is a risk measure (often called the **standard deviation principle**). The coefficient k is usually chosen to ensure that losses will exceed the risk measure for some distribution, such as the normal distribution, with some specified small probability. The standard deviation principle is not a coherent risk measure. Why? While properties 1, 3, and 4 hold, property 2 does not. Can you construct a counterexample?* □

If X follows the normal distribution, a value of $k = 1.645$ results in an exceedance probability of $\Pr(X > \mu + k\sigma) = 5\%$. Similarly, if $k = 2.576$, then $\Pr(X > \mu + k\sigma) = 0.5\%$. However, if the distribution is not normal, the same multiples of the standard deviation will lead to different exceedance probabilities. One can also begin with the exceedance probability, obtaining the quantile $\mu + k\sigma$ and the equivalent value of k. This is the key idea behind Value-at-Risk.

Definition 3.3 *Let X denote a loss random variable. The* Value-at-Risk *of X at the $100p\%$ level, denoted $\mathrm{VaR}_p(X)$ or x_p, is the $100p$ percentile (or quantile) of the distribution of X.*

For continuous distributions, we can simply write $\mathrm{VaR}_p(X)$ for random variable X as the value of x_p satisfying

$$\Pr(X > x_p) = p.$$

It is well known that VaR does not satisfy one of the four criteria for coherence, the subadditivity requirement. The failure of VaR to be subadditive can been shown by a simple counter but extreme example inspired by a more complicated one from Wirch [128].

Example 3.4 (Incoherence of VaR) *Let Z denote a loss random variable of the continuous type with cdf at \$1, \$90, and \$100 satisfying the following three equations:*

$$F_Z(1) = 0.91,$$
$$F_Z(90) = 0.95,$$
$$F_Z(100) = 0.96.$$

The 95% quantile, the $\mathrm{VaR}_{95\%}(Z)$ is \$90 because there is a 5% chance of exceeding \$90.

Suppose that we now split the risk Z into two separate (but dependent) risks X and Y such that the two separate risks in total are equivalent to risk Z, that is, $X + Y = Z$. One way to do this is by defining risk X as the loss if it falls up to $100, and zero otherwise. Similarly define risk Y as the loss if it falls over $100, zero otherwise. The cdf for risk X satisfies

$$F_X(1) = 0.95,$$
$$F_X(90) = 0.99,$$
$$F_X(100) = 1.$$

indicating a 95% quantile of $1.

Similarly the cdf for risk Y satisfies $F_Z(0) = 0.96$ indicating that there is a 96% chance of no loss. Therefore the 95% quantile cannot exceed $0. Consequently, the sum of the 95% quantiles for X and Y is less than the $VaR_{95\%}(Z)$ which violates subadditivity. □

Although this example may appear to be somewhat artificial, the existence of such possibilities creates opportunities for strange or unproductive manipulation. Therefore we focus on risk measures that are coherent.

3.3   TAIL-VALUE-AT-RISK

As a risk measure, Value-at-Risk is used extensively in financial risk management of trading risk over a fixed (usually relatively short) time period. In these situations, the normal distribution are often used for describing gains or losses. If distributions of gains or losses are restricted to the normal distribution, Value-at-Risk satisfies all coherency requirements. This is true more generally for elliptical distributions, for which the normal distribution is a special case. However, the normal distribution is generally not used for describing operational risk losses as most loss distributions have considerable skewness. Consequently, the use of VaR is problematic because of the lack of subadditivity.

Definition 3.5 *Let X denote a loss random variable. The Tail-Value-at-Risk of X at the $100p\%$ confidence level, denoted $TVaR_p(X)$, is the expected loss given that the loss exceeds the $100p$ percentile (or quantile) of the distribution of X.*

For the sake of notational convenience, we shall restrict consideration to continuous distributions. This avoids ambiguity about the definition of VaR. In general, we can extend the results to discrete distributions or distributions of mixed type by appropriately modifying definitions. For practical purposes, it is generally sufficient to think in terms of continuous distributions.

We can simply write $\text{TVaR}_p(X)$ for random variable X as

$$\text{TVaR}_p(X) = \text{E}\left(X \mid X > x_p\right) = \frac{\int_{x_p}^{\infty} x \, dF(x)}{1 - F(x_p)}$$

where $F(x)$ is the cdf of X. Furthermore, for continuous distributions, if the above quantity is finite, we can use integration by parts and substitution to rewrite this as

$$\text{TVaR}_p(X) = \frac{\int_{x_p}^{\infty} x f(x) \, dx}{1 - F(x_p)}$$

$$= \frac{\int_p^1 \text{VaR}_u(X) \, du}{1 - p}.$$

Thus, TVaR can be seen to average all VaR values above confidence level p. This means that TVaR tells us much more about the tail of the distribution than VaR alone.

Finally, TVaR can also be written as

$$\text{TVaR}_p(X) = \text{E}\left(X \mid X > x_p\right)$$

$$= x_p + \frac{\int_{x_p}^{\infty} (x - x_p) \, dF(x)}{1 - F(x_p)}$$

$$= \text{VaR}_p(x) + e(x_p)$$

where $e(x_p)$ is the mean excess loss function. Thus TVaR is larger than the corresponding VaR by the average excess of all losses that exceed VaR. TVaR has also been developed independently in the insurance field and called **Conditional Tail Expectation** (CTE) by Wirch [128] and widely known by that term in North America. It has also been called **Tail Conditional Expectation** (TCE). In Europe, it has also been called **Expected Shortfall** (ES). (See Tasche [113] and Acerbi and Tasche [3]).

Overbeck [87] also discusses VaR and TVaR as risk measures. He argues that VaR is an "all or nothing" risk measure, in that if an extreme event in excess of the VaR threshold occurs, there is no capital to cushion losses. He also argues that the VaR quantile in TVaR provides a definition of "bad times," which are those where losses exceed the VaR threshold, thereby not using up all available capital when TVaR is used to determine capital. Then TVaR provides the average excess loss in "bad times," that is, when the VaR "bad times" threshold has been exceeded.

Example 3.6 (Normal distribution)   *Consider a normal distribution with mean μ, standard deviation σ, and pdf*

$$f(x) = \frac{1}{\sqrt{2\pi}\sigma} \exp\left[-\frac{1}{2}\left(\frac{x - \mu}{\sigma}\right)^2\right].$$

Let $\phi(x)$ and $\Phi(x)$ denote the pdf and the cdf of the standard normal distribution ($\mu = 0$, $\sigma = 1$). Then

$$VaR_p(X) = \mu + \sigma\Phi^{-1}(p)$$

and, with a bit of calculus, it can be shown that

$$TVaR_p(X) = \mu + \sigma\frac{\phi\left[\Phi^{-1}(p)\right]}{1-p}.$$

Note that, in both cases, the risk measure can be translated to the standard deviation principle with an appropriate choice of k. □

Example 3.7 (t distribution) *Consider a t distribution with location parameter μ, scale parameter σ, with ν degrees of freedom and pdf*

$$f(x) = \frac{\Gamma\left(\frac{\nu+1}{2}\right)}{\sqrt{\pi\nu}\sigma\Gamma\left(\frac{\nu}{2}\right)}\left[1 + \frac{1}{\nu}\left(\frac{x-\mu}{\sigma}\right)^2\right]^{-\frac{\nu+1}{2}}.$$

Let $t(x)$ and $T(x)$ denote the pdf and the cdf of the standardized t distribution ($\mu = 0$, $\sigma = 1$) with $\nu > 2$ degrees of freedom. Then

$$VaR_p(X) = \mu + \sigma T^{-1}(p)$$

and, with some more calculus, it can be shown that

$$TVaR_p(X) = \mu + \sigma\frac{t\left[T^{-1}(p)\right]}{1-p}\left\{\frac{\nu + \left[T^{-1}(p)\right]^2}{\nu - 1}\right\}.$$

□

Example 3.8 (Exponential distribution) *Consider an exponential distribution with mean θ and pdf*

$$f(x) = \frac{1}{\theta}\exp\left(-\frac{x}{\theta}\right), \quad x > 0.$$

Then

$$VaR_p(X) = \theta\ln(1-p)$$

and

$$TVaR_p(X) = VaR_p(X) + \theta.$$

The excess of TVaR over VaR is a constant θ for all values of p because of the memoryless property of the exponential distribution. □

TVaR is a coherent measure. This has been shown by Artzner et al. [6]. Therefore, when using it, we never run into the problem of subadditivity of the VaR. TVaR is one of many possible coherent risk measures. However, it is particularly well-suited to applications in operational risk where you may want to reflect the shape of the tail beyond the VaR threshold in some way. TVaR represents that shape through a single number, the mean excess or expected shortfall.

Part II

Probabilistic tools for operational risk modeling

4

Models for the size of losses: Continuous distributions

If everything seems to be going well, you have probably overlooked something.
—Murphy

4.1 INTRODUCTION

In this chapter, we will focus on models that can be used for the size of losses. We restrict ourselves to distributions that do not take on negative values. Negative losses are positive gains. Because our focus is on losses, we will not consider, for example, errors that result in gains. Random variables that cannot take on negative values are said to have nonnegative support. The set of all possible distribution functions with nonnegative support is the set of all possible nondecreasing functions that take on value 0 for all negative values of the random variable and take on, or approach, value 1 as the random variable becomes very large. When searching for a distribution function to use as a model for a random phenomenon, it can be helpful if the field can be narrowed from this infinitely large set to a small set containing distribution functions with a sufficiently large variety of shapes to capture shapes of distributions encountered in practice. Beyond classification into discrete, continuous, and mixed distributions, we can classify distributions according to other criteria. Section 4.2 lists many distributions. They are ordered on the basis of the number of parameters in the model. Section 4.3 provides a unified approach to these distributions by combining them into "families." Several subsequent sections examine the shape of the distributions and methods for creating even

more distributions. By the end of this chapter, most of the distributions whose
details appear in this book will have been introduced.

4.2   AN INVENTORY OF CONTINUOUS DISTRIBUTIONS

We will examine a number of distributions that can be used for modeling losses
from operational events. By definition, losses can only take on values that
are nonnegative. Hence we only look at distributions whose random variable
can only take on nonnegative values. For most distributions, the domain runs
from zero to infinity. In practice, however, losses are limited by some large
amount (such as the total assets of the firm). Often in modeling losses we
ignore this fact because the probability of such an event is extremely small.
If the probability of such a loss is sufficiently large to be material we could
apply a limit x to the loss random variable X, and consider the distribution
of $X \wedge x$.

   We now introduce a selected set of continuous distributions with support
on $(0, \infty)$. In the descriptions of the distributions given in the next subsections
are the moments of both X and $X \wedge x$. We list the distributions and their
properties for easy later reference. Relationships between the distributions
are discussed in the Section 4.3. The gamma function $\Gamma(\alpha)$, the incomplete
gamma function $\Gamma(\alpha; x)$, and the beta function $\beta(\tau, \alpha; x)$ that are used are
defined in Appendix A.

4.2.1   One-parameter distributions

4.2.1.1 Exponential distribution   The exponential is the only continuous distribution with a hazard rate that is constant, $h(x) = 1/\theta$, and a conditional
expected excess loss that is also constant, $e_d(x) = \theta$. Therefore, the expected
size of the excess loss above a threshold doesn't depend on the threshold.

$$f(x) = \frac{1}{\theta}e^{-x/\theta}$$

$$F(x) = 1 - e^{-x/\theta}$$

$$E[X^k] = \theta^k \Gamma(k+1), \quad k > -1$$

$$E[X^k] = \theta^k k! \quad \text{if } k \text{ is an integer}$$

$$E[X \wedge x] = \theta(1 - e^{-x/\theta})$$

$$E[(X \wedge x)^k] = \theta^k \Gamma(k+1)\Gamma(k+1; x/\theta) + x^k e^{-x/\theta}, \quad k > -1$$

$$E[(X \wedge x)^k] = \theta^k k! \Gamma(k+1; x/\theta) + x^k e^{-x/\theta} \quad \text{if } k > -1 \text{ is an integer}$$

$$M(t) = (1 - \theta t)^{-1}, \quad t < 1/\theta$$

$$\text{Mode} = 0$$

4.2.1.2 Inverse exponential distribution The inverse exponential is closely related to the exponential distribution. Further discussion of inverse distributions is in Section 4.7. Note that the inverse exponential has an infinite mean (and higher moments), indicating a very heavy tail.

$$f(x) = \frac{\theta e^{-\theta/x}}{x^2}$$
$$F(x) = e^{-\theta/x}$$
$$E[X^k] = \theta^k \Gamma(1-k), \quad k < 1$$
$$E[(X \wedge x)^k] = \theta^k \Gamma(1-k; \theta/x) + x^k (1 - e^{-\theta/x}), \quad \text{all } k$$
$$\text{Mode} = \theta/2$$

4.2.1.3 Single-parameter Pareto distribution The support of this distribution begins at θ. Usually the value of θ is known and therefore not considered a parameter. The Pareto distribution is described as heavy tailed because it has only a finite number of moments. From the following information you should be able to deduce that the mean excess function is linear in d.

$$f(x) = \alpha \theta^\alpha x^{-\alpha-1}, \quad x > \theta$$
$$F(x) = 1 - \left(\frac{\theta}{x}\right)^\alpha, \quad x > \theta$$
$$E[X^k] = \frac{\alpha \theta^k}{\alpha - k}, \quad k < \alpha$$
$$E[(X \wedge x)^k] = \frac{\alpha \theta^k}{\alpha - k} - \frac{k \theta^\alpha}{(\alpha - k)x^{\alpha-k}}, \quad x > \theta$$
$$\text{Mode} = \theta$$

4.2.2 Two-parameter distributions

4.2.2.1 Gamma distribution The gamma distribution is commonly used for many applications. If α is an integer, the gamma distribution can be considered as the distribution of the sum of α independent and identically (iid) exponential random variables.

$$f(x) = \frac{(x/\theta)^\alpha e^{-x/\theta}}{x\Gamma(\alpha)}$$
$$F(x) = \Gamma(\alpha; x/\theta)$$
$$E[X^k] = \frac{\theta^k \Gamma(\alpha + k)}{\Gamma(\alpha)}, \quad k > -\alpha$$

$$\mathrm{E}[X^k] = \theta^k(\alpha + k - 1) \cdots \alpha \quad \text{if } k \text{ is an integer}$$

$$\mathrm{E}[(X \wedge x)^k] = \frac{\theta^k \Gamma(\alpha + k)}{\Gamma(\alpha)} \Gamma(\alpha + k; x/\theta) + x^k[1 - \Gamma(\alpha; x/\theta)], \quad k > -\alpha$$

$$\mathrm{E}[(X \wedge x)^k] = \alpha(\alpha + 1) \cdots (\alpha + k - 1)\theta^k \Gamma(\alpha + k; x/\theta)$$
$$+ x^k[1 - \Gamma(\alpha; x/\theta)] \quad \text{if } k \text{ is an integer}$$

$$M(t) = (1 - \theta t)^{-\alpha}, \quad t < 1/\theta$$

$$\text{Mode} = \theta(\alpha - 1), \quad \text{if } \alpha > 1, \text{ else mode is at } 0$$

4.2.2.2 Inverse gamma distribution   The inverse gamma distribution (also known as the Vinci distribution).

$$f(x) = \frac{(\theta/x)^\alpha e^{-\theta/x}}{x\Gamma(\alpha)}$$

$$F(x) = 1 - \Gamma(\alpha; \theta/x)$$

$$\mathrm{E}[X^k] = \frac{\theta^k \Gamma(\alpha - k)}{\Gamma(\alpha)}, \quad k < \alpha$$

$$\mathrm{E}[(X \wedge x)^k] = \frac{\theta^k \Gamma(\alpha - k)}{\Gamma(\alpha)}[1 - \Gamma(\alpha - k; \theta/x)] + x^k \Gamma(\alpha; \theta/x)$$

$$= \frac{\theta^k \Gamma(\alpha - k; \theta/x)}{\Gamma(\alpha)} + x^k \Gamma(\alpha; \theta/x), \text{ for all } k$$

$$\text{Mode} = \theta/(\alpha + 1)$$

4.2.2.3 Lognormal distribution   The cdf of the lognormal distribution is obtained from the normal cdf by replacing x by $\ln x$.

$$f(x) = \frac{1}{x\sigma\sqrt{2\pi}} \exp\left[-\frac{1}{2}\left(\frac{\ln x - \mu}{\sigma}\right)^2\right] = \frac{\phi\left(\frac{\ln x - \mu}{\sigma}\right)}{\sigma x}$$

$$F(x) = \Phi\left(\frac{\ln x - \mu}{\sigma}\right)$$

$$\mathrm{E}[X^k] = \exp\left(k\mu + \tfrac{1}{2}k^2\sigma^2\right)$$

$$\mathrm{E}[(X \wedge x)^k] = \exp\left(k\mu + \tfrac{1}{2}k^2\sigma^2\right) \Phi\left(\frac{\ln x - \mu - k\sigma^2}{\sigma}\right) + x^k[1 - F(x)]$$

$$\text{Mode} = \exp(\mu - \sigma^2)$$

4.2.2.4 Inverse Gaussian distribution   The inverse Gaussian distribution is also known as the inverse normal or the Hadwiger distribution.

$$f(x) = \left(\frac{\theta}{2\pi x^3}\right)^{1/2} \exp\left(-\frac{\theta}{2x}\left(\frac{x-\mu}{\mu}\right)^2\right)$$

$$F(x) = \Phi\left[\frac{x-\mu}{\mu}\left(\frac{\theta}{x}\right)^{1/2}\right] + \exp\left(\frac{2\theta}{\mu}\right)\Phi\left[-\frac{x+\mu}{\mu}\left(\frac{\theta}{x}\right)^{1/2}\right]$$

$$E[X] = \mu, \quad Var[X] = \mu^3/\theta$$

$$E[X \wedge x] = x - (x-\mu)\Phi\left[\frac{x-\mu}{\mu}\left(\frac{\theta}{x}\right)^{1/2}\right] - (x+\mu)\exp\left(\frac{2\theta}{\mu}\right)\Phi\left[-\frac{x+\mu}{\mu}\left(\frac{\theta}{x}\right)^{1/2}\right]$$

$$M(t) = \exp\left[\frac{\theta}{\mu}\left(1 - \sqrt{1 - \frac{2\mu^2}{\theta}t}\right)\right], \quad t < \frac{\theta}{2\mu^2}$$

4.2.2.5 Weibull distribution   The Weibull cdf can be obtained from the exponential cdf by replacing x/θ by $(x/\theta)^\tau$.

$$f(x) = \frac{\tau(x/\theta)^\tau e^{-(x/\theta)^\tau}}{x}$$

$$F(x) = 1 - e^{-(x/\theta)^\tau}$$

$$E[X^k] = \theta^k \Gamma(1 + k/\tau), \quad k > -\tau$$

$$E[(X \wedge x)^k] = \theta^k \Gamma(1 + k/\tau)\Gamma[1 + k/\tau; (x/\theta)^\tau] + x^k e^{-(x/\theta)^\tau}, \quad k > -\tau$$

$$\text{Mode} = \theta\left(\frac{\tau-1}{\tau}\right)^{1/\tau}, \quad \text{if } \tau > 1, \text{ else the mode is at } 0$$

4.2.2.6 Inverse Weibull distribution   The inverse Weibull distribution is also known as the log-Gompertz distribution.

$$f(x) = \frac{\tau(\theta/x)^\tau e^{-(\theta/x)^\tau}}{x}$$

$$F(x) = e^{-(\theta/x)^\tau}$$

$$E[X^k] = \theta^k \Gamma(1 - k/\tau), \quad k < \tau$$

$$E[(X \wedge x)^k] = \theta^k \Gamma(1 - k/\tau)\{1 - \Gamma[1 - k/\tau; (\theta/x)^\tau]\} + x^k\left[1 - e^{-(\theta/x)^\tau}\right]$$

$$= \theta^k G[1 - k/\tau; (\theta/x)^\tau] + x^k\left[1 - e^{-(\theta/x)^\tau}\right], \quad \text{for all } k$$

$$\text{Mode} = \theta\left(\frac{\tau}{\tau+1}\right)^{1/\tau}$$

4.2.2.7 Loglogistic distribution   The loglogistic distribution looks a lot like the lognormal distribution but with much heavier tails. It is also known as the Fisk distribution.

$$f(x) = \frac{\gamma(x/\theta)^\gamma}{x[1 + (x/\theta)^\gamma]^2}$$

$$F(x) = u, \quad u = \frac{(x/\theta)^\gamma}{1 + (x/\theta)^\gamma}$$

$$\mathrm{E}[X^k] = \theta^k \Gamma(1 + k/\gamma)\Gamma(1 - k/\gamma), \quad -\gamma < k < \gamma$$

$$\mathrm{E}[(X \wedge x)^k] = \theta^k \Gamma(1 + k/\gamma)\Gamma(1 - k/\gamma)\beta(1 + k/\gamma, 1 - k/\gamma; u) + x^k(1 - u)$$

$$\text{Mode} = \theta \left(\frac{\gamma - 1}{\gamma + 1}\right)^{1/\gamma}, \quad \text{if } \gamma > 1, \text{ else mode is at } 0$$

4.2.2.8 Pareto distribution   The Pareto distribution has a very heavy tail and is used extensively in loss modeling when there is a high probability of very large losses. It is also known as the Pareto Type II or Lomax distribution.

$$f(x) = \frac{\alpha\theta^\alpha}{(x + \theta)^{\alpha+1}}$$

$$F(x) = 1 - \left(\frac{\theta}{x + \theta}\right)^\alpha$$

$$\mathrm{E}[X^k] = \frac{\theta^k \Gamma(k + 1)\Gamma(\alpha - k)}{\Gamma(\alpha)}, \quad -1 < k < \alpha$$

$$\mathrm{E}[X^k] = \frac{\theta^k k!}{(\alpha - 1) \cdots (\alpha - k)} \quad \text{if } k \text{ is an integer}$$

$$\mathrm{E}[X \wedge x] = \frac{\theta}{\alpha - 1}\left[1 - \left(\frac{\theta}{x + \theta}\right)^{\alpha-1}\right], \quad \alpha \neq 1$$

$$\mathrm{E}[X \wedge x] = -\theta \ln\left(\frac{\theta}{x + \theta}\right), \quad \alpha = 1$$

$$\mathrm{E}[(X \wedge x)^k] = \frac{\theta^k \Gamma(k + 1)\Gamma(\alpha - k)}{\Gamma(\alpha)}\beta[k + 1, \alpha - k; x/(x + \theta)]$$

$$+ x^k \left(\frac{\theta}{x + \theta}\right)^\alpha, \quad \text{for all } k$$

$$\text{Mode} = 0$$

4.2.2.9 Inverse Pareto distribution

$$f(x) = \frac{\tau\theta x^{\tau-1}}{(x+\theta)^{\tau+1}}$$

$$F(x) = \left(\frac{x}{x+\theta}\right)^{\tau}$$

$$E[X^k] = \frac{\theta^k \Gamma(\tau+k)\Gamma(1-k)}{\Gamma(\tau)}, \quad -\tau < k < 1$$

$$E[X^k] = \frac{\theta^k(-k)!}{(\tau-1)\cdots(\tau+k)} \quad \text{if } k \text{ is a negative integer}$$

$$E[(X \wedge x)^k] = \theta^k \tau \int_0^{x/(x+\theta)} y^{\tau+k-1}(1-y)^{-k}dy$$

$$+ x^k\left[1 - \left(\frac{x}{x+\theta}\right)^{\tau}\right], \quad k > -\tau$$

$$\text{Mode} = \theta\frac{\tau-1}{2}, \quad \text{if } \tau > 1, \text{ else the mode is at } 0$$

4.2.2.10 Paralogistic distribution

$$f(x) = \frac{\alpha^2(x/\theta)^{\alpha}}{x[1+(x/\theta)^{\alpha}]^{\alpha+1}}$$

$$F(x) = 1 - \left(\frac{1}{1+(x/\theta)^{\alpha}}\right)^{\alpha}$$

$$E[X^k] = \frac{\theta^k \Gamma(1+k/\alpha)\Gamma(\alpha-k/\alpha)}{\Gamma(\alpha)}, \quad -\alpha < k < \alpha^2$$

$$E[(X \wedge x)^k] = \frac{\theta^k \Gamma(1+k/\alpha)\Gamma(\alpha-k/\alpha)}{\Gamma(\alpha)}\beta(1+k/\alpha, \alpha-k/\alpha; 1-u)$$

$$+ x^k\left(\frac{1}{1+(x/\theta)^{\alpha}}\right)^{\alpha}, \quad k > -\alpha$$

$$\text{Mode} = \theta\left(\frac{\alpha-1}{\alpha^2+1}\right)^{1/\alpha}, \quad \text{if } \alpha > 1, \text{ else the mode is at } 0$$

4.2.2.11   Inverse paralogistic distribution

$$f(x) = \frac{\tau^2 (x/\theta)^{\tau^2}}{x[1 + (x/\theta)^\tau]^{\tau+1}}$$

$$F(x) = \left(\frac{(x/\theta)^\tau}{1 + (x/\theta)^\tau} \right)^\tau$$

$$\mathrm{E}[X^k] = \frac{\theta^k \Gamma(\tau + k/\tau)\Gamma(1 - k/\tau)}{\Gamma(\tau)}, \quad -\tau^2 < k < \tau$$

$$\mathrm{E}[(X \wedge x)^k] = \frac{\theta^k \Gamma(\tau + k/\tau)\Gamma(1 - k/\tau)}{\Gamma(\tau)} \beta(\tau + k/\tau, 1 - k/\tau; u) + x^k[1 - u^\tau]$$

$$\mathrm{Mode} = \theta \, (\tau - 1)^{1/\tau}, \quad \text{if } \tau > 1, \text{ else mode is at } 0$$

4.2.3   Three-parameter distributions

4.2.3.1   Transformed gamma distribution   The transformed (or generalized) gamma cdf is obtained from the gamma by replacing x/θ by $(x/\theta)^\tau$. Such transformations are discussed further in Section 4.7.

$$f(x) = \frac{\tau u^\alpha e^{-u}}{x \Gamma(\alpha)}, \quad u = (x/\theta)^\tau$$

$$F(x) = \Gamma(\alpha; u)$$

$$\mathrm{E}[X^k] = \frac{\theta^k \Gamma(\alpha + k/\tau)}{\Gamma(\alpha)}, \quad k > -\alpha\tau$$

$$\mathrm{E}[(X \wedge x)^k] = \frac{\theta^k \Gamma(\alpha + k/\tau)}{\Gamma(\alpha)} \Gamma(\alpha + k/\tau; u)$$

$$+ x^k[1 - \Gamma(\alpha; u)], \quad k > -\alpha\tau$$

$$\mathrm{Mode} = \theta \left(\frac{\alpha\tau - 1}{\tau} \right)^{1/\tau}, \quad \text{if } \alpha\tau > 1, \text{ else mode is at } 0$$

4.2.3.2 Inverse transformed gamma distribution   The inverse transformed gamma distribution is also known as the inverse generalized gamma distribution.

$$f(x) = \frac{\tau u^\alpha e^{-u}}{x\Gamma(\alpha)}, \quad u = (\theta/x)^\tau$$

$$F(x) = 1 - \Gamma(\alpha; u)$$

$$E[X^k] = \frac{\theta^k \Gamma(\alpha - k/\tau)}{\Gamma(\alpha)}, \quad k < \alpha\tau$$

$$E[(X \wedge x)^k] = \frac{\theta^k \Gamma(\alpha - k/\tau)}{\Gamma(\alpha)}[1 - \Gamma(\alpha - k/\tau; u)] + x^k \Gamma(\alpha; u)$$

$$= \frac{\theta^k G(\alpha - k/\tau; u)}{\Gamma(\alpha)} + x^k \Gamma(\alpha; u), \quad \text{all } k$$

$$\text{Mode} = \theta \left(\frac{\tau}{\alpha\tau + 1}\right)^{1/\tau}$$

4.2.3.3 Generalized Pareto distribution   The generalized Pareto distribution is also known as the beta of the second kind distribution.

$$f(x) = \frac{\Gamma(\alpha + \tau)}{\Gamma(\alpha)\Gamma(\tau)} \frac{\theta^\alpha x^{\tau-1}}{(x + \theta)^{\alpha+\tau}}$$

$$F(x) = \beta(\tau, \alpha; u), \quad u = \frac{x}{x + \theta}$$

$$E[X^k] = \frac{\theta^k \Gamma(\tau + k)\Gamma(\alpha - k)}{\Gamma(\alpha)\Gamma(\tau)}, \quad -\tau < k < \alpha$$

$$E[X^k] = \frac{\theta^k \tau(\tau + 1) \cdots (\tau + k - 1)}{(\alpha - 1) \cdots (\alpha - k)} \quad \text{if } k \text{ is an integer}$$

$$E[(X \wedge x)^k] = \frac{\theta^k \Gamma(\tau + k)\Gamma(\alpha - k)}{\Gamma(\alpha)\Gamma(\tau)}\beta(\tau + k, \alpha - k; u) + x^k [1 - F(x)], \quad k > -\tau$$

$$E[(X \wedge x)^k] = \frac{\theta^k \Gamma(\tau + k)\Gamma(\alpha - k)}{\Gamma(\alpha)\Gamma(\tau)}\beta(\tau + k, \alpha - k; u)$$

$$\text{Mode} = \theta\frac{\tau - 1}{\alpha + 1}, \quad \text{if } \tau > 1, \text{ else mode is at } 0$$

4.2.3.4 *Burr distribution* This distribution is also known as the Burr Type XII or Singh–Maddala distribution.

$$f(x) = \frac{\alpha\gamma(x/\theta)^\gamma}{x[1 + (x/\theta)^\gamma]^{\alpha+1}}$$

$$F(x) = 1 - u^\alpha, \quad u = \frac{1}{1 + (x/\theta)^\gamma}.$$

$$E[X^k] = \frac{\theta^k \Gamma(1 + k/\gamma)\Gamma(\alpha - k/\gamma)}{\Gamma(\alpha)}, \quad -\gamma < k < \alpha\gamma$$

$$E[(X \wedge x)^k] = \frac{\theta^k \Gamma(1 + k/\gamma)\Gamma(\alpha - k/\gamma)}{\Gamma(\alpha)}\beta(1 + k/\gamma, \alpha - k/\gamma; 1 - u)$$

$$+ x^k u^\alpha, \quad k > -\gamma.$$

$$\text{Mode} = \theta\left(\frac{\gamma - 1}{\alpha\gamma + 1}\right)^{1/\gamma}, \quad \text{if } \gamma > 1, \text{ else the mode is at } 0.$$

4.2.3.5 *Inverse Burr distribution* The inverse Burr (or Dagum) cdf is obtained from the Burr by replacing x/θ by $(x/\theta)^{-1}$

$$f(x) = \frac{\tau\gamma(x/\theta)^{\gamma\tau}}{x[1 + (x/\theta)^\gamma]^{\tau+1}}$$

$$F(x) = u^\tau, \quad u = \frac{(x/\theta)^\gamma}{1 + (x/\theta)^\gamma}$$

$$E[X^k] = \frac{\theta^k \Gamma(\tau + k/\gamma)\Gamma(1 - k/\gamma)}{\Gamma(\tau)}, \quad -\tau\gamma < k < \gamma$$

$$E[(X \wedge x)^k] = \frac{\theta^k \Gamma(\tau + k/\gamma)\Gamma(1 - k/\gamma)}{\Gamma(\tau)}\beta(\tau + k/\gamma, 1 - k/\gamma; u)$$

$$+ x^k[1 - u^\tau], \quad k > -\tau\gamma$$

$$\text{Mode} = \theta\left(\frac{\tau\gamma - 1}{\gamma + 1}\right)^{1/\gamma}, \quad \text{if } \tau\gamma > 1, \text{ else mode is at } 0$$

4.2.3.6 Log-t distribution   Let Y have a t distribution with r degrees of freedom. Then $X = \exp(\sigma Y + \mu)$ has the log-t distribution. Positive moments do not exist for this distribution. Just as the t distribution has a heavier tail than the normal distribution, this distribution has a heavier tail than the lognormal distribution.

$$f(x) = \frac{\Gamma\left(\dfrac{r+1}{2}\right)}{x\sigma\sqrt{\pi r}\,\Gamma\left(\dfrac{r}{2}\right)\left[1 + \dfrac{1}{r}\left(\dfrac{\ln x - \mu}{\sigma}\right)^2\right]^{(r+1)/2}}$$

$$F(x) = F_r\left(\frac{\ln x - \mu}{\sigma}\right) \quad \text{with } F_r(t) \text{ the cdf of a } t \text{ distribution with } r \text{ degrees of freedom}$$

$$F(x) = \begin{cases} \dfrac{1}{2}\beta\left[\dfrac{r}{2}, \dfrac{1}{2}; \dfrac{r}{r + \left(\dfrac{\ln x - \mu}{\sigma}\right)^2}\right], & 0 < x \le e^\mu \\[4ex] 1 - \dfrac{1}{2}\beta\left[\dfrac{r}{2}, \dfrac{1}{2}; \dfrac{r}{r + \left(\dfrac{\ln x - \mu}{\sigma}\right)^2}\right], & x \ge e^\mu \end{cases}$$

4.2.4 Four-parameter distributions

4.2.4.1 Transformed beta distribution   This distribution is also known as the generalized beta of the second kind, or Pearson Type VI distribution.

$$f(x) = \frac{\Gamma(\alpha + \tau)}{\Gamma(\alpha)\Gamma(\tau)} \frac{\gamma(x/\theta)^{\gamma\tau}}{x[1 + (x/\theta)^\gamma]^{\alpha+\tau}}$$

$$F(x) = \beta(\tau, \alpha; u), \quad u = \frac{(x/\theta)^\gamma}{1 + (x/\theta)^\gamma}$$

$$\mathrm{E}[X^k] = \frac{\theta^k \Gamma(\tau + k/\gamma)\Gamma(\alpha - k/\gamma)}{\Gamma(\alpha)\Gamma(\tau)}, \quad -\tau\gamma < k < \alpha\gamma$$

$$\mathrm{E}[(X \wedge x)^k] = \frac{\theta^k \Gamma(\tau + k/\gamma)\Gamma(\alpha - k/\gamma)}{\Gamma(\alpha)\Gamma(\tau)}\beta(\tau + k/\gamma, \alpha - k/\gamma; u)$$
$$+ x^k[1 - F(x)], \quad k > -\tau\gamma$$

$$\text{Mode} = \theta\left(\frac{\tau\gamma - 1}{\alpha\gamma + 1}\right)^{1/\gamma}, \quad \text{if } \tau\gamma > 1, \text{ else the mode is at } 0$$

We now introduce some distributions with finite support. Such distributions can be used in connection with describing losses as percentages of maximum losses with support on $[0, 1]$. In the distributions listed below, the support is on $[0, \theta]$. A shift to support to $[d, \theta + d]$ is accomplished by replacing x by $x - d$ in the formulas given below.

4.2.5   Distributions with finite support

4.2.5.1   Beta distribution

$$f(x) = \frac{\Gamma(a+b)}{\Gamma(a)\Gamma(b)} u^a (1-u)^{b-1} \frac{1}{x}, \quad 0 < x < \theta, \quad u = x/\theta$$

$$F(x) = \beta(a, b; u)$$

$$\mathrm{E}[X^k] = \frac{\theta^k \Gamma(a+b)\Gamma(a+k)}{\Gamma(a)\Gamma(a+b+k)}, \quad k > -a$$

$$\mathrm{E}[X^k] = \frac{\theta^k a(a+1)\cdots(a+k-1)}{(a+b)(a+b+1)\cdots(a+b+k-1)} \quad \text{if } k \text{ is an integer,}$$

$$\mathrm{E}[(X \wedge x)^k] = \frac{\theta^k a(a+1)\cdots(a+k-1)}{(a+b)(a+b+1)\cdots(a+b+k-1)} \beta(a+k, b; u)$$
$$+ x^k [1 - \beta(a, b; u)]$$

4.2.5.2   Generalized beta distribution

$$f(x) = \frac{\Gamma(a+b)}{\Gamma(a)\Gamma(b)} u^a (1-u)^{b-1} \frac{\tau}{x}, \quad 0 < x < \theta, \quad u = (x/\theta)^\tau$$

$$F(x) = \beta(a, b; u)$$

$$\mathrm{E}[X^k] = \frac{\theta^k \Gamma(a+b)\Gamma(a+k/\tau)}{\Gamma(a)\Gamma(a+b+k/\tau)}, \quad k > -a\tau$$

$$\mathrm{E}[(X \wedge x)^k] = \frac{\theta^k \Gamma(a+b)\Gamma(a+k/\tau)}{\Gamma(a)\Gamma(a+b+k/\tau)} \beta(a+k/\tau, b; u) + x^k [1 - \beta(a, b; u)]$$

4.3   SELECTED DISTRIBUTIONS AND THEIR RELATIONSHIPS

4.3.1   Introduction

There are many ways to organize distributions into groups. Families such as Pearson (13 types including the normal distribution), Burr (12 types), Stoppa (5 types), and Dagum (11 types) are discussed in Chapter 2 of the book by Kleiber and Kotz [67]. The same distribution can appear in more than one system, indicating that there are many relationships among the distributions beyond those presented here. The systems presented in Section 4.3.2 are particularly useful for risk modeling because all the members have

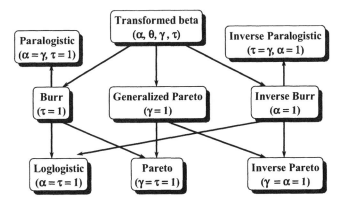

Fig. 4.1 Transformed beta family

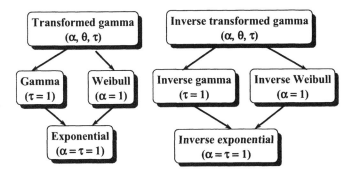

Fig. 4.2 Transformed/inverse transformed gamma family

support on the positive real line and all tend to be skewed to the right. For a comprehensive set of continuous distributions, the two volumes by Johnson, Kotz, and Balakrishnan ([63], [64]) are a valuable reference. In addition, there are entire books devoted to single distributions (such as Arnold [5] for the Pareto distribution).

4.3.2   Two important parametric families

As noted when defining parametric families, many of the distributions presented in this section are special cases of others. For example, a Weibull distribution with $\tau = 1$ and θ arbitrary is an exponential distribution. Through this process, many of our distributions can be organized into related groupings, as illustrated in Figures 4.1 and 4.2. The transformed beta family includes two special cases of a different nature. The paralogistic and inverse paralogistic distributions are created by setting the two nonscale parameters of the Burr

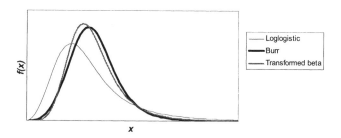

Fig. 4.3   Transformed beta nested members - I

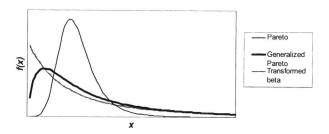

Fig. 4.4   Transformed beta nested members -II

and inverse Burr distributions equal to each other rather than to a specified value.

Figure 4.3 and 4.4 each show three nested members of the transformed beta family. "Nested" means that the distribution with fewer parameters can be obtained as special cases by setting one or more parameters to a fixed number.

Figures 4.5 and 4.6 show some nested members from the transformed and inverse transformed gamma families.

4.4 LIMITING DISTRIBUTIONS

The classification in Section 4.3 involved distributions that are special cases of other distributions. Another way to relate distributions is to see what happens as parameters go to their limiting values of zero or infinity.

Example 4.1 *Show that the transformed gamma distribution is a limiting case of the transformed beta distribution as $\theta \to \infty$, $\alpha \to \infty$, and $\theta/\alpha^{1/\gamma} \to \xi$, a constant.*

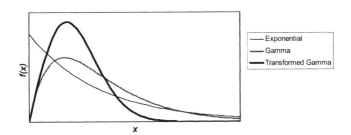

Fig. 4.5   Transformed gamma nested members

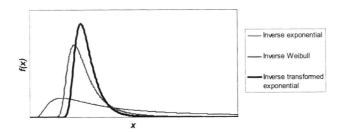

Fig. 4.6   Inverse transformed gamma nested members

The demonstration relies on two facts concerning limits:

$$\lim_{\alpha \to \infty} \frac{e^{-\alpha}\alpha^{\alpha-1/2}(2\pi)^{1/2}}{\Gamma(\alpha)} = 1 \tag{4.1}$$

and

$$\lim_{a \to \infty} \left(1 + \frac{x}{a}\right)^{a+b} = e^x. \tag{4.2}$$

The limit in equation (4.1) is known as Stirling's formula and provides an approximation for the gamma function. The limit in equation (4.2) is a standard result found in most calculus texts. To ensure that the ratio $\theta/\alpha^{1/\gamma}$ goes to a constant, it is sufficient to force it to be constant as α and θ become larger and larger. This can be accomplished by substituting $\xi\alpha^{1/\gamma}$ for θ in the transformed beta pdf and then letting $\alpha \to \infty$. The first steps, which also include using Stirling's formula to replace two of the gamma function terms, are

$$
\begin{aligned}
f(x) &= \frac{\Gamma(\alpha+\tau)\gamma x^{\gamma\tau-1}}{\Gamma(\alpha)\Gamma(\tau)\theta^{\gamma\tau}(1+x^\gamma\theta^{-\gamma})^{\alpha+\tau}} \\
&= \frac{e^{-\alpha-\tau}(\alpha+\tau)^{\alpha+\tau-1/2}(2\pi)^{1/2}\gamma x^{\gamma\tau-1}}{e^{-\alpha}\alpha^{\alpha-1/2}(2\pi)^{1/2}\Gamma(\tau)(\xi\alpha^{1/\gamma})^{\gamma\tau}(1+x^\gamma\xi^{-\gamma}\alpha^{-1})^{\alpha+\tau}} \\
&= \frac{e^{-\tau}[(\alpha+\tau)/\alpha]^{\alpha+\tau-1/2}\gamma x^{\gamma\tau-1}}{\Gamma(\tau)\xi^{\gamma\tau}\left[1+(x/\xi)^\gamma/\alpha\right]^{\alpha+\tau}}.
\end{aligned}
$$

The two limits

$$\lim_{\alpha \to \infty} \left(1 + \frac{\tau}{\alpha}\right)^{\alpha+\tau-1/2} = e^\tau, \qquad \lim_{\alpha \to \infty} \left[1 + \frac{(x/\xi)^\gamma}{\alpha}\right]^{\alpha+\tau} = e^{(x/\xi)^\gamma}$$

can be substituted to yield

$$\lim_{\alpha \to \infty} f(x) = \frac{\gamma x^{\gamma\tau-1}e^{-(x/\xi)^\gamma}}{\Gamma(\tau)\xi^{\gamma\tau}}$$

which is the pdf of the transformed gamma distribution.   □

With a similar argument, the inverse transformed gamma distribution is obtained by letting τ go to infinity instead of α (see Exercise 4.3).

Because the Burr distribution is a transformed beta distribution with $\tau = 1$, its limiting case is the transformed gamma with $\tau = 1$ (using the parameterization in the previous example), which is the Weibull distribution. Similarly, the inverse Burr has the inverse Weibull as a limiting case. Finally, letting $\tau = \gamma = 1$ shows that the limiting case for the Pareto distribution is the exponential (and similarly for their inverse distributions).

As a final illustration of a limiting case, consider the transformed gamma distribution as parameterized above. Let $\gamma^{-1}\sqrt{\xi^\gamma} \to \sigma$ and $\gamma^{-1}(\xi^\gamma\tau - 1) \to \mu$.

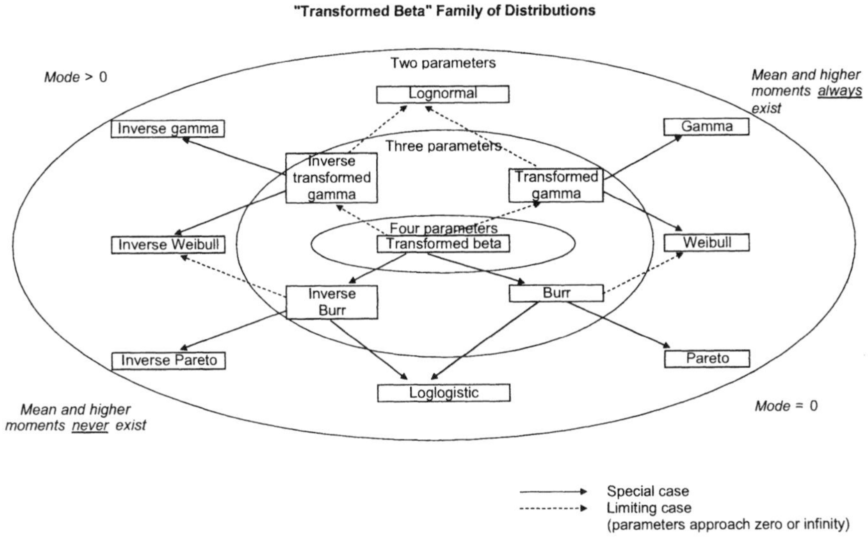

Fig. 4.7 Distributional relationships and characteristics

If this is done by letting $\tau \to \infty$ (so both γ and ξ must go to zero), the limiting distribution will be lognormal.

In Figure 4.7 some of the limiting and special case relationships are shown. Other interesting facts about the various distributions are also given.[1]

4.5   THE ROLE OF PARAMETERS

One way to classify models is on the basis of the number of parameters in the model. The number of parameters needed in the model is an indication of the complexity of the model. Arguments for a simple model include the following:

- With few parameters required in its specification, it is more likely that each one can be determined more accurately.

- A simple model is more likely to be stable when used across time and across settings. That is, if the model does well today, it (perhaps with necessary changes to reflect inflation or other temporal phenomena) will probably do well tomorrow and will also do well in other, similar, situations.

---

[1] Thanks to David Clark for creating this picture.

- Because data can often be irregular, a simple model may provide necessary smoothing.

Of course, a complex model also has advantages:

- With many parameters required in its specification, it can more closely match reality.

- With many parameters required in its specification, it can more closely match irregularities that are observed in the data.

Another way to express the difference is that simpler models can be estimated more accurately, but the simple model itself may not be a good description of the underlying phenomenon. The principle of parsimony states that the simplest model that adequately reflects reality should be used. The definition of "adequately" will depend on the purpose for which the model is to be used.

In the following subsections, we will move from simpler models to more complex models. There is some difficulty in naming the various classifications because there is not universal agreement on the definitions. With the exception of parametric distributions, the other category names have been created by the authors. It should also be understood that these categories do not cover the universe of possible models, nor will every model be easy to categorize. These should be considered as qualitative descriptions.

4.5.1 Parametric and scale distributions

These models are simple enough to be specified by a few key numbers.

Definition 4.2 *A **parametric distribution** is a set of distribution functions, each member of which is determined by specifying one or more values called **parameters**. The number of parameters is fixed and finite.*

The most familiar parametric distribution is the normal distribution with parameters μ and σ. When values for these two parameters are specified, the distribution function is completely known.

These are the simplest distributions in this subsection, because typically only a small number of values need to be specified. Within the class of parametric distributions, distributions with fewer parameters are simpler than those with more parameters.

For much of risk modeling work, it is especially convenient if the form of the distribution is unchanged when the random variable is multiplied by a constant. The most common uses for this phenomenon are to model the effect of inflation and to accommodate a change in the monetary unit.

Definition 4.3 *A parametric distribution is a **scale distribution** if, when a random variable from that set of distributions is multiplied by a positive constant, the resulting random variable is also in that set of distributions.*

Example 4.4 *Demonstrate that the exponential distribution is a scale distribution.*

The distribution function of the exponential distribution is

$$F_X(x) = 1 - e^{-x/\theta}, \quad x > 0.$$

. Let $Y = cX$, where $c > 0$. Then,

$$\begin{aligned}
F_Y(y) &= \Pr(Y \le y) \\
&= \Pr(cX \le y) \\
&= \Pr\left(X \le \frac{y}{c}\right) \\
&= 1 - e^{-y/c\theta}, \quad y > 0.
\end{aligned}$$

This is an exponential distribution with parameter $c\theta$. So the form of the distribution has not changed, only the parameter value. □

Definition 4.5 *For random variables with nonnegative support, a* **scale parameter** *is a parameter for a scale distribution that meets two conditions. First, when the random variable of a member of the scale distribution is multiplied by a positive constant, the parameter is multiplied by the same constant. Second, when the random variable of a member of the scale distribution is multiplied by a positive constant, all other parameters are unchanged.*

Example 4.6 *Demonstrate that the gamma distribution has a scale parameter.*

Let X have the gamma distribution and $Y = cX$. Then, using the incomplete gamma notation given in Appendix A,

$$\begin{aligned}
F_Y(y) &= \Pr\left(X \le \frac{y}{c}\right) \\
&= \Gamma\left(\alpha; \frac{y}{c\theta}\right)
\end{aligned}$$

indicating that Y has a gamma distribution with parameters α and $c\theta$. Therefore, the parameter θ is a scale parameter. □

It is often possible to recognize a scale parameter from looking at the distribution or density function. In particular, the distribution function would have x always appear together with the scale parameter θ as x/θ.

4.5.2 Finite mixture distributions

Distributions that are finite mixtures have distributions that are weighted averages of other distribution functions.

Definition 4.7 *A random variable Y is a **k-point mixture**[2] of the random variables $X_1, X_2, \ldots, X_k$ if its cdf is given by*

$$F_Y(y) = a_1 F_{X_1}(y) + a_2 F_{X_2}(y) + \cdots + a_k F_{X_k}(y), \tag{4.3}$$

where all $a_j > 0$ and $a_1 + a_2 + \cdots + a_k = 1$.

This essentially assigns weight a_j to the jth distribution. The weights are usually considered as parameters. Thus the total number of parameters is the sum of the parameters on the k distributions plus $k - 1$. Note that, if we have 20 different distributions, a two-point mixture allows us to create over 200 new distributions.[3] This may be sufficient for most modeling situations. Nevertheless, these are still parametric distributions, though perhaps with many parameters.

Example 4.8 *Models used in insurance can provide some insight into models that could be used for operational risk losses, particularly those that are insurable risks. For models involving general liability insurance, the Insurance Services Office has had some success with a mixture of two Pareto distributions. They also found that five parameters were not necessary. The distribution they selected has cdf*

$$F(x) = 1 - a \left(\frac{\theta_1}{\theta_1 + x} \right)^{\alpha} - (1 - a) \left(\frac{\theta_2}{\theta_2 + x} \right)^{\alpha+2}.$$

Note that the shape parameters in the two Pareto distributions differ by 2. The second distribution places more probability on smaller values. This might be a model for frequent, small losses while the first distribution covers large, but infrequent losses. This distribution has only four parameters, bringing some parsimony to the modeling process. ☐

Suppose we do not know how many distributions should be in the mixture. Then the value of k itself also becomes a parameter, as indicated in the following definition.

Definition 4.9 *A **variable-component mixture distribution** has a distribution function that can be written as*

$$F(x) = \sum_{j=1}^{K} a_j F_j(x), \quad \sum_{j=1}^{K} a_j = 1, \ a_j > 0, \ j = 1, \ldots, K, \ K = 1, 2, \ldots.$$

---

[2] The words "mixed" and "mixture" have been used interchangeably to refer to the type of distribution described here as well as distributions that are partly discrete and partly continuous. This text will not attempt to resolve that confusion. The context will make clear which type of distribution is being considered.

[3] There are actually $\binom{20}{2} + 20 = 210$ choices. The extra 20 represent the cases where both distributions are of the same type but with different parameters.

THE ROLE OF PARAMETERS   77

These models have been called *semiparametric* because in complexity they are between parametric models and nonparametric models (see Section 4.5.3). This distinction becomes more important when model selection is discussed in Chapter 12. When the number of parameters is to be estimated from data, hypothesis tests to determine the appropriate number of parameters become more difficult. When all of the components have the same parametric distribution (but different parameters), the resulting distribution is called a "variable mixture of gs" distribution, where g stands for the name of the component distribution.

Example 4.10 *Determine the distribution, density, and hazard rate functions for the variable mixture of exponential distributions.*

A combination of exponential distribution functions can be written

$$F(x) = 1 - a_1 e^{-x/\theta_1} - a_2 e^{-x/\theta_2} - \cdots - a_K e^{-x/\theta_K},$$

$$\sum_{j=1}^{K} a_j = 1,\ a_j, \theta_j > 0,\ j = 1, \ldots, K,\ K = 1, 2, \ldots.$$

and then the other functions are

$$f(x) = a_1 \theta_1^{-1} e^{-x/\theta_1} + a_2 \theta_2^{-1} e^{-x/\theta_2} + \cdots + a_K \theta_K^{-1} e^{-x/\theta_K},$$

$$h(x) = \frac{a_1 \theta_1^{-1} e^{-x/\theta_1} + a_2 \theta_2^{-1} e^{-x/\theta_2} + \cdots + a_K \theta_K^{-1} e^{-x/\theta_K}}{a_1 e^{-x/\theta_1} + a_2 e^{-x/\theta_2} + \cdots + a_K e^{-x/\theta_K}}.$$

The number of parameters is not fixed nor is it even limited. For example, when $K = 2$ there are three parameters $(a_1, \theta_1, \theta_2)$, noting that a_2 is not a parameter because once a_1 is set the value of a_2 is determined. However, when $K = 4$ there are seven parameters. □

Example 4.11 *Illustrate how a two-point mixture of gamma variables can create a bimodal distribution.*

Consider a mixture of two gamma distributions with equal weights. One has parameters $\alpha = 4$ and $\theta = 7$ (for a mode of 21) and the other has parameters $\alpha = 15$ and $\theta = 7$ (for a mode of 98). The density function is

$$f(x) = 0.5 \frac{x^3 e^{-x/7}}{3! 7^4} + 0.5 \frac{x^{14} e^{-x/7}}{14! 7^{15}}$$

and a graph appears in Figure 4.8. □

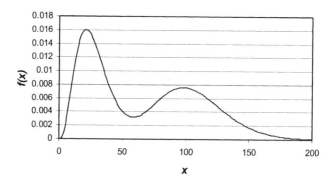

Fig. 4.8 Two-point mixture of gammas distribution.

4.5.3 Data-dependent distributions

For Models 1–5 and many of the examples, we postulate a shape for a distribution by assuming that the distribution is of a particular form (e.g., uniform, lognormal, gamma). The distribution is completely specified when its parameters are specified. It is also possible to construct models for which we do not specify the form a priori. We can require data in the determination of shape. Such models also have parameters but are often called nonparametric. It is convenient to think of parameters in a broader sense: as an independent piece of information required in specifying a distribution. Then the number of independent pieces of information required to fully specify a distribution is the number of parameters.

Definition 4.12 *A **data-dependent distribution** is at least as complex as the data or knowledge that produced it, and the number of "parameters" increases as the number of data points or amount of knowledge increases.*

Essentially, these models have as many (or more) "parameters" than observations in the data set. The empirical distribution as illustrated by Model 6 on page 31 is a data-dependent distribution. Each data point contributes probability $1/n$ to the probability function, so the n parameters are the n observations in the data set that produced the empirical distribution.

Another example of a data-dependent model is the kernel smoothing density model. Rather than placing a mass of probability $1/n$ at each data point, a continuous density function with weight $1/n$ replaces the data point. This continuous density function is usually centered at the data point. Such a continuous density function surrounds each data point. The kernel-smoothed distribution is the weighted average of all the continuous density functions. As a result, the kernel smoothed distribution follows the shape of data in a general sense, but not exactly as in the case of the empirical distribution.

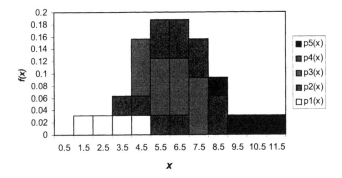

Fig. 4.9   Kernel density distribution

A simple example is given below. The idea of kernel density smoothing is illustrated in Example 4.13. Included, without explanation, is the concept of bandwidth. The role of bandwidth is self-evident.

Example 4.13 *Construct a kernel smoothing model from Model 6 using the uniform kernel and a bandwidth of 2.*

The probability density function is

$$f(x) = \sum_{j=1}^{5} p_6(x_j) K_j(x),$$

$$K_j(x) = \begin{cases} 0, & |x - x_j| > 2, \\ 0.25, & |x - x_j| \le 2, \end{cases}$$

where the sum is taken over the five points where the original model has positive probability. For example, the first term of the sum is the function

$$p_6(x_1) K_1(x) = \begin{cases} 0, & x < 1, \\ 0.03125, & 1 \le x \le 5, \\ 0, & x > 5. \end{cases}$$

The complete density function is the sum of five such functions, which are illustrated in Figure 4.9. $\square$

Note that both the kernel smoothing model and the empirical distribution can also be written as mixture distributions. The reason that these models are classified separately is that the number of components is directly related to the sample size. This is not the case with finite mixture models where the number of components in the model is not a function of the amount of data.

4.6 TAILS OF DISTRIBUTIONS

The **tail** of a distribution (more properly, the right tail) is the portion of the distribution corresponding to large values of the random variable. Understanding large possible operational risk loss values is important because these have the greatest impact on the total of operational risk losses. Random variables that tend to assign higher probabilities to larger values are said to be heavier-tailed. Tail weight can be a relative concept (model A has a heavier tail than model B) or an absolute concept (distributions with a certain property are classified as heavy-tailed). When choosing models, tail weight can help narrow the choices or can confirm a choice for a model. Heavy-tailed distributions are particularly important of operational risk in connection with extreme value theory (see Chapter 7).

4.6.1 Classification based on moments

Recall that in the continuous case the kth raw moment for a random variable that takes on only positive values (like most insurance payment variables) is given by $\int_0^\infty x^k f(x)dx$. Depending on the density function and the value of k, this integral may not exist (that is, it may be infinite). One way of classifying distribution is on the basis of whether all moments exist. It is generally agreed that the existence of all positive moments indicates a light right tail, while the existence of only positive moments up to a certain value (or existence of no positive moments at all) indicates a heavy right tail.

Example 4.14 *Demonstrate that for the gamma distribution all positive moments exist but for the Pareto distribution they do not.*

For the gamma distribution, the raw moments are

$$\mu_k' = \int_0^\infty x^k \frac{x^{\alpha-1}e^{-x/\theta}}{\Gamma(\alpha)\theta^\alpha}dx$$

$$= \int_0^\infty (y\theta)^k \frac{(y\theta)^{\alpha-1}e^{-y}}{\Gamma(\alpha)\theta^\alpha}\theta dy, \text{ making the substitution } y = x/\theta$$

$$= \frac{\theta^k}{\Gamma(\alpha)}\Gamma(\alpha+k) < \infty \text{ for all } k > 0.$$

For the Pareto distribution, they are

$$\mu_k' = \int_0^\infty x^k \frac{\alpha\theta^\alpha}{(x+\theta)^{\alpha+1}}dx$$

$$= \int_\theta^\infty (y-\theta)^k \frac{\alpha\theta^\alpha}{y^{\alpha+1}}dy, \text{ making the substitution } y = x+\theta$$

$$= \alpha\theta^\alpha \int_\theta^\infty \sum_{j=0}^k \binom{k}{j} y^{j-\alpha-1}(-\theta)^{k-j}dy \text{ for integer values of } k.$$

The integral exists only if all of the exponents on y in the sum are less than -1. That is, if $j - \alpha - 1 < -1$ for all j, or, equivalently, if $k < \alpha$. Therefore, only some moments exist. □

By this classification, the Pareto distribution is said to have a heavy tail and the gamma distribution is said to have a light tail. A look at the moment formulas in this chapter reveals which distributions have heavy tails and which do not, as indicated by the existence of moments.

4.6.2 Classification based on tail behavior

One commonly used indication that one distribution has a heavier tail than another distribution with the same mean is that the ratio of the two survival functions should diverge to infinity (with the heavier-tailed distribution in the numerator) as the argument becomes large. This classification is based on asymptotic properties of the distributions. The divergence implies that the numerator distribution puts significantly more probability on large values. Note that it is equivalent to examine the ratio of density functions. The limit of the ratio will be the same, as can be seen by an application of L'Hôpital's rule:

$$\lim_{x \to \infty} \frac{\overline{F}_1(x)}{\overline{F}_2(x)} = \lim_{x \to \infty} \frac{\overline{F}'_1(x)}{\overline{F}'_2(x)} = \lim_{x \to \infty} \frac{-f_1(x)}{-f_2(x)}.$$

Example 4.15 *Demonstrate that the Pareto distribution has a heavier tail than the gamma distribution using the limit of the ratio of their density functions.*

To avoid confusion, the letters τ and λ will be used for the parameters of the gamma distribution instead of the customary α and θ. Then the required limit is

$$\lim_{x \to \infty} \frac{f_{\text{Pareto}}(x)}{f_{\text{gamma}}(x)} = \lim_{x \to \infty} \frac{\alpha \theta^\alpha (x + \theta)^{-\alpha-1}}{x^{\tau-1} e^{-x/\lambda} \lambda^{-\tau} \Gamma(\tau)^{-1}}$$

$$= c \lim_{x \to \infty} \frac{e^{x/\lambda}}{(x + \theta)^{\alpha+1} x^{\tau-1}}$$

$$> c \lim_{x \to \infty} \frac{e^{x/\lambda}}{(x + \theta)^{\alpha+\tau}}$$

and, either by application of L'Hôpital's rule or by remembering that exponentials go to infinity faster than polynomials, the limit is infinity. Figure 4.10 shows a portion of the density functions for a Pareto distribution with parameters $\alpha = 3$ and $\theta = 10$ and a gamma distribution with parameters $\alpha = \frac{1}{3}$ and $\theta = 15$. Both distributions have a mean of 5 and a variance of 75. The graph is consistent with the algebraic derivation. □

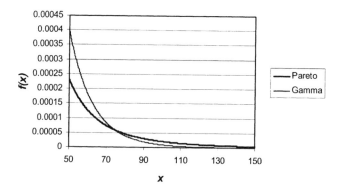

Fig. 4.10   Tails of gamma and Pareto distributions

4.6.3   Classification based on hazard rate function

The hazard rate function also reveals information about the tail of the distribution. Distributions with decreasing hazard rate functions have heavy tails.
Distributions with increasing hazard rate functions have light tails. The distribution with constant hazard rate, the exponential distribution, has neither
increasing nor decreasing failure rates. For distributions with (asymptotically) monotone hazard rates, distributions with exponential tails divide the
distributions into heavy-tailed and light-tailed distributions.

Comparisons between distributions can be made on the basis of the rate of
increase or decrease of the hazard rate function. For example, a distribution
has a lighter tail than another if, for large values of the argument, its hazard
rate function is increasing at a faster rate.

Example 4.16 *Compare the tails of the Pareto and gamma distributions by
looking at their hazard rate functions.*

The hazard rate function for the Pareto distribution is

$$h(x) = \frac{f(x)}{\overline{F}(x)} = \frac{\alpha\theta^{\alpha}(x+\theta)^{-\alpha-1}}{\theta^{\alpha}(x+\theta)^{-\alpha}} = \frac{\alpha}{x+\theta}$$

which is decreasing. For the gamma distribution we need to be a bit more
clever because there is no closed form expression for $\overline{F}(x)$. Observe that

$$\frac{1}{h(x)} = \frac{\int_x^{\infty} f(t)dt}{f(x)} = \frac{\int_0^{\infty} f(x+y)dy}{f(x)}$$

and so, if $f(x+y)/f(x)$ is an increasing function of x for any fixed y, then
$1/h(x)$ will be increasing in x and so the random variable will have a decreasing

hazard rate. Now, for the gamma distribution

$$\frac{f(x+y)}{f(x)} = \frac{(x+y)^{\alpha-1}e^{-(x+y)/\theta}}{x^{\alpha-1}e^{-x/\theta}} = \left(1 + \frac{y}{x}\right)^{\alpha-1} e^{-y/\theta},$$

which is strictly increasing in x provided $\alpha < 1$ and strictly decreasing in x if $\alpha > 1$. By this measure, some gamma distributions have a heavy tail (those with $\alpha < 1$) and some have a light tail. Note that when $\alpha = 1$ we have the exponential distribution and a constant hazard rate. Also, even though $h(x)$ is complicated in the gamma case, we know what happens for large x. Because $f(x)$ and $\overline{F}(x)$ both go to 0 as $x \to \infty$, L'Hôpital's rule yields

$$\lim_{x\to\infty} h(x) = \lim_{x\to\infty} \frac{f(x)}{\overline{F}(x)} = -\lim_{x\to\infty} \frac{f'(x)}{f(x)} = -\lim_{x\to\infty}\left[\frac{d}{dx}\ln f(x)\right]$$

$$= -\lim_{x\to\infty}\frac{d}{dx}\left[(\alpha-1)\ln x - \frac{x}{\theta}\right] = \lim_{x\to\infty}\left(\frac{1}{\theta} - \frac{\alpha-1}{x}\right) = \frac{1}{\theta}.$$

That is, $h(x) \to 1/\theta$ as $x \to \infty$. □

The mean excess function also gives information about tail weight. If the mean excess function is increasing in d, the distribution is considered to have a heavy tail. If the mean excess function is decreasing in d, the distribution is considered to have a light tail. Comparisons between distributions can be made on the basis of the rate of increase or decrease of the mean excess function. For example, a distribution has a heavier tail than another if, for large values of the argument, its mean excess function is increasing at a lower rate.

In fact, the mean excess loss function and the hazard rate are closely related in several ways. First, note that

$$\frac{\overline{F}(y+d)}{\overline{F}(d)} = \frac{\exp\left[-\int_0^{y+d} h(x)dx\right]}{\exp\left[-\int_0^d h(x)dx\right]} = \exp\left[-\int_d^{y+d} h(x)dx\right]$$

$$= \exp\left[-\int_0^y h(d+t)dt\right].$$

Therefore, if the hazard rate is decreasing, then for fixed y it follows that $\int_0^y h(d+t)dt$ is a decreasing function of d, and from the above $\overline{F}(y+d)/\overline{F}(d)$ is an increasing function of d. But from (2.5), the mean excess loss function may be expressed as

$$e(d) = \frac{\int_d^\infty \overline{F}(x)dx}{\overline{F}(d)} = \int_0^\infty \frac{\overline{F}(y+d)}{\overline{F}(d)}dy.$$

Thus, if the hazard rate is a decreasing function, then the mean excess loss function $e(d)$ is an increasing function of d because the same is true of $\overline{F}(y+$

$d)/\overline{F}(d)$ for fixed y. Similarly, if the hazard rate is an increasing function, then the mean excess loss function is a decreasing function. It is worth noting (and is perhaps counterintuitive), however, that the converse implication is not true. Exercise 4.16 gives an example of a distribution that has a decreasing mean excess loss function, but the hazard rate is not increasing for all values. Nevertheless, the implications described above are generally consistent with the above discussions of heaviness of the tail.

There is a second relationship between the mean excess loss function and the hazard rate. As $d \to \infty$, $\overline{F}(d)$ and $\int_d^\infty \overline{F}(x)dx$ go to 0. Thus, the limiting behavior of the mean excess loss function as $d \to \infty$ may be ascertained using L'Hôpital's rule because formula (2.5) holds. We have

$$\lim_{d\to\infty} e(d) = \lim_{d\to\infty} \frac{\int_d^\infty \overline{F}(x)dx}{\overline{F}(d)} = \lim_{d\to\infty} \frac{-\overline{F}(d)}{-f(d)} = \lim_{d\to\infty} \frac{1}{h(d)}$$

as long as the indicated limits exist. These limiting relationships may useful if the form of $F(x)$ is complicated.

Example 4.17 *Examine the behavior of the mean excess loss function of the gamma distribution.*

Because $e(d) = \int_d^\infty \overline{F}(x)dx/\overline{F}(d)$ and $\overline{F}(x)$ is complicated, $e(d)$ is complicated. But $e(0) = \mathrm{E}(X) = \alpha\theta$, and, using Example 4.16, we have

$$\lim_{x\to\infty} e(x) = \lim_{x\to\infty} \frac{1}{h(x)} = \frac{1}{\lim_{x\to\infty} h(x)} = \theta.$$

Also, from Example 4.16, $h(x)$ is strictly decreasing in x for $\alpha < 1$ and strictly increasing in x for $\alpha > 1$, implying that $e(d)$ is strictly increasing from $e(0) = \alpha\theta$ to $e(\infty) = \theta$ for $\alpha < 1$ and strictly decreasing from $e(0) = \alpha\theta$ to $e(\infty) = \theta$ for $\alpha > 1$. For $\alpha = 1$, we have the exponential distribution for which $e(d) = \theta$. □

4.7 CREATING NEW DISTRIBUTIONS

4.7.1 Introduction

This section indicates how new parametric distributions can be created from existing ones. Many of the distributions in this chapter were created this way. In each case, a new random variable is created by transforming the original random variable in some way or using some other method.

4.7.2 Multiplication by a constant

This transformation is equivalent to applying loss size inflation uniformly across all loss levels and is known as a change of scale. For example, if this year's losses are given by the random variable X, then uniform loss inflation of 5% indicates that next year's losses can be modeled with the random variable $Y = 1.05X$.

Theorem 4.18 *Let X be a continuous random variable with pdf $f_X(x)$ and cdf $F_X(x)$. Let $Y = \theta X$ with $\theta > 0$. Then*

$$F_Y(y) = F_X\left(\frac{y}{\theta}\right), \quad f_Y(y) = \frac{1}{\theta}f_X\left(\frac{y}{\theta}\right).$$

Proof:

$$F_Y(y) = \Pr(Y \le y) = \Pr(\theta X \le y) = \Pr\left(X \le \frac{y}{\theta}\right) = F_X\left(\frac{y}{\theta}\right)$$
$$f_Y(y) = \frac{d}{dy}F_Y(y) = \frac{1}{\theta}f_X\left(\frac{y}{\theta}\right).$$

$\square$

Corollary 4.19 *The parameter θ is a scale parameter for the random variable Y.*

Example 4.20 illustrates this process.

Example 4.20 *Let X have pdf $f(x) = e^{-x}$, $x > 0$. Determine the cdf and pdf of $Y = \theta X$.*

$$F_X(x) = 1 - e^{-x},$$
$$F_Y(y) = 1 - e^{-y/\theta},$$
$$f_Y(y) = \frac{1}{\theta}e^{-y/\theta}.$$

We recognize this as the exponential distribution. $\square$

4.7.3 Transformation by raising to a power

Theorem 4.21 *Let X be a continuous random variable with pdf $f_X(x)$ and cdf $F_X(x)$ with $F_X(0) = 0$. Let $Y = X^{1/\tau}$. Then, if $\tau > 0$,*

$$F_Y(y) = F_X(y^\tau), \quad f_Y(y) = \tau y^{\tau-1}f_X(y^\tau), \quad y > 0$$

while, if $\tau < 0$,

$$F_Y(y) = 1 - F_X(y^\tau), \quad f_Y(y) = -\tau y^{\tau-1}f_X(y^\tau). \tag{4.4}$$

Proof: If $\tau > 0$
$$F_Y(y) = \Pr(X \le y^\tau) = F_X(y^\tau),$$
while if $\tau < 0$
$$F_Y(y) = \Pr(X \ge y^\tau) = 1 - F_X(y^\tau).$$
The pdf follows by differentiation. $\quad\square$

It is more common to keep parameters positive and so, when τ is negative, we can create a new parameter $\tau^* = -\tau$. Then (4.4) becomes
$$F_Y(y) = 1 - F_X(y^{-\tau^*}), \quad f_Y(y) = \tau^* y^{-\tau^*-1} f_X(y^{-\tau^*}).$$
We will drop the asterisk for future use of this positive parameter.

Definition 4.22 *When raising a distribution to a power, if $\tau > 0$ the resulting distribution is called **transformed**, if $\tau = -1$ it is called **inverse**, and if $\tau < 0$ (but is not -1) it is called **inverse transformed**. To create the distributions in Section 4.2 and to retain θ as a scale parameter, the random variable of the original distribution should be raised to a power before being multiplied by θ.*

Example 4.23 *Suppose X has the exponential distribution. Determine the cdf of the inverse, transformed, and inverse transformed exponential distributions.*

The inverse exponential distribution with no scale parameter has cdf
$$F(y) = 1 - [1 - e^{-1/y}] = e^{-1/y}.$$
With the scale parameter added it is $F(y) = e^{-\theta/y}$.

The transformed exponential distribution with no scale parameter has cdf
$$F(y) = 1 - \exp(-y^\tau).$$
With the scale parameter added it is $F(y) = 1 - \exp[-(y/\theta)^\tau]$. This distribution is more commonly known as the **Weibull distribution**.

The inverse transformed exponential distribution with no scale parameter has cdf
$$F(y) = 1 - [1 - \exp(-y^{-\tau})] = \exp(-y^{-\tau}).$$
With the scale parameter added it is $F(y) = \exp[-(\theta/y)^\tau]$. This distribution is the **inverse Weibull**. $\quad\square$

Another base distribution has pdf $f(x) = x^{\alpha-1} e^{-x}/\Gamma(\alpha)$. When a scale parameter is added, this becomes the **gamma distribution.** It has inverse and transformed versions that can be created using the results in this section. Unlike the distributions introduced to this point, this one does not have a closed form cdf. The best we can do is define notation for the function.

Definition 4.24 *The **incomplete gamma function** with parameter $\alpha > 0$ is denoted and defined by*

$$\Gamma(\alpha; x) = \frac{1}{\Gamma(\alpha)} \int_0^x t^{\alpha-1} e^{-t} \, dt$$

*while the **gamma function** is denoted and defined by*

$$\Gamma(\alpha) = \int_0^\infty t^{\alpha-1} e^{-t} \, dt.$$

In addition, $\Gamma(\alpha) = (\alpha - 1)\Gamma(\alpha - 1)$ and for positive integer values of n, $\Gamma(n) = (n - 1)!$. Appendix A provides details on numerical methods of evaluating these quantities. Furthermore, these functions are built into most spreadsheets and many statistical and numerical analysis software packages.

4.7.4   Transformation by exponentiation

Theorem 4.25 *Let X be a continuous random variable with pdf $f_X(x)$ and cdf $F_X(x)$ with $f_X(x) > 0$ for all real x, that is support on the entire real line. Let $Y = \exp(X)$. Then, for $y > 0$,*

$$F_Y(y) = F_X(\ln y), \quad f_Y(y) = \frac{1}{y} f_X(\ln y).$$

Proof: $F_Y(y) = \Pr(e^X \le y) = \Pr(X \le \ln y) = F_X(\ln y).$ □

Example 4.26 *Let X have the normal distribution with mean μ and variance σ^2. Determine the cdf and pdf of $Y = e^X$.*

$$F_Y(y) = \Phi\left(\frac{\ln y - \mu}{\sigma}\right)$$

$$f_Y(y) = \frac{1}{y\sigma} \phi\left(\frac{\ln y - \mu}{\sigma}\right) = \frac{1}{y\sigma\sqrt{2\pi}} \exp\left[-\frac{1}{2}\left(\frac{\ln y - \mu}{\sigma}\right)^2\right].$$

□

We could try to add a scale parameter by creating $W = \theta Y$, but this adds no value, as is demonstrated in Exercise 4.21. This example created the **lognormal** distribution (the name has become the convention even though "expnormal" would seem more descriptive).

4.7.5 Continuous mixture of distributions

The concept of mixing can be extended from mixing a finite number of random variables to mixing an uncountable number. In Theorem 4.27, the pdf $f_\Lambda(\lambda)$ plays the role of the discrete "probabilities" a_j in the k-point mixture.

Theorem 4.27 *Let X have pdf $f_{X|\Lambda}(x|\lambda)$ and cdf $F_{X|\Lambda}(x|\lambda)$, where λ is a parameter. Let λ be a realization of the random variable Λ with pdf $f_\Lambda(\lambda)$. Then the unconditional pdf of X is*

$$f_X(x) = \int f_{X|\Lambda}(x|\lambda) f_\Lambda(\lambda)\, d\lambda, \tag{4.5}$$

*where the integral is taken over all values of λ with positive probability. The resulting distribution is a **mixture distribution**. The distribution function can be determined from*

$$
\begin{aligned}
F_X(x) &= \int_{-\infty}^{x} \int f_{X|\Lambda}(y|\lambda) f_\Lambda(\lambda) d\lambda\, dy \\
&= \int \int_{-\infty}^{x} f_{X|\Lambda}(y|\lambda) f_\Lambda(\lambda) dy\, d\lambda \\
&= \int F_{X|\Lambda}(x|\lambda) f_\Lambda(\lambda) d\lambda.
\end{aligned}
$$

Moments of the mixture distribution can be found from

$$\mathrm{E}(X^k) = \mathrm{E}[\mathrm{E}(X^k|\Lambda)]$$

and, in particular,

$$\mathrm{Var}(X) = \mathrm{E}[\mathrm{Var}(X|\Lambda)] + \mathrm{Var}[\mathrm{E}(X|\Lambda)].$$

Proof: The integrand is, by definition, the joint density of X and Λ. The integral is then the marginal density. For the expected value (assuming the order of integration can be reversed),

$$
\begin{aligned}
\mathrm{E}(X^k) &= \int \int x^k f_{X|\Lambda}(x|\lambda) f_\Lambda(\lambda)\, d\lambda\, dx \\
&= \int \mathrm{E}(X^k|\lambda) f_\Lambda(\lambda) d\lambda \\
&= \mathrm{E}[\mathrm{E}(X^k|\Lambda)].
\end{aligned}
$$

For the variance,

$$
\begin{aligned}
\mathrm{Var}(X) &= \mathrm{E}(X^2) - [\mathrm{E}(X)]^2 \\
&= \mathrm{E}[\mathrm{E}(X^2|\Lambda)] - \{\mathrm{E}[\mathrm{E}(X|\Lambda)]\}^2 \\
&= \mathrm{E}\{\mathrm{Var}(X|\Lambda) + [\mathrm{E}(X|\Lambda)]^2\} - \{\mathrm{E}[\mathrm{E}(X|\Lambda)]\}^2 \\
&= \mathrm{E}[\mathrm{Var}(X|\Lambda)] + \mathrm{Var}[\mathrm{E}(X|\Lambda)].
\end{aligned}
$$

□

Note that, if $f_\Lambda(\lambda)$ is a discrete distribution, the integrals are replaced with sums. An alternative way to write the results is $f_X(x) = E_\Lambda[f_{X|\Lambda}(x|\Lambda)]$ and $F_X(x) = E_\Lambda[F_{X|\Lambda}(x|\Lambda)]$, where the subscript on E indicates that the random variable is Λ.

An interesting phenomenon is that mixture distributions are often heavy-tailed; Therefore, mixing is a good way to generate a heavy-tailed model. In particular, if $f_{X|\Lambda}(x|\lambda)$ has a decreasing hazard rate function for all λ, then the mixture distribution will also have a decreasing hazard rate function (see Ross [103], pp. 407–409). Example 4.28 shows how a familiar heavy-tailed distribution may be obtained by mixing.

Example 4.28 *Let $X|\Lambda$ have an exponential distribution with parameter $1/\Lambda$. Let Λ have a gamma distribution. Determine the unconditional distribution of X.*

We have (note that the parameter θ in the gamma distribution has been replaced by its reciprocal)

$$
\begin{aligned}
f_X(x) &= \frac{\theta^\alpha}{\Gamma(\alpha)} \int_0^\infty \lambda e^{-\lambda x} \lambda^{\alpha-1} e^{-\theta\lambda} d\lambda \\
&= \frac{\theta^\alpha}{\Gamma(\alpha)} \int_0^\infty \lambda^\alpha e^{-\lambda(x+\theta)} d\lambda \\
&= \frac{\theta^\alpha}{\Gamma(\alpha)} \frac{\Gamma(\alpha+1)}{(x+\theta)^{\alpha+1}} \\
&= \frac{\alpha\theta^\alpha}{(x+\theta)^{\alpha+1}}.
\end{aligned}
$$

This is a Pareto distribution.   □

Example 4.29 is adapted from Hayne [50]. It illustrates how this type of mixture distribution can arise naturally as a description of uncertainty about the parameter of interest. Continuous mixtures are particularly useful in providing a model for parameter uncertainty. The exact value of a parameter is not known, but a probability density function can be elucidated to describe possible values of that parameter. The example arises in insurance. It is easy to imagine how the same type model of uncertainty can be used in the operational risk framework to describe the lack of precision of quantifying a scale parameter. A scale parameter can be used as a basis for measuring a company's exposure to risk.

Example 4.29 *In considering risks associated with automobile driving, it is important to recognize that the distance driven varies from driver to driver. It is also the case that for a particular driver the number of miles varies from* *year to year. Suppose the distance for a randomly selected driver has the inverse Weibull distribution but that the year-to-year variation in the scale parameter has the transformed gamma distribution with the same value for τ. Determine the distribution for the distance driven in a randomly selected year by a randomly selected driver.*

The inverse Weibull distribution for miles driven in a year has parameters Λ (in place of Θ) and τ while the transformed gamma distribution for the scale parameter Λ has parameters τ, θ, and α. The marginal density is

$$
\begin{aligned}
f(x) &= \int_0^\infty \frac{\tau \lambda^\tau}{x^{\tau+1}} e^{-(\lambda/x)^\tau} \frac{\tau \lambda^{\tau\alpha-1}}{\theta^{\tau\alpha}\Gamma(\alpha)} e^{-(\lambda/\theta)^\tau} \, d\lambda \\
&= \frac{\tau^2}{\theta^{\tau\alpha}\Gamma(\alpha)x^{\tau+1}} \int_0^\infty \lambda^{\tau+\tau\alpha-1} \exp[-\lambda^\tau(x^{-\tau}+\theta^{-\tau})] \, d\lambda \\
&= \frac{\tau^2}{\theta^{\tau\alpha}\Gamma(\alpha)x^{\tau+1}} \int_0^\infty [y^{1/\tau}(x^{-\tau}+\theta^{-\tau})^{-1/\tau}]^{\tau+\tau\alpha-1} e^{-y} \\
&\qquad \times y^{\tau^{-1}-1}\tau^{-1}(x^{-\tau}+\theta^{-\tau})^{-1/\tau} \, dy \\
&= \frac{\tau}{\theta^{\tau\alpha}\Gamma(\alpha)x^{\tau+1}(x^{-\tau}+\theta^{-\tau})^{\alpha+1}} \int_0^\infty y^\alpha e^{-y} \, dy \\
&= \frac{\tau\Gamma(\alpha+1)}{\theta^{\tau\alpha}\Gamma(\alpha)x^{\tau+1}(x^{-\tau}+\theta^{-\tau})^{\alpha+1}} \\
&= \frac{\tau\alpha\theta^\tau x^{\tau\alpha-1}}{(x^\tau+\theta^\tau)^{\alpha+1}}.
\end{aligned}
$$

In the above, the third line is obtained by the transformation $y = \lambda^\tau(x^{-\tau}+\theta^{-\tau})$. The final line uses the fact that $\Gamma(\alpha+1) = \alpha\Gamma(\alpha)$. The result is an inverse Burr distribution. Note that this distribution applies to a particular driver. Another driver may have a different Weibull shape parameter τ. As well, the driver's Weibull scale parameter Θ may have a different distribution and, in particular, a different mean. □

In an operational risk context, it is easy to imagine replacing the driver by a machine that processes transactions, and the mixing distribution as describing the level of the number of transactions over all such machines.

4.7.6 Frailty models

An important type of mixture distribution is a frailty model. Although the physical motivation for this particular type of mixture is originally from the analysis of lifetime distributions in survival analysis, the resulting mathematical convenience implies that the approach may also be viewed as a useful way to generate new distributions by mixing.

We begin by introducing a **frailty** random variable $\Lambda > 0$ and define the conditional hazard rate (given $\Lambda = \lambda$) of X to be

$$h_{X|\Lambda}(x|\lambda) = \lambda a(x)$$

, where $a(x)$ is a known function of x; that is, $a(x)$ is to be specified in a particular application. The frailty is meant to quantify uncertainty associated with the hazard rate. In the above specification of the conditional hazard rate, the uncertain quantity λ acts in a multiplicative manner. Thus, the level of the hazard rate is the uncertain quantity, not the shape of the hazard function.

The conditional survival function of $X|\Lambda$ is therefore

$$\overline{F}_{X|\Lambda}(x|\lambda) = e^{-\int_0^x h_{X|\Lambda}(t|\lambda)dt} = e^{-\lambda A(x)},$$

where $A(x) = \int_0^x a(t)dt$. In order to specify the mixture distribution (that is, the marginal distribution of X), we define the moment generating function of the frailty random variable Λ to be $M_\Lambda(t) = \mathrm{E}(e^{t\Lambda})$. Then the marginal survival function is

$$\overline{F}_X(x) = \mathrm{E}[e^{-\Lambda A(x)}] = M_\Lambda[-A(x)], \tag{4.6}$$

and obviously $F_X(x) = 1 - \overline{F}_X(x)$.

The most important subclass of the frailty models is the class of exponential mixtures with $a(x) = 1$, so that $A(x) = x$ and $\overline{F}_{X|\Lambda}(x|\lambda) = e^{-\lambda x}$, $x \geq 0$. Other useful mixtures include Weibull mixtures with $a(x) = \gamma x^{\gamma-1}$ and $A(x) = x^\gamma$.

Evaluation of the frailty distribution requires an expression for the moment generating function $M_\Lambda(t)$ of Λ. The most common choice is gamma frailty, but other choices such as inverse Gaussian frailty are also used in practice.

Example 4.30 *Let Λ have a gamma distribution and let $X|\Lambda$ have a Weibull distribution with conditional survival function $\overline{F}_{X|\Lambda}(x|\lambda) = e^{-\lambda x^\gamma}$. Determine the unconditional or marginal distribution of X.*

It follows from Example 2.29 that the gamma moment generating function is $M_\Lambda(t) = (1 - \theta t)^{-\alpha}$, and from formula (4.6) that X has survival function

$$\overline{F}_X(x) = M_\Lambda(-x^\gamma) = (1 + \theta x^\gamma)^{-\alpha}.$$

This is a Burr distribution with the usual parameter θ replaced by $\theta^{-1/\gamma}$. Note that when $\gamma = 1$ this is an exponential mixture which is a Pareto distribution, considered previously in Example 4.28. □

As mentioned earlier, mixing tends to create heavy-tailed distributions, and in particular a mixture of distributions that all have decreasing hazard rates also has a decreasing hazard rate. In Exercise 4.29 the reader is asked to prove this fact for frailty models. For an extensive treatment of frailty models, see the book by Hougaard [56].

4.7.7   Splicing pieces of distributions

Another method for creating a new distribution is splicing together pieces of different distributions. This approach is similar to mixing in that it might be believed that two or more separate processes are responsible for generating the losses. With mixing, the various processes operate on subsets of the population. Once the subset is identified, a simple loss model suffices. For splicing, the processes differ with regard to the loss amount. That is, one model governs the behavior of losses in some interval of possible losses while other models cover the other intervals. Definition 4.31 makes this precise.

Definition 4.31 *A k-component spliced distribution has a density function that can be expressed as follows:*

$$f_X(x) = \begin{cases} a_1 f_1(x), & c_0 < x < c_1, \\ a_2 f_2(x), & c_1 < x < c_2, \\ \vdots & \vdots \\ a_k f_k(x), & c_{k-1} < x < c_k. \end{cases}$$

For $j = 1, \ldots, k$, each $a_j > 0$ and each $f_j(x)$ must be a legitimate density function with all probability on the interval (c_{j-1}, c_j). Also, $a_1 + \cdots + a_k = 1$.

Example 4.32 *Demonstrate that Model 5 on page 28 is a two-component spliced model.*

The density function is

$$f(x) = \begin{cases} 0.01, & 0 \le x < 50, \\ 0.02, & 50 \le x < 75 \end{cases}$$

and the spliced model is created by letting $f_1(x) = 0.02$, $0 \le x < 50$, which is a uniform distribution on the interval from 0 to 50, and $f_2(x) = 0.04$, $50 \le x < 75$, which is a uniform distribution on the interval from 50 to 75. The coefficients are then $a_1 = 0.5$ and $a_2 = 0.5$.   □

When using parametric models, the motivation for splicing is that the tail behavior for large losses may be different from the behavior for small losses. For example, experience (based on knowledge beyond that available in the current, perhaps small, data set) may indicate that the tail has the shape of the Pareto distribution, but that the body of the distribution is more in keeping with distributions that have a shape similar to the lognormal or inverse Gaussian distributions.

Similarly, when there is a large amount of data below some value but a limited amount of information above, for theoretical or practical reasons, we may want to use some distribution up to a certain point and a parametric model beyond that point. One such theoretical basis for models for large losses is given by extreme value theory. In this book, extreme value theory is given separate treatment in Chapter 7.

The above Definition 4.31 of spliced models assumes that the break points $c_0, \ldots, c_k$ are known in advance. Another way to construct a spliced model is to use standard distributions over the range from c_0 to c_k. Let $g_j(x)$ be the jth such density function. Then, in Definition 4.31, one can replace $f_j(x)$ with $g_j(x)/[G(c_j) - G(c_{j-1})]$. This formulation makes it easier to have the break points become parameters that can be estimated.

Neither approach to splicing ensures that the resulting density function will be continuous (that is, the components will meet at the break points). Such a restriction could be added to the specification.

Example 4.33 *Create a two-component spliced model using an exponential distribution from 0 to c and a Pareto distribution (using γ in place of θ) from c to ∞.*

The basic format is

$$
f_X(x) = \begin{cases} a_1 \dfrac{\theta^{-1} e^{-x/\theta}}{1 - e^{-c/\theta}}, & 0 < x < c, \\ a_2 \dfrac{\alpha \gamma^\alpha (x + \gamma)^{-\alpha-1}}{\gamma^\alpha (c + \gamma)^{-\alpha}}, & c < x < \infty. \end{cases}
$$

However, we must force the density function to integrate to 1. All that is needed is to let $a_1 = v$ and $a_2 = 1 - v$. The spliced density function becomes

$$
f_X(x) = \begin{cases} v \dfrac{\theta^{-1} e^{-x/\theta}}{1 - e^{-c/\theta}}, & 0 < x < c, \\ (1 - v) \dfrac{\alpha (c + \gamma)^\alpha}{(x + \gamma)^{\alpha+1}}, & c < x < \infty \end{cases}, \quad \theta, \alpha, \gamma, c > 0, \ 0 < v < 1.
$$

Figure 4.11 illustrates this density function using the values $c = 100$, $v = 0.6$, $\theta = 100$, $\gamma = 200$, and $\alpha = 4$. It is clear that this density function is not continuous. □

4.8 TVaR FOR CONTINUOUS DISTRIBUTIONS

The Tail-Value-at-Risk (TVaR) for any quantile x_p can be computed directly for any continuous distribution with a finite mean. From Exercise 2.12, it follows that

$$
\begin{aligned}
\mathrm{E}(X) &= \mathrm{E}(X \wedge x_p) + \overline{F}(x_p) e(x_p) \\
&= \mathrm{E}(X \wedge x_p) + \mathrm{E}\left[(X - x_p)_+\right]
\end{aligned}
$$

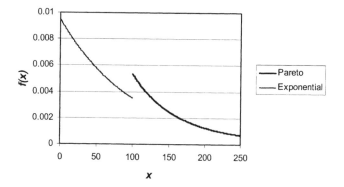

Fig. 4.11   Two-component spliced density.

and

$$\mathrm{TVaR}_p(X) = \mathrm{E}\left(X \mid X > x_p\right)$$
$$= x_p + \frac{\int_{x_p}^{\infty}(x - x_p)\ \mathrm{d}F(x)}{1 - F(x_p)}$$
$$= x_p + e(x_p)$$
$$= x_p + \frac{\mathrm{E}(X) - \mathrm{E}(X \wedge x_p)}{\overline{F}(x_p)}.$$

For the each distribution in Section 4.2, the elements in the second term are listed there. The TVaR is easily computed. The specific results for each distribution do not provide much insight into the relationship between the TVaR and the shape of the distribution.   Sections 4.8.1 and 4.8.2 provide general formulas for two large families of continuous distributions.

4.8.1   Continuous elliptical distributions

"Elliptical distributions" are distributions where the contours of the multivariate version of the distribution form ellipses. Univariate elliptical distributions are the corresponding marginal distributions. The normal and t distributions are both univariate elliptical distributions. The exponential distribution is not. In fact, the class of elliptical distribution consists of all symmetric distributions with support on the entire real line. These distributions are not normally used for modeling losses because they have positive and negative support. However they can be used for modeling random variables, such as rates of return, that can take on positive or negative values. The normal and other distributions have been used in the fields of finance and risk management. Landsman and Valdez [73] provide an analysis of TVaR for such elliptical distributions. In an earlier paper, Panjer [89] showed that the Tail-Value-at-Risk for the normal distribution can be written as

$$\text{TVaR}_p(X) = \mu + \frac{\frac{1}{\sigma}\phi\left(\frac{x_p - \mu}{\sigma}\right)}{1 - \Phi\left(\frac{x_p - \mu}{\sigma}\right)}\sigma^2$$

where $x_p = \text{VaR}_p(X)$. Landsman and Valdez [73] show that this formula can be generalized to all univariate elliptical distributions with finite mean and variance. They show that any univariate elliptical distributions with finite mean and variance can be written as

$$f(x) = \frac{c}{\sigma}g\left[\frac{1}{2}\left(\frac{x - \mu}{\sigma}\right)^2\right]$$

where $g(x)$ is a function on $[0, \infty)$ with $\int_0^\infty g(x)dx < \infty$. Now let $G(x) = c\int_0^x g(y)dy$ and $\overline{G}(x) = G(\infty) - G(x)$. Similarly let $F(x) = \int_{-\infty}^x f(y)dy$ and $\overline{F}(x) = 1 - F(x)$.

Theorem 4.34 *Consider any univariate elliptical distribution with finite mean and variance. Then the Tail-Value-at-Risk at p-quantile x_p, where $p > 1/2$, can be written as*

$$TVaR_p(X) = \mu + \lambda\sigma^2$$

where

$$\lambda = \frac{\frac{1}{\sigma}\overline{G}\left[\frac{1}{2}\left(\frac{x_p - \mu}{\sigma}\right)^2\right]}{\overline{F}(x_p)}.$$

Proof: From the definition of TVaR,

$$\text{TVaR}_p(X) = \frac{1}{\overline{F}(x_p)}\int_{x_p}^\infty x \cdot f(x)dx$$

$$= \frac{1}{\overline{F}(x_p)}\int_{x_p}^\infty x \cdot \frac{c}{\sigma} \cdot g\left[\frac{1}{2}\left(\frac{x - \mu}{\sigma}\right)^2\right]dx.$$

Letting $z = (x - \mu)/\sigma$,

$$\text{TVaR}_p(X) = \frac{1}{\overline{F}(x_p)}\int_{\frac{x_p - \mu}{\sigma}}^\infty (\mu + \sigma z) \cdot c \cdot g\left(\frac{1}{2}z^2\right)dz$$

$$= \mu + \frac{c\sigma}{\overline{F}(x_p)}\int_{\frac{x_p - \mu}{\sigma}}^\infty z \cdot g\left(\frac{1}{2}z^2\right)dz$$

$$= \mu + \lambda\sigma^2$$

where

$$\lambda = \frac{c}{\sigma \overline{F}(x_p)} \int_{\frac{1}{2}\left(\frac{x_p-\mu}{\sigma}\right)^2}^{\infty} g(u)\,du$$

$$= \frac{1}{\sigma \overline{F}(x_p)} \overline{G}\left(\frac{1}{2}\left(\frac{x_p-\mu}{\sigma}\right)^2\right).$$

□

Example 4.35 (Logistic distribution) *The logistic distribution has density of the form*

$$f(x) = \frac{c}{\sigma} g\left[\frac{1}{2}\left(\frac{x-\mu}{\sigma}\right)^2\right]$$

where

$$g(u) = \frac{\exp(-u)}{(1+\exp(-u))^2}$$

and c=1/2. Thus

$$G(x) = \frac{1}{2}\int_0^x g(u)\,du$$

$$= \frac{1}{2}\int_0^x \frac{\exp(-u)}{(1+\exp(-u))^2}\,du$$

$$= \frac{1}{2}\left[\frac{1}{1+\exp(-x)} - \frac{1}{2}\right]$$

and

$$\frac{1}{\sigma}\overline{G}\left[\frac{1}{2}\left(\frac{x_p-\mu}{\sigma}\right)^2\right] = \frac{1}{2\sigma}\left\{1 - \frac{1}{1+\exp\left[-\frac{1}{2}\left(\frac{x_p-\mu}{\sigma}\right)^2\right]}\right\}$$

$$= \frac{1}{2\sigma}\left\{\frac{\exp\left[-\frac{1}{2}\left(\frac{x_p-\mu}{\sigma}\right)^2\right]}{1+\exp\left[-\frac{1}{2}\left(\frac{x_p-\mu}{\sigma}\right)^2\right]}\right\}$$

$$= \frac{1}{2}\left[\frac{\frac{1}{\sigma}\phi\left(\frac{x_p-\mu}{\sigma}\right)}{\frac{1}{\sqrt{2\pi}}+\phi\left(\frac{x_p-\mu}{\sigma}\right)}\right].$$

Therefore, we see that

$$\lambda = \frac{1}{2}\left[\frac{\frac{1}{\sigma}\phi\left(\frac{x_p-\mu}{\sigma}\right)}{\frac{1}{\sqrt{2\pi}}+\phi\left(\frac{x_p-\mu}{\sigma}\right)} \frac{\frac{1}{\sigma}\phi\left(\frac{x_p-\mu}{\sigma}\right)}{\overline{F}\left(\frac{x_p-\mu}{\sigma}\right)}\right].$$

□

4.8.2   Continuous exponential dispersion distributions

Landsman and Valdez [74] also obtain analytic results for a broad class of distributions generalizing the results for the normal distribution but also extending to random variables that have support only on positive numbers. Examples include distributions such as the gamma and inverse Gaussian. We consider two exponential dispersion models, the additive exponential dispersion family and the reproductive exponential dispersion family. The definitions are the same except for the role of one parameter λ.

Definition 4.36 *A continuous random variable X has a distribution from the **additive exponential dispersion family (AEDF)** if its pdf may be parameterized in terms of parameters θ and λ and expressed as*

$$f(x; \theta, \lambda) = e^{\theta x - \lambda \kappa(\theta)} q(x; \lambda). \tag{4.7}$$

Definition 4.37 *A continuous random variable X has a distribution from the **reproductive exponential dispersion family (REDF)** if its pdf may be parameterized in terms of parameters θ and λ and expressed as*

$$f(x; \theta, \lambda) = e^{\lambda[\theta x - \kappa(\theta)]} q(x; \lambda). \tag{4.8}$$

The mean and variance of these distributions are

Mean:	AEDF	$\mu = \lambda \kappa'(\theta)$
	REDF	$\mu = \kappa'(\theta)$
Variance:	AEDF	$\mathrm{Var}(X) = \lambda \kappa''(\theta) = \kappa''(\theta)/\sigma^2$
	REDF	$\mathrm{Var}(X) = \kappa''(\theta)/\lambda = \kappa''(\theta)\sigma^2$

where $1/\lambda = \sigma^2$ is called the dispersion parameter.

Example 4.38 (Normal distribution) *The normal distribution has density*

$$f(x) = \frac{1}{\sqrt{2\pi}\sigma} \exp\left[-\frac{1}{2} \left(\frac{x-\mu}{\sigma} \right)^2 \right],$$

which can be rewritten as

$$f(x) = \frac{1}{\sqrt{2\pi}\sigma} \exp\left[-\frac{1}{2} \left(\frac{x}{\sigma} \right)^2 \right] \exp\left[\frac{1}{\sigma^2} \left(\mu x - \frac{1}{2}\mu^2 \right) \right].$$

By setting $\lambda = 1/\sigma^2$, $\kappa(\theta) = \theta^2/2$ and

$$q(x; \lambda) = \frac{1}{\sqrt{2\pi}\sigma} \exp\left[-\frac{1}{2} \left(\frac{x}{\sigma} \right)^2 \right],$$

we can see that the normal density satisfies equation (4.8) and so the normal distribution is a member of the REDF. $\square$

Example 4.39 (Gamma distribution) *The gamma distribution has density*

$$f(x) = \frac{1}{x\Gamma(\alpha)} \left(\frac{x}{\beta}\right)^{\alpha} \exp\left(-\frac{x}{\beta}\right)$$

where we have chosen β to denote the scale parameter to avoid confusion between θs. By setting $\theta = -1/\beta$, $\lambda = \alpha$, $\kappa(\theta) = -\ln(-\theta)$ and

$$q(x;\lambda) = \frac{x^{\alpha-1}}{\Gamma(\alpha)}$$

we can see that the gamma density satisfies equation (4.7) and so the gamma distribution is a member of the AEDF. □

Example 4.40 (Inverse Gaussian distribution) *The inverse Gaussian distribution has density that can be written as*

$$f(x) = \sqrt{\frac{\lambda}{2x^3}} \exp\left[-\frac{\lambda(x-\mu)^2}{2\mu^2 x}\right]$$

which is equivalent, but with a different parametrization, to the form given in Section 4.2. By setting $\theta = -1/\left(2\mu^2\right)$, $\kappa(\theta) = -1/\mu = -\sqrt{-2\theta}$ and

$$q(x;\lambda) = \sqrt{\frac{\lambda}{2x^3}} \exp\left(-\frac{\lambda}{2x}\right),$$

we can see that the inverse Gaussian density satisfies equation (4.8) and so the inverse Gaussian distribution is a member of the REDF. □

We now consider the main results of this section. We consider random variables from the AEDF and REDF. For the purpose of this section, we will also require that the support of the random variable is an open set that does not depend on θ and the function $\kappa(\theta)$ is a differentiable function. These are technical requirements that will be satisfied by most commonly used distributions.

Theorem 4.41 *Let X be a member of the AEDF subject to the above conditions. Then the Tail-Value-at-Risk can be written as*

$$TVaR_p(X) = \mu + h$$

where $h = \frac{\partial}{\partial \theta} \ln \left[\overline{F}(x_p; \theta, \lambda)\right]$.

Proof: We have

$$
\begin{aligned}
\frac{\partial}{\partial \theta} \ln \left(\overline{F}\left(x_p; \theta, \lambda\right)\right) &= \frac{1}{\overline{F}\left(x_p; \theta, \lambda\right)} \int_{x_p}^{\infty} \frac{\partial}{\partial \theta} \left\{ e^{[\theta x - \lambda \kappa(\theta)]} q(x; \lambda) \right\} dx \\
&= \frac{1}{\overline{F}\left(x_p; \theta, \lambda\right)} \int_{x_p}^{\infty} \left\{ [x - \lambda \kappa'(\theta)]\, e^{\lambda[\theta x - \kappa(\theta)]} q(x; \lambda) \right\} dx \\
&= \frac{1}{\overline{F}\left(x_p; \theta, \lambda\right)} \int_{x_p}^{\infty} x f\left(x; \theta, \lambda\right) dx - \lambda \kappa'(\theta) \\
&= \mathrm{TVaR}_p(X) - \mu
\end{aligned}
$$

and the result follows by rearrangement. □

The case of the REDF follows in similar fashion.

Theorem 4.42 *Let X be a member of the REDF subject to the above conditions. Then the Tail-Value-at-Risk can be written as*

$$
TVaR_p(X) = \mu + h\sigma^2
$$

where $\sigma^2 = 1/\lambda$ and

$$
h = \frac{\partial}{\partial \theta} \ln \left[\overline{F}\left(x_p; \theta, \lambda\right)\right].
$$

Proof: We have

$$
\begin{aligned}
\frac{\partial}{\partial \theta} \ln \left(\overline{F}\left(x_p; \theta, \lambda\right)\right) &= \frac{1}{\overline{F}\left(x_p; \theta, \lambda\right)} \int_{x_p}^{\infty} \frac{\partial}{\partial \theta} \left\{ e^{\lambda[\theta x - \kappa(\theta)]} q(x; \lambda) \right\} dx \\
&= \frac{1}{\overline{F}\left(x_p; \theta, \lambda\right)} \int_{x_p}^{\infty} \left\{ \lambda\, [x - \kappa'(\theta)]\, e^{\lambda[\theta x - \kappa(\theta)]} q(x; \lambda) \right\} dx \\
&= \frac{\lambda}{\overline{F}\left(x_p; \theta, \lambda\right)} \int_{x_p}^{\infty} x f\left(x; \theta, \lambda\right) dx - \lambda \kappa'(\theta) \\
&= \lambda\left[\mathrm{TVaR}_p(X) - \mu\right] \\
&= \left[\mathrm{TVaR}_p(X) - \mu\right] / \sigma^2
\end{aligned}
$$

and the result follows by rearrangement. □

Example 4.43 (Normal distribution) *because the normal distribution is a member of the REDF, its TVaR is*

$$
TVaR_p(X) = \mu + h\sigma^2
$$

where $\sigma^2 = 1/\lambda$ and

$$
\begin{aligned}
h &= \frac{\partial}{\partial \theta} \ln \left(\overline{F} \left(x_p; \theta, \lambda \right) \right) \\
&= \frac{\partial}{\partial \theta} \ln \left(1 - \Phi \left[\sqrt{\lambda} \left(x_p - \theta \right) \right] \right) \\
&= \frac{\sqrt{\lambda} \phi \left[\sqrt{\lambda} \left(x_p - \theta \right) \right]}{1 - \Phi \left[\sqrt{\lambda} \left(x_p - \theta \right) \right]}.
\end{aligned}
$$

Then the TVaR of the normal distribution is

$$
TVaR_p(X) = \mu + \frac{1}{\sigma} \frac{\phi \left[\sqrt{\lambda} \left(x_p - \theta \right) \right]}{1 - \Phi \left[\sqrt{\lambda} \left(x_p - \theta \right) \right]} \sigma^2.
$$

□

Example 4.44 (Gamma distribution) *The gamma distribution is a member of the AEDF, so its TVaR is*

$$
TVaR_p(X) = \mu + h
$$

where

$$
\begin{aligned}
h &= \frac{\partial}{\partial \theta} \ln \left(\overline{F} \left(x_p; \theta, \lambda \right) \right) \\
&= \frac{1}{\overline{F} \left(x_p; \theta, \lambda \right)} \frac{\partial}{\partial \theta} \int_{x_p}^{\infty} \frac{x^{\lambda - 1}}{\Gamma(\lambda)} \exp \left[\theta x + \lambda \ln \left(-\theta \right) \right] dx \\
&= \frac{1}{\overline{F} \left(x_p; \theta, \lambda \right)} \int_{x_p}^{\infty} \frac{x^{\lambda - 1}}{\Gamma(\lambda)} \frac{\partial}{\partial \theta} \exp \left[\theta x + \lambda \ln \left(-\theta \right) \right] dx \\
&= \frac{1}{\overline{F} \left(x_p; \theta, \lambda \right)} \int_{x_p}^{\infty} \frac{x^{\lambda - 1}}{\Gamma(\lambda)} \left(x + \frac{\lambda}{\theta} \right) \exp \left[\theta x + \lambda \ln \left(-\theta \right) \right] dx \\
&= \frac{1}{\overline{F} \left(x_p; \theta, \lambda \right)} \left[-\frac{1}{\theta} \frac{\Gamma(\lambda + 1)}{\Gamma(\lambda)} \int_{x_p}^{\infty} f(x; \theta, \lambda + 1) dx \right] + \frac{\lambda}{\theta} \\
&= -\frac{\lambda}{\theta} \left[\frac{\overline{F} \left(x_p; \theta, \lambda + 1 \right)}{\overline{F} \left(x_p; \theta, \lambda \right)} - 1 \right] \\
&= \mu \left[\frac{\overline{F} \left(x_p; \theta, \lambda + 1 \right)}{\overline{F} \left(x_p; \theta, \lambda \right)} - 1 \right].
\end{aligned}
$$

Then the TVaR of the gamma distribution is

$$
TVaR_p(X) = \mu \frac{\overline{F} \left(x_p; \theta, \lambda + 1 \right)}{\overline{F} \left(x_p; \theta, \lambda \right)}.
$$

☐

Example 4.45 (Inverse Gaussian distribution) *The inverse Gaussian distribution is a member of the AEDF, so its TVaR is*

$$TVaR_p(X) = \mu + h\sigma^2.$$

The cdf of the inverse Gaussian distribution is

$$F(x;\theta,\lambda) = \Phi\left(\frac{1}{\mu}\sqrt{\lambda x} - \sqrt{\lambda/x}\right) + \exp\left(2\frac{\lambda}{\mu}\right)\Phi\left(-\frac{1}{\mu}\sqrt{\lambda x} - \sqrt{\lambda/x}\right)$$

so that

$$h = \frac{\partial}{\partial\theta}\ln\left(\overline{F}(x_p;\theta,\lambda)\right)$$

$$= \frac{-1}{\overline{F}(x_p;\theta,\lambda)}\frac{\partial}{\partial\mu}\left[\begin{array}{c}\Phi\left(\frac{1}{\mu}\sqrt{\lambda x_p} - \sqrt{\lambda/x_p}\right) + \\ \exp\left(2\frac{\lambda}{\mu}\right)\Phi\left(-\frac{1}{\mu}\sqrt{\lambda x_p} - \sqrt{\lambda/x_p}\right)\end{array}\right]\frac{d\mu}{d\theta}$$

$$= \frac{1}{\overline{F}(x_p;\theta,\lambda)}\left[\begin{array}{c}\mu\sqrt{\lambda x_p}\phi\left(\frac{1}{\mu}\sqrt{\lambda x_p} - \sqrt{\lambda/x_p}\right) \\ +\mu\exp\left(2\frac{\lambda}{\mu}\right)\cdot 2\lambda\Phi\left(-\frac{1}{\mu}\sqrt{\lambda x_p} - \sqrt{\lambda/x_p}\right) \\ -\mu\exp\left(2\frac{\lambda}{\mu}\right)\sqrt{\lambda x_p}\phi\left(-\frac{1}{\mu}\sqrt{\lambda x_p} - \sqrt{\lambda/x_p}\right)\end{array}\right].$$

Let

$$z_p^* = \frac{1}{\mu}\sqrt{\lambda x_p} - \sqrt{\lambda/x_p}$$

so that

$$-z_p^* - 2\sqrt{\lambda/x_p} = -\frac{1}{\mu}\sqrt{\lambda x_p} - \sqrt{\lambda/x_p},$$

we have

$$h = \frac{\mu}{\overline{F}(x_p;\theta,\lambda)}\left\{\sqrt{\lambda x_p}\phi(z_p^*) + \exp\left(2\frac{\lambda}{\mu}\right)\left[\begin{array}{c}2\lambda\Phi\left(-z_p^* - 2\sqrt{\lambda/x_p}\right) \\ -\sqrt{\lambda x_p}\phi\left(-z_p^* - 2\sqrt{\lambda/x_p}\right)\end{array}\right]\right\}.$$

Then the TVaR of the inverse Gaussian distribution is

$$TVaR_p(X) = \mu + h\sigma^2 = \mu + \frac{h}{\lambda}.$$

☐

4.9 EXERCISES

4.1 For a Pareto distribution, let both α and θ go to infinity with the ratio α/θ held constant. Show that the result is an exponential distribution.

4.2 Determine the limiting distribution of the generalized Pareto distribution as α and θ both go to infinity.

4.3 Show that as $\tau \to \infty$ in the transformed beta distribution the result is the inverse transformed gamma distribution.

4.4 Demonstrate that the lognormal distribution is a scale distribution but has no scale parameter. Display an alternative parametrization of this distribution that does have a scale parameter.

4.5 Which of Models 1–6 could be considered as members of a parametric distribution? For those that are, name or describe the distribution.

4.6 Losses have a Pareto distribution with $\alpha = 2$ and θ unknown. Losses the following year experience additional inflation of 6%. Let r be the ratio of the proportion of losses that will exceed d next year to the proportion of losses that exceed d this year. Determine the limit of r as d goes to infinity.

4.7 Determine the mean and second moment of the two-point mixture distribution in Example 4.8. The solution to this exercise provides general formulas for raw moments of a mixture distribution.

4.8 Determine expressions for the mean and variance of the mixture of gammas distribution.

4.9 Which of Models 1–6 could be considered to be from parametric distribution families? Which could be considered to be from variable-component mixture distributions?

4.10 There are two types of losses. Seventy-five percent of losses have a normal distribution with a mean of $3000 and a standard deviation of $1000. The remaining 25% have a normal distribution with a mean of $4000 and a standard deviation of $1000. Determine the probability that a randomly selected loss exceeds $5000.

4.11 Let X have a Burr distribution with parameters $\alpha = 1$, $\gamma = 2$, and $\theta = \sqrt{1000}$ and let Y have a Pareto distribution with parameters $\alpha = 1$ and $\theta = 1000$. Let Z be a mixture of X and Y with equal weight on each component. Determine the median of Z. Let $W = 1.1Z$. Demonstrate that W is also a mixture of a Burr and a Pareto distribution and determine the parameters of W.

4.12 Demonstrate that the model in Example 4.13 is a mixture of uniform distributions.

4.13 Show that the Weibull distribution has a scale parameter.

4.14 Using the methods in this section (except for the mean excess loss), compare the tail weight of the Weibull and inverse Weibull distributions.

4.15 Arguments as in Example 4.15 place the lognormal distribution between the gamma and Pareto distributions with regard to tail weight. To reinforce this conclusion, consider a gamma distribution with parameters $\alpha = 0.2$, $\theta = 500$; a lognormal distribution with parameters $\mu = 3.709290$, $\sigma = 1.338566$; and a Pareto distribution with parameters $\alpha = 2.5$, $\theta = 150$. First, demonstrate that all three distributions have the same mean and variance. Then numerically demonstrate that there is a value of the argument such that the gamma pdf is smaller than the lognormal and Pareto pdfs for all larger arguments and that there is another value of the argument such that the lognormal pdf is smaller than the Pareto pdf for all arguments above that value.

4.16 You are given that the random variable X has probability density function $f(x) = (1 + 2x^2)e^{-2x}$, $x \geq 0$.

(a) Determine the survival function $\overline{F}(x)$.

(b) Determine the hazard rate $h(x)$.

(c) Determine the mean excess loss function $e(x)$.

(d) Determine $\lim_{x \to \infty} h(x)$ and $\lim_{x \to \infty} e(x)$.

(e) Prove that $e(x)$ is strictly decreasing but $h(x)$ is not strictly increasing.

4.17 Let X have cdf $F_X(x) = 1 - (1 + x)^{-\alpha}$, $x, \alpha > 0$. Determine the pdf and cdf of $Y = \theta X$.

4.18 For a large bank, with 100 observed losses resulting from a certain type of error, the amounts of such losses that occurred in the year 2005 were arranged grouped by size (in hundreds of thousands of dollars): 42 were below $300, 3 were between $300 and $350, 5 were between $350 and $400, 5 were between $400 and $450, 0 were between $450 and $500, 5 were between $500 and $600, and the remaining 40 were above $600. For the next three years, all losses are inflated by 10% per year. Based on the empirical distribution from the year 2005, determine a range for the probability that a loss exceeds $500 in the year 2008. (There is not enough information to determine the probability exactly.)

4.19 Let X have the Pareto distribution. Determine the cdf of the transformed, inverse, and inverse transformed distributions. Determine which of these distributions appear in Chapter 4 .

4.20 Let X have the loglogistic distribution. loglogistic distribution Demonstrate that the inverse distribution also has the loglogistic distribution. This shows that there is no need to identify a separate inverse loglogistic distribution.

4.21 Let Y have the lognormal distribution with parameters μ and σ. Let $Z = \theta Y$. Show that Z also has the lognormal distribution and therefore the addition of a third parameter has not created a new distribution.

4.22 Let X have a Pareto distribution with parameters α and θ. Let $Y = \ln(1 + X/\theta)$. Determine the name of the distribution of Y and its parameters.

4.23 Venter [120] noted that if X has the transformed gamma distribution and its scale parameter θ has an inverse transformed gamma distribution (where the parameter τ is the same in both distributions), the resulting mixture has the transformed beta distribution. Demonstrate that this is true.

4.24 Given a value of $\Theta = \theta$, the random variable X has an exponential distribution with hazard rate function $h(x) = \theta$, a constant. The random variable Θ has a uniform distribution on the interval $(1, 11)$. Determine $\overline{F}_X(0.5)$ for the unconditional distribution.

4.25 Determine the probability density function and the hazard rate of the frailty distribution.

4.26 Suppose that $X|\Lambda$ has the Weibull survival function $\overline{F}_{X|\Lambda}(x|\lambda) = e^{-\lambda x^\gamma}$, $x \geq 0$, and Λ has an exponential distribution. Demonstrate that the unconditional distribution of X is loglogistic.

4.27 Consider the exponential–inverse Gaussian frailty model with $a(x) = \theta/(2\sqrt{1 + \theta x})$, where $\theta > 0$.

   (a) Verify that the conditional hazard rate $h_{X|\Lambda}(x|\lambda)$ of $X|\Lambda$ is indeed a valid hazard rate.

   (b) Determine the conditional survival function $\overline{F}_{X|\Lambda}(x|\lambda)$.

   (c) If Λ has a gamma distribution with parameters $\theta = 1$ and α replaced by 2α, determine the marginal or unconditional survival function of X.

   (d) Use (c) to argue that a given frailty model may arise from more than one combination of conditional distributions of $X|\Lambda$ and frailty distributions of Λ.

4.28 Suppose that X has survival function $\overline{F}_X(x) = 1 - F_X(x)$ given by equation (4.6). Show that $\overline{F}_1(x) = F_X(x)/[\mathrm{E}(\Lambda)A(x)]$ is again a survival function of the form (4.6), and identify the distribution of Λ associated with $\overline{F}_1(x)$.

4.29 Fix $s \geq 0$, and define an "Esscher-transformed" frailty random variable Λ_s with probability density function (or discrete probability mass function in the discrete case) $f_{\Lambda_s}(\lambda) = e^{-s\lambda} f_\Lambda(\lambda)/M_\Lambda(-s)$, $\lambda \geq 0$.

(a) Show that Λ_s has moment generating function

$$M_{\Lambda_s}(t) = E(e^{t\Lambda_s}) = \frac{M_\Lambda(t-s)}{M_\Lambda(-s)}.$$

(b) The cumulant generating function of Λ is defined as $c_\Lambda(t) = \ln[M_\Lambda(t)]$.

Use (a) to prove that

$$c_\Lambda'(-s) = \mathrm{E}(\Lambda_s) \text{ and } c_\Lambda''(-s) = \mathrm{Var}(\Lambda_s).$$

(c) For the frailty model with survival function given by equation (4.6), prove that the associated hazard rate may be expressed as

$$h_X(x) = a(x)c_\Lambda'[-A(x)],$$

where c_Λ is defined in (b).

(d) Use (c) to show that

$$h_X'(x) = a'(x)c_\Lambda'[-A(x)] - [a(x)]^2 c_\Lambda''[-A(x)].$$

(e) Prove using (d) that, if the conditional hazard rate $h_{X|\Lambda}(x|\lambda)$ is nonincreasing in x, then $h_X(x)$ is also nonincreasing in x.

4.30 Write the density function for a two-component spliced model in which the density function is proportional to a uniform density over the interval from 0 to 1,000 and is proportional to an exponential density function from 1,000 to ∞. Ensure that the resulting density function is continuous.

4.31 Let X have pdf $f(x) = \exp(-|x/\theta|)/2\theta$ for $-\infty < x < \infty$. Let $Y = e^X$. Determine the pdf and cdf of Y.

4.32 Losses in 2006 follow the density function $f(x) = 3x^{-4}$, $x \geq 1$, where x is the loss size expressed in millions of dollars. It is expected that individual loss sizes in 2007 will be 10% greater. Determine the cdf of losses for 2007 and use it to determine the probability that a 2007 loss exceeds $2.2 millions.

4.33 Consider the inverse Gaussian random variable X with pdf

$$f(x) = \sqrt{\frac{\theta}{2\pi x^3}} \exp\left[-\frac{\theta}{2x}\left(\frac{x-\mu}{\mu}\right)^2\right], \quad x > 0,$$

where $\theta > 0$ and $\mu > 0$ are parameters.

(a) Derive the pdf of the reciprocal inverse Gaussian random variable $1/X$.

(b) Prove that the "joint" moment generating function of X and $1/X$ is given by

$$M(t_1, t_2) = \mathrm{E}\left(e^{t_1 X + t_2 X^{-1}}\right)$$
$$= \sqrt{\frac{\theta}{\theta - 2t_2}} \exp\left(\frac{\theta - \sqrt{(\theta - 2\mu^2 t_1)(\theta - 2t_2)}}{\mu}\right),$$

where $t_1 < \theta/\left(2\mu^2\right)$ and $t_2 < \theta/2$.

(c) Use (b) to show that the moment generating function of X is

$$M_X(t) = \mathrm{E}\left(e^{tX}\right) = \exp\left[\frac{\theta}{\mu}\left(1 - \sqrt{1 - \frac{2\mu^2}{\theta}t}\right)\right], \quad t < \frac{\theta}{2\mu^2}.$$

(d) Use (b) to show that the reciprocal inverse Gaussian random variable $1/X$ has moment generating function

$$M_{1/X}(t) = \mathrm{E}\left(e^{tX^{-1}}\right)$$
$$= \sqrt{\frac{\theta}{\theta - 2t}} \exp\left[\frac{\theta}{\mu}\left(1 - \sqrt{1 - \frac{2}{\theta}t}\right)\right], \quad t < \frac{\theta}{2}.$$

Hence prove that $1/X$ has the same distribution as $Z_1 + Z_2$, where Z_1 has a gamma distribution, Z_2 has an inverse Gaussian distribution, and Z_1 is independent of Z_2. Also, identify the gamma and inverse Gaussian parameters in this representation.

(e) Use (b) to show that

$$Z = \frac{1}{X}\left(\frac{X-\mu}{\mu}\right)^2$$

has a gamma distribution with parameters $\alpha = \frac{1}{2}$ and the usual parameter θ replaced by $2/\theta$.

5

Models for the number of losses: Counting distributions

If anything simply cannot go wrong, it will anyway.

—Murphy

5.1 INTRODUCTION

The purpose of this chapter is to introduce a large class of counting distributions. Counting distributions are discrete distributions with probabilities only on the nonnegative integers; that is, probabilities are defined only at the points $0, 1, 2, 3, 4, \ldots$. In an operational risk context, counting distributions describe the number of losses or the number of events causing losses such as power outages that cause business interruption. With an understanding of both the number of losses and the size of losses, we can have a deeper understanding of a variety of issues surrounding operational risk than if we have only information about historical total losses. The impact of risk mitigation strategies that address either the frequency of losses or the size of losses can be better understood. Another reason for separating numbers and amounts of losses is that models for the number of losses are fairly easy to obtain and experience has shown that the commonly used frequency distributions perform well in modeling the propensity to generate losses. In this chapter, we introduce many frequency distributions.

We now formalize some of the notation that will be used for models for discrete phenomena. The **probability function** (pf) p_k denotes the probability that exactly k events (such as losses) occur. Let N be a random variable representing the number of such events. Then

$$p_k = \Pr(N = k), \qquad k = 0, 1, 2, \ldots.$$

As a reminder, the probability generating function (pgf) of a discrete random variable N with pf p_k is

$$P(z) = P_N(z) = \mathrm{E}\left(z^N\right) = \sum_{k=0}^{\infty} p_k z^k. \tag{5.1}$$

As is true with the moment generating function, the pgf can be used to generate moments. In particular, $P'(1) = \mathrm{E}(N)$ and $P''(1) = \mathrm{E}[N(N-1)]$ (see Exercise 5.3). To see how the probabilities are obtained from the pgf, the mth derivative of the pgf and its value when the argument z is set to zero are:

$$P^{(m)}(z) = \mathrm{E}\left(\frac{d^m}{dz^m} z^N\right) = \mathrm{E}[N(N-1)\cdots(N-m+1)z^{N-m}]$$

$$= \sum_{k=m}^{\infty} k(k-1)\cdots(k-m+1)z^{k-m} p_k.$$

$$P^{(m)}(0) = m! p_m \text{ so that } p_m = \frac{P^{(m)}(0)}{m!}.$$

5.2   THE POISSON DISTRIBUTION

The probability function for the Poisson distribution is

$$p_k = \frac{e^{-\lambda} \lambda^k}{k!}, \qquad k = 0, 1, 2, \ldots.$$

The probability generating function from Example 2.30 is

$$P(z) = e^{\lambda(z-1)}, \qquad \lambda > 0.$$

The mean and variance can be computed from the probability generating function as follows:

$$\mathrm{E}(N) = P'(1) = \lambda$$

$$\mathrm{E}[N(N-1)] = P''(1) = \lambda^2$$

$$\mathrm{Var}(N) = \mathrm{E}[N(N-1)] + \mathrm{E}(N) - [\mathrm{E}(N)]^2$$

$$= \lambda^2 + \lambda - \lambda^2$$

$$= \lambda.$$

Thus, for the Poisson distribution the variance is equal to the mean. The Poisson distribution can arise from a Poisson process. The Poisson distribution and Poisson processes are also discussed in many books including those by Panjer and Willmot [93] and Ross [104].

The Poisson distribution has at least two additional useful properties. The first is given in Theorem 5.1.

Theorem 5.1 *Let $N_1, \ldots, N_n$ be independent Poisson variables with parameters $\lambda_1, \ldots, \lambda_n$. Then $N = N_1 + \cdots + N_n$ has a Poisson distribution with parameter $\lambda_1 + \cdots + \lambda_n$.*

Proof: The pgf of the sum of independent random variables is the product of the individual pgfs. For the sum of Poisson random variables we have

$$P_N(z) = \prod_{j=1}^{n} P_{N_j}(z) = \prod_{j=1}^{n} \exp[\lambda_j(z-1)]$$

$$= \exp\left[\sum_{j=1}^{n} \lambda_j(z-1)\right]$$

$$= e^{\lambda(z-1)},$$

where $\lambda = \lambda_1 + \cdots + \lambda_n$. Just as is true with moment generating functions, the pgf is unique and therefore N must have a Poisson distribution with parameter λ. □

The second property is particularly useful in modeling operational risk events. Suppose that the number of losses in a fixed time period, such as one year, follows a Poisson distribution. Further suppose that the losses can be classified into m distinct types. For example, losses could be classified by size, such as those below a fixed threshold and those above the threshold. It turns out that, if we are interested in studying the number of losses above the threshold, that new distribution is also Poisson but with a new Poisson parameter.

This is also useful when considering the impact of removing or adding a type of risk to the definition of operational risks. Suppose that the number of losses for a particular set of types of operational risks follows a Poisson distribution. If one of the types of losses is eliminated, the distribution of the number of losses of the remaining types will still have a Poisson distribution but with a new parameter.

In each of the cases mentioned in the previous paragraphs, the number of losses of the different types will not only be Poisson distributed but will also be independent of each other; that is, the distributions of the number of losses above the threshold and the number below the threshold will be independent. We now formalize these ideas in Theorem 5.2.

Theorem 5.2 *Suppose that the number of events N is a Poisson random variable with mean λ. Further suppose that each event can be classified into one of m types with probabilities $p_1, \ldots, p_m$ independent of all other events. Then the number of events $N_1, \ldots, N_m$ corresponding to event types $1, \ldots, m$*

respectively, are mutually independent Poisson random variables with means $\lambda p_1, \ldots, \lambda p_m$, *respectively.*

Proof: For fixed $N = n$, the conditional joint distribution of $(N_1, \ldots, N_m)$ is multinomial with parameters $(n, p_1, \ldots, p_m)$. Also, for fixed $N = n$, the conditional marginal distribution of N_j is binomial with parameters (n, p_j).

The joint pf of $(N_1, \ldots, N_m)$ is given by

$$\Pr(N_1 = n_1, \ldots, N_m = n_m) = Pr(N_1 = n_1, \ldots, N_m = n_m | N = n)$$
$$\times \Pr(N = n)$$
$$= \frac{n!}{n_1! n_2! \cdots n_m!} p_1^{n_1} \cdots p_m^{n_m} \frac{e^{-\lambda} \lambda^n}{n!}$$
$$= \prod_{j=1}^{m} e^{-\lambda p_j} \frac{(\lambda p_j)^{n_j}}{n_j!},$$

where $n = n_1 + n_2 + \cdots + n_m$. Similarly, the marginal pf of N_j is determined below.

$$\Pr(N_j = n_j) = \sum_{n=n_j}^{\infty} \Pr(N_j = n_j | N = n) \Pr(N = n)$$
$$= \sum_{n=n_j}^{\infty} \binom{n}{n_j} p_j^{n_j} (1 - p_j)^{n - n_j} \frac{e^{-\lambda} \lambda^n}{n!}$$
$$= e^{-\lambda} \frac{(\lambda p_j)^{n_j}}{n_j!} \sum_{n=n_j}^{\infty} \frac{[\lambda(1 - p_j)]^{n - n_j}}{(n - n_j)!}$$
$$= e^{-\lambda} \frac{(\lambda p_j)^{n_j}}{n_j!} e^{\lambda(1 - p_j)}$$
$$= e^{-\lambda p_j} \frac{(\lambda p_j)^{n_j}}{n_j!}.$$

Hence the joint pf is the product of the marginal pfs, establishing mutual independence. $\square$

5.3   THE NEGATIVE BINOMIAL DISTRIBUTION

The negative binomial distribution has been used extensively as an alternative to the Poisson distribution. Like the Poisson distribution, it has positive probabilities on the nonnegative integers. Because it has two parameters, it has more flexibility in shape than the Poisson.

The probability function of the **negative binomial distribution** is given by

$$\Pr(N = k) = p_k = \binom{k + r - 1}{k} \left(\frac{1}{1+\beta}\right)^r \left(\frac{\beta}{1+\beta}\right)^k,$$
$$k = 0, 1, 2, \ldots, \quad r > 0, \ \beta > 0. \tag{5.2}$$

The binomial coefficient is to be evaluated using

$$\binom{x}{k} = \frac{x(x-1)\cdots(x-k+1)}{k!}.$$

While k must be an integer, x may be any real number. When $x > k - 1$, it can also be written as

$$\binom{x}{k} = \frac{\Gamma(x+1)}{\Gamma(k+1)\Gamma(x-k+1)},$$

which may be useful because the gamma function $\Gamma(x)$ is available in most spreadsheets, programming languages, and mathematics packages.

It is not difficult to show that the probability generating function for the negative binomial distribution is

$$P(z) = [1 - \beta(z - 1)]^{-r}.$$

From this it follows that the mean and variance of the negative binomial distribution are

$$E(N) = r\beta \quad \text{and} \quad \text{Var}(N) = r\beta(1 + \beta).$$

Because β is positive, the variance of the negative binomial distribution can be seen to exceed the mean. This is in contrast to the Poisson distribution, for which the variance is equal to the mean. This suggests that for a particular set of data, if the observed variance is larger than the observed mean, the negative binomial might be a better candidate than the Poisson distribution as a model to be used.

The negative binomial distribution is a generalization of the Poisson in at least two different ways, namely as a mixed Poisson distribution with a gamma mixing distribution (demonstrated later in this subsection) and as a compound Poisson distribution with a logarithmic secondary distribution (see Section 5.7).

The **geometric distribution** is the special case of the negative binomial distribution when $r = 1$. The geometric distribution is, in some senses, the discrete analogue of the continuous exponential distribution. Both the geometric and exponential distributions have an exponentially decaying probability function and hence the memoryless property. The memoryless property can be interpreted in various contexts as follows. If the exponential distribution is a distribution of lifetimes, then the expected future lifetime is constant for any age. This is often the case for electronic components. If the exponential distribution describes the size of operational risk losses, then the memoryless property can be interpreted as follows: *Given that a loss exceeds a threshold d, the expected amount of the loss in excess of d is constant and so does not depend on d.* If the geometric distribution describes the number of losses, then the memoryless property can be interpreted as follows: *Given that there are at least m losses, the probability distribution of the number of losses in excess of m does not depend on m.* Among continuous distributions, the exponential distribution is used to distinguish between *subexponential* distributions with heavy (or fat) tails and distributions with light (or thin) tails. Similarly for frequency distributions, distributions that decay in the tail slower than the geometric distribution are often considered to have heavy tails, whereas distributions that decay more rapidly than the geometric have light tails. The negative binomial distribution has a heavy tail (decays more slowly than the geometric distribution) when $r < 1$ and a lighter tail than the geometric distribution when $r > 1$.

As noted earlier, one way to create the negative binomial as Poisson mixture distribution is as a mixture of Poisson distributions. Suppose that it is known that an operational risk has a Poisson distribution for the number of losses when the risk parameter λ is known. We now treat λ as being the outcome of a random variable Λ. Denoting the pf of Λ by $u(\lambda)$, where Λ may be continuous or discrete, and denoting its the cdf by $U(\lambda)$, the idea is that λ is the outcome of a random variable can be justified in several ways. First, we can think of the population of risks as being heterogeneous with respect to the risk parameter Λ. In practice this makes sense. The parameter λ measures the expected number of losses, but there is a degree of uncertainty associated with λ. The true value of λ is unobservable because we observe the number of losses arising from the risk and not the risk parameter itself. Compared to the Poisson distribution, there is an additional degree of uncertainty, that is, uncertainty about the parameter, in the mixed Poisson model.

This is the same mixing process that was discussed with regard to continuous distributions in Section 4.7.5. As discussed above, this is often referred to as *parameter uncertainty*. In the Bayesian context, the distribution of Λ is called a *prior distribution* and the parameters of its distribution are sometimes called *hyperparameters*.

When the parameter λ is unknown, the probability that exactly k losses will arise can be written as the weighted average of the same probability conditional on $\Lambda = \lambda$ where the weights are the probabilities from the distribution of Λ. From the law of total probability, we can write

$$
\begin{aligned}
p_k &= \Pr(N = k) \\
&= E[\Pr(N = k|\Lambda)] \\
&= \int_0^\infty \Pr(N = k|\Lambda = \lambda)u(\lambda)\, d\lambda \\
&= \int_0^\infty \frac{e^{-\lambda}\lambda^k}{k!}u(\lambda)\, d\lambda.
\end{aligned}
$$

Now suppose Λ has a gamma distribution. Then

$$
p_k = \int_0^\infty \frac{e^{-\lambda}\lambda^k}{k!}\frac{\lambda^{\alpha-1}e^{-\frac{\lambda}{\theta}}}{\theta^\alpha\Gamma(\alpha)}\, d\lambda = \frac{1}{k!}\frac{1}{\theta^\alpha\Gamma(\alpha)}\int_0^\infty e^{-\lambda(1+\frac{1}{\theta})}\lambda^{k+\alpha-1}\, d\lambda.
$$

From the definition of the gamma distribution in Appendix A, this expression can be evaluated as

$$
\begin{aligned}
p_k &= \frac{\Gamma(k+\alpha)}{k!\Gamma(\alpha)}\frac{\theta^k}{(1+\theta)^{k+\alpha}} \\
&= \binom{k+\alpha-1}{k}\left(\frac{\theta}{1+\theta}\right)^k\left(\frac{1}{1+\theta}\right)^\alpha.
\end{aligned}
$$

This formula is of the same form as formula (5.2), demonstrating that the mixed Poisson, with a gamma mixing distribution, is a negative binomial distribution.

It is worth noting that the Poisson distribution is a limiting case of the negative binomial distribution. To see this, let r go to infinity and β go to zero while keeping their product constant. Let $\lambda = r\beta$ be that constant. Substituting $\beta = \lambda/r$ in the pgf leads to (using L'Hôpital's rule in lines 3 and 5 below)

$$
\begin{aligned}
\lim_{r\to\infty}\left[1 - \frac{\lambda(z-1)}{r}\right]^{-r} &= \exp\left\{\lim_{r\to\infty} -r\ln\left[1 - \frac{\lambda(z-1)}{r}\right]\right\} \\
&= \exp\left\{-\lim_{r\to\infty}\frac{\ln[1 - \lambda(z-1)/r]}{r^{-1}}\right\} \\
&= \exp\left\{\lim_{r\to\infty}\frac{[1 - \lambda(z-1)/r]^{-1}\lambda(z-1)/r^2}{r^{-2}}\right\} \\
&= \exp\left[\lim_{r\to\infty}\frac{r\lambda(z-1)}{r - \lambda(z-1)}\right] \\
&= \exp\left\{\lim_{r\to\infty}[\lambda(z-1)]\right\} \\
&= \exp[\lambda(z-1)]
\end{aligned}
$$

which is the pgf of the Poisson distribution.

5.4   THE BINOMIAL DISTRIBUTION

The binomial distribution is another counting distribution that arises naturally in loss number modeling. It possesses some properties different from the
Poisson and the negative binomial that make it particularly useful. First, its
variance is smaller than its mean. This makes it potentially useful for data
sets in which the observed sample variance is less than the sample mean. This
contrasts with the negative binomial, where the variance exceeds the mean,
and the Poisson distribution, where the variance is equal to the mean.

Second, it describes a physical situation in which m risks are each subject to
loss. We can formalize this as follows. Consider m independent and identical
transactions each with probability q of making a loss. Then the number of
losses for a single transactions follows a Bernoulli distribution, a distribution
with probability $1 - q$ at 0 and probability q at 1. The probability generating
function of the number of losses per transaction is then given by

$$P(z) = (1 - q)z^0 + qz^1 = 1 + q(z - 1).$$

Now, if there are m such independent transactions, then the probability generating functions can be multiplied together to give the probability generating
function of the total number of losses arising from the m transactions. That
probability generating function is

$$P(z) = [1 + q(z - 1)]^m, \qquad 0 < q < 1.$$

Then from this it is easy to show that the probability of exactly k losses is

$$p_k = \Pr(N = k) = \binom{m}{k} q^k (1 - q)^{m-k}, \quad k = 0, 1, \ldots, m,$$

the pf for a binomial distribution with parameters m and q.   From this
Bernoulli trial framework, it is clear that at most m losses can occur. Hence,
the distribution only has positive probabilities on the nonnegative integers up
to and including m.

Consequently, an additional attribute of the binomial distribution that is
sometimes useful is that it has finite support; that is, the range of values for
which there exist positive probabilities has finite length. In many cases, it
may be reasonable to have an upper limit on the range of possible values.
The mean and variance of the binomial distribution are given by

$$E(N) = mq, \quad \text{Var}(N) = mq(1 - q).$$

5.5   THE $(a, b, 0)$ CLASS

The following definition characterizes the members of this class of distributions.

Table 5.1   Members of the $(a, b, 0)$ class

Distribution	a	b	p_0
Poisson	0	λ	$e^{-\lambda}$
Binomial	$-\dfrac{q}{1-q}$	$(m+1)\dfrac{q}{1-q}$	$(1-q)^m$
Negative binomial	$\dfrac{\beta}{1+\beta}$	$(r-1)\dfrac{\beta}{1+\beta}$	$(1+\beta)^{-r}$
Geometric	$\dfrac{\beta}{1+\beta}$	0	$(1+\beta)^{-1}$

Definition 5.3 *Let p_k be the pf of a discrete random variable. It is a member of the* **(a, b, 0)** *class of distributions, provided that there exists constants a and b such that*

$$\frac{p_k}{p_{k-1}} = a + \frac{b}{k}, \qquad k = 1, 2, 3, \ldots .$$

This recursive relation describes the relative size of successive probabilities in the counting distribution. The probability at zero, p_0, can be obtained from the recursive formula because the probabilities must add up to 1. This provides a boundary condition, which, in addition to the recursive formula, will uniquely define the probabilities. The $(a, b, 0)$ class of distributions is a two-parameter class, the two parameters being a and b. By substituting in the probability function for each of the Poisson, binomial, and negative binomial distributions on the left-hand side of the recursion, it can be seen that each of these three distributions satisfies the recursion and that the values of a and b are as given in Table 5.1. In addition, the table gives the value of p_0, the starting value for the recursion. Also in the table is the geometric distribution, the one-parameter special case $(r = 1)$ of the negative binomial distribution.

It is well known (see Panjer and Willmot [93, Chapter 6]) that these are the only possible distributions satisfying this recursive formula.

The recursive formula can be rewritten as

$$k\frac{p_k}{p_{k-1}} = ak + b, \qquad k = 1, 2, 3, \ldots .$$

The expression on the left-hand side is a linear function in k. Note from Table 5.1 that the slope a of the linear function is 0 for the Poisson distribution, is negative for the binomial distribution, and is positive for the negative binomial distribution, including the geometric. This suggests a graphical way of indicating which of the three distributions might be selected for fitting. First, we can plot the observed sample probabilities (indicated by "hats")

$$k\frac{\hat{p}_k}{\hat{p}_{k-1}} = k\frac{n_k}{n_{k-1}}$$

Table 5.2 Accident profile

Number of accidents, k	Number of automobiles, n_k	$k\dfrac{n_k}{n_{k-1}}$
0	7840	
1	1317	0.17
2	239	0.36
3	42	0.53
4	14	1.33
5	4	1.43
6	4	6.00
7	1	1.75
8+	0	
Total	9461	

against k. The observed values should form approximately a straight line if one of these models is to be selected, and the value of the slope should be an indication of which of the models should be selected. Note that this cannot be done if any of the n_k are 0. Hence this procedure is less useful for a small number of observations.

Example 5.4 *This example is from insurance data, where we are interested in finding a distribution for the number of accidents per automobile. Consider the accident data in Table 5.2, which is taken from Thyrion [117]. For the 9461 automobiles studied, the number of accidents is recorded in the table. Also recorded in the table is the observed value of the quantity that should be linear.*

Figure 5.1 plots the value of the quantity of interest against k, the number of accidents. It can be seen from the graph that the quantity of interest looks approximately linear except for the point at $k = 6$. The reliability of the quantities as k increases diminishes because the number of observations becomes small and the variability of the results grows. This illustrates the weakness of this ad hoc procedure. Visually, all the points appear to have equal value. However, the points on the left are more reliable than the points on the right. From the graph, it can be seen that the slope is positive and the data appear approximately linear. This suggests the negative binomial distribution is an appropriate candidate for a model. Whether or not the slope is significantly different from 0 is also not easily judged from the graph. By rescaling the vertical axis of the graph, the slope can be made to look steeper and hence the slope could be made to appear to be significantly different from 0. Graphically, it is difficult to distinguish between the Poisson and the negative binomial distribution because the Poisson requires a slope of 0.

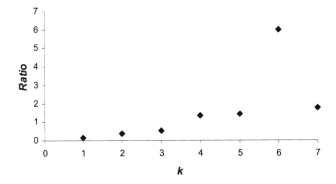

Fig. 5.1 Plot of the ratio kn_k/n_{k-1} against k.

However, we can say that the binomial distribution is probably not a good choice because there is no evidence of a negative slope. In this case, it is advisable to try the Poisson and negative binomial distributions and conduct a more formal test to choose between them. $\square$

It is also possible to compare the appropriateness of the distributions by looking at the relationship of the variance to the mean. For this data set, the mean number of losses per policy is 0.2144. The variance is 0.2889. Because the variance exceeds the mean, the negative binomial should be considered as an alternative to the Poisson distribution. Again this is a qualitative comment because we have, at this point, no formal way of determining whether the variance is sufficiently larger than the mean to warrant use of the negative binomial distribution. In order to do some formal analysis, Table 5.3 gives the results of maximum likelihood estimation (to be discussed in Chapter 10) of the parameters of the Poisson and negative binomial distributions and the negative loglikelihood in each case. In Chapter 12 formal selection methods are presented. They would indicate that the negative binomial is superior to the Poisson as a model for this data set. However, those methods also indicate that, in many cases, the negative binomial is not a particularly good model, and some of the distributions yet to be introduced should be considered.

In subsequent subsections we will expand the class of the distributions beyond the three discussed in this section by constructing more general models related to the Poisson, binomial, and negative binomial distributions.

Table 5.3 Poisson–negative binomial comparison

Distribution	Parameter estimates	$-$Loglikelihood
Poisson	$\hat{\lambda} = 0.2143537$	5,490.78
Negative binomial	$\hat{\beta} = 0.3055594$ $\hat{r} = 0.7015122$	5,348.04

5.6 THE $(a, b, 1)$ CLASS

At times, the distributions discussed previously do not adequately describe the characteristics of some data sets encountered in practice. This may be because the tail of the negative binomial is not heavy enough or because the distributions in the $(a, b, 0)$ class cannot capture the shape of the data set in some other part of the distribution.

In this section, we address the problem of a poor fit at the left-hand end of the distribution, in particular the probability at zero.

For loss count data, the probability at zero is the probability that no losses occur during the period under study. When the probability of occurrence of a loss is low (as is often the case in insurance), the probability at zero has the largest value. Thus, it is important to pay special attention to the fit at this point. By analogy in the operational risk context, if the probability of a loss for a particular business process is low, the probability at zero is largest.

Similarly, it is possible to have situations in which there is less than the expected number, or even zero, occurrences at zero. Any adjustment of the probability at zero is easily handled by modifying the Poisson, binomial, and negative binomial distributions.

Definition 5.5 *A counting distribution is a member of the* **(a,b,1)** *class of distributions provided that there exist constants a and b such that*

$$\frac{p_k}{p_{k-1}} = a + \frac{b}{k}, \qquad k = 2, 3, 4, \dots .$$

Note that the only difference from the $(a, b, 0)$ class is that the recursion begins at p_1 rather than p_0. This forces the distribution from $k = 1$ to $k = \infty$ to have the same shape as the $(a, b, 0)$ class in the sense that the probabilities are the same up to a constant of proportionality because $\sum_{k=1}^{\infty} p_k$ can be set to any number in the interval $(0, 1]$. The remaining probability is at $k = 0$.

We will distinguish between the situations in which $p_0 = 0$ and those where $p_0 > 0$. The first subclass is called the **truncated** (more specifically, **zero-truncated**) distributions. The members are the zero-truncated Poisson, zero-truncated binomial, and zero-truncated negative binomial (and its special case, the zero-truncated geometric) distributions.

The second subclass will be referred to as the **zero-modified** distributions because the probability is modified from that for the $(a, b, 0)$ class. These distributions can be viewed as a mixture of an $(a, b, 0)$ distribution and a degenerate distribution with all the probability at zero. Alternatively, they can be called **truncated with zeros** distributions because the distribution can be viewed as a mixture of a truncated distribution and a degenerate distribution with all the probability at zero. We now show this more formally. Note that all zero-truncated distributions can be considered as zero-modified distributions, with the particular modification being to set $p_0 = 0$.

With three types of distributions, notation can become confusing. When writing about discrete distributions in general, we will continue to let $p_k = \Pr(N = k)$. When referring to a zero-truncated distribution, we will use p_k^T, and when referring to a zero-modified distribution, we will use p_k^M. Once again, it is possible for a zero-modified distribution to be a zero-truncated distribution.

Let $P(z) = \sum_{k=0}^{\infty} p_k z^k$ denote the pgf of a member of the $(a, b, 0)$ class. Let $P^M(z) = \sum_{k=0}^{\infty} p_k^M z^k$ denote the pgf of the corresponding member of the $(a, b, 1)$ class; that is,

$$p_k^M = c p_k, \qquad k = 1, 2, 3, \ldots,$$

and p_0^M is an arbitrary number. Then

$$P^M(z) = p_0^M + \sum_{k=1}^{\infty} p_k^M z^k$$

$$= p_0^M + c \sum_{k=1}^{\infty} p_k z^k$$

$$= p_0^M + c[P(z) - p_0].$$

Because $P^M(1) = P(1) = 1$,

$$1 = p_0^M + c(1 - p_0),$$

resulting in

$$c = \frac{1 - p_0^M}{1 - p_0} \quad \text{or} \quad p_0^M = 1 - c(1 - p_0).$$

This relationship is necessary to ensure that the p_k^M sum to 1. We then have

$$P^M(z) = p_0^M + \frac{1 - p_0^M}{1 - p_0}[P(z) - p_0]$$

$$= \left(1 - \frac{1 - p_0^M}{1 - p_0}\right) 1 + \frac{1 - p_0^M}{1 - p_0} P(z). \tag{5.3}$$

This is a weighted average of the pgfs of the degenerate distribution and the corresponding $(a, b, 0)$ member. Furthermore,

$$p_k^M = \frac{1 - p_0^M}{1 - p_0} p_k, \qquad k = 1, 2, \dots . \tag{5.4}$$

Let $P^T(z)$ denote the pgf of the zero-truncated distribution corresponding to an $(a, b, 0)$ pgf $P(z)$. Then, by setting $p_0^M = 0$ in formulas (5.3) and (5.4),

$$P^T(z) = \frac{P(z) - p_0}{1 - p_0}$$

and

$$p_k^T = \frac{p_k}{1 - p_0}, \qquad k = 1, 2, \dots . \tag{5.5}$$

Then from formula (5.4)

$$p_k^M = (1 - p_0^M) p_k^T, \qquad k = 1, 2, \dots, \tag{5.6}$$

and

$$P^M(z) = p_0^M(1) + (1 - p_0^M) P^T(z). \tag{5.7}$$

Then the zero-modified distribution is also the weighted average of a degenerate distribution and the zero-truncated member of the $(a, b, 0)$ class. The following example illustrates these relationships.

Example 5.6 *Consider a negative binomial random variable with parameters $\beta = 0.5$ and $r = 2.5$. Determine the first four probabilities for this random variable. Then determine the corresponding probabilities for the zero-truncated and zero-modified (with $p_0^M = 0.6$) versions.*

From Table 5.4 on Page 123 we have, for the negative binomial distribution,

$$p_0 = (1 + 0.5)^{-2.5} = 0.362887,$$
$$a = \frac{0.5}{1.5} = \frac{1}{3},$$
$$b = \frac{(2.5 - 1)(0.5)}{1.5} = \frac{1}{2}.$$

The first three recursions yield

$$p_1 = 0.362887 \left(\tfrac{1}{3} + \tfrac{1}{2} \tfrac{1}{1} \right) = 0.302406,$$
$$p_2 = 0.302406 \left(\tfrac{1}{3} + \tfrac{1}{2} \tfrac{1}{2} \right) = 0.176404,$$
$$p_3 = 0.176404 \left(\tfrac{1}{3} + \tfrac{1}{2} \tfrac{1}{3} \right) = 0.088202.$$

For the zero-truncated random variable, $p_0^T = 0$ by definition. The recursions start with [from formula (5.5)] $p_1^T = 0.302406/(1 - 0.362887) = 0.474651$. Then

$$p_2^T = 0.474651 \left(\tfrac{1}{3} + \tfrac{1}{2} \tfrac{1}{2} \right) = 0.276880,$$
$$p_3^T = 0.276880 \left(\tfrac{1}{3} + \tfrac{1}{2} \tfrac{1}{3} \right) = 0.138440.$$

If the original values were all available, then the zero-truncated probabilities could have all been obtained by multiplying the original values by $1/(1 - 0.362887) = 1.569580$.

For the zero-modified random variable, $p_0^M = 0.6$ arbitrarily. From (5.4), $p_1^M = (1 - 0.6)(0.302406)/(1 - 0.362887) = 0.189860$. Then

$$p_2^M = 0.189860 \left(\tfrac{1}{3} + \tfrac{1}{2} \tfrac{1}{2} \right) = 0.110752,$$
$$p_3^M = 0.110752 \left(\tfrac{1}{3} + \tfrac{1}{2} \tfrac{1}{3} \right) = 0.055376.$$

In this case, each original negative binomial probability has been multiplied by $(1 - 0.6)/(1 - 0.362887) = 0.627832$. Also note that, for $j \geq 1$, $p_j^M = 0.4 p_j^T$. $\qquad\square$

Although we have only discussed the zero-modified distributions of the $(a, b, 0)$ class, the $(a, b, 1)$ class admits additional distributions. The (a, b) parameter space can be expanded to admit an extension of the negative binomial distribution to include cases where $-1 < r < 0$. For the $(a, b, 0)$ class, $r > 0$ is required. By adding the additional region to the sample space, the "extended" truncated negative binomial (ETNB) distribution has parameter restrictions $\beta > 0$, $r > -1$, $r \neq 0$.

To show that the recursive equation

$$p_k = p_{k-1} \left(a + \frac{b}{k} \right), \qquad k = 2, 3, \ldots, \tag{5.8}$$

with $p_0 = 0$ defines a proper distribution, it is sufficient to show that for any value of p_1, the successive values of p_k obtained recursively are each positive and that $\sum_{k=1}^{\infty} p_k < \infty$. For the ETNB, this must be done for the parameter space

$$a = \frac{\beta}{1 + \beta}, \quad \beta > 0,$$
$$b = (r - 1) \frac{\beta}{1 + \beta}, \quad r > -1, r \neq 0$$

(see Exercise 5.5).

When $r \to 0$, the limiting case of the ETNB is the logarithmic distribution with

$$p_k^T = \frac{[\beta/(1 + \beta)]^k}{k \ln(1 + \beta)}, \qquad k = 1, 2, 3, \ldots \tag{5.9}$$

(see Exercise 5.6). The pgf of the logarithmic distribution is

$$P^T(z) = 1 - \frac{\ln[1 - \beta(z - 1)]}{\ln(1 + \beta)} \tag{5.10}$$

(see Exercise 5.7). The zero-modified logarithmic distribution is created by assigning an arbitrary probability at zero and reducing the remaining probabilities.

It is also interesting that the special extreme case with $-1 < r < 0$ and $\beta \to \infty$ is a proper distribution, sometimes called the Sibuya distribution. It has pgf $P(z) = 1 - (1 - z)^{-r}$, and no moments exist (see Exercise 5.8). Distributions with no moments are not particularly interesting for modeling loss numbers (unless the right tail is subsequently modified) because an infinite number of losses are expected. If this is the case, the risk manager should be fired!

Example 5.7 *Determine the probabilities for an ETNB distribution with $r = -0.5$ and $\beta = 1$. Do this both for the truncated version and for the modified version with $p_0^M = 0.6$ set arbitrarily.*

We have $a = 1/(1 + 1) = 0.5$ and $b = (-0.5 - 1)(1)/(1 + 1) = -0.75$. We also have $p_1^T = -0.5(1)/[(1 + 1)^{0.5} - (1 + 1)] = 0.853553$. Subsequent values are

$$p_2^T = \left(0.5 - \frac{0.75}{2}\right)(0.853553) = 0.106694,$$

$$p_3^T = \left(0.5 - \frac{0.75}{3}\right)(0.106694) = 0.026674.$$

For the modified probabilities, the truncated probabilities need to be multiplied by 0.4 to produce $p_1^M = 0.341421$, $p_2^M = 0.042678$, and $p_3^M = 0.010670$.

Note: A reasonable question is to ask if there is a "natural" member of the ETNB distribution, that is, one for which the recursion would begin with p_1 rather than p_2. For that to be the case, the natural value of p_0 would have to satisfy $p_1 = (0.5 - 0.75/1)p_0 = -0.25p_0$. This would force one of the two probabilities to be negative and so there is no acceptable solution. It is easy to show that this occurs for any $r < 0$.   □

There are no other members of the $(a, b, 1)$ class beyond those discussed above. A summary is given in Table 5.4.

5.7   COMPOUND FREQUENCY MODELS

A larger class of distributions can be created by the processes of compounding any two discrete distributions. The term **compounding** reflects the idea that the pgf of the new distribution $P(z)$ is written as

$$P(z) = P_N[P_M(z)], \tag{5.11}$$

where $P_N(z)$ and $P_M(z)$ are called the **primary** and **secondary** distributions, respectively.

The compound distributions arise naturally as follows. Let N be a counting random variable with pgf $P_N(z)$. Let $M_1, M_2, \ldots$ be identically and

Table 5.4 Members of the $(a, b, 1)$ class

Distribution[a]	p_0	a	b	Parameter space
Poisson	$e^{-\lambda}$	0	λ	$\lambda > 0$
ZT Poisson	0	0	λ	$\lambda > 0$
ZM Poisson	Arbitrary	0	λ	$\lambda > 0$
Binomial	$(1-q)^m$	$-\dfrac{q}{1-q}$	$(m+1)\dfrac{q}{1-q}$	$0 < q < 1$
ZT binomial	0	$-\dfrac{q}{1-q}$	$(m+1)\dfrac{q}{1-q}$	$0 < q < 1$
ZM binomial	Arbitrary	$-\dfrac{q}{1-q}$	$(m+1)\dfrac{q}{1-q}$	$0 < q < 1$
Negative binomial	$(1+\beta)^{-r}$	$\dfrac{\beta}{1+\beta}$	$(r-1)\dfrac{\beta}{1+\beta}$	$r > 0,\ \beta > 0$
ETNB	0	$\dfrac{\beta}{1+\beta}$	$(r-1)\dfrac{\beta}{1+\beta}$	$r > -1,^b\ \beta > 0$
ZM ETNB	Arbitrary	$\dfrac{\beta}{1+\beta}$	$(r-1)\dfrac{\beta}{1+\beta}$	$r > -1,^b\ \beta > 0$
Geometric	$(1+\beta)^{-1}$	$\dfrac{\beta}{1+\beta}$	0	$\beta > 0$
ZT geometric	0	$\dfrac{\beta}{1+\beta}$	0	$\beta > 0$
ZM geometric	Arbitrary	$\dfrac{\beta}{1+\beta}$	0	$\beta > 0$
Logarithmic	0	$\dfrac{\beta}{1+\beta}$	$-\dfrac{\beta}{1+\beta}$	$\beta > 0$
ZM logarithmic	Arbitrary	$\dfrac{\beta}{1+\beta}$	$-\dfrac{\beta}{1+\beta}$	$\beta > 0$

[a]ZT = zero truncated, ZM = zero modified.
[b]Excluding $r = 0$, which is the logarithmic distribution.

independently distributed counting random variables with pgf $P_M(z)$. Assuming that the M_js do not depend on N, the pgf of the random sum $S = M_1 + M_2 + \cdots + M_N$ (where $N = 0$ implies that $S = 0$) is $P_S(z) = P_N[P_M(z)]$. This is shown as

$$
\begin{aligned}
P_S(z) &= \sum_{k=0}^{\infty} \Pr(S = k) z^k \\
&= \sum_{k=0}^{\infty} \sum_{n=0}^{\infty} \Pr(S = k \mid N = n) \Pr(N = n) z^k \\
&= \sum_{n=0}^{\infty} \Pr(N = n) \sum_{k=0}^{\infty} \Pr(M_1 + \cdots + M_n = k \mid N = n) z^k \\
&= \sum_{n=0}^{\infty} \Pr(N = n) [P_M(z)]^n \\
&= P_N[P_M(z)].
\end{aligned}
$$

In operational risk contexts, this distribution can arise naturally. If N represents the number of loss-causing events and $\{M_k;\ k = 1, 2, \ldots, N\}$ represents the number of losses (errors, injuries, failures, etc.) from the events, then S represents the total number of losses for all such events. This kind of interpretation is not necessary to justify the use of a compound distribution. If a compound distribution fits data well, that may be enough justification itself. Also, there are other motivations for these distributions, as presented in Section 5.9.

Example 5.8 *Demonstrate that any zero-modified distribution is a compound distribution.*

Consider a primary Bernoulli distribution. It has pgf $P_N(z) = 1 - q + qz$. Then consider an arbitrary secondary distribution with pgf $P_M(z)$. Then, from formula (5.11) we obtain

$$
P_S(z) = P_N[P_M(z)] = 1 - q + qP_M(z).
$$

From formula (5.3), it is clear that this is the pgf of a ZM distribution with

$$
q = \frac{1 - p_0^M}{1 - p_0}.
$$

That is, the ZM distribution has assigned arbitrary probability p_0^M at zero, while p_0 is the probability assigned at zero by the secondary distribution. □

Example 5.9 *Consider the case where both M and N have the Poisson distribution. Determine the pgf of this distribution.*

This distribution is called the Poisson–Poisson or Neyman Type A distribution. Let $P_N(z) = e^{\lambda_1(z-1)}$ and $P_M(z) = e^{\lambda_2(z-1)}$. Then

$$
P_S(z) = e^{\lambda_1[e^{\lambda_2(z-1)} - 1]}.
$$

When λ_2 is a lot larger than λ_1 (for example, $\lambda_1 = 0.1$ and $\lambda_2 = 10$) the resulting distribution will have two local modes.   □

Example 5.10 *Demonstrate that the Poisson–logarithmic distribution is a negative binomial, as compound Poisson-logarithmic distribution.*

The negative binomial distribution has pgf

$$P(z) = [1 - \beta(z - 1)]^{-r}.$$

Suppose $P_N(z)$ is Poisson(λ) and $P_M(z)$ is logarithmic(β); then

$$
\begin{aligned}
P_N[P_M(z)] &= \exp\{\lambda[P_M(z) - 1]\} \\
&= \exp\left\{\lambda\left[1 - \frac{\ln[1 - \beta(z - 1)]}{\ln(1 + \beta)} - 1\right]\right\} \\
&= \exp\left\{\frac{-\lambda}{\ln(1 + \beta)}\ln[1 - \beta(z - 1)]\right\} \\
&= [1 - \beta(z - 1)]^{-\lambda/\ln(1+\beta)} \\
&= [1 - \beta(z - 1)]^{-r},
\end{aligned}
$$

where $r = \lambda/\ln(1+\beta)$. This shows that the negative binomial distribution can be written as a compound Poisson distribution with a logarithmic secondary distribution.   □

The above example shows that the "Poisson–logarithmic" distribution does not create a new distribution beyond the $(a, b, 0)$ and $(a, b, 1)$ classes. As a result, this combination of distributions is not useful to us. Another combination that does not create a new distribution beyond the $(a, b, 1)$ class is the compound geometric distribution where both the primary and secondary distributions are geometric. The resulting distribution is a zero-modified geometric distribution, as shown in Exercise 5.12. The following theorem shows that certain other combinations are also of no use in expanding the class of distributions through compounding. Suppose $P_S(z) = P_N[P_M(z); \theta]$ as before. Now, $P_M(z)$ can always be written as

$$P_M(z) = f_0 + (1 - f_0)P_M^*(z) \tag{5.12}$$

where $P_M^*(z)$ is the pgf of the conditional distribution over the positive range (in other words, the zero-truncated version).

Theorem 5.11 *Suppose the pgf $P_N(z; \theta)$ satisfies*

$$P_N(z; \theta) = B[\theta(z - 1)]$$

for some parameter θ and some function $B(z)$ that is independent of θ. That is, the parameter θ and the argument z only appear in the pgf as $\theta(z - 1)$.

There may be other parameters as well, and they may appear anywhere in the pgf. Then $P_S(z) = P_N[P_M(z); \theta]$ *can be rewritten as*

$$P_S(z) = P_N[P_M^T(z); \theta(1 - f_0)].$$

Proof:

$$\begin{aligned} P_S(z) &= P_N[P_M(z); \theta] \\ &= P_N[f_0 + (1 - f_0)P_M^T(z); \theta] \\ &= B\{\theta[f_0 + (1 - f_0)P_M^T(z) - 1]\} \\ &= B\{\theta(1 - f_0)[P_M^T(z) - 1]\} \\ &= P_N[P_M^T(z); \theta(1 - f_0)]. \end{aligned}$$

$\square$

This shows that adding, deleting, or modifying the probability at zero in the secondary distribution does not add a new distribution because it is equivalent to modifying the parameter θ of the primary distribution. This means that, for example, a Poisson primary distribution with a Poisson, zero-truncated Poisson, or zero-modified Poisson secondary distribution will still lead to a Neyman Type A (Poisson–Poisson) distribution.

5.8   RECURSIVE CALCULATION OF COMPOUND PROBABILITIES

The probability of exactly k losses can be written as

$$\begin{aligned} \Pr(S = k) &= \sum_{n=0}^{\infty} \Pr(S = k | N = n) \Pr(N = n) \\ &= \sum_{n=0}^{\infty} \Pr(M_1 + \cdots + M_N = k | N = n) \Pr(N = n) \\ &= \sum_{n=0}^{\infty} \Pr(M_1 + \cdots + M_n = k) \Pr(N = n). \end{aligned} \tag{5.13}$$

Letting $g_n = \Pr(S = n)$, $p_n = \Pr(N = n)$, and $f_n = \Pr(M = n)$, this is rewritten as

$$g_k = \sum_{n=0}^{\infty} p_n f_k^{*n} \tag{5.14}$$

where f_k^{*n}, $k = 0, 1, \ldots$, is the n-fold convolution of the function f_k, $k = 0, 1, \ldots$, that is, the probability that the sum of n random variables which are each independent and identically distributed (iid) with probability function f_k will take on value k.

When $P_N(z)$ is chosen to be a member of the $(a, b, 0)$ class,

$$p_k = \left(a + \frac{b}{k}\right) p_{k-1}, \qquad k = 1, 2, \ldots, \tag{5.15}$$

and a simple recursive formula can be used. This formula avoids the use of convolutions and thus reduces the computations considerably.

Theorem 5.12 (Panjer recursion) *If the primary distribution is a member of the $(a, b, 0)$ class, the recursive formula is*

$$g_k = \frac{1}{1 - af_0} \sum_{j=1}^{k} \left(a + \frac{bj}{k}\right) f_j g_{k-j}, \qquad k = 1, 2, 3, \ldots. \tag{5.16}$$

Proof: From formula (5.15),

$$n p_n = a(n - 1)p_{n-1} + (a + b)p_{n-1}.$$

Multiplying each side by $[P_M(z)]^{n-1} P_M'(z)$ and summing over n yields

$$\sum_{n=1}^{\infty} n p_n [P_M(z)]^{n-1} P_M'(z) = a \sum_{n=1}^{\infty} (n - 1)p_{n-1}[P_M(z)]^{n-1} P_M'(z)$$

$$+ (a + b) \sum_{n=1}^{\infty} p_{n-1}[P_M(z)]^{n-1} P_M'(z).$$

Because $P_S(z) = \sum_{n=0}^{\infty} p_n [P_M(z)]^n$, the previous equation is

$$P_S'(z) = a \sum_{n=0}^{\infty} n p_n [P_M(z)]^n P_M'(z) + (a + b) \sum_{n=0}^{\infty} p_n [P_M(z)]^n P_M'(z).$$

Therefore

$$P_S'(z) = a P_S'(z) P_M(z) + (a + b) P_S(z) P_M'(z).$$

Each side can be expanded in powers of z. The coefficients of z^{k-1} in such an expansion must be the same on both sides of the equation. Hence, for $k = 1, 2, \ldots$ we have

$$k g_k = a \sum_{j=0}^{k} (k - j) f_j g_{k-j} + (a + b) \sum_{j=0}^{k} j f_j g_{k-j}$$

$$= a k f_0 g_k + a \sum_{j=1}^{k} (k - j) f_j g_{k-j} + (a + b) \sum_{j=1}^{k} j f_j g_{k-j}$$

$$= a k f_0 g_k + a k \sum_{j=1}^{k} f_j g_{k-j} + b \sum_{j=1}^{k} j f_j g_{k-j}.$$

Therefore,

$$g_k = af_0g_k + \sum_{j=1}^{k}\left(a + \frac{bj}{k}\right)f_jg_{k-j}.$$

Rearrangement yields the recursive formula (5.16).   □

This recursion (5.16) has become known as the Panjer recursion after its introduction as a computational tool for aggregate losses by Panjer [88]. Its use here is numerically equivalent to its use for aggregate losses in Chapter 6. In order to use the recursive formula (5.16), the starting value g_0 is required and is given in Theorem 5.15.

Theorem 5.13 *If the primary distribution is a member of the $(a,b,1)$ class, the recursive formula is*

$$g_k = \frac{[p_1 - (a+b)p_0]f_k + \sum_{j=1}^{k}(a+bj/k)f_jg_{k-j}}{1 - af_0}, \quad k = 1,2,3,\dots . \quad (5.17)$$

Proof: It is similar to the proof of Theorem 5.12 and is left to the reader. □

Example 5.14 *Develop the Panjer recursive formula for the case where the primary distribution is Poisson.*

In this case $a = 0$ and $b = \lambda$, yielding the recursive form

$$g_k = \frac{\lambda}{k}\sum_{j=1}^{k}jf_jg_{k-j}.$$

The starting value is, from (5.11),

$$\begin{aligned}g_0 &= \Pr(S = 0) = P(0) \\ &= P_N[P_M(0)] = P_N(f_0) \\ &= e^{-\lambda(1-f_0)}.\end{aligned} \quad (5.18)$$

Distributions of this type are called compound Poisson distributions[1]. When the secondary distribution is specified, the compound distribution is called Poisson–X, where X is the name of the secondary distribution.   □

The method used to obtain g_0 applies to any compound distribution.

Theorem 5.15 *For any compound distribution, $g_0 = P_N(f_0)$, where $P_N(z)$ is the pgf of the primary distribution and f_0 is the probability that the secondary distribution takes on the value zero.*

[1]In some textbooks, the term compound distribution, as in "compound Poisson," refers to what are called in this book "mixed distributions."

Proof: See the second line of equation (5.18). □

Note that the secondary distribution is not required to be in any special form. However, to keep the number of distributions manageable, secondary distributions will be selected from the $(a, b, 0)$ or the $(a, b, 1)$ class.

Example 5.16 *Calculate the probabilities for the Poisson–ETNB distribution where $\lambda = 3$ for the Poisson distribution and the ETNB distribution has $r = -0.5$ and $\beta = 1$.*

From Example 5.7 the secondary probabilities are $f_0 = 0$, $f_1 = 0.853553$, $f_2 = 0.106694$, and $f_3 = 0.026674$. From equation (5.18), $g_0 = \exp[-3(1 - 0)] = 0.049787$. For the Poisson primary distribution, $a = 0$ and $b = 3$. The recursive formula (5.16) becomes

$$g_k = \frac{\sum_{j=1}^{k}(3j/k)f_j g_{k-j}}{1 - 0(0)} = \sum_{j=1}^{k}\frac{3j}{k}f_j g_{k-j}.$$

Then,

$$g_1 = \frac{3(1)}{1}0.853553(0.049787) = 0.127488,$$

$$g_2 = \frac{3(1)}{2}0.853553(0.127488) + \frac{3(2)}{2}0.106694(0.049787) = 0.179163,$$

$$g_3 = \frac{3(1)}{3}0.853553(0.179163) + \frac{3(2)}{3}0.106694(0.127488)$$

$$+\frac{3(3)}{3}0.026674(0.049787) = 0.184114.$$

□

The following example uses the Panjer recursion to illustrate the equivalence between the Poisson-X and Poisson-zero-modified-X distributions, where X can be any distribution.

Example 5.17 *Determine the probabilities for a Poisson–zero-modified ETNB distribution where the parameters are $\lambda = 7.5$, $p_0^M = 0.6$, $r = -0.5$, and $\beta = 1$.*

From Example 5.7 the secondary probabilities are $f_0 = 0.6$, $f_1 = 0.341421$, $f_2 = 0.042678$, and $f_3 = 0.010670$. From equation (5.18), $g_0 = \exp[-7.5(1 - 0.6)] = 0.049787$. For the Poisson primary distribution, $a = 0$ and $b = 7.5$. The recursive formula (5.16) becomes

$$g_k = \frac{\sum_{j=1}^{k}(7.5j/k)f_j g_{k-j}}{1 - 0(0.6)} = \sum_{j=1}^{k}\frac{7.5j}{k}f_j g_{k-j}.$$

Then,

$$g_1 = \frac{7.5(1)}{1}0.341421(0.049787) = 0.127487,$$

$$g_2 = \frac{7.5(1)}{2}0.341421(0.127487) + \frac{7.5(2)}{2}0.042678(0.049787) = 0.179161,$$

$$g_3 = \frac{7.5(1)}{3}0.341421(0.179161) + \frac{7.5(2)}{3}0.042678(0.127487)$$

$$+ \frac{7.5(3)}{3}0.010670(0.049787) = 0.184112.$$

Except for slight rounding differences, these probabilities are the same as those obtained in Example 5.16. ☐

5.9 AN INVENTORY OF DISCRETE DISTRIBUTIONS

In the previous sections of this chapter, we have introduced the simple $(a, b, 0)$ class, generalized to the $(a, b, 1)$ class, and then used compounding to create a larger class of distributions. In this section, we summarize the distributions introduced in those sections.

There are relationships among the various distributions similar to those of Section 4.3.2. The specific relationships are given in Table 5.5.

It is clear from earlier developments that members of the $(a, b, 0)$ class are special cases of members of the $(a, b, 1)$ class and that zero-truncated distributions are special cases of zero-modified distributions. The limiting cases are best discovered through the probability generating function, as was done on page 113, where the Poisson distribution is shown to be a limiting case of the negative binomial distribution.

We have not listed compound distributions where the primary distribution is one of the two parameter models such as the negative binomial or Poisson–inverse Gaussian. This was done because these distributions are often themselves compound Poisson distributions and, as such, are generalizations of distributions already presented. This collection forms a particularly rich set of distributions in terms of shape. However, many other distributions are also possible. Many others are discussed in Johnson, Kotz, and Kemp [65], Douglas [24], and Panjer and Willmot [93].

5.9.1 The $(a, b, 0)$ class

The distributions in this class have support on $0, 1, \ldots.$ For this class, a particular distribution is specified by setting p_0 and then using $p_k = (a + b/k)p_{k-1}.$ Specific members are created by setting p_0, a, and b. For any member, $\mu_{(1)} = (a + b)/(1 - a)$, and for higher j, $\mu_{(j)} = (aj + b)\mu_{(j-1)}/(1 - a)$. The variance is $(a + b)/(1 - a)^2.$

Table 5.5   Relationships among discrete distributions

Distribution	Is a special case of	Is a limiting case of
Poisson	ZM Poisson	Negative binomial
		Poisson–binomial
		Poisson–inv. Gaussian
		Polya–Aeppli[a]
		Neyman–A[b]
ZT Poisson	ZM Poisson	ZT negative binomial
ZM Poisson		ZM negative binomial
Geometric	Negative binomial,	Geometric–Poisson
	ZM geometric	
ZT geometric	ZT negative binomial	
ZM geometric	ZM negative binomial	
Logarithmic		ZT negative binomial
ZM logarithmic		ZM negative binomial
Binomial	ZM binomial	
Negative binomial	ZM negative binomial,	
	Poisson–ETNB	
Poisson–inverse Gaussian	Poisson–ETNB	
Polya–Aeppli	Poisson–ETNB	
Neyman–A		Poisson–ETNB

[a] Also called Poisson-geometric.
[b] Also called Poisson-Poisson.

5.9.1.1 Poisson

$$p_0 = e^{-\lambda}, \quad a = 0, \quad b = \lambda,$$
$$p_k = \frac{e^{-\lambda}\lambda^k}{k!},$$
$$E[N] = \lambda, \quad \text{Var}[N] = \lambda,$$
$$P(z) = e^{\lambda(z-1)}.$$

5.9.1.2 Geometric

$$p_0 = \frac{1}{1+\beta}, \quad a = \frac{\beta}{1+\beta}, \quad b = 0,$$
$$p_k = \frac{\beta^k}{(1+\beta)^{k+1}},$$
$$E[N] = \beta, \quad \text{Var}[N] = \beta(1+\beta),$$
$$P(z) = [1 - \beta(z-1)]^{-1}.$$

This is a special case of the negative binomial with $r = 1$.

5.9.1.3 Binomial

$$p_0 = (1-q)^m, \quad a = -\frac{q}{1-q}, \quad b = \frac{(m+1)q}{1-q},$$

$$p_k = \binom{m}{k} q^k (1-q)^{m-k}, \quad k = 0, 1, \ldots, m,$$

$$E[N] = mq, \quad \text{Var}[N] = mq(1-q),$$

$$P(z) = [1 + q(z-1)]^m.$$

5.9.1.4 Negative binomial

$$p_0 = (1+\beta)^{-r}, \quad a = \frac{\beta}{1+\beta}, \quad b = \frac{(r-1)\beta}{1+\beta},$$

$$p_k = \frac{r(r+1)\cdots(r+k-1)\beta^k}{k!(1+\beta)^{r+k}},$$

$$E[N] = r\beta, \quad \text{Var}[N] = r\beta(1+\beta),$$

$$P(z) = [1 - \beta(z-1)]^{-r}.$$

5.9.2   The $(a, b, 1)$ class

To distinguish this class from the $(a, b, 0)$ class, the probabilities are denoted $\Pr(N = k) = p_k^M$ or $\Pr(N = k) = p_k^T$ depending on which subclass is being represented. For this class, p_0^M is arbitrary (that is, it is a parameter) and then p_1^M or p_1^T is a specified function of the parameters a and b. Subsequent probabilities are obtained recursively as in the $(a, b, 0)$ class: $p_k^M = (a + b/k)p_{k-1}^M$, $k = 2, 3, \ldots$, with the same recursion for p_k^T There are two subclasses of this class. When discussing their members, we often refer to the "corresponding" member of the $(a, b, 0)$ class. This refers to the member of that class with the same values for a and b. The notation p_k will continue to be used for probabilities for the corresponding $(a, b, 0)$ distribution.

5.9.3   The zero-truncated subclass

The members of this class have $p_0^T = 0$ and therefore it need not be estimated. These distributions should only be used when a value of zero is impossible. The first factorial moment is $\mu_{(1)} = (a + b)/[(1 - a)(1 - p_0)]$, where p_0 is the value for the corresponding member of the $(a, b, 0)$ class. For the logarithmic distribution (which has no corresponding member), $\mu_{(1)} = \beta/\ln(1+\beta)$. Higher factorial moments are obtained recursively with the same formula as with the $(a, b, 0)$ class. The variance is $(a + b)[1 - (a + b + 1)p_0]/[(1 - a)(1 - p_0)]^2$.For those members of the subclass that have corresponding $(a, b, 0)$ distributions, $p_k^T = p_k/(1 - p_0)$.

5.9.3.1 Zero-truncated Poisson

$$p_1^T = \frac{\lambda}{e^\lambda - 1}, \quad a = 0, \quad b = \lambda,$$

$$p_k^T = \frac{\lambda^k}{k!(e^\lambda - 1)},$$

$$\mathrm{E}[N] = \lambda/(1 - e^{-\lambda}), \quad \mathrm{Var}[N] = \lambda[1 - (\lambda + 1)e^{-\lambda}]/(1 - e^{-\lambda})^2,$$

$$P(z) = \frac{e^{\lambda z} - 1}{e^\lambda - 1}.$$

5.9.3.2 Zero-truncated geometric

$$p_1^T = \frac{1}{1 + \beta}, \quad a = \frac{\beta}{1 + \beta}, \quad b = 0,$$

$$p_k^T = \frac{\beta^{k-1}}{(1 + \beta)^k},$$

$$\mathrm{E}[N] = 1 + \beta, \quad \mathrm{Var}[N] = \beta(1 + \beta),$$

$$P(z) = \frac{[1 - \beta(z - 1)]^{-1} - (1 + \beta)^{-1}}{1 - (1 + \beta)^{-1}}.$$

This is a special case of the zero-truncated negative binomial with $r = 1$.

5.9.3.3 Logarithmic

$$p_1^T = \frac{\beta}{(1 + \beta)\ln(1 + \beta)}, \quad a = \frac{\beta}{1 + \beta}, \quad b = -\frac{\beta}{1 + \beta},$$

$$p_k^T = \frac{\beta^k}{k(1 + \beta)^k \ln(1 + \beta)},$$

$$\mathrm{E}[N] = \beta/\ln(1 + \beta), \quad \mathrm{Var}[N] = \frac{\beta[1 + \beta - \beta/\ln(1 + \beta)]}{\ln(1 + \beta)},$$

$$P(z) = 1 - \frac{\ln[1 - \beta(z - 1)]}{\ln(1 + \beta)}.$$

This is a limiting case of the zero-truncated negative binomial as $r \to 0$.

5.9.3.4 Zero-truncated binomial

$$p_1^T = \frac{m(1-q)^{m-1}q}{1-(1-q)^m}, \quad a = -\frac{q}{1-q}, \quad b = \frac{(m+1)q}{1-q},$$

$$p_k^T = \frac{\binom{m}{k}q^k(1-q)^{m-k}}{1-(1-q)^m}, \quad k = 1,2,\ldots,m,$$

$$\mathrm{E}[N] = \frac{mq}{1-(1-q)^m},$$

$$\mathrm{Var}[N] = \frac{mq[(1-q)-(1-q+mq)(1-q)^m]}{[1-(1-q)^m]^2},$$

$$P(z) = \frac{[1+q(z-1)]^m - (1-q)^m}{1-(1-q)^m}.$$

5.9.3.5 Zero-truncated negative binomial

$$p_1^T = \frac{r\beta}{(1+\beta)^{r+1} - (1+\beta)}, \quad a = \frac{\beta}{1+\beta}, \quad b = \frac{(r-1)\beta}{1+\beta},$$

$$p_k^T = \frac{r(r+1)\cdots(r+k-1)}{k![(1+\beta)^r - 1]}\left(\frac{\beta}{1+\beta}\right)^k,$$

$$\mathrm{E}[N] = \frac{r\beta}{1-(1+\beta)^{-r}},$$

$$Var[N] = \frac{r\beta[(1+\beta) - (1+\beta+r\beta)(1+\beta)^{-r}]}{[1-(1+\beta)^{-r}]^2},$$

$$P(z) = \frac{[1-\beta(z-1)]^{-r} - (1+\beta)^{-r}}{1-(1+\beta)^{-r}}.$$

This distribution is sometimes called the extended truncated negative binomial distribution because the parameter r can extend below 0.

5.9.4 The zero-modified subclass

A zero-modified distribution is created by starting with a truncated distribution and then placing an arbitrary amount of probability at zero. This probability, p_0^M, is a parameter. The remaining probabilities are adjusted accordingly. Values of p_k^M can be determined from the corresponding zero-truncated distribution as $p_k^M = (1-p_0^M)p_k^T$ or from the corresponding $(a,b,0)$ distribution as $p_k^M = (1-p_0^M)p_k/(1-p_0)$. The same recursion used for the zero-truncated subclass applies.

The mean is $1 - p_0^M$ times the mean for the corresponding zero-truncated distribution. The variance is $1 - p_0^M$ times the zero-truncated variance plus $p_0^M(1-p_0^M)$ times the square of the zero-truncated mean. The probability generating function is $P^M(z) = p_0^M + (1-p_0^M)P(z)$, where $P(z)$ is the probability generating function for the corresponding zero-truncated distribution.

5.9.5   The compound class

Members of this class are obtained by compounding one distribution with another. That is, let N be a discrete distribution, called the **primary distribution** and let $M_1, M_2, \ldots$ be identically and independently distributed with another discrete distribution, called the **secondary distribution**. The compound distribution is $S = M_1 + \cdots + M_N$. The probabilities for the compound distributions are found from the Panjer recursion

$$g_k = \frac{1}{1 - af_0} \sum_{j=1}^{k} (a + b\frac{j}{k}) f_j g_{k-j}$$

for $k = 1, 2, \ldots$, where a and b are the usual values for the primary distribution [which must be a member of the $(a, b, 0)$ class] and f_j is the probability from the secondary distribution. The only two primary distributions listed here are Poisson (for which $p_0 = \exp[-\lambda(1 - f_0)]$) and geometric [for which $p_0 = 1/[1 + \beta - \beta f_0]$]. The probability generating function is $P(z) = P_N[P_M(z)]$. In the following list the primary distribution is always named first. For the first, second, and fourth distributions, the secondary distribution is the $(a, b, 0)$ class member with that name.

5.9.5.1   Poisson–binomial

This distribution has a Poisson primary distribution and a binomial secondary or, equivalently, a Poisson primary and a zero-truncated secondary distribution.

5.9.5.2   Poisson–Poisson

The parameter λ_1 is for the primary Poisson distribution, and λ_2 is for the secondary Poisson distribution. This distribution is also called the **Neyman Type A**.

5.9.5.3   Geometric–extended truncated negative binomial

The parameter β_1 is for the primary geometric distribution. The last two parameters are for the secondary distribution, noting that for $r = 0$ the secondary distribution is logarithmic. The truncated version is used so that the extension of r is available.

5.9.5.4   Geometric–Poisson

This is a special case of a negative binomial-Poisson, which could itself be described as a Poisson-logarithmic-Poisson.

5.9.5.5   Poisson–extended truncated negative binomial

When $r = 0$ the secondary distribution is logarithmic, resulting in the negative binomial distribution. This distribution is also called the **generalized Poisson–Pascal**.

5.9.5.6   *Polya–Aeppli*

This is a special case of the Poisson–extended truncated negative binomial with $r = 1$. It is actually a Poisson-geometric or, equivalently, a Poisson–truncated geometric distribution.

5.9.5.7   *Poisson–inverse Gaussian*

This is a special case of the Poisson–extended truncated negative binomial with $r = -0.5$.

5.10   A HIERARCHY OF DISCRETE DISTRIBUTIONS

The following table indicates which distributions are special or limiting cases of others. For the special cases, one parameter is set equal to a constant to create the special case. For the limiting cases, two parameters go to infinity or zero in some special way.

Distribution	Is a special case of	Is a limiting case of
Poisson	ZM Poisson	Negative binomial, Poisson–binomial, Poisson–inv. Gaussian, Polya–Aeppli, Neyman–A
ZT Poisson	ZM Poisson	ZT negative binomial
ZM Poisson		ZM negative binomial
Geometric	Negative binomial ZM geometric	Geometric–Poisson
ZT geometric	ZT negative binomial	
ZM geometric	ZM negative binomial	
Logarithmic		ZT negative binomial
ZM logarithmic		ZM negative binomial
Binomial	ZM binomial	
Negative binomial	ZM negative binomial	Poisson–ETNB
Poisson–inverse Gaussian	Poisson–ETNB	
Polya–Aeppli	Poisson–ETNB	
Neyman–A		Poisson–ETNB

5.11 FURTHER PROPERTIES OF THE COMPOUND POISSON CLASS

Of central importance within the class of compound frequency models is the class of compound Poisson frequency distributions. Physical motivation for this model arises from the fact that the Poisson distribution is often a good model to describe the number of loss-causing accidents, and the number of losses from an accident is often itself a random variable. In addition, there are numerous convenient mathematical properties enjoyed by the compound Poisson class. In particular, those involving recursive evaluation of the probabilities were also discussed in Section 5.9.5. In addition, there is a close connection between the compound Poisson distributions and the mixed Poisson frequency distributions which is discussed in more detail in Section 5.13. Here we consider some other properties of these distributions. The compound Poisson pgf may be expressed as

$$P(z) = \exp\{\lambda[Q(z) - 1]\}, \tag{5.19}$$

where $Q(z)$ is the pgf of the secondary distribution.

Example 5.18 *Obtain the pgf for the Poisson–ETNB distribution and show that it looks like the pgf of a Poisson–negative binomial distribution.*

The ETNB distribution has pgf

$$Q(z) = \frac{[1 - \beta(z - 1)]^{-r} - (1 + \beta)^{-r}}{1 - (1 + \beta)^{-r}}$$

for $\beta > 0$, $r > -1$, and $r \neq 0$. Then the Poisson–ETNB distribution has as the logarithm of its pgf

$$
\begin{aligned}
\ln P(z) &= \lambda \left\{ \frac{[1 - \beta(z - 1)]^{-r} - (1 + \beta)^{-r}}{1 - (1 + \beta)^{-r}} - 1 \right\} \\
&= \lambda \left\{ \frac{[1 - \beta(z - 1)]^{-r} - 1}{1 - (1 + \beta)^{-r}} \right\} \\
&= \mu\{[1 - \beta(z - 1)]^{-r} - 1\},
\end{aligned}
$$

where $\mu = \lambda/[1 - (1 + \beta)^{-r}]$. This defines a compound Poisson distribution with primary mean μ and secondary pgf $[1 - \beta(z - 1)]^{-r}$, which is the pgf of a negative binomial random variable, as long as r and hence μ are positive. This illustrates that the probability at zero in the secondary distribution has no impact on the compound Poisson form. Also, the above calculation demonstrates that the Poisson–ETNB pgf $P(z)$, with $\ln P(z) = \mu\{[1 - \beta(z - 1)]^{-r} - 1\}$, has parameter space $\{\beta > 0, r > -1, \mu r > 0\}$, a useful observation with respect to estimation and analysis of the parameters.   □

We can compare the skewness (third moment) of these distributions to develop an appreciation of the amount by which the skewness, and hence the tails of these distributions, can vary even when the mean and variance are fixed. From equation (5.19) (see Exercise 5.14) and Definition 2.18, the mean and second and third central moments of the compound Poisson distribution are

$$\mu_1' = \mu = \lambda m_1',$$
$$\mu_2 = \sigma^2 = \lambda m_2',$$
$$\mu_3 = \lambda m_3',$$
(5.20)

where m_j' is the jth raw moment of the secondary distribution. The coefficient of skewness is

$$\gamma_1 = \frac{\mu_3}{\sigma^3} = \frac{m_3'}{\lambda^{1/2}(m_2')^{3/2}}.$$

For the Poisson–binomial distribution, with a bit of algebra (see Exercise 5.15) we obtain

$$\mu = \lambda m q,$$
$$\sigma^2 = \mu[1 + (m-1)q],$$
$$\mu_3 = 3\sigma^2 - 2\mu + \frac{m-2}{m-1}\frac{(\sigma^2 - \mu)^2}{\mu}.$$
(5.21)

Carrying out similar exercises for the negative binomial, Polya–Aeppli (Poisson-geometric), Neyman Type A, and Poisson–ETNB distributions yields

$$\text{Negative binomial: } \mu_3 = 3\sigma^2 - 2\mu + 2\frac{(\sigma^2 - \mu)^2}{\mu}$$

$$\text{Polya–Aeppli: } \mu_3 = 3\sigma^2 - 2\mu + \frac{3}{2}\frac{(\sigma^2 - \mu)^2}{\mu}$$

$$\text{Neyman Type A: } \mu_3 = 3\sigma^2 - 2\mu + \frac{(\sigma^2 - \mu)^2}{\mu}$$

$$\text{Poisson–ETNB: } \mu_3 = 3\sigma^2 - 2\mu + \frac{r+2}{r+1}\frac{(\sigma^2 - \mu)^2}{\mu}$$

For the Poisson–ETNB distribution, the range of r is $-1 < r < \infty$, $r \neq 0$. Note that as $r \to 0$ the secondary distribution is logarithmic, resulting in the negative binomial distribution.

Note that for fixed mean and variance the third moment only changes through the coefficient in the last term for each of the five distributions. For the Poisson distribution, $\mu_3 = \lambda = 3\sigma^2 - 2\mu$, and so the third term for each expression for μ_3 represents the change from the Poisson distribution. For the Poisson–binomial distribution, if $m = 1$, the distribution is Poisson because it is equivalent to a Poisson–zero-truncated binomial as truncation at zero leaves only probability at 1. Another view is that from the formula for the third moment (5.21), we have

$$\mu_3 = 3\sigma^2 - 2\mu + \frac{m-2}{m-1}\frac{(m-1)^2 q^4 \lambda^2 m^2}{\lambda m q}$$
$$= 3\sigma^2 - 2\mu + (m-2)(m-1)q^3 \lambda m,$$

which reduces to the Poisson value for μ_3 when $m = 1$. Hence, it is necessary that $m \geq 2$ for non-Poisson distributions to be created. Then the coefficient satisfies

$$0 \leq \frac{m-2}{m-1} < 1.$$

For the Poisson–ETNB, because $r > -1$, the coefficient satisfies

$$1 < \frac{r+2}{r+1} < \infty,$$

Hence, the Poisson–ETNB distribution provides any desired degree of skewness greater than that of the Poisson distribution. Note that the Polya–Aeppli and the negative binomial distributions are special and limiting cases of the Poisson–ETNB with $r = 1$ and $r \to 0$, respectively.

Example 5.19 *The data in Table 5.6 are taken from Hossack et al. [55] and give the distribution of the number of losses on accidents involving automobiles in Australia. Determine an appropriate frequency model based on the skewness results of this section.*

The mean, variance, and third central moment are 0.1254614, 0.1299599, and 0.1401737, respectively. For these numbers,

$$\frac{\mu_3 - 3\sigma^2 + 2\mu}{(\sigma^2 - \mu)^2/\mu} = 7.543865.$$

From among the Poisson–binomial, negative binomial, Polya–Aeppli, Neyman Type A, and Poisson–ETNB distributions, only the latter is appropriate. For this distribution, an estimate of r can be obtained from

$$7.543865 = \frac{r+2}{r+1}$$

resulting in $r = -0.8471851$. In Example 12.13 a more formal estimation and selection procedure will be applied, but the conclusion will be the same. $\square$

A very useful property of the compound Poisson class of probability distributions is the fact that it is closed under convolution. We have the following theorem.

Table 5.6   Hossack et al. data

No. of losses	No. of cars
0	565,664
1	68,714
2	5,177
3	365
4	24
5	6
6+	0

Theorem 5.20 *Suppose that S_i has a compound Poisson distribution with Poisson parameter λ_i and secondary distribution $\{q_n(i);\ n = 0, 1, 2, \ldots\}$ for $i = 1, 2, 3, \ldots, k$. Suppose also that $S_1, S_2, \ldots, S_k$ are independent random variables. Then $S = S_1 + S_2 + \cdots + S_k$ also has a compound Poisson distribution with Poisson parameter $\lambda = \lambda_1 + \lambda_2 + \cdots + \lambda_k$ and secondary distribution $\{q_n;\ n = 0, 1, 2, \ldots\}$, where $q_n = [\lambda_1 q_n(1) + \lambda_2 q_n(2) + \cdots + \lambda_k q_n(k)]/\lambda$.*

Proof: Let $Q_i(z) = \sum_{n=0}^{\infty} q_n(i) z^n$ for $i = 1, 2, \ldots, k$. Then S_i has pgf $P_{S_i}(z) = \mathrm{E}(z^{S_i}) = \exp\{\lambda_i[Q_i(z) - 1]\}$. Because the S_is are independent, S has pgf

$$
\begin{aligned}
P_S(z) &= \prod_{i=1}^{k} P_{S_i}(z) \\
&= \prod_{i=1}^{k} \exp\{\lambda_i[Q_i(z) - 1]\} \\
&= \exp\left[\sum_{i=1}^{k} \lambda_i Q_i(z) - \sum_{i=1}^{k} \lambda_i\right] \\
&= \exp\{\lambda[Q(z) - 1]\}
\end{aligned}
$$

where $\lambda = \sum_{i=1}^{k} \lambda_i$ and $Q(z) = \sum_{i=1}^{k} \lambda_i Q_i(z)/\lambda$. The result follows by the uniqueness of the generating function.   □

One main advantage of this result is computational. If we are interested in the sum of independent compound Poisson random variables, then we do not need to compute the distribution of each compound Poisson random variable separately (i.e., recursively using Example 5.14) because Theorem 5.20 implies that a single application of the compound Poisson recursive formula in Example 5.14 will suffice. The following example illustrates this idea.

Example 5.21 *Suppose that $k = 2$ and S_1 has a compound Poisson distribution with $\lambda_1 = 2$ and secondary distribution $q_1(1) = 0.2, q_2(1) = 0.7$, and $q_3(1) = 0.1$. Also, S_2 (independent of S_1) has a compound Poisson distribution with $\lambda_2 = 3$ and secondary distribution $q_2(2) = 0.25, q_3(2) = 0.6$, and $q_4(2) = 0.15$. Determine the distribution of $S = S_1 + S_2$.*

We have $\lambda = \lambda_1 + \lambda_2 = 2 + 3 = 5$. Then

$$
\begin{aligned}
q_1 &= 0.4(0.2) + 0.6(0) = 0.08, \\
q_2 &= 0.4(0.7) + 0.6(0.25) = 0.43, \\
q_3 &= 0.4(0.1) + 0.6(0.6) = 0.40, \\
q_4 &= 0.4(0) + 0.6(0.15) = 0.09.
\end{aligned}
$$

Thus, S has a compound Poisson distribution with Poisson parameter $\lambda = 5$ and secondary distribution $q_1 = 0.08, q_2 = 0.43, q_3 = 0.40$, and $q_4 = 0.09$. Numerical values of the distribution of S may be obtained using the recursive formula

$$
\Pr(S = x) = \frac{5}{x} \sum_{n=1}^{x} n q_n \Pr(S = x - n), \quad x = 1, 2, \ldots,
$$

beginning with $\Pr(S = 0) = e^{-5}$. □

In various situations the convolution of negative binomial distributions is of interest. Example 5.22 indicates how this distribution may be evaluated.

Example 5.22 (Convolutions of negative binomial distributions). *Suppose that N_i has a negative binomial distribution with parameters r_i and β_i for $i = 1, 2, \ldots, k$ and that $N_1, N_2, \ldots, N_k$ are independent. Determine the distribution of $N = N_1 + N_2 + \cdots + N_k$.*

The pgf of N_i is $P_{N_i}(z) = [1 - \beta_i(z - 1)]^{-r_i}$ and that of N is $P_N(z) = \prod_{i=1}^{k} P_{N_i}(z) = \prod_{i=1}^{k}[1 - \beta_i(z - 1)]^{-r_i}$. If $\beta_i = \beta$ for $i = 1, 2, \ldots, k$, then $P_N(z) = [1 - \beta(z - 1)]^{-(r_1 + r_2 + \cdots + r_k)}$, and N has a negative binomial distribution with parameters $r = r_1 + r_2 + \cdots + r_k$ and β.

If not all the β_is are identical, however, we may proceed as follows. From Example 5.10,

$$
P_{N_i}(z) = [1 - \beta_i(z - 1)]^{-r_i} = e^{\lambda_i[Q_i(z) - 1]}
$$

where $\lambda_i = r_i \ln(1 + \beta_i)$ and

$$
Q_i(z) = 1 - \frac{\ln[1 - \beta_i(z - 1)]}{\ln(1 + \beta_i)} = \sum_{n=1}^{\infty} q_n(i) z^n
$$

with

$$
q_n(i) = \frac{[\beta_i/(1 + \beta_i)]^n}{n \ln(1 + \beta_i)}; \quad n = 1, 2, \ldots.
$$

But Theorem 5.20 implies that $N = N_1 + N_2 + \cdots + N_k$ has a compound Poisson distribution with Poisson parameter

$$
\lambda = \sum_{i=1}^{k} r_i \ln(1 + \beta_i)
$$

and secondary distribution

$$
\begin{aligned}
q_n &= \sum_{i=1}^{k} \frac{\lambda_i}{\lambda} q_n(i) \\
&= \frac{\sum_{i=1}^{k} r_i [\beta_i/(1+\beta_i)]^n}{n \sum_{i=1}^{k} r_i \ln(1+\beta_i)}, \quad n = 1, 2, 3, \ldots .
\end{aligned}
$$

The distribution of N may be computed recursively using the formula

$$
\Pr(N = n) = \frac{\lambda}{n} \sum_{k=1}^{n} k q_k \Pr(N = n - k), \quad n = 1, 2, \ldots,
$$

beginning with $\Pr(N = 0) = e^{-\lambda} = \prod_{i=1}^{k}(1 + \beta_i)^{-r_i}$ and with λ and q_n as given above. □

It is not hard to see that Theorem 5.20 is a generalization of Theorem 5.1, which may be recovered with $q_1(i) = 1$ for $i = 1, 2, \ldots, k$. Similarly, the decomposition result of Theorem 5.2 may also be extended to compound Poisson random variables, where the decomposition is on the basis of the region of support of the secondary distribution. See Panjer and Willmot [93], Section 6.4 or Karlin and Taylor [66], Section 16.9 for further details.

5.12   MIXED FREQUENCY MODELS

Many compound distributions can arise in a way that is very different from compounding. In this section, we examine mixture distributions by treating one or more parameters as being "random" in some sense. This section expands on the ideas discussed in Section 5.3 in connection with the gamma mixture of the Poisson distribution being negative binomial.

We assume that the parameter is distributed over the population under consideration (the **collective**) and that the sampling scheme that generates our data has two stages. First, a value of the parameter is selected. Then, given that parameter value, an observation is generated using that parameter value.

Let $P(z|\theta)$ denote the pgf of the number of events (e.g., losses) if the risk parameter is known to be θ. The parameter, θ, might be the Poisson mean, for example, in which case the measurement of risk is the expected number of events in a fixed time period.

Let $U(\theta) = \Pr(\Theta \leq \theta)$ be the cdf of Θ, where Θ is the risk parameter, which is viewed as a random variable. Then $U(\theta)$ represents the probability that, when a value of Θ is selected (e.g., a driver is included in our sample), the value of the risk parameter does not exceed θ. Let $u(\theta)$ be the pf or pdf of Θ. Then

$$
P(z) = \int P(z|\theta) u(\theta)\, d\theta \text{ or } P(z) = \sum P(z|\theta_j) u(\theta_j) \tag{5.22}
$$

is the unconditional pgf of the number of events (where the formula selected depends on whether Θ is discrete or continuous[2]). The corresponding probabilities are denoted by

$$p_k = \int p_k(\theta)u(\theta)d\theta \text{ or } p_k = \sum p_k(\theta_j)u(\theta_j).\qquad(5.23)$$

The **mixing distribution** denoted by $U(\theta)$ may be of the discrete or continuous type or even a combination of discrete and continuous types. **Discrete mixtures** are mixtures of distributions where the mixing function is of the discrete type. Similarly, **continuous mixtures** are mixtures of distributions where the mixing function is of the continuous type. This phenomenon of mixing was introduced for continuous mixtures of severity distributions in Section 4.7.5 and for finite discrete mixtures in Section 4.5.2.

It should be noted that the mixing distribution is unobservable because the data are drawn from the mixed distribution.

Example 5.23 *Demonstrate that the zero-modified distributions may be created by using a two-point mixture.*

Suppose

$$P(z) = p \cdot 1 + (1 - p)P_2(z).$$

This is a (discrete) two-point mixture of a degenerate distribution that places all probability at zero and a distribution with pgf $P_2(z)$. From formula (5.12), this is also a compound Bernoulli distribution. □

Many mixed models can be constructed beginning with a simple distribution. Two examples are given here.

Example 5.24 *Determine the pf for a mixed binomial with a beta mixing distribution. This distribution is called binomial–beta, negative hypergeometric, or Polya–Eggenberger.*

The beta distribution has pdf

$$u(q) = \frac{\Gamma(a+b)}{\Gamma(a)\Gamma(b)}q^{a-1}(1-q)^{b-1}, \quad a > 0, b > 0.$$

---

[2]We could have written the more general $P(z) = \int P(z|\theta)\,dU(\theta)$, which would include situations where Θ has a distribution that is partly continuous and partly discrete.

Then the mixed distribution has probabilities

$$
\begin{aligned}
p_k &= \int_0^1 \binom{m}{k} q^k (1-q)^{m-k} \frac{\Gamma(a+b)}{\Gamma(a)\Gamma(b)} q^{a-1}(1-q)^{b-1}\, dq \\
&= \frac{\Gamma(a+b)\Gamma(m+1)\Gamma(a+k)\Gamma(b+m-k)}{\Gamma(a)\Gamma(b)\Gamma(k+1)\Gamma(m-k+1)\Gamma(a+b+m)} \\
&= \frac{\binom{-a}{k}\binom{-b}{m-k}}{\binom{-a-b}{m}}, \quad k = 0,1,2,\ldots.
\end{aligned}
$$

□

Example 5.25 *Determine the pf for a mixed negative binomial distribution with mixing on the parameter $p = (1+\beta)^{-1}$. Let p have a beta distribution. The mixed distribution is called the generalized Waring distribution.*

Arguing as in Example 5.24 we have

$$
\begin{aligned}
p_k &= \frac{\Gamma(r+k)}{\Gamma(r)\Gamma(k+1)} \frac{\Gamma(a+b)}{\Gamma(a)\Gamma(b)} \int_0^1 p^{a+r-1}(1-p)^{b+k-1}\, dp \\
&= \frac{\Gamma(r+k)}{\Gamma(r)\Gamma(k+1)} \frac{\Gamma(a+b)}{\Gamma(a)\Gamma(b)} \frac{\Gamma(a+r)\Gamma(b+k)}{\Gamma(a+r+b+k)}, \quad k = 0,1,2,\ldots.
\end{aligned}
$$

When $b = 1$, this distribution is called the Waring distribution. When $r = b = 1$, it is termed the Yule distribution.   □

5.13 POISSON MIXTURES

If we let $p_k(\theta)$ in formula (5.23) have the Poisson distribution, this leads to a class of distributions with useful properties. A simple example of a Poisson mixture is the two-point mixture.

Example 5.26 *Suppose risks can be classified as "good risks" and "bad risks," each group with its own Poisson distribution. Determine the pf for this model and fit it to the data from Example 11.5. This model and its application to the data set are from Tröbliger [118] in connection with automobile drivers.*

From formula (5.23) the pf is

$$
p_k = p \frac{e^{-\lambda_1}\lambda_1^k}{k!} + (1-p)\frac{e^{-\lambda_2}\lambda_2^k}{k!}.
$$

The maximum likelihood estimates[3] were calculated by Tröbliger to be $\hat{p} = 0.94, \hat{\lambda}_1 = 0.11$, and $\hat{\lambda}_2 = 0.70$. This means that about 94% of drivers were "good" with a risk of $\lambda_1 = 0.11$ expected accidents per year and 6% were "bad" with a risk of $\lambda_2 = 0.70$ expected accidents per year. □

This example illustrates two important points about finite mixtures. First, the model is probably oversimplified in the sense that risks (e.g., drivers) probably exhibit a continuum of risk levels rather than just two. The second point is that finite mixture models have a lot of parameters to be estimated. The simple two-point Poisson mixture above has three parameters. Increasing the number of distributions in the mixture to r will then involve $r - 1$ mixing parameters (i.e., the coefficients) in addition to the total number of parameters in the r component distributions. As a result of this, continuous mixtures are frequently preferred.

The class of mixed Poisson distributions has some interesting properties that will be developed here.

Let $P(z)$ be the pgf of a mixed Poisson distribution with arbitrary mixing distribution $U(\theta)$. Then (with formulas given for the continuous case), by introducing a scale parameter λ, we have

$$P(z) = \int e^{\lambda\theta(z-1)}u(\theta)\,d\theta = \int \left[e^{\lambda(z-1)}\right]^\theta u(\theta)\,d\theta$$
$$= E\left\{\left[e^{\lambda(z-1)}\right]^\theta\right\} = M_\Theta\left[\lambda(z-1)\right], \qquad (5.24)$$

where $M_\Theta(z)$ is the mgf of the mixing distribution.

Therefore, $P'(z) = \lambda M'_\Theta[\lambda(z-1)]$ and with $z = 1$ we obtain $E(N) = \lambda E(\Theta)$, where N has the mixed Poisson distribution. Also, $P''(z) = \lambda^2 M''_\Theta[\lambda(z-1)]$, implying that $E[N(N-1)] = \lambda^2 E(\Theta^2)$ and therefore

$$\begin{aligned}\text{Var}(N) &= E[N(N-1)] + E(N) - [E(N)]^2 \\ &= \lambda^2 E(\Theta^2) + E(N) - \lambda^2[E(\Theta)]^2 \\ &= \lambda^2 \text{Var}(\Theta) + E(N) \\ &> E(N)\end{aligned}$$

and thus for mixed Poisson distributions the variance is always greater than the mean.

Douglas [24] proves that for any mixed Poisson distribution the mixing distribution is unique. This means that two different mixing distributions cannot lead to the same mixed Poisson distribution. This allows us to identify the mixing distribution in some cases.

There is also an important connection between mixed Poisson distributions and compound Poisson distributions.

[3]Maximum likelihood estimation is discussed in Section 10.3.

Definition 5.27 *A distribution is said to be **infinitely divisible** if for all values of $n = 1, 2, 3, \ldots$ its characteristic function $\varphi(z)$ can be written as*

$$\varphi(z) = [\varphi_n(z)]^n,$$

where $\varphi_n(z)$ is the characteristic function of some random variable.

In other words, taking the $(1/n)$th power of the characteristic function still results in a characteristic function. The characteristic function is defined as follows.

Definition 5.28 *The **characteristic function** of a random variable X is*

$$\varphi_X(z) = \mathrm{E}(e^{izX}) = \mathrm{E}(\cos zX + i\sin zX),$$

where $i = \sqrt{-1}$.

In Definition 5.27, "characteristic function" could have been replaced by "moment generating function" or "probability generating function," or some other transform. That is, if the definition is satisfied for one of these transforms, it will be satisfied for all others for the same random variable. We choose the characteristic function because it exists for all distributions whereas the moment generating function does not exist for some distributions with heavy tails. Because many earlier results involved probability generating functions, it is useful to note the relationship between it and the characteristic function.

Theorem 5.29 *If the probability generating function exists for a random variable X, then $P_X(z) = \varphi(-i\ln z)$ and $\varphi_X(z) = P(e^{iz})$.*

Proof:

$$P_X(z) = \mathrm{E}(z^X) = \mathrm{E}(e^{X\ln z}) = \mathrm{E}[e^{-i(i\ln z)X}] = \varphi_X(-i\ln z)$$

and

$$\varphi_X(z) = \mathrm{E}(e^{izX}) = \mathrm{E}[(e^{iz})^X] = P_X(e^{iz}).$$

$\square$

The following distributions, among others, are infinitely divisible: normal, gamma, Poisson, negative binomial. The binomial distribution is not infinitely divisible because the exponent m in its pgf must take on integer values. Dividing m by $n = 1, 2, 3, \ldots$ will result in nonintegral values. In fact, no distributions with a finite range of support (the range over which positive probabilities exist) can be infinitely divisible. Now to the important result.

Theorem 5.30 *Suppose $P(z)$ is a mixed Poisson pgf with an infinitely divisible mixing distribution. Then $P(z)$ is also a compound Poisson pgf and may be expressed as*

$$P(z) = e^{\lambda[P_2(z)-1]},$$

where $P_2(z)$ is a pgf. If we also adopt the convention that $P_2(0) = 0$, then $P_2(z)$ is unique.

A proof can be found in Feller [35], Chapter 12. If we choose any infinitely divisible mixing distribution, the corresponding mixed Poisson distribution can be equivalently described as a compound Poisson distribution. For some distributions, this is a distinct advantage when carrying out numerical work because the recursive formula (5.16) can be used in evaluating the probabilities once the secondary distribution is identified. For most cases, this identification is easily carried out. A second advantage is that, because the same distribution can be motivated in two different ways, a specific explanation is not required in order to use it. Conversely, the fact that one of these models fits well does not imply that it is the result of mixing or compounding. For example, the fact that losses follow a negative binomial distribution does not imply that individuals have the Poisson distribution and the Poisson parameter has a gamma distribution.

Example 5.31 *Use the above results and formula (5.24) to demonstrate that a gamma mixture of Poisson variables is negative binomial.*

If the mixing distribution is gamma, it has the following moment generating function (as derived in Example 2.29 and where β plays the role of $1/\theta$):

$$M_\Theta(t) = \left(\frac{\beta}{\beta - t} \right)^\alpha, \quad \beta > 0, \ \alpha > 0, \ t < \beta.$$

It is clearly infinitely divisible because $[M_\Theta(t)]^{1/n}$ is the mgf of a gamma distribution with parameters α/n and β. Then the pgf of the mixed Poisson distribution is

$$P(z) = \left[\frac{\beta}{\beta - \lambda(z - 1)} \right]^\alpha = \left[1 - \frac{\lambda}{\beta}(z - 1) \right]^{-\alpha},$$

which is the form of the pgf of the negative binomial distribution where the negative binomial parameter r is equal to α and the parameter β is equal to λ/β. □

It was shown in Example 5.10 that a compound Poisson distribution with a logarithmic secondary distribution is a negative binomial distribution. Therefore the theorem holds true for this case. It is not difficult to see that, if $u(\theta)$ is the pf for any discrete random variable with pgf $P_\Theta(z)$, then the pgf of the mixed Poisson distribution is $P_\Theta \left[e^{\lambda(z-1)} \right]$, a compound distribution with a Poisson secondary distribution.

Example 5.32 *Demonstrate that the Neyman Type A distribution can be obtained by mixing.*

If in formula (5.24) the mixing distribution has pgf

$$P_\Theta(z) = e^{\mu(z-1)},$$

then the mixed Poisson distribution has pgf

$$P(z) = \exp\{\mu[e^{\lambda(z-1)} - 1]\},$$

the pgf of a compound Poisson with a Poisson secondary distribution, that is, the Neyman Type A distribution.   □

A further interesting result obtained by Holgate [54] is that if a mixing distribution is absolutely continuous and unimodal, then the resulting mixed Poisson distribution is also unimodal. Multimodality can occur when discrete mixing functions are used. For example, the Neyman Type A distribution can have more than one mode. The reader should try this calculation for various combinations of the two parameters.

Most continuous distributions in this book involve a scale parameter. This means that scale changes to distributions do not cause a change in the form of the distribution, only in the value of its scale parameter. For the mixed Poisson distribution, with pgf (5.24), any change in λ is equivalent to a change in the scale parameter of the mixing distribution. Hence, it may be convenient to simply set $\lambda = 1$ where a mixing distribution with a scale parameter is used.

Example 5.33 *Show that a mixed Poisson with an inverse Gaussian mixing distribution is the same as a Poisson–ETNB distribution with* $r = -0.5$.

The inverse Gaussian distribution has pdf

$$f(x) = \left(\frac{\theta}{2\pi x^3}\right)^{1/2} \exp\left[-\frac{\theta}{2x}\left(\frac{x-\mu}{\mu}\right)^2\right], \quad x > 0,$$

which is conveniently rewritten as

$$f(x) = \frac{\mu}{(2\pi\beta x^3)^{1/2}} \exp\left[-\frac{(x-\mu)^2}{2\beta x}\right], \quad x > 0,$$

where $\beta = \mu^2/\theta$. The mgf of this distribution is

$$M(t) = \exp\left\{-\frac{\mu}{\beta}[(1 - 2\beta t)^{1/2} - 1]\right\}.$$

Hence, the inverse Gaussian distribution is infinitely divisible ($[M(t)]^{1/n}$ is the mgf of an inverse Gaussian distribution with μ replaced by μ/n). From (formula 5.24) with $\lambda = 1$, the pgf of the mixed distribution is

$$P(z) = \exp\left(-\frac{\mu}{\beta}\{[1 + 2\beta(1 - z)]^{1/2} - 1\}\right).$$

Table 5.7 Pairs of compound and mixed Poisson distributions

Name	Compound secondary distribution	Mixing distribution
Negative binomial	Logarithmic	Gamma
Neyman–A	Poisson	Poisson
Poisson–inverse Gaussian	ETNB $(r = -0.5)$	Inverse Gaussian

By setting

$$\lambda = \frac{\mu}{\beta}[(1 + 2\beta)^{1/2} - 1]$$

and

$$P_2(z) = \frac{[1 - 2\beta(z - 1)]^{1/2} - (1 + 2\beta)^{1/2}}{1 - (1 + 2\beta)^{1/2}},$$

we see that

$$P(z) = \exp\{\lambda[P_2(z) - 1]\},$$

where $P_2(z)$ is the pgf of the extended truncated negative binomial distribution with $r = -\frac{1}{2}$.

Hence, the Poisson–inverse Gaussian distribution is a compound Poisson distribution with an ETNB $(r = -\frac{1}{2})$ secondary distribution. ☐

The relationships between mixed and compound Poisson distributions are given in Table 5.7.

In this chapter, we have focused on distributions that are easily handled computationally. Although many other discrete distributions are available, we believe that those discussed here form a sufficiently rich class for most problems in modeling count data.

5.14 EFFECT OF EXPOSURE ON LOSS COUNTS

Assume that the current set of risks consists of n entities, each of which could produce losses. Let N_j be the number of losses produced by the jth entity. Then $N = N_1 + \cdots + N_n$. If we assume that the N_j are independent and identically distributed, then

$$P_N(z) = [P_{N_1}(z)]^n.$$

Now suppose the set of risks is expected to expand to n^* entities with frequency N^*. Then

$$P_{N^*}(z) = [P_{N_1}(z)]^{n^*} = [P_N(z)]^{n^*/n}.$$

Thus, if N is infinitely divisible, the distribution of N^* will have the same form as that of N, but with modified parameters.

Example 5.34 *It has been determined from past studies that the number of losses for a group of 300 machines carrying on certain transactions (e.g., a cash-dispensing machine) has the negative binomial distribution with $\beta = 0.3$ and $r = 10$. Determine the frequency distribution for a group of 500 such machines.*

The pgf of N^* is

$$P_{N^*}(z) = [P_N(z)]^{500/300} = \{[1 - 0.3(z-1)]^{-10}\}^{500/300}$$
$$= [1 - 0.3(z-1)]^{-16.67},$$

which is negative binomial with $\beta = 0.3$ and $r = 16.67$. □

For the $(a, b, 0)$ class, all members except the binomial have this property. For the $(a, b, 1)$ class, none of the members does. For compound distributions, it is the primary distribution that must be infinitely divisible. In particular, compound Poisson and compound negative binomial (including the geometric) distributions will be preserved under an increase in exposure. Earlier, some reasons were given to support the use of zero-modified distributions. If exposure adjustments are anticipated, it may be better to choose a compound model, even if the fit is not quite as good. It should be noted that compound models have the ability to place large amounts of probability at zero.

5.15 TVaR FOR DISCRETE DISTRIBUTIONS

In general, in operational risk modeling, we will not compute risk measures for the number of losses, although this is possible. We are generally interested in the sum of the total losses measured in dollar terms. A Tail-Value-at-Risk measure for the number of losses would give the expected number of losses conditional on the fact that a certain quantile was exceeded. This may be useful for gaining insight into risk processes but has not yet been used in operational risk management. For discrete distributions, the definition of the quantile is not unique because the cdf $F(x)$ is a step function that is constant between successive points on the x-axis. It is possible to refine the definition of quantile to deal with this problem. However, it is probably easier, from a pedagogical perspective, to consider only the quantiles corresponding to the points of support of the distribution. We then consider only the quantiles x_p that are points of support of the probability distribution[4] $f(x)$. Thus we

---

[4]We will use the letter f to denote the pf for discrete distributions in this section rather than p as in earlier sections because of the use of the letter p as a probability in this section.

consider only the probabilities p that correspond to those points of support through the relation[5]

$$p = \Pr\left(X \le x_p\right).$$

This restriction will allow us to use the formulas that are in the same form as for continuous distributions. Then the Tail-Value-at-Risk for any quantile x_p can be computed directly for any discrete distribution with a finite mean because from Exercise 2.12

$$\mathrm{TVaR}_p\left(X\right) = \mathrm{E}\left(X \mid X > x_p\right)$$

$$= x_p + \frac{\sum_x \left(x - x_p\right)_+ f(x)}{1 - F(x_p)} \qquad (5.25)$$

where the sum needs only to be taken over all possible values of x that are greater than x_p. The (possibly) infinite sum in formula (5.25) is easily avoided by rewriting that infinite sum as

$$\sum_x \left(x - x_p\right)_+ f(x) = \sum_x \left(x - x_p\right) f(x) + \sum_x \left(x_p - x\right)_+ f(x)$$

$$= \mathrm{E}(X) - x_p + \sum_x \left(x_p - x\right)_+ f(x)$$

$$= \mathrm{E}(X) - x_p + \sum_{x < x_p} \left(x_p - x\right) f(x) \qquad (5.26)$$

and noticing that this last summation has a finite number of nonzero terms. Hence, Tail-Value-at-Risk is easily computed for any discrete distribution with nonnegative support using formula (5.26) and substituting the result into (5.25).

As with the case of continuous distributions, the specific results for each distribution do not provide much insight into the relationship between the TVaR and the shape of the distribution. Section 5.15.1 provides general formulas for large families of discrete distributions.

5.15.1   TVaR for discrete exponential dispersion distributions

Landsman and Valdez [74] obtain analytic results for a broad class of distributions that includes both continuous and discrete distributions. The results for continuous distributions were discussed in Chapter 4. We now consider the two exponential dispersion models, the additive exponential dispersion family and the reproductive exponential dispersion family, but apply them to discrete distributions.

---

[5] This is not very restrictive. For example, if you are interested in the 99% quantile, the nearest points of support will correspond to quantiles close to and on either side of 99%.

Definition 5.35 *A discrete random variable X has a distribution from the* **additive exponential dispersion family (AEDF)** *if its probability function may be parameterized in terms of parameters θ and λ and expressed as*

$$f(x; \theta, \lambda) = e^{\theta x - \lambda \kappa(\theta)} q(x; \lambda). \tag{5.27}$$

Definition 5.36 *A discrete random variable X has a distribution from the* **reproductive exponential dispersion family (REDF)** *if its probability function may be parameterized in terms of parameters θ and λ and expressed as*

$$f(x; \theta, \lambda) = e^{\lambda [\theta x - \kappa(\theta)]} q(x; \lambda). \tag{5.28}$$

As in the case of continuous distributions, the mean and variance of these distributions are

Mean: AEDF $\mu = \lambda \kappa'(\theta)$
         REDF $\mu = \kappa'(\theta)$
Variance: AEDF $\mathrm{Var}(X) = \lambda \kappa''(\theta) = \kappa''(\theta)/\sigma^2$
           REDF $\mathrm{Var}(X) = \kappa''(\theta)/\lambda = \kappa''(\theta)\sigma^2$

where $1/\lambda = \sigma^2$ is called the "dispersion parameter."

Example 5.37 *Show that the Poisson distribution is a member of the AEDF class.*

The Poisson distribution with mean μ has probability function

$$f(x) = \frac{\mu^x}{x!} e^{-\mu}, \quad x = 0, 1, 2, \dots$$

which can be rewritten as

$$f(x) = \frac{1}{x!} \exp \left(x \ln \mu - \mu \right).$$

By setting $\lambda = 1$, $\theta = \ln \mu$, $\kappa(\theta) = e^\theta$ and $q(x; \lambda) = 1/x!$,

$$f(x) = \frac{1}{x!} \exp \left(\theta x - e^\theta \right)$$

and so we can see that the Poisson distribution has the form 5.27. Therefore the Poisson distribution is a member of the AEDF.   □

Example 5.38 *Show that the binomial distribution is a member of the AEDF class.*

The binomial distribution with mean $\mu = mq$ has probability function

$$f(x) = \binom{m}{x} q^x (1 - q)^{m-x}, \quad x = 0, 1, 2, \dots$$

where m is an integer. By letting $\theta = \ln\left(\frac{q}{1-q}\right)$, we can rewrite the pf as

$$f(x) = \binom{m}{x} e^{\theta x} \left(1 + e^{\theta}\right)^{-m}$$

$$= \binom{m}{x} \exp\left[\theta x - m \ln\left(1 + e^{\theta}\right)\right], \quad x = 0, 1, 2, ...$$

Now by setting $\lambda = m$, $\kappa(\theta) = \ln\left(1 + e^{\theta}\right)$ and $q(x; \lambda) = \binom{m}{x}$, we can see that the binomial pf has the form 5.27. Therefore the binomial distribution is a member of the AEDF. □

Example 5.39 *Show that the negative binomial distribution is a member of the AEDF class.*

The negative binomial distribution with mean $\mu = r\beta$ has probability function

$$f(x) = \binom{r+x}{x} p^r \left(1 - p\right)^x, \quad x = 0, 1, 2, ...$$

where $p = \frac{1}{1+\beta}$. We can rewrite the pf as

$$f(x) = \binom{r+x-1}{x} \exp\left[\theta \ln\left(1 - p\right) + r \ln\left(p\right)\right], \quad x = 0, 1, 2, ...$$

Now by setting $\theta = \ln\left(1 - p\right)$, $\lambda = r$, $\kappa(\theta) = -\ln\left(1 + e^{\theta}\right)$ and $q(x; \lambda) = \binom{r+x-1}{x}$, we can see that the negative binomial pf has the form 5.27. Therefore the negative binomial distribution is a member of the AEDF. □

We now consider the main results of this section. We consider random variables from the AEDF and the REDF. For the purpose of this section, we will also require that the support of the random variable is an open set that does not depend on θ and the function $\kappa(\theta)$ is a differentiable function. These are technical requirements that will be satisfied by most commonly used distributions. We repeat, for convenience, the statement of a theorem already used in the case of continuous distributions. The theorem applies equally to discrete distributions.

Theorem 5.40 *Let X be a member of the AEDF subject to the above conditions. Then the Tail-Value-at-Risk can be written as*

$$TVaR_p(X) = \mu + h$$

where $\sigma^2 = 1/\lambda$ and $h = \frac{\partial}{\partial \theta} \ln\left(\overline{F}\left(x_p; \theta, \lambda\right)\right).$ □

Example 5.41 *Obtain the TVaR for the Poisson distribution.*

The Tail-Value-at-Risk is $\mu + h$ where

$$h = \frac{\partial}{\partial \theta} \ln \left(\overline{F}(x_p; \theta, , \lambda) \right)$$

$$= \frac{1}{\overline{F}(x_p; \theta, \lambda)} \frac{\partial}{\partial \theta} \left[\sum_{x = x_p + 1}^{\infty} f(x; \theta, \lambda) \right]$$

$$= \frac{1}{\overline{F}(x_p; \theta, 1)} \frac{\partial}{\partial \theta} \left[\sum_{x = x_p + 1}^{\infty} \frac{1}{x!} \exp \left(\theta x - e^{\theta} \right) \right]$$

$$= \frac{1}{\overline{F}(x_p; \theta, 1)} \left[\sum_{x = x_p + 1}^{\infty} \frac{1}{x!} (x - e^{\theta}) \exp \left(\theta x - e^{\theta} \right) \right]$$

$$= \frac{e^{\theta}}{\overline{F}(x_p; \theta, 1)} \left[\sum_{y = x_p}^{\infty} \frac{1}{y!} \exp \left(\theta y - e^{\theta} \right) \right] - e^{\theta}$$

$$= e^{\theta} \left[\frac{\overline{F}(x_p - 1; \theta, 1)}{\overline{F}(x_p; \theta, 1)} - 1 \right]$$

$$= \mu \frac{f(x_p; \theta, 1)}{\overline{F}(x_p; \theta, 1)}.$$

Hence the TVaR for the Poisson distribution is

$$\text{TVaR}_p(X) = \mu \left[1 + \frac{f(x_p; \theta, 1)}{\overline{F}(x_p; \theta, 1)} \right]$$

or, equivalently,

$$\text{TVaR}_p(X) = \mu + \frac{f(x_p; \theta, 1)}{\overline{F}(x_p; \theta, 1)} \mu.$$

Recall that the mean and variance are equal for the Poisson distribution. It is curious that the above formula is of the same form as for the normal distribution. □

Example 5.42 *Obtain the TVaR for the binomial distribution.*

The Tail-Value-at-Risk is $\mu + h$ where

$$
\begin{aligned}
h &= \frac{\partial}{\partial \theta} \ln \left(\overline{F}\left(x_p; \theta, , \lambda\right)\right) \\
&= \frac{1}{\overline{F}\left(x_p; \theta, \lambda\right)} \frac{\partial}{\partial \theta} \left[\sum_{x=x_p+1}^{m} f(x; \theta, \lambda) \right] \\
&= \frac{1}{\overline{F}\left(x_p; \theta, m\right)} \frac{\partial}{\partial \theta} \left[\sum_{x=x_p+1}^{m} \binom{m}{x} \exp\left[\theta x - m \ln\left(1 + e^{\theta}\right)\right] \right] \\
&= \frac{1}{\overline{F}\left(x_p; \theta, m\right)} \left[\sum_{x=x_p+1}^{m} \binom{m}{x} (x - m\frac{e^{\theta}}{1 + e^{\theta}}) \exp\left[\theta x - m \ln\left(1 + e^{\theta}\right)\right] \right] \\
&= \frac{1}{\overline{F}\left(x_p; \theta, m\right)} \left[\sum_{x=x_p+1}^{m} \binom{m}{x} (x - mq) q^x (1 - q)^{m-x} \right] \\
&= \frac{1}{\overline{F}\left(x_p; \theta, m\right)} \left[\sum_{x=x_p+1}^{m} x \binom{m}{x} q^x (1 - q)^{m-x} - mq \overline{F}\left(x_p; \theta, m\right) \right] \\
&= \frac{mq}{\overline{F}\left(x_p; \theta, m\right)} \left[\sum_{y=x_p}^{m-1} \binom{m-1}{y} q^y (1 - q)^{m-1-y} \right] - mq \\
&= mq \left[\frac{\overline{F}\left(x_p - 1; \theta, m - 1\right)}{\overline{F}\left(x_p; \theta, m\right)} - 1 \right] \\
&= \mu \left[\frac{\overline{F}\left(x_p - 1; \theta, m - 1\right)}{\overline{F}\left(x_p; \theta, m\right)} - 1 \right].
\end{aligned}
$$

Hence the TVaR for the binomial distribution is

$$
\text{TVaR}_p(X) = \mu \left[\frac{\overline{F}\left(x_p - 1; \theta, m - 1\right)}{\overline{F}\left(x_p; \theta, m\right)} \right].
$$

□

Example 5.43 *Obtain the TVaR for the negative binomial distribution.*

The Tail-Value-at-Risk is $\mu + h$ where

$$h = \frac{\partial}{\partial \theta} \ln \left(\overline{F} \left(x_p; \theta,, \lambda \right) \right)$$

$$= \frac{1}{\overline{F} \left(x_p; \theta, \lambda \right)} \frac{\partial}{\partial \theta} \left[\sum_{x=x_p+1}^{\infty} f(x; \theta, \lambda) \right]$$

$$= \frac{1}{\overline{F} \left(x_p; \theta, r \right)} \frac{\partial}{\partial \theta} \left[\sum_{x=x_p+1}^{\infty} \binom{r+x-1}{x} \exp \left[\theta x + r \ln \left(1 - e^\theta \right) \right] \right]$$

$$= \frac{1}{\overline{F} \left(x_p; \theta, r \right)} \left[\sum_{x=x_p+1}^{\infty} \binom{r+x-1}{x} \left(x - r \frac{1-p}{p} \right) p^r (1-p)^x \right]$$

$$= \frac{1}{\overline{F} \left(x_p; \theta, r \right)} \left[\sum_{x=x_p+1}^{\infty} x \binom{r+x-1}{x} p^r (1-p)^x - r \frac{1-p}{p} \overline{F} \left(x_p; \theta, r \right) \right]$$

$$= \frac{1}{\overline{F} \left(x_p; \theta, r \right)} r \frac{1-p}{p} \left[\sum_{y=x_p}^{\infty} \binom{r+y}{y} p^{r+1} (1-p)^y \right] - r \frac{1-p}{p}$$

$$= r \frac{1-p}{p} \left[\frac{\overline{F} \left(x_p - 1; \theta, r+1 \right)}{\overline{F} \left(x_p; \theta, r \right)} - 1 \right]$$

$$= \mu \left[\frac{\overline{F} \left(x_p - 1; \theta, r+1 \right)}{\overline{F} \left(x_p; \theta, r \right)} - 1 \right].$$

Hence the TVaR for the negative binomial distribution is

$$\text{TVaR}_p(X) = \mu \left[\frac{\overline{F} \left(x_p - 1; \theta, r+1 \right)}{\overline{F} \left(x_p; \theta, r \right)} \right].$$

□

5.16 EXERCISES

5.1 For each of the data sets in Exercises 11.3 and 11.5 calculate values similar to those in Table 5.2. For each, determine the most appropriate model from the $(a, b, 0)$ class.

5.2 Calculate $\Pr(N = 0)$, $\Pr(N = 1)$, and $\Pr(N = 2)$ for each of the following distributions.

    (a) Poisson $(\lambda = 4)$

(b) Geometric ($\beta = 4$)

(c) Negative binomial ($r = 2, \beta = 2$)

(d) Binomial ($m = 8, q = 0.5$)

(e) Logarithmic ($\beta = 4$)

(f) ETNB ($r = -0.5, \beta = 4$)

(g) Poisson–inverse Gaussian ($\lambda = 2, \beta = 4$)

(h) Zero-modified geometric ($p_0^M = 0.5, \beta = 4$)

(i) Poisson–Poisson(Neyman Type A) ($\lambda_{primary} = 4, \lambda_{secondary} = 1$)

(j) Poisson–ETNB ($\lambda = 4, r = 2, \beta = 0.5$)

(k) Poisson–zero-modified geometric distribution ($\lambda = 8, p_0^M = 0.5, r = 2, \beta = 0.5$)

5.3 The **moment generating function** (mgf) for discrete variables is defined as

$$M_N(z) = \mathrm{E}\left(e^{zN}\right) = \sum_{k=0}^{\infty} p_k e^{zk}.$$

Demonstrate that $P_N(z) = M_N(\ln z)$. Use the fact that $\mathrm{E}(N^k) = M_N^{(k)}(0)$ to show that $P'(1) = \mathrm{E}(N)$ and $P''(1) = \mathrm{E}[N(N-1)]$.

5.4 Use your knowledge of the permissible ranges for the parameters of the Poisson, negative binomial, and binomial to determine all possible values of a and b for these members of the $(a, b, 0)$ class. Because these are the only members of the class, all other pairs must not lead to a legitimate probability distribution (nonnegative values that sum to 1). Show that the pair $a = -1$ and $b = 1.5$ (which is not on the list of possible values) does not lead to a legitimate distribution.

5.5 Show that for the negative binomial distribution with any $\beta > 0$ and $r > -1$, but $r \neq 0$, the successive values of p_k given by formula (5.8) are, for any p_1, positive and $\sum_{k=1}^{\infty} p_k < \infty$.

5.6 Show that when, in the zero-truncated negative binomial distribution, $r \to 0$ the pf is as given by equation (5.9).

5.7 Show that the pgf of the logarithmic distribution is as given by equation (5.10).

5.8 Show that for the Sibuya distribution, which is the ETNB distribution with $-1 < r < 0$ and $\beta \to \infty$, the mean does not exist (that is, the sum which defines the mean does not converge). Because this random variable takes on nonnegative values, this also shows that no other positive moments exist.

5.9 A frequency model that has not been mentioned to this point is the **zeta distribution**. It is a zero-truncated distribution with $p_k^T = k^{-(\rho+1)}/\zeta(\rho + 1)$, $k = 1, 2, \ldots, \rho > 0$. The denominator is the zeta function, which must be evaluated numerically as $\zeta(\rho + 1) = \sum_{k=1}^{\infty} k^{-(\rho+1)}$. The zero-modified zeta distribution can be formed in the usual way. More information can be found in the article by Luong and Doray [78]. Verify that the zeta distribution is not a member of the $(a, b, 1)$ class.

5.10 Do all the members of the $(a, b, 0)$ class satisfy the condition of Theorem 5.11? For those that do, identify the parameter (or function of its parameters) that plays the role of θ in the theorem.

5.11 For $i = 1, \ldots, n$ let S_i have independent compound Poisson frequency distributions with Poisson parameter λ_i and a secondary distribution with pgf $P_2(z)$. Note that all n of the variables have the same secondary distribution. Determine the distribution of $S = S_1 + \cdots + S_n$.

5.12 Show that the following three distributions are identical: (1) geometric–geometric, (2) Bernoulli–geometric, (3) zero-modified geometric. That is, for any one of the distributions with arbitrary parameters, show that there is a member of the other two distribution types that has the same pf or pgf.

5.13 Show that the binomial–geometric and negative binomial–geometric (with negative binomial parameter r a positive integer) distributions are identical.

5.14 Show that, for any pgf, $P^{(k)}(1) = \mathrm{E}[N(N-1)\cdots(N-k+1)]$ provided the expectation exists. Here $P^{(k)}(z)$ indicates the kth derivative. Use this result to confirm the three moments as given by equations (5.20).

5.15 Verify the three moments as given by equations (5.21).

5.16 Show that the negative binomial–Poisson compound distribution is the same as a mixed Poisson distribution with a negative binomial mixing distribution.

5.17 For $i = 1, \ldots, n$ let N_i have a mixed Poisson distribution with parameter λ. Let the mixing distribution for N_i have pgf $P_i(z)$. Show that $N = N_1 + \cdots + N_n$ has a mixed Poisson distribution and determine the pgf of the mixing distribution.

5.18 Let N have a Poisson distribution with (given that $\Theta = \theta$) parameter $\lambda\theta$. Let the distribution of the random variable Θ have a scale parameter. Show that the mixed distribution does not depend on the value of λ.

5.19 Let N have a Poisson distribution with (given that $\Theta = \theta$) parameter θ. Let the distribution of the random variable Θ have pdf $u(\theta) = \alpha^2(\alpha + 1)^{-1}(\theta + 1)e^{-\alpha\theta}$, $\theta > 0$. Determine the pf of the mixed distribution. Also, show that the mixed distribution is also a compound distribution.

5.20 For the discrete counting random variable N with probabilities $p_n = \Pr(N = n)$; $n = 0, 1, 2, \ldots$, let $a_n = \Pr(N > n) = \sum_{k=n+1}^{\infty} p_k$; $n = 0, 1, 2, \ldots$.

(a) Demonstrate that $E(N) = \sum_{n=0}^{\infty} a_n$.

(b) Demonstrate that $A(z) = \sum_{n=0}^{\infty} a_n z^n$ and $P(z) = \sum_{n=0}^{\infty} p_n z^n$ are related by $A(z) = [1 - P(z)] / (1 - z)$. What happens as $z \to 1$?

(c) Suppose that N has the negative binomial distribution

$$p_n = \binom{n+r-1}{n} \left(\frac{1}{1+\beta} \right)^r \left(\frac{\beta}{1+\beta} \right)^n, \quad n = 0, 1, 2, \ldots,$$

where r is a positive integer. Prove that

$$a_n = \beta \sum_{k=1}^{r} \binom{n+k-1}{n} \left(\frac{1}{1+\beta} \right)^k \left(\frac{\beta}{1+\beta} \right)^n, \quad n = 0, 1, 2, \ldots.$$

(d) Suppose that N has the Sibuya distribution with pgf $P(z) = 1 - (1 - z)^{-r}$, $-1 < r < 0$. Prove that

$$p_n = \frac{(-r)\Gamma(n+r)}{n!\Gamma(1+r)}, \quad n = 1, 2, 3, \ldots,$$

and that

$$a_n = \binom{n+r}{n}, \quad n = 0, 1, 2, \ldots.$$

(e) Suppose that N has the mixed Poisson distribution with

$$p_n = \int_0^{\infty} \frac{(\lambda\theta)^n e^{-\lambda\theta}}{n!} \, dU(\theta), \quad n = 0, 1, 2, \ldots,$$

where $U(\theta)$ is a cumulative distribution function. Prove that

$$a_n = \lambda \int_0^{\infty} \frac{(\lambda\theta)^n e^{-\lambda\theta}}{n!} [1 - U(\theta)] \, d\theta, \quad n = 0, 1, 2, \ldots.$$

5.21 Consider the mixed Poisson distribution

$$p_n = \Pr(N = n) = \int_0^1 \frac{(\lambda\theta)^n e^{-\lambda\theta}}{n!} U'(\theta) d\theta, \quad n = 0, 1, \ldots,$$

where $U(\theta) = 1 - (1 - \theta)^k$, $0 < \theta < 1$, $k = 1, 2, \ldots$. Prove that

$$p_n = k e^{-\lambda} \sum_{m=0}^{\infty} \frac{\lambda^{m+n}(m+k-1)!}{m!(m+k+n)!}, \quad n = 0, 1, \ldots.$$

5.22 Using Exercise 5.20, prove that

$$\Pr(N > n) = e^{-\lambda} \sum_{m=0}^{\infty} \frac{\lambda^{m+n+1}(m+k)!}{m!(m+k+n+1)!}.$$

(a) When $k = 1$, prove that

$$p_n = \frac{1 - \sum_{m=0}^{n} \lambda^m e^{-\lambda}/m!}{\lambda}, \quad n = 0, 1, 2, \ldots.$$

5.23 Consider the mixed Poisson distribution

$$p_n = \int_0^{\infty} \frac{(\lambda\theta)^n e^{-\lambda\theta}}{n!} u(\theta)d\theta, \quad n = 0, 1, \ldots,$$

where the pdf $u(\theta)$ is that of the positive stable distribution (see, for example, Feller [36], pp. 448, 583) given by

$$u(\theta) = \frac{1}{\pi} \sum_{k=1}^{\infty} \frac{\Gamma(k\alpha + 1)}{k!}(-1)^{k-1}\theta^{-k\alpha-1} \sin(k\alpha\pi), \quad \theta > 0,$$

where $0 < \alpha < 1$. The Laplace transform is $\int_0^{\infty} e^{-s\theta} u(\theta)d\theta = \exp(-s^{\alpha})$, $s \geq 0$. Prove that $\{p_n; n = 0, 1, \ldots\}$ is a compound Poisson distribution with Sibuya secondary distribution (this mixed Poisson distribution is sometimes called a discrete stable distribution).

5.24 Consider a mixed Poisson distribution with a reciprocal inverse Gaussian distribution as the mixing distribution.

(a) Use Exercise 4.33 to show that this distribution is the convolution of a negative binomial distribution and a Poisson–ETNB distribution with $r = -\frac{1}{2}$ (i.e., a Poisson–inverse Gaussian distribution).

(b) Show that the mixed Poisson distribution in (a) is a compound Poisson distribution and identify the secondary distribution.

6

Aggregate loss models

Left to themselves, things tend to go from bad to worse.

—Murphy

6.1 INTRODUCTION

The purpose of this chapter is to develop models of aggregate losses, the total amount of all losses occurring in a fixed time period.

We can represent the aggregate losses as the sum, S, of a random number, N, of the individual loss amounts $(X_1, X_2, \ldots, X_N)$. Hence,

$$S = X_1 + X_2 + \cdots + X_N, \quad N = 0, 1, 2, \ldots, \tag{6.1}$$

where it is understood that $S = 0$ when $N = 0$.

The distribution of S is obtained from the distribution of N and the distribution of the X_js. Using this approach, the frequency and the severity of losses are modeled separately. The information about these distributions is used to obtain information about S. An alternative to this approach is to simply gather information about S (e.g., total losses each month for a period of months) and to use some model from Chapter 4 to model the distribution of S. Modeling the distribution of N and the distribution of the X_js separately has some distinct advantages:

1. When the expected number of operational risk losses changes as the company grows, growth needs to be accounted for in forecasting the

number of operational risk losses in future years based on past years' data.

2. The effects of general economic inflation may need to be reflected in the sizes of losses that are subject to inflationary pressures.

3. The impact of changing limits that result from covering excess losses with insurance as a risk mitigation strategy is more easily studied. This is done by changing the specification of the severity distribution.

4. The impact on loss frequencies of changing thresholds for small losses is better understood.

5. Data that are heterogeneous in terms of thresholds and limits can be combined to obtain the hypothetical loss size distribution. This is useful when data from several years are combined.

6. The shape of the distribution of S depends on the shapes of both distributions of N and X. For example, if the severity distribution has a much heavier tail than the frequency distribution, the shape of the tail of the distribution of aggregate losses or losses will be determined by the severity distribution and will be insensitive to the choice of frequency distribution.

In summary, a more accurate and flexible model can be constructed by examining frequency and severity separately.

Because the random variables N, $X_1, X_2, \ldots$, and S provide much of the focus for this chapter and the two that follow, we want to be especially careful when referring to them. We will refer to N as the **loss count (or frequency) random variable** and will refer to its distribution as the **loss count (or frequency) distribution**. The expression **number of losses** will also be used. The X_js are the **individual** or **single loss (or severity) random variables**. The modifier **individual** or **single** will be dropped when the reference is clear. Finally, S is the **aggregate loss random variable** or the **total loss random variable**.

6.2 MODEL CHOICES

In many cases of fitting frequency or severity distributions to real data, several distributions may be good candidates for models. However, some distributions may be preferable for a variety of practical reasons.

In general, it is useful for the severity distribution to be a scale distribution (see Definition 4.3) because the choice of currency (e.g., U.S. dollars or Euros) should not affect the result. Also, scale families are easy to adjust for inflationary effects over time (this is, in effect, a change in currency; e.g., 2004 U.S. dollars to 2005 U.S. dollars). When forecasting the costs for a future year, the anticipated rate of inflation can be factored in easily by adjusting the parameters.

A similar consideration applies to frequency distributions. As a company's business grows, the number of operational losses can be expected to grow, all other things being equal. If we choose models that have probability generating functions of the form

$$P_N(z; \alpha) = Q(z)^\alpha \qquad (6.2)$$

for some parameter α, then the expected number of losses is proportional to α. Increasing the volume of business by $100r\%$ results in expected losses being proportional to $\alpha^* = (1+r)\alpha$. This was discussed in Section 5.14. Because r is any value satisfying $r > -1$, the distributions satisfying equation (6.2) should allow α to take on any positive values. Such distributions can be seen to be infinitely divisible (see Definition 5.27).

A related consideration also suggests frequency distributions that are infinitely divisible. This relates to the concept of invariance over the time period of study. Ideally the model selected should not depend on the length of the time period used in the study of loss frequency. The expected frequency should be proportional to the length of the time period after any adjustment for growth in business. This means that a study conducted over a period of 5 years can be used to develop loss frequency distributions for periods of a month, a year, or any other period. Furthermore, the form of the distribution for a one-year period is the same as for a one-month period with a change of parameter. The parameter α corresponds to the length of a time period. For example, if $\alpha = 1.7$ in equation (6.2) for a one-month period, then the identical model with $\alpha = 20.4$ is an appropriate model for a one-year period.

6.3   THE COMPOUND MODEL FOR AGGREGATE LOSSES

Let S denote aggregate losses associated with a set of N observed losses $X_1, X_2, \cdots, X_N$ satisfying the following independence assumption: Given that there are n losses, the loss sizes are mutually independent random variables whose common distribution does not depend on n.

The approach in this chapter is to:

1. Develop a model for the distribution of N based on data.

2. Develop a model for the common distribution of the X_js based on data.

3. Using these two models, carry out necessary calculations to obtain the distribution of S.

Completion of the first two steps follows the ideas in earlier chapters. We now presume that these two models are developed and that we only need to carry out numerical work in obtaining solutions to problems associated with the distribution of S.

The random sum

$$S = X_1 + X_2 + \cdots + X_N$$

(where N has a counting distribution) has distribution function

$$F_S(x) = \Pr(S \leq x)$$

$$= \sum_{n=0}^{\infty} p_n \Pr(S \leq x | N = n)$$

$$= \sum_{n=0}^{\infty} p_n F_X^{*n}(x), \tag{6.3}$$

where $F_X(x) = \Pr(X \leq x)$ is the common distribution function of the X_js and $p_n = \Pr(N = n)$. In (6.3), $F_X^{*n}(x)$ is the "n-fold convolution" of the cdf of X. It can be obtained as

$$F_X^{*0}(x) = \begin{cases} 0, & x < 0, \\ \\ 1, & x \geq 0, \end{cases}$$

and

$$F_X^{*k}(x) = \int_{-\infty}^{\infty} F_X^{*(k-1)}(x - y) \, dF_X(y) \text{ for } k = 1, 2, \ldots. \tag{6.4}$$

If X is a continuous random variable with probability zero on negative values, (6.4) reduces to

$$F_X^{*k}(x) = \int_0^x F_X^{*(k-1)}(x - y) f_X(y) \, dy \text{ for } k = 2, 3, \ldots.$$

For $k = 1$ this equation reduces to $F_X^{*1}(x) = F_X(x)$. By differentiating, the pdf is

$$f_X^{*k}(x) = \int_0^x f_X^{*(k-1)}(x - y) f_X(y) \, dy \text{ for } k = 2, 3, \ldots.$$

In the case of discrete random variables with positive probabilities at $0, 1, 2, \ldots$, Equation (6.4) reduces to

$$F_X^{*k}(x) = \sum_{y=0}^{x} F_X^{*(k-1)}(x - y) f_X(y) \text{ for } x = 0, 1, \ldots, \; k = 2, 3, \ldots.$$

The corresponding pf is

$$f_X^{*k}(x) = \sum_{y=0}^{x} f_X^{*(k-1)}(x - y) f_X(y) \text{ for } x = 0, 1, \ldots, \; k = 2, 3, \ldots.$$

The distribution (6.3) is called a **compound distribution,** and the pf for the distribution of aggregate losses is

$$f_S(x) = \sum_{n=0}^{\infty} p_n f_X^{*n}(x).$$

Arguing as in Section 5.7, the pgf of S is

$$P_S(z) = E[z^S]$$

$$= \sum_{n=0}^{\infty} E[z^{X_1 + X_2 + \cdots + X_n} | N = n] \Pr(N = n)$$

$$= \sum_{n=0}^{\infty} E\left[\prod_{j=1}^{n} z^{X_j} \right] \Pr(N = n)$$

$$= \sum_{n=0}^{\infty} \Pr(N = n)[P_X(z)]^n$$

$$= E[P_X(z)^N] = P_N[P_X(z)] \tag{6.5}$$

because of the independence of $X_1, \ldots, X_n$ for fixed n.

A similar relationship exists for the other generating functions. It is sometimes more convenient to use the characteristic function

$$\varphi_S(z) = E(e^{izS}) = P_N[\varphi_X(z)],$$

which always exists. Panjer and Willmot [93] use the Laplace transform

$$L_S(z) = E(e^{-zS}) = P_N[L_X(z)],$$

which always exists for random variables defined on nonnegative values. With regard to the moment generating function, we have

$$M_S(z) = P_N[M_X(z)].$$

The pgf of compound distributions was discussed in Section 5.7 where the "secondary" distribution plays the role of the loss size distribution in this chapter.

In the case where $P_N(z) = P_1[P_2(z)]$ (that is, N is itself a compound distribution), the pgf of aggregate losses is $P_S(z) = P_1\{P_2[P_X(z)]\}$, which in itself produces no additional difficulties.

From equation (6.5), the moments of S can be obtained in terms of the moments of N and the X_js. The first three moments are

$$E(S) = \mu'_{S1} = \mu'_{N1}\mu'_{X1} = E(N)E(X),$$
$$Var(S) = \mu_{S2} = \mu'_{N1}\mu_{X2} + \mu_{N2}(\mu'_{X1})^2, \tag{6.6}$$
$$E\{[S - E(S)]^3\} = \mu_{S3} = \mu'_{N1}\mu_{X3} + 3\mu_{N2}\mu'_{X1}\mu_{X2} + \mu_{N3}(\mu'_{X1})^3.$$

Here, the first subscript indicates the appropriate random variable, the second subscript indicates the order of the moment, and the superscript is a prime (') for raw moments (moments about the origin) and is unprimed for central moments (moments about the mean). The moments can be used on their own to provide approximations for probabilities of aggregate losses by matching the first few model and sample moments.

Example 6.1 *The observed mean (and standard deviation) of the number of losses and the individual losses over the past 10 months are 6.7 (2.3) and 179,247 (52,141), respectively. Determine the mean and variance of aggregate losses per month.*

$$E(S) = 6.7(179{,}247) = 1{,}200{,}955,$$
$$\text{Var}(S) = 6.7(52{,}141)^2 + (2.3)^2(179{,}247)^2$$
$$= 1.88180 \times 10^{11}.$$

Hence, the mean and standard deviation of aggregate losses are 1,200,955 and 433,797, respectively. □

Example 6.2 (Example 6.1 continued) *Using normal and lognormal distributions as approximating distributions for aggregate losses, calculate the probability that losses will exceed 140% of expected costs. That is,*

$$\Pr(S > 1.40 \times 1{,}200{,}955) = \Pr(S > 1{,}681{,}337).$$

For the normal distribution

$$\Pr(S > 1{,}681{,}337) = \Pr\left(\frac{S - E(S)}{\sqrt{\text{Var}(S)}} > \frac{1{,}681{,}337 - 1{,}200{,}955}{433{,}797}\right)$$
$$= \Pr(Z > 1.107) = 1 - \Phi(1.107) = 0.134.$$

The mean and second raw moment of the lognormal distribution are

$$E(S) = \exp(\mu + \tfrac{1}{2}\sigma^2) \quad \text{and} \quad E(S^2) = \exp(2\mu + 2\sigma^2).$$

Equating these to 1.200955×10^6 and $1.88180 \times 10^{11} + (1.200955 \times 10^6)^2 = 1.63047 \times 10^{12}$ and taking logarithms results in the following two equations in two unknowns:

$$\mu + \tfrac{1}{2}\sigma^2 = 13.99863, \quad 2\mu + 2\sigma^2 = 28.11989.$$

From this, $\mu = 13.93731$ and $\sigma^2 = 0.1226361$. Then

$$\Pr(S > 1{,}681{,}337) = 1 - \Phi\left[\frac{\ln 1{,}681{,}337 - 13.93731}{(0.1226361)^{0.5}}\right]$$

$$= 1 - \Phi(1.135913) = 0.128.$$

□

The normal distribution provides a good approximation when $E(N)$ is large. In particular, if N has the Poisson, binomial, or negative binomial distribution, a version of the central limit theorem indicates that, as λ, m, or r, respectively, goes to infinity, the distribution of S becomes normal. In this example, $E(N)$ is small so the distribution of S is likely to be skewed. In this case the lognormal distribution may provide a good approximation, although there is no theory to support this choice.

Example 6.3 (Illustration of convolution calculations) *Suppose individual losses follow the distribution given in Table 6.1 (given in units of $\$1000$).*

Table 6.1   Loss distribution for Example 6.3

x	$f_X(x)$
1	0.150
2	0.200
3	0.250
4	0.125
5	0.075
6	0.050
7	0.050
8	0.050
9	0.025
10	0.025

Furthermore, the frequency distribution is given in Table 6.2.

Table 6.2   Frequency distribution for Example 6.3

n	p_n
0	0.05
1	0.10
2	0.15
3	0.20
4	0.25
5	0.15
6	0.06
7	0.03
8	0.01

Table 6.3 Aggregate probabilities for Example 6.3

x	f_X^{*0}	f_X^{*1}	f_X^{*2}	f_X^{*3}	f_X^{*4}	f_X^{*5}	f_X^{*6}	f_X^{*7}	f_X^{*8}	$f_S(x)$
0	1	0	0	0	0	0	0	0	0	.05000
1	0	.150	0	0	0	0	0	0	0	.01500
2	0	.200	.02250	0	0	0	0	0	0	.02338
3	0	.250	.06000	.00338	0	0	0	0	0	.03468
4	0	.125	.11500	.01350	.00051	0	0	0	0	.03258
5	0	.075	.13750	.03488	.00270	.00008	0	0	0	.03579
6	0	.050	.13500	.06144	.00878	.00051	.00001	0	0	.03981
7	0	.050	.10750	.08569	.01999	.00198	.00009	.00000	0	.04356
8	0	.050	.08813	.09750	.03580	.00549	.00042	.00002	.00000	.04752
9	0	.025	.07875	.09841	.05266	.01194	.00136	.00008	.00000	.04903
10	0	.025	.07063	.09338	.06682	.02138	.00345	.00031	.00002	.05190
11	0	0	.06250	.08813	.07597	.03282	.00726	.00091	.00007	.05138
12	0	0	.04500	.08370	.08068	.04450	.01305	.00218	.00022	.05119
13	0	0	.03125	.07673	.08266	.05486	.02062	.00448	.00060	.05030
14	0	0	.01750	.06689	.08278	.06314	.02930	.00808	.00138	.04818
15	0	0	.01125	.05377	.08081	.06934	.03826	.01304	.00279	.04576
16	0	0	.00750	.04125	.07584	.07361	.04677	.01919	.00505	.04281
17	0	0	.00500	.03052	.06811	.07578	.05438	.02616	.00829	.03938
18	0	0	.00313	.02267	.05854	.07552	.06080	.03352	.01254	.03575
19	0	0	.00125	.01673	.04878	.07263	.06573	.04083	.01768	.03197
20	0	0	.00063	.01186	.03977	.06747	.06882	.04775	.02351	.02832
21	0	0	0	.00800	.03187	.06079	.06982	.05389	.02977	.02479
p_n	.05	.10	.15	.20	.25	.15	.06	.03	.01	

The probability that the aggregate loss is x thousand dollars is

$$f_S(x) = \sum_{n=0}^{8} p_n f_X^{*n}(x).$$

Determine the pf of S up to $\$21,000$. Determine the mean and standard deviation of total losses.

The distribution up to amounts of $\$21,000$ is given in Table 6.3. To obtain $f_S(x)$, each row of the matrix of convolutions of $f_X(x)$ is multiplied by the probabilities from the row below the table and the products are summed.

The reader may wish to verify using (6.6) that the first two moments of the distribution $f_S(x)$ are

$$E(S) = 12.58, \quad \text{Var}(S) = 58.7464.$$

Hence the aggregate loss has mean $\$12,580$ and standard deviation $\$7664$. (Why can't the calculations be done from Table 6.3 ?) □

6.4 SOME ANALYTIC RESULTS

For most choices of distributions of N and the X_js, the compound distributional values can only be obtained numerically. Subsequent sections of this chapter are devoted to such numerical procedures. However, for certain combinations of choices, simple analytic results are available, thus reducing the computational problems considerably.

Example 6.4 (Compound geometric–exponential) *Suppose* $X_1, X_2, \ldots$ *are iid with common exponential distribution with mean* θ *and that* N *has a geometric distribution with parameter* β. *Determine the (aggregate loss) distribution of* S.

The mgf of X is $M_X(z) = (1 - \theta z)^{-1}$. The mgf of N is $P_N(z) = [1 - \beta(z - 1)]^{-1}$ (see Chapter 5). Therefore, the mgf of S is

$$M_S(z) = P_N[M_X(z)]$$
$$= \{1 - \beta[(1 - \theta z)^{-1} - 1]\}^{-1}$$
$$= \frac{1}{1 + \beta} 1 + \frac{\beta}{1 + \beta} [1 - \theta(1 + \beta)z]^{-1}$$

with a bit of algebra.

This is a two-point mixture of a degenerate distribution with probability 1 at zero and an exponential distribution with mean $\theta(1 + \beta)$. Hence, $\Pr(S = 0) = (1 + \beta)^{-1}$, and for $x > 0$, S has pdf

$$f_S(x) = \frac{\beta}{\theta(1 + \beta)^2} \exp\left[-\frac{x}{\theta(1 + \beta)}\right].$$

It has a point mass of $(1 + \beta)^{-1}$ at zero and an exponentially decaying density over the positive axis. Its cdf can be written as

$$F_S(x) = 1 - \frac{\beta}{1 + \beta} \exp\left[-\frac{x}{\theta(1 + \beta)}\right], \quad x \geq 0.$$

It has a jump at zero and is continuous otherwise. □

Example 6.5 (Exponential severities) *Determine the cdf of* S *for any compound distribution with exponential severities.*

The mgf of the sum of n independent exponential random variables each with mean θ is

$$M_{X_1 + X_2 + \cdots + X_n}(z) = (1 - \theta z)^{-n},$$

which is the mgf of the gamma distribution with cdf $F_X^{*n}(x) = \Gamma\left(n; \frac{x}{\theta}\right)$.

For integer values of α, the values of $\Gamma(\alpha; x)$ can be calculated exactly (see Appendix A for the derivation) as

$$\Gamma(n; x) = 1 - \sum_{j=0}^{n-1} \frac{x^j e^{-x}}{j!}, \quad n = 1, 2, 3, \ldots. \tag{6.7}$$

From equation (6.3)

$$F_S(x) = p_0 + \sum_{n=1}^{\infty} p_n \Gamma\left(n; \frac{x}{\theta}\right).$$

Substituting in equation (6.7) yields

$$F_S(x) = 1 - \sum_{n=1}^{\infty} p_n \sum_{j=0}^{n-1} \frac{(x/\theta)^j e^{-x/\theta}}{j!}, \quad x \geq 0. \tag{6.8}$$

Interchanging the order of summation yields

$$F_S(x) = 1 - e^{-x/\theta} \sum_{j=0}^{\infty} \frac{(x/\theta)^j}{j!} \sum_{n=j+1}^{\infty} p_n$$

$$= 1 - e^{-x/\theta} \sum_{j=0}^{\infty} \bar{P}_j \frac{(x/\theta)^j}{j!}, \quad x \geq 0,$$

where $\bar{P}_j = \sum_{n=j+1}^{\infty} p_n$ for $j = 0, 1, \ldots$. $\qquad \Box$

The approach of Example 6.5 may be extended to the larger class of mixed Erlang severity distributions, as shown in Exercise 6.10.

For frequency distributions that assign positive probability to all nonnegative integers, the right-hand side of equation (6.8) can be evaluated by taking sufficient terms in the first summation. For distributions for which $\Pr(N > n^*) = 0$, the first summation becomes finite. For example, for the binomial frequency distribution, equation (6.8) becomes

$$F_S(x) = 1 - \sum_{n=1}^{m} \binom{m}{n} q^n (1-q)^{m-n} \sum_{j=0}^{n-1} \frac{(x/\theta)^j e^{-x/\theta}}{j!}. \tag{6.9}$$

Example 6.6 (Compound negative binomial–exponential) *Determine the distribution of S when the frequency distribution is negative binomial with an integer value for the parameter r and the severity distribution is exponential.*

The mgf of S is

$$M_S(z) = P_N[M_X(z)]$$
$$= P_N[(1 - \theta z)^{-1}]$$
$$= \{1 - \beta[(1 - \theta z)^{-1} - 1]\}^{-r}.$$

With a bit of algebra, this can be rewritten as

$$M_S(z) = \left(1 + \frac{\beta}{1+\beta}\{[1 - \theta(1+\beta)z]^{-1} - 1\}\right)^r,$$

which is of the form
$$M_S(z) = P_N^*[M_X^*(z)],$$
where
$$P_N^*(z) = \left[1 + \frac{\beta}{1+\beta}(z-1)\right]^r,$$
the pgf of the binomial distribution with parameters r and $\beta/(1+\beta)$, and $M_X^*(z)$ is the mgf of the exponential distribution with mean $\theta(1+\beta)$.

This transformation reduces the computation of the distribution function to the finite sum of the form (6.9), that is,

$$F_S(x) = 1 - \sum_{n=1}^{r} \binom{r}{n} \left(\frac{\beta}{1+\beta}\right)^n \left(\frac{1}{1+\beta}\right)^{r-n}$$
$$\times \sum_{j=0}^{n-1} \frac{[x\theta^{-1}(1+\beta)^{-1}]^j e^{-x\theta^{-1}(1+\beta)^{-1}}}{j!}.$$

$\square$

Example 6.7 (Severity distributions closed under convolution) *A distribution is said to be **closed under convolution** if adding iid members of a family produces another member of that family. Further assume that adding n members of a family produces a member with all but one parameter unchanged and the remaining parameter is multiplied by n. Determine the distribution of S when the severity distribution has this property.*

The condition means that, if $f_X(x; a)$ is the pf of each X_j, then the pf of $X_1 + X_2 + \cdots + X_n$ is $f_X(x; na)$. This means that

$$f_S(x) = \sum_{n=1}^{\infty} p_n f_X^{*n}(x; a)$$
$$= \sum_{n=1}^{\infty} p_n f_X(x; na),$$

eliminating the need to carry out evaluation of the convolution. Severity distributions that are closed under convolution include the gamma and inverse Gaussian distributions. See Exercise 6.7. $\square$

6.5 EVALUATION OF THE AGGREGATE LOSS DISTRIBUTION

The computation of the compound distribution function

$$F_S(x) = \sum_{n=0}^{\infty} p_n F_X^{*n}(x) \tag{6.10}$$

or the corresponding probability (density) function is generally not an easy task, even in the simplest of cases. In this section we discuss a number of approaches to numerical evaluation of the right-hand side of equation (6.10) for specific choices of the frequency and severity distributions as well as for arbitrary choices of one or both distributions.

One approach is to use an **approximating distribution** to avoid direct calculation of formula (6.10). This approach was used in Example 6.2 where the method of moments was used to estimate the parameters of the approximating distribution. The advantage of this method is that it is simple and easy to apply. However, the disadvantages are significant. First, there is no way of knowing how good the approximation is. Choosing different approximating distributions can result in very different results, particularly in the right-hand tail of the distribution. Of course, the approximation should improve as more moments are used; but after four moments, we quickly run out of distributions!

The approximating distribution may also fail to accommodate special features of the true distribution. For example, when the loss distribution is of the continuous type and there is a maximum possible loss (for example, when there is insurance in place that covers any losses in excess of a threshold), the severity distribution may have a point mass ("atom" or "spike") at the maximum. The true aggregate loss distribution is of the mixed type with spikes at integral multiples of the maximum corresponding to $1, 2, 3, \ldots$ losses of maximum size. These spikes, if large, can have a significant effect on the probabilities near such multiples. These jumps in the aggregate loss distribution function cannot be replicated by a smooth approximating distribution.

A second method to evaluate the right-hand side of equation (6.10) or the corresponding pdf is **direct calculation**. The most difficult (or computer intensive) part is the evaluation of the n-fold convolutions of the severity distribution for $n = 2, 3, 4, \ldots$. In some situations, there is an analytic form— for example, when the severity distribution is closed under convolution, as defined in Example 6.7 and illustrated in Examples 6.4–6.6. Otherwise the convolutions must be evaluated numerically using

$$F_X^{*k}(x) = \int_{-\infty}^{\infty} F_X^{*(k-1)}(x - y)\, dF_X(y). \tag{6.11}$$

When the losses are limited to nonnegative values (as is usually the case), the range of integration becomes finite, reducing formula (6.11) to

$$F_X^{*k}(x) = \int_{0-}^{x} F_X^{*(k-1)}(x - y)\, dF_X(y). \tag{6.12}$$

These integrals are written in Lebesgue–Stieltjes form because of possible jumps in the cdf $F_X(x)$ at zero and at other points.[1] Numerical evaluation

---

[1] Without going into the formal definition of the Lebesgue–Stieltjes integral, it suffices to interpret $\int g(y)\, dF_X(y)$ as to be evaluated by integrating $g(y)f_X(y)$ over those y values for

of (6.12) requires numerical integration methods. Because of the first term inside the integral, the right-hand side of (6.12) needs to be evaluated for all possible values of x and all values of k. This can quickly become technically overpowering!

A simple way to avoid these technical problems is to replace the severity distribution by a discrete distribution defined at multiples $0, 1, 2 \ldots$ of some convenient monetary unit such as \$1,000. This reduces formula (6.12) to (in terms of the new monetary unit)

$$F_X^{*k}(x) = \sum_{y=0}^{x} F_X^{*(k-1)}(x - y) f_X(y).$$

The corresponding pf is

$$f_X^{*k}(x) = \sum_{y=0}^{x} f_X^{*(k-1)}(x - y) f_X(y).$$

In practice, the monetary unit can be made sufficiently small to accommodate spikes at maximum loss amounts. One needs only the maximum to be a multiple of the monetary unit to have it located at exactly the right point. As the monetary unit of measurement becomes smaller, the discrete distribution function will approach the true distribution function. The simplest approach is to round all amounts to the nearest multiple of the monetary unit; for example, round all losses or losses to the nearest \$1,000. More sophisticated methods will be discussed later in this chapter.

When the severity distribution is defined on nonnegative integers $0, 1, 2, \ldots$, calculating $f_X^{*k}(x)$ for integral x requires $x + 1$ multiplications. Then carrying out these calculations for all possible values of k and x up to m requires a number of multiplications that are of order m^3, written as $O(m^3)$, to obtain the distribution (6.10) for $x = 0$ to $x = m$. When the maximum value, m, for which the aggregate losses distribution is calculated is large, the number of computations quickly becomes prohibitive, even for fast computers. For example, in real applications n can easily be as large as 1,000. This requires about 10^9 multiplications. Further, if $\Pr(X = 0) > 0$, an infinite number of calculations are required to obtain any single probability exactly. This is because $F_X^{*n}(x) > 0$ for all n and all x and so the sum in (6.10) contains an infinite number of terms. When $\Pr(X = 0) = 0$, we have $F_X^{*n}(x) = 0$ for $n > x$ and so the right-hand side (6.10) has no more than $x + 1$ positive terms. Table 6.3 provides an example of this latter case.

Alternative methods to more quickly evaluate the aggregate losses distribution are discussed in Sections 6.6 and 6.7. The first such method, **the**

---

which X has a continuous distribution and then adding $g(y_i) \Pr(X = y_i)$ over those points where $\Pr(X = y_i) > 0$. This allows for a single notation to be used for continuous, discrete, and mixed random variables.

recursive method, reduces the number of computations discussed above to $O(m^2)$, which is a considerable savings in computer time, a reduction of about 99.9% when $m = 1000$ compared to direct calculation. However, the method is limited to certain frequency distributions. Fortunately, it includes all frequency distributions discussed in Chapter 5.

The second method, **the inversion method**, numerically inverts a transform, such as the characteristic function or Fourier transform, using general or specialized inversion software.

6.6   THE RECURSIVE METHOD

Suppose that the severity distribution $f_X(x)$ is defined on $0, 1, 2, \ldots, m$ representing multiples of some convenient monetary unit. The number m represents the largest possible loss and could be infinite. Further, suppose that the frequency distribution, p_k, is a member of the $(a, b, 1)$ class and therefore satisfies

$$p_k = \left(a + \frac{b}{k}\right)p_{k-1}, \quad k = 2, 3, 4, \ldots.$$

Then the following result holds.

Theorem 6.8 (Extended Panjer recursion) *For the* $(a, b, 1)$ *class,*

$$f_S(x) = \frac{[p_1 - (a+b)p_0]f_X(x) + \sum_{y=1}^{x \wedge m}(a + by/x)f_X(y)f_S(x-y)}{1 - af_X(0)}, \quad (6.13)$$

noting that $x \wedge m$ *is notation for* $\min(x, m)$.

Proof: This result is identical to Theorem 5.13 with appropriate substitution of notation and recognition that the argument of $f_X(x)$ cannot exceed m. □

Corollary 6.9 (Panjer recursion) *For the* $(a, b, 0)$ *class, the result* (6.13) *reduces to*

$$f_S(x) = \frac{\sum_{y=1}^{x \wedge m}(a + by/x)\,f_X(y)f_S(x-y)}{1 - af_X(0)}. \quad (6.14)$$

Note that when the severity distribution has no probability at zero, the denominators of equations (6.13) and (6.14) are equal to 1. The recursive formula (6.14) has become known as the Panjer formula in recognition of the introduction to the actuarial literature by Panjer [88]. The recursive formula (6.13) is an extension of the original Panjer formula. It was first proposed by Sundt and Jewell [112].

In the case of the Poisson distribution, equation (6.14) reduces to

$$f_S(x) = \frac{\lambda}{x}\sum_{y=1}^{x \wedge m} yf_X(y)f_S(x-y), \quad x = 1, 2, \ldots. \quad (6.15)$$

The starting value of the recursive schemes (6.13) and (6.14) is $f_S(0) = P_N[f_X(0)]$ following Theorem 5.15 with an appropriate change of notation. In the case of the Poisson distribution, we have

$$f_S(0) = e^{-\lambda[1-f_X(0)]}.$$

Table 6.4 gives the corresponding initial values for all distributions in the $(a, b, 1)$ class using the convenient simplifying notation $f_0 = f_X(0)$.

Table 6.4 Starting values $(f_S(0))$ for recursions

Distribution	$f_S(0)$
Poisson	$\exp[\lambda(f_0 - 1)]$
Geometric	$[1 + \beta(1 - f_0)]^{-1}$
Binomial	$[1 + q(f_0 - 1)]^m$
Negative binomial	$[1 + \beta(1 - f_0)]^{-r}$
ZM Poisson	$p_0^M + (1 - p_0^M)\dfrac{\exp(\lambda f_0) - 1}{\exp(\lambda) - 1}$
ZM geometric	$p_0^M + (1 - p_0^M)\dfrac{f_0}{1 + \beta(1 - f_0)}$
ZM binomial	$p_0^M + (1 - p_0^M)\dfrac{[1 + q(f_0 - 1)]^m - (1 - q)^m}{1 - (1 - q)^m}$
ZM negative binomial	$p_0^M + (1 - p_0^M)\dfrac{[1 + \beta(1 - f_0)]^{-r} - (1 + \beta)^{-r}}{1 - (1 + \beta)^{-r}}$
ZM logarithmic	$p_0^M + (1 - p_0^M)\left\{1 - \dfrac{\ln[1 + \beta(1 - f_0)]}{\ln(1 + \beta)}\right\}$

6.6.1 Compound frequency models

When the frequency distribution can be represented as a compound distribution (e.g., Neyman Type A, Poisson–inverse Gaussian) involving only distributions from the $(a, b, 0)$ or $(a, b, 1)$ classes, the recursive formula (6.13) can be used two or more times to obtain the aggregate loss distribution. If the frequency distribution can be written as

$$P_N(z) = P_1[P_2(z)],$$

then the aggregate loss distribution has pgf

$$P_S(z) = P_N[P_X(z)]$$
$$= P_1\{P_2[P_X(z)]\},$$

which can be rewritten as

$$P_S(z) = P_1[P_{S_1}(z)] \tag{6.16}$$

where

$$P_{S_1}(z) = P_2[P_X(z)]. \tag{6.17}$$

Now equation (6.17) has the same form as an aggregate loss distribution. Thus, if $P_2(z)$ is in the $(a, b, 0)$ or $(a, b, 1)$ class, the distribution of S_1 can be calculated using (6.13). The resulting distribution is the "severity" distribution in (6.17). A second application of formula (6.13) in (6.16) results in the distribution of S.

The following example illustrates the use of this algorithm.

Example 6.10 *The number of losses has a Poisson–ETNB distribution with Poisson parameter $\lambda = 2$ and ETNB parameters $\beta = 3$ and $r = 0.2$. The loss size distribution has probabilities 0.3, 0.5, and 0.2 at 0, 10, and 20, respectively. Determine the total loss distribution recursively.*

In the above terminology, N has pgf $P_N(z) = P_1[P_2(z)]$, where $P_1(z)$ and $P_2(z)$ are the Poisson and ETNB pgfs, respectively. Then the total dollars of losses has pgf $P_S(z) = P_1[P_{S_1}(z)]$, where $P_{S_1}(z) = P_2[P_X(z)]$ is a compound ETNB pgf. We will first compute the distribution of S_1. We have (in monetary units of 10) $f_X(0) = 0.3$, $f_X(1) = 0.5$, and $f_X(2) = 0.2$. In order to use the compound ETNB recursion, we start with

$$f_{S_1}(0) = P_2[f_X(0)]$$
$$= \frac{\{1 + \beta[1 - f_X(0)]\}^{-r} - (1 + \beta)^{-r}}{1 - (1 + \beta)^{-r}}$$
$$= \frac{\{1 + 3(1 - 0.3)\}^{-0.2} - (1 + 3)^{-0.2}}{1 - (1 + 3)^{-0.2}}$$
$$= 0.16369.$$

The remaining values of $f_{S_1}(x)$ may be obtained using formula (6.13) with S replaced by S_1. In this case we have $a = 3/(1 + 3) = 0.75$, $b = (0.2 - 1)a = -0.6$, $p_0 = 0$ and $p_1 = (0.2)(3)/\left[(1 + 3)^{0.2+1} - (1 + 3)\right] = 0.46947$. Then formula (6.13) becomes

$$f_{S_1}(x) = \frac{[0.46947 - (0.75 - 0.6)(0)] f_X(x) + \sum_{y=1}^{x} (0.75 - 0.6y/x) f_X(y) f_{S_1}(x-y)}{1 - (0.75)(0.3)}$$

$$= 0.60577 f_X(x) + 1.29032 \sum_{y=1}^{x} \left(0.75 - 0.6\frac{y}{x}\right) f_X(y) f_{S_1}(x-y).$$

The first few probabilities are

$$f_{S_1}(1) = 0.60577(0.5) + 1.29032 \left[0.75 - 0.6\left(\tfrac{1}{1}\right)\right](0.5)(0.16369)$$
$$= 0.31873,$$

$$f_{S_1}(2) = 0.60577(0.2) + 1.29032 \left\{\left[0.75 - 0.6\left(\tfrac{1}{2}\right)\right](0.5)(0.31873)\right.$$
$$\left. + \left[0.75 - 0.6\left(\tfrac{2}{2}\right)\right](0.2)(0.16369)\right\} = 0.22002,$$

$$f_{S_1}(3) = 1.29032 \left\{\left[0.75 - 0.6\left(\tfrac{1}{3}\right)\right](0.5)(0.22002)\right.$$
$$\left. + \left[0.75 - 0.6\left(\tfrac{2}{3}\right)\right](0.2)(0.31873)\right\} = 0.10686,$$

$$f_{S_1}(4) = 1.29032 \left\{\left[0.75 - 0.6\left(\tfrac{1}{4}\right)\right](0.5)(0.10686)\right.$$
$$\left. + \left[0.75 - 0.6\left(\tfrac{2}{4}\right)\right](0.2)(0.22002)\right\} = 0.06692.$$

We now turn to evaluation of the distribution of S with compound Poisson pgf

$$P_S(z) = P_1[P_{S_1}(z)] = e^{\lambda[P_{S_1}(z)-1]}.$$

Thus the distribution $\{f_{S_1}(x), \ x = 0, 1, 2, \ldots\}$ becomes the "secondary" or "loss size" distribution in an application of the compound Poisson recursive formula. Therefore,

$$f_S(0) = P_S(0) = e^{\lambda[P_{S_1}(0)-1]} = e^{\lambda[f_{S_1}(0)-1]} = e^{2(0.16369-1)} = 0.18775.$$

The remaining probabilities may be found from the recursive formula

$$f_S(x) = \frac{2}{x} \sum_{y=1}^{x} y f_{S_1}(y) f_S(x-y), \quad x = 1, 2, \ldots.$$

The first few probabilities are

$$f_S(1) = 2\left(\tfrac{1}{1}\right)(0.31873)(0.18775) = 0.11968,$$

$$f_S(2) = 2\left(\tfrac{1}{2}\right)(0.31873)(0.11968) + 2\left(\tfrac{2}{2}\right)(0.22002)(0.18775) = 0.12076,$$

$$f_S(3) = 2\left(\tfrac{1}{3}\right)(0.31873)(0.12076) + 2\left(\tfrac{2}{3}\right)(0.22002)(0.11968)$$
$$+ 2\left(\tfrac{3}{3}\right)(0.10686)(0.18775) = 0.10090,$$

$$f_S(4) = 2\left(\tfrac{1}{4}\right)(0.31873)(0.10090) + 2\left(\tfrac{2}{4}\right)(0.22002)(0.12076)$$
$$+ 2\left(\tfrac{3}{4}\right)(0.10686)(0.11968) + 2\left(\tfrac{4}{4}\right)(0.06692)(0.18775)$$
$$= 0.08696.$$

$\square$

This simple idea can be extended to higher levels of compounding by repeatedly applying the same concepts. The computer time required to carry out two applications will be about twice that of one application of formula (6.13). However, the total number of computations is still of order $O(m^2)$ rather than $O(m^3)$ as in the direct method.

When the severity distribution has a maximum possible value at r, the computations are speeded up even more because the sum in formula (6.13) will be restricted to at most r nonzero terms. In this case, then, the computations can be considered to be of order $O(m)$.

6.6.2 Underflow/overflow problems

The recursion (6.13) starts with the calculated value of $P(S = 0) = P_N[f_X(0)]$. For a very large portfolio of risks, this probability is very small, sometimes smaller than the smallest number that can be represented on the computer. When this occurs, this initial value is represented on the computer as zero and the recursion (6.13) fails. This problem can be overcome in several different ways (see Panjer and Willmot [92]). One of the easiest ways is to start with an arbitrary set of values for $f_S(0), f_S(1), \dots, f_S(k)$ such as $(0, 0, 0, \dots, 0, 1)$, where k is sufficiently far to the left in the distribution so that $F_S(k)$ is still negligible. Setting k to a point that lies six standard deviations to the left of the mean is usually sufficient. The recursive formula (6.13) is used to generate values of the distribution with this set of starting values until the values are consistently less than $f_S(k)$. The "probabilities" are then summed and divided by the sum so that the "true" probabilities add to 1. Trial and error will dictate how small k should be for a particular problem.

Another method to obtain probabilities when the starting value is too small is to carry out the calculations for a smaller risk set. For example, for the Poisson distribution with a very large mean λ, we can find a value of $\lambda^* = \lambda/2^n$ so that the probability at zero is representable on the computer when λ^* is used as the Poisson mean. Equation (6.13) is now used to obtain the aggregate losses distribution when λ^* is used as the Poisson mean. If $P_*(z)$ is the pgf of the aggregate losses using Poisson mean λ^*, then $P_S(z) = [P_*(z)]^{2^n}$. Hence, we can obtain successively the distributions with pgfs $[P_*(z)]^2, [P_*(z)]^4, [P_*(z)]^8, \dots, [P_*(z)]^{2^n}$ by convoluting the result at each stage with itself. This requires an additional n convolutions in carrying out the calculations but involves no approximations. This procedure can be carried out for any frequency distributions that are closed under convolution. For the negative binomial distribution, the analogous procedure starts with $r^* = r/2^n$. For the binomial distribution, the parameter m must be integer valued. A slight modification can be used. Let $m^* = \lfloor m/2^n \rfloor$ when $\lfloor \cdot \rfloor$ indicates the **integer part of** function. When the n convolutions are carried out, we still need to carry out the calculations using formula (6.13) for parameter $m - m^* 2^n$. This result is then convoluted with the result of the n convolutions. For compound frequency distributions, only the primary distribution needs to be closed under convolution.

6.6.3 Numerical stability

Any recursive formula requires accurate computation of values because each such value will be used in computing subsequent values. Some recursive schemes suffer the risk of errors propagating through all subsequent values and potentially blowing up. In the recursive formula (6.13), errors are introduced through rounding or truncation at each stage because computers represent numbers with a finite number of significant digits. The question about stability is, *"How fast do the errors in the calculations grow as the computed values are used in successive computations?"*

The question of error propagation in recursive formulas has been a subject of study of numerical analysts. This work has been extended by Panjer and Wang [91] to study the recursive formula (6.13). The analysis is quite complicated and well beyond the scope of this book. However, some general conclusions can be made here.

Errors are introduced in subsequent values through the summation

$$\sum_{y=1}^{x} \left(a + \frac{by}{x} \right) f_X(y) f_S(x - y)$$

in recursion (6.13). In the extreme right-hand tail of the distribution of S, this sum is positive (or at least nonnegative), and subsequent values of the sum will be decreasing. The sum will stay positive, even with rounding errors, when each of the three factors in each term in the sum is positive. In this case, the recursive formula is stable, producing relative errors that do not grow fast. For the Poisson and negative binomial -based distributions, the factors in each term are always positive.

On the other hand, for the binomial distribution, the sum can have negative terms because a is negative, b is positive, and y/x is a positive function not exceeding 1. In this case, the negative terms can cause the successive values to blow up with alternating signs. When this occurs, the nonsensical results are immediately obvious. Although this does not happen frequently in practice, the reader should be aware of this possibility in models based on the binomial distribution.

6.6.4 Continuous severity

The recursive method has been developed for discrete severity distributions, while it is customary to use continuous distributions for severity. In the case of continuous severities, the analog of the recursion (6.13) is an integral equation, the solution of which is the aggregate loss distribution.

Theorem 6.11 *For the* $(a, b, 1)$ *class of frequency distributions and any continuous severity distribution with probability on the positive real line, the following integral equation holds:*

$$f_S(x) = p_1 f_X(x) + \int_0^x \left(a + \frac{by}{x} \right) f_X(y) f_S(x - y) \, dy. \qquad (6.18)$$

For a detailed proof, see Theorems 6.14.1 and 6.16.1 of Panjer and Willmot [93], along with the associated corollaries. They consider the more general (a, b, m) class of distributions, which allow for arbitrary modification of m initial values of the distribution. Note that the initial term in the right-hand side of equation 6.18 is $p_1 f_X(x)$, not $[p_1 - (a + b)p_0] f_X(x)$ as in equation (6.13). It should also be noted that equation (6.18) holds for members of the $(a, b, 0)$.

Integral equations of the form (6.18) are Volterra integral equations of the second kind. Numerical solution of this type of integral equation has been studied in the book by Baker [8]. We will develop a method using a discrete approximation of the severity distribution in order to use the recursive method (6.13) and avoid the more complicated methods. The more sophisticated methods of Baker for solving equation (6.18) are described in detail by Panjer and Willmot [93].

6.6.5   Constructing arithmetic distributions

In order to implement recursive methods, the easiest approach is to construct a discrete severity distribution on multiples of a convenient unit of measurement h, the **span**. Such a distribution is called arithmetic because it is defined on the nonnegative integers. In order to arithmetize a distribution, it is important to preserve the properties of the original distribution both locally through the range of the distribution and globally—that is, for the entire distribution. This should preserve the general shape of the distribution and at the same time preserve global quantities such as moments.

The methods suggested here apply to the discretization (arithmetization) of continuous, mixed, and nonarithmetic discrete distributions.

6.6.5.1 Method of rounding (mass dispersal) Let f_j denote the probability placed at jh, $j = 0, 1, 2, \ldots$. Then set[2]

$$f_0 = \Pr\left(X < \frac{h}{2}\right) = F_X\left(\frac{h}{2} - 0\right),$$

$$f_j = \Pr\left(jh - \frac{h}{2} \leq X < jh + \frac{h}{2}\right)$$

$$= F_X\left(jh + \frac{h}{2} - 0\right) - F_X\left(jh - \frac{h}{2} - 0\right), \quad j = 1, 2, \ldots.$$

This method splits the probability between $(j + 1)h$ and jh and assigns it to $j + 1$ and j. This, in effect, rounds all amounts to the nearest convenient monetary unit, h, the span of the distribution.

6.6.5.2 Method of local moment matching In this method we construct an arithmetic distribution that matches p moments of the arithmetic and the true severity distributions. Consider an arbitrary interval of length ph, denoted by $[x_k, x_k + ph)$. We will locate point masses $m_0^k, m_1^k, \cdots, m_p^k$ at points x_k, $x_k + h, \cdots, x_k + ph$ so that the first p moments are preserved. The system of $p + 1$ equations reflecting these conditions is

$$\sum_{j=0}^{p}(x_k + jh)^r m_j^k = \int_{x_k - 0}^{x_k + ph - 0} x^r \, dF_X(x), \quad r = 0, 1, 2, \ldots, p, \qquad (6.19)$$

where the notation "-0" at the limits of the integral indicates that discrete probability at x_k is to be included but discrete probability at $x_k + ph$ is to be excluded.

Arrange the intervals so that $x_{k+1} = x_k + ph$ and so the endpoints coincide. Then the point masses at the endpoints are added together. With $x_0 = 0$, the resulting discrete distribution has successive probabilities:

$$\begin{array}{llll} f_0 = m_0^0, & f_1 = m_1^0, & f_2 = m_2^0, \ldots, \\ f_p = m_p^0 + m_0^1, & f_{p+1} = m_1^1, & f_{p+2} = m_2^1, \ldots. \end{array} \qquad (6.20)$$

By summing equation (6.19) for all possible values of k, with $x_0 = 0$, it is clear that the first p moments are preserved for the entire distribution and that the probabilities add to 1 exactly. It only remains to solve the system of equations (6.19).

Theorem 6.12 *The solution of* (6.19) *is*

$$m_j^k = \int_{x_k - 0}^{x_k + ph - 0} \prod_{i \neq j} \frac{x - x_k - ih}{(j - i)h} \, dF_X(x), \quad j = 0, 1, \ldots, p. \qquad (6.21)$$

---

[2] The notation $F_X(x - 0)$ indicates that discrete probability at x should not be included. For continuous distributions this will make no difference.

Proof: The Lagrange formula for collocation of a polynomial $f(y)$ at points $y_0, y_1, \ldots, y_n$ is

$$f(y) = \sum_{j=0}^{n} f(y_j) \prod_{i \neq j} \frac{y - y_i}{y_j - y_i}.$$

Applying this formula to the polynomial $f(y) = y^r$ over the points x_k, $x_k + h, \ldots, x_k + ph$ yields

$$x^r = \sum_{j=0}^{p} (x_k + jh)^r \prod_{i \neq j} \frac{x - x_k - ih}{(j - i)h}, \quad r = 0, 1, \ldots, p.$$

Integrating over the interval $[x_k, x_k + ph)$ with respect to the severity distribution results in

$$\int_{x_k - 0}^{x_k + ph - 0} x^r \, dF_X(x) = \sum_{j=0}^{p} (x_k + jh)^r m_j^k,$$

where m_j^k is given by (6.21). Hence, the solution (6.21) preserves the first p moments, as required. □

Example 6.13 *Suppose X has the exponential distribution with pdf $f(x) = 0.1e^{-0.1x}$. Use a span of $h = 2$ to discretize this distribution by the method of rounding and by matching the first moment.*

For the method of rounding, the general formulas are

$$f_0 = F(1) = 1 - e^{-0.1(1)} = 0.09516,$$
$$f_j = F(2j + 1) - F(2j - 1) = e^{-0.1(2j-1)} - e^{-0.1(2j+1)}.$$

The first few values are given in Table 6.5.

For matching the first moment we have $p = 1$ and $x_k = 2k$. The key equations become

$$m_0^k = \int_{2k}^{2k+2} \frac{x - 2k - 2}{-2}(0.1)e^{-0.1x}\,dx = 5e^{-0.1(2k+2)} - 4e^{-0.1(2k)},$$

$$m_1^k = \int_{2k}^{2k+2} \frac{x - 2k}{2}(0.1)e^{-0.1x}\,dx = -6e^{-0.1(2k+2)} + 5e^{-0.1(2k)},$$

and then

$$f_0 = m_0^0 = 5e^{-0.2} - 4 = 0.09365,$$
$$f_j = m_1^{j-1} + m_0^j = 5e^{-0.1(2j-2)} - 10e^{-0.1(2j)} + 5e^{-0.1(2j+2)}.$$

The first few values also are given in Table 6.5. A more direct solution for matching the first moment is provided in Exercise 6.11. □

Table 6.5 Discretization of the exponential distribution by two methods

j	f_j rounding	f_j matching
0	0.09516	0.09365
1	0.16402	0.16429
2	0.13429	0.13451
3	0.10995	0.11013
4	0.09002	0.09017
5	0.07370	0.07382
6	0.06034	0.06044
7	0.04940	0.04948
8	0.04045	0.04051
9	0.03311	0.03317
10	0.02711	0.02716

This method of local moment matching was introduced by Gerber and Jones [48] and Gerber [47] and further studied by Panjer and Lutek [90] for a variety of empirical and analytical severity distributions. In assessing the impact of errors, Panjer and Lutek [90] found that two moments were usually sufficient and that adding a third moment requirement adds only marginally to the accuracy. Furthermore, the rounding method and the first-moment method ($p = 1$) had similar errors while the second-moment method ($p = 2$) provided significant improvement. The specific formulas for the method of rounding and the method of matching the first moment are given in Appendix B. A reason to favor matching zero or one moment is that the resulting probabilities will always be nonnegative. When matching two or more moments, this cannot be guaranteed.

The methods described here are qualitatively similar to numerical methods used to solve Volterra integral equations such as equation (6.18) developed in numerical analysis (see, for example, Baker [8]).

6.7 FAST FOURIER TRANSFORM METHODS

Inversion methods discussed in this section are used to obtain numerically the probability function, from a known expression for a transform, such as the pgf, mgf, or cf of the desired function.

Compound distributions lend themselves naturally to this approach because their transforms are compound functions and are easily evaluated when both frequency and severity components are known. The pgf and cf of the aggregate loss distribution are

$$P_S(z) = P_N[P_X(z)]$$

and
$$\varphi_S(z) = \mathrm{E}[e^{iSz}] = P_N[\varphi_X(z)], \tag{6.22}$$

respectively. The characteristic function always exists and is unique. Conversely, for a given characteristic function, there always exists a unique distribution. The objective of inversion methods is to obtain the distribution numerically from the characteristic function (6.22).

It is worth mentioning that there has recently been much research in other areas of applied probability on obtaining the distribution numerically from the associated Laplace–Stieltjes transform. These techniques are applicable to the evaluation of compound distributions in the present context but will not be discussed further here. A good survey is in the article [1].

The FFT is an algorithm that can be used for inverting characteristic functions to obtain densities of discrete random variables. The FFT comes from the field of signal processing. It was first used for the inversion of characteristic functions of compound distributions by Bertram [16] and is explained in detail with applications to aggregate loss calculation by Robertson [101].

Definition 6.14 *For any continuous function $f(x)$, the **Fourier transform** is the mapping*

$$\tilde{f}(z) = \int_{-\infty}^{\infty} f(x)e^{izx}\, dx. \tag{6.23}$$

The original function can be recovered from its Fourier transform as

$$f(x) = \frac{1}{2\pi} \int_{-\infty}^{\infty} \tilde{f}(z)e^{-izx}\, dz.$$

When $f(x)$ is a probability density function, $\tilde{f}(z)$ is its characteristic function. For our applications, $f(x)$ will be real valued. From formula (6.23), $\tilde{f}(z)$ is complex valued. When $f(x)$ is a probability function of a discrete (or mixed) distribution, the definitions can be easily generalized (see, for example, Fisz [38]).

Definition 6.15 *Let f_x denote a function defined for all integer values of x that is periodic with period length n (that is, $f_{x+n} = f_x$ for all x). For the vector $(f_0, f_1, \ldots, f_{n-1})$, the **discrete Fourier transform** is the mapping $\tilde{f}_x$, $x = \ldots, -1, 0, 1, \ldots$, defined by*

$$\tilde{f}_k = \sum_{j=0}^{n-1} f_j \exp\left(\frac{2\pi i}{n} jk\right), \quad k = \ldots, -1, 0, 1, \ldots. \tag{6.24}$$

This mapping is bijective. In addition, $\tilde{f}_k$ is also periodic with period length n. The inverse mapping is

$$f_j = \frac{1}{n} \sum_{k=0}^{n-1} \tilde{f}_k \exp\left(-\frac{2\pi i}{n} kj\right), \quad j = \ldots, -1, 0, 1, \ldots. \tag{6.25}$$

This inverse mapping recovers the values of the original function.

Because of the periodic nature of f and $\tilde{f}$, we can think of the discrete Fourier transform as a bijective mapping of n points into n points. From formula (6.24), it is clear that, in order to obtain n values of $\tilde{f}_k$, the number of terms that need to be evaluated is of order n^2, that is, $O(n^2)$.

The **Fast Fourier Transform (FFT)** is an algorithm that reduces the number of computations required to be of order $O(n \ln_2 n)$. This can be a dramatic reduction in computations when n is large. The algorithm exploits the property that a discrete Fourier transform of length n can be rewritten as the sum of two discrete transforms, each of length $n/2$, the first consisting of the even-numbered points and the second consisting of the odd-numbered points.

$$
\begin{aligned}
\tilde{f}_k &= \sum_{j=0}^{n-1} f_j \exp\left(\frac{2\pi i}{n} jk\right) \\
&= \sum_{j=0}^{n/2-1} f_{2j} \exp\left(\frac{2\pi i}{n} 2jk\right) + \sum_{j=0}^{n/2-1} f_{2j+1} \exp\left[\frac{2\pi i}{n}(2j+1)k\right] \\
&= \sum_{j=0}^{m-1} f_{2j} \exp\left(\frac{2\pi i}{m} jk\right) + \exp\left(\frac{2\pi i}{n}k\right) \sum_{j=0}^{m-1} f_{2j+1} \exp\left(\frac{2\pi i}{m} jk\right),
\end{aligned}
$$

when $m = n/2$. Hence

$$
\tilde{f}_k = \tilde{f}_k^a + \exp\left(\frac{2\pi i}{n}k\right) \tilde{f}_k^b. \tag{6.26}
$$

These can, in turn, be written as the sum of two transforms of length $m/2$. This can be continued successively. For the lengths $n/2$, $m/2$,... to be integers, the FFT algorithm begins with a vector of length $n = 2^r$. The successive writing of the transforms into transforms of half the length will result, after r times, in transforms of length 1. Knowing the transform of length 1 will allow us to successively compose the transforms of length 2, 2^2, 2^3, ..., 2^r by simple addition using formula (6.26). Details of the methodology are found in Press et al. [96].

In our applications, we use the FFT to invert the characteristic function when discretization of the severity distribution is done. This is carried out as follows:

1. Discretize the severity distribution using some methods such as those described in Section 6.6, obtaining the discretized severity distribution

$$
f_X(0), f_X(1), \ldots, f_X(n-1),
$$

where $n = 2^r$ for some integer r and n is the number of points desired in the distribution $f_S(x)$ of aggregate losses.

2. Apply the FFT to this vector of values, obtaining $\varphi_X(z)$, the characteristic function of the **discretized** distribution. The result is also a vector of $n = 2^r$ values.

3. Transform this vector using the pgf transformation of the loss frequency distribution, obtaining $\varphi_S(z) = P_N[\varphi_X(z)]$, which is the characteristic function, that is, the discrete Fourier transform of the aggregate losses distribution, a vector of $n = 2^r$ values.

4. Apply the Inverse Fast Fourier Transform (IFFT), which is identical to the FFT except for a sign change and a division by n [see formula (6.25)]. This gives a vector of length $n = 2^r$ values representing the exact distribution of aggregate losses for the discretized severity model.

The FFT procedure requires a discretization of the severity distribution. When the number of points in the severity distribution is less than $n = 2^r$, the severity distribution vector must be padded with zeros until it is of length n.

When the severity distribution places probability on values beyond $x = n$, as is the case with most distributions discussed in Chapter 4, the probability that is missed in the right-hand tail beyond n can introduce some minor error in the final solution because the function and its transform are both assumed to be periodic with period n, when in reality they are not. The authors suggest putting all the remaining probability at the final point at $x = n$ so that the probabilities add up to 1 exactly. This allows for periodicity to be used for the severity distribution in the FFT algorithm and ensures that the final set of aggregate probabilities will sum to 1. However, it is imperative that n be selected to be large enough so that most all the aggregate probability occurs by the nth point. Example 6.16 provides an extreme illustration.

Example 6.16 *Suppose the random variable X takes on the values 1, 2, and 3 with probabilities 0.5, 0.4, and 0.1, respectively. Further suppose the number of losses has the Poisson distribution with parameter $\lambda = 3$. Use the FFT to obtain the distribution of S using $n = 8$ and $n = 4096$.*

In either case, the probability distribution of X is completed by adding one zero at the beginning (because S places probability at zero, the initial representation of X must also have the probability at zero given) and either 4 or 4092 zeros at the end. The results from employing the FFT and IFFT appear in Table 6.6. For the case $n = 8$, the eight probabilities sum to 1. For the case $n = 4096$, the probabilities also sum to 1, but there is not room here to show them all. It is easy to apply the recursive formula to this problem, which verifies that all of the entries for $n = 4096$ are accurate to the five decimal places presented. On the other hand, with $n = 8$, the FFT gives values that are clearly distorted. If any generalization can be made, it is that more of the extra probability has been added to the smaller values of S.   □

Table 6.6   Aggregate probabilities computed by the FFT and IFFT

s	$n = 8$ $f_S(s)$	$n = 4{,}096$ $f_S(s)$
0	0.11227	0.04979
1	0.11821	0.07468
2	0.14470	0.11575
3	0.15100	0.13256
4	0.14727	0.13597
5	0.13194	0.12525
6	0.10941	0.10558
7	0.08518	0.08305

Because the FFT and IFFT algorithms are available in many computer software packages and because the computer code is short, easy to write, and available (e.g., [96], pp. 411–412), no further technical details about the algorithm are given here. The reader can read any one of numerous books dealing with FFTs for a more detailed understanding of the algorithm. The technical details that allow the speeding up of the calculations from $O(n^2)$ to $O(\log_2 n)$ relate to the detailed properties of the discrete Fourier transform. Robertson [101] gives a good explanation of the FFT as applied to calculating the distribution of aggregate loss.

6.8   USING APPROXIMATING SEVERITY DISTRIBUTIONS

Whenever the severity distribution is calculated using an approximate method, the result is, of course, an approximation to the true aggregate distribution. In particular, the true aggregate distribution is often continuous (except, perhaps, with discrete probability at zero or at an aggregate censoring limit) while the approximate distribution either is discrete with probability at equally spaced values as with recursion and Fast Fourier Transform (FFT),or is discrete with probability $1/n$ at arbitrary values as with simulation. In this section we introduce reasonable ways to obtain values of $F_S(x)$ and $\mathrm{E}[(S \wedge x)^k]$ from those approximating distributions. In all cases we assume that the true distribution of aggregate losses is continuous, except perhaps with discrete probability at $S = 0$.

6.8.1   Arithmetic distributions

For both recursion and FFT methods, the approximating distribution can be written as $p_0, p_1, \ldots$, where $p_j = \Pr(S^* = jh)$ and S^* refers to the approximating distribution. While several methods of undiscretizing this distribu-

Table 6.7 Discrete approximation to the aggregate loss distribution

j	x	$f_X(x)$	$p_j = f_{S^*}(x)$
0	0	0.009934	0.335556
1	2	0.019605	0.004415
2	4	0.019216	0.004386
3	6	0.018836	0.004356
4	8	0.018463	0.004327
5	10	0.018097	0.004299
6	12	0.017739	0.004270
7	14	0.017388	0.004242
8	16	0.017043	0.004214
9	18	0.016706	0.004186
10	20	0.016375	0.004158

tion are possible, we will introduce only one. It assumes that we can obtain $g_0 = \Pr(S = 0)$, the true probability that aggregate losses are zero. The method is based on constructing a continuous approximation to S^* by assuming that the probability p_j is uniformly spread over the interval $(j - \frac{1}{2})h$ to $(j + \frac{1}{2})h$ for $j = 1, 2, \ldots$. For the interval from 0 to $h/2$, a discrete probability of g_0 is placed at zero and the remaining probability, $p_0 - g_0$, is spread uniformly over the interval. Let S^{**} be the random variable with this mixed distribution. All quantities of interest are then computed using S^{**}.

Example 6.17 *Let N have the geometric distribution with $\beta = 2$ and let X have the exponential distribution with $\theta = 100$. Use recursion with a span of 2 to approximate the distribution of aggregate losses and then obtain a continuous approximation.*

The exponential distribution was discretized using the method that preserves the first moment. The probabilities appear in Table 6.7. Also presented are the aggregate probabilities computed using the recursive formula. We also note that $g_0 = \Pr(N = 0) = (1 + \beta)^{-1} = \frac{1}{3}$. For $j = 1, 2, \ldots$ the continuous approximation has pdf $f_{S^{**}}(x) = f_{S^*}(2j)/2$, $2j-1 < x \le 2j+1$. We also have $\Pr(S^{**} = 0) = \frac{1}{3}$ and $f_{S^{**}}(x) = (0.335556 - \frac{1}{3})/1 = 0.002223$, $0 < x \le 1$. $\square$

Returning to the original problem, it is possible to work out the general formulas for the basic quantities. For the cdf,

$$F_{S^{**}}(x) = g_0 + \int_0^x \frac{p_0 - g_0}{h/2} ds$$

$$= g_0 + \frac{2x}{h}(p_0 - g_0), \quad 0 \le x \le \frac{h}{2},$$

and

$$F_{S^{**}}(x) = \sum_{i=0}^{j-1} p_i + \int_{(j-1/2)h}^{x} \frac{p_j}{h} \, ds$$

$$= \sum_{i=0}^{j-1} p_i + \frac{x - (j - 1/2)h}{h} p_j, \quad \left(j - \frac{1}{2}\right) h < x \leq \left(j + \frac{1}{2}\right) h.$$

For the limited expected value (LEV),

$$E[(S^{**} \wedge x)^k] = 0^k g_0 + \int_0^x s^k \frac{p_0 - g_0}{h/2} \, ds + x^k [1 - F_{S^{**}}(x)]$$

$$= \frac{2x^{k+1}(p_0 - g_0)}{h(k+1)} + x^k[1 - F_{S^{**}}(x)], \quad 0 < x \leq \frac{h}{2},$$

and

$$E[(S^{**} \wedge x)^k] = 0^k g_0 + \int_0^{h/2} s^k \frac{p_0 - g_0}{h/2} \, ds + \sum_{i=1}^{j-1} \int_{(i-1/2)h}^{(i+1/2)h} s^k \frac{p_i}{h} \, ds$$

$$+ \int_{(j-1/2)h}^{x} s^k \frac{p_j}{h} ds + x^k [1 - F_{S^{**}}(x)]$$

$$= \frac{(h/2)^k (p_0 - g_0)}{k+1} + \sum_{i=1}^{j-1} \frac{h^k [(i + 1/2)^{k+1} - (i - 1/2)^{k+1}]}{k+1} p_i$$

$$+ \frac{x^{k+1} - [(j - 1/2)h]^{k+1}}{h(k+1)} p_j$$

$$+ x^k [1 - F_{S^{**}}(x)], \quad \left(j - \frac{1}{2}\right) h < x \leq \left(j + \frac{1}{2}\right) h.$$

For $k = 1$ this reduces to

$$E(S^{**} \wedge x) = \begin{cases} x(1 - g_0) - \dfrac{x^2}{h}(p_0 - g_0), & 0 < x \leq \dfrac{h}{2}, \\ \dfrac{h}{4}(p_0 - g_0) + \displaystyle\sum_{i=1}^{j-1} ihp_i + \dfrac{x^2 - [(j - 1/2)h]^2}{2h} p_j \\ \qquad + x[1 - F_{S^{**}}(x)], & \left(j - \dfrac{1}{2}\right) h < x \leq \left(j + \dfrac{1}{2}\right) h. \end{cases} \tag{6.27}$$

These formulas are summarized in Appendix B.

Example 6.18 (Example 6.17 continued) *Compute the cdf and LEV at integral values from 1 to 10 using S^*, S^{**}, and the exact distribution of aggregate losses.*

The exact distribution is available for this example. It was developed in Example 6.4 where it was determined that $\Pr(S = 0) = (1 + \beta)^{-1} = \frac{1}{3}$ and

Table 6.8 Comparison of true aggregate payment values and two approximations

x	cdf			LEV		
	S	S^*	S^{**}	S	S^*	S^{**}
1	0.335552	0.335556	0.335556	0.66556	0.66444	0.66556
2	0.337763	0.339971	0.337763	1.32890	1.32889	1.32890
3	0.339967	0.339971	0.339970	1.99003	1.98892	1.99003
4	0.342163	0.344357	0.342163	2.64897	2.64895	2.64896
5	0.344352	0.344357	0.344356	3.30571	3.30459	3.30570
6	0.346534	0.348713	0.346534	3.96027	3.96023	3.96025
7	0.348709	0.348713	0.348712	4.61264	4.61152	4.61263
8	0.350876	0.353040	0.350876	5.26285	5.26281	5.26284
9	0.353036	0.353040	0.353039	5.91089	5.90977	5.91088
10	0.355189	0.357339	0.355189	6.55678	6.55673	6.55676

the pdf for the continuous part is

$$f_S(x) = \frac{\beta}{\theta(1+\beta)^2} \exp\left[-\frac{x}{\theta(1+\beta)}\right] = \frac{2}{900} e^{-x/300}, \quad x > 0.$$

From this we have

$$F_S(x) = \tfrac{1}{3} + \int_0^x \frac{2}{900} e^{-s/300}\, ds = 1 - \tfrac{2}{3} e^{-x/300}$$

and

$$E(S \wedge x) = \int_0^x \frac{2s}{900} e^{-s/300}\, ds + x\tfrac{2}{3} e^{-x/300} = 200(1 - e^{-x/300}).$$

The requested values are given in Table 6.8. □

6.9 COMPARISON OF METHODS

The recursive method has some significant advantages over the direct method using convolutions. The time required to compute an entire distribution of n points is reduced to $O(n^2)$ from $O(n^3)$ for the direct convolution method when its support is unlimited and to $O(n)$ when its support is limited. Furthermore, it provides exact values when the severity distribution is itself discrete (arithmetic). The only source of error is in the discretization of the severity distribution. Except for binomial models, the calculations are guaranteed to be numerically stable. This method is very easy to program in a few lines of computer code. However, it has a few disadvantages. The recursive method only works for the classes of frequency distributions described in

Chapter 5. Using distributions not based on the $(a, b, 0)$ and $(a, b, 1)$ classes requires modification of the formula or developing a new recursion. Numerous other recursions have been developed in the actuarial and statistical literature recently.

The FFT method is easy to use in that it uses standard routines available with many software packages. It is faster than the recursive method when n is large because it requires calculations of order $n \ln_2 n$ rather than n^2. However, if the severity distribution has a fixed (and not too large) number of points, the recursive method will require fewer computations because the sum in formula (6.13) will have at most m terms, reducing the order of required computations to be of order n, rather than n^2 in the case of no upper limit of the severity. The FFT method can be extended to the case where the severity distribution can take on negative values. Like the recursive method, it produces the entire distribution.

6.10 TVaR FOR AGGREGATE LOSSES

The calculation of the Tail-Value-at-Risk for continuous and discrete distributions was discussed in Sections 4.8 and 5.15. So far in the current chapter, we have dealt with the calculation of the exact (or approximating) distribution of the sum of a random number of losses. Clearly, the shape of this distribution depends on the shape of both the discrete frequency distribution and the continuous (or possibly discrete) severity distribution. If the severity distribution is light-tailed and the frequency distribution is not, then one could expect the tail of the aggregate loss distribution to be largely determined by the frequency distribution. Indeed, in the extreme case where all losses are of equal size, the shape of the aggregate loss distribution is completely determined by the frequency distribution. On the other hand, if the severity distribution is heavy-tailed and the frequency is not, then one could expect the shape of the tail of the aggregate loss distribution to be determined by the shape of the severity distribution because extreme outcomes will be determined with high probability by a single, or at least very few, large losses. In practice, if both the frequency and severity distribution are specified, it is easy to compute the TVaR at a specified quantile.

6.10.1 TVaR for discrete aggregate loss distributions

As discussed in earlier sections in this chapter, the numerical evaluation of the aggregate loss distribution requires a discretization of the severity distribution resulting in a discretized aggregate loss distribution. We, therefore, give formulas for the discrete case. Consider the random variable S representing the aggregate losses. The overall mean is the product of the means of the frequency and severity distributions Then the TVaR at quantile x_p for this distribution is[3]

$$\mathrm{TVaR}_p\,(S) = \mathrm{E}\,(S \mid S > x_p)$$

$$= x_p + \frac{\sum_x (x - x_p)_+ f_S(x)}{1 - F_S(x_p)}. \tag{6.28}$$

Noting that

$$\sum_x (x - x_p)_+ f_S(x) = \sum_x (x - x_p) f_S(x) + \sum_x (x_p - x)_+ f_S(x)$$

$$= \mathrm{E}(S) - x_p + \sum_x (x_p - x)_+ f_S(x)$$

$$= \mathrm{E}(S) - x_p + \sum_{x < x_p} (x_p - x) f_S(x), \tag{6.29}$$

we see that, because $S \geq 0$, the last sum in equation (6.29) is taken over a finite number of points, the points of support up to the quantile x_p.

Then the result of the equation (6.29) can be substituted into equation (6.28) to obtain the value of the TVaR. The value of the TVaR at high quantiles (as are required in operational risk) depends on the shape of the aggregate loss distribution. For certain distributions, we have analytic results that can give us very good estimates of the TVaR. To do this we first need to give some results on the extreme tail behavior of the aggregate loss distribution. We first focus on frequency distributions and then on severity distributions.

6.10.2   TVaR for some frequency distributions

We shall use the notation $A(x) \sim B(x)$ as $x \to \infty$ to denote that

$$\lim_{x \to \infty} \frac{A(x)}{B(x)} = 1.$$

Definition 6.19 *A function $C(x)$ is said to be slowly **varying at infinity** if $C(tx) \sim C(x)$ as $x \to \infty$ for all $t > 0$.*

The logarithm function $\ln(x)$ and any constant function are slowly varying at infinity while the exponential function $\exp(x)$ is not.

We now consider frequency distributions that satisfy

---

[3]The quantile must be one of the points of support of the aggregate loss distributions. If the selected quantile is not such a point, the TVaR can be calculated at the two adjacent points and the results interpolated to get an approximate value of the desired TVaR.

$$p_n \sim \theta^n n^\gamma C(n) \qquad (6.30)$$

where $0 < \theta < 1$ and $C(n)$ is slowly varying at infinity. Distributions satisfying formula (6.30) include the negative binomial, the geometric, the logarithmic, Poisson-ETNB (when $-1 < r < 0$) (see Teugels and Willmot [116]) including the Poisson-inverse Gaussian, and mixed Poisson distributions with mixing distributions that are sufficiently heavy-tailed (see Willmot [127]) and many compound distributions (see Willmot [126]).

We also consider severity distributions that have a moment generating function. In addition, we assume that there exists a number $\kappa > 0$ satisfying

$$M(\kappa) = \frac{1}{\theta}. \qquad (6.31)$$

In very general terms, this condition ensures that the severity distribution is not too heavy-tailed. For distributions whose moment generating functions increase indefinitely, the condition is always satisfied. However, some distributions (e.g. inverse Gaussian) have moment generating functions that have an upper limit, in which case condition (6.31) is satisfied only for some values of θ.

The following theorem of Embrechts, Maejima, and Teugels [32] gives the asymptotic shape of the tail of the aggregate loss distribution for large quantiles.

Theorem 6.20 *Let p_n denote that probability function of a counting distribution satisfying condition (6.30) and let $M(z)$ denote the mgf of a non-arithmetic severity distribution satisfying condition (6.31). Then if $-M'(\kappa) < \infty$, the tail of the corresponding aggregate loss distribution satisfies*

$$\overline{F}_S(x) \sim \frac{x^\gamma e^{-\kappa x} C(x)}{\kappa \left[-\theta M'(\kappa) \right]^{\gamma+1}}, \qquad x \to \infty. \qquad (6.32)$$

This theorem shows that the tail of the aggregate loss distribution looks like the product of a gamma density and a slowly varying function. The terms in the denominator form the necessary normalizing constant. The asymptotic formula for the tail in Theorem 6.20 can be used as an approximation for the tail for high quantiles. Having obtained this, we can obtain approximate values of the TVaR from

$$\mathrm{TVaR}_p\,(S) = \mathrm{E}\,(S \mid S > x_p)$$

$$= x_p + \frac{\int_{x_p}^\infty (x - x_p)\, f_S(x) dx}{1 - F_S(x_p)}$$

$$= x_p + \frac{\int_{x_p}^\infty \overline{F}_S\,(x)\, dx}{\overline{F}_S(x_p)}.$$

In some situations, we can get an asymptotic formula for the TVaR. It is often the case that the slowly varying function $C(x)$ in the asymptotic formula (6.32) is constant. This is the case for all examples given above, except possibly for the mixed Poisson case with certain mixing functions. When $C(x)$ is constant, we can rewrite formula (6.32) as

$$\overline{F}_S(x) \sim cx^\gamma e^{-\kappa x}, \quad x \to \infty$$

where the constant c absorbs all the constant terms in (6.32) (including the constant $C(x)$). Then using L'Hôpital's rule,

$$
\begin{aligned}
\lim_{x_p \to \infty} \frac{\int_{x_p}^\infty \overline{F}_S(x)\, dx}{\overline{F}_S(x_p)} &= \lim_{x_p \to \infty} \frac{\int_{x_p}^\infty \overline{F}_S(x)\, dx}{cx_p^\gamma e^{-\kappa x_p}} \\
&= \lim_{x_p \to \infty} \frac{-\overline{F}_S(x_p)}{c\gamma x_p^{\gamma-1} e^{-\kappa x_p} - c\kappa x_p^\gamma e^{-\kappa x_p}} \\
&= \lim_{x_p \to \infty} \frac{\overline{F}_S(x_p)}{cx_p^\gamma e^{-\kappa x_p}\left[\kappa - \frac{\gamma}{x_p}\right]} \\
&= \frac{1}{\kappa}.
\end{aligned}
$$

Thus, we obtain the TVaR approximately as

$$\mathrm{TVaR}_p\,(S) = \mathrm{E}\,(S \mid S > x_p)$$

$$\approx x_p + \frac{1}{\kappa}$$

which is exactly the TVaR for the exponential distribution with mean $1/\kappa$. In this case, the extreme tail becomes approximately exponential and so the conditional expected excess over the quantile x_p is constant.

6.10.3 TVaR for some severity distributions

In this subsection, we consider a class of severity distributions for which (6.31) does not hold. However, using different arguments than those used in the last Section 6.10.2, we can still obtain asymptotic results for the tail and the TVaR of the aggregate loss distribution. We consider the class of **subexponential distributions** with distribution functions satisfying

$$\lim_{x \to \infty} \frac{1 - F^{*2}(x)}{1 - F(x)} = 2. \tag{6.33}$$

It can be shown that if condition (6.33) holds then also

$$\lim_{x \to \infty} \frac{1 - F^{*n}(x)}{1 - F(x)} = n.$$

This class is quite broad and includes many of the distributions discussed in Section 4.2. We consider this class of severity distributions together with a general class of frequency distributions. The following theorem of Embrechts, Goldie and Veraverbeke [29] provides the asymptotic form of the tail of the distribution of aggregate losses.

Theorem 6.21 *Let N denote a random variable from a counting distribution with finite mean $E(N)$ and with mgf $M(z)$ that exists for some $z > 0$. Let X denote a continuous random variable whose cdf satisfies condition (6.33). Then*

$$\lim_{x \to \infty} \frac{1 - F_S(x)}{1 - F_X(x)} = E(N).$$

All discrete distributions with finite means that were considered in Chapter 5 have moment generating functions. This theorem means that for subexponential severity distributions the asymptotic tail of the aggregate loss distribution mirrors that of the severity distribution but multiplied by a factor reflecting the expected number of losses. It is interesting to note that the subexponential class includes those distributions satisfying

$$\overline{F}(x) \sim x^{-\gamma} C(x), \quad x \to \infty \tag{6.34}$$

where $C(x)$ is slowly varying at infinity and $|\gamma| < \infty$.

Example 6.22 *Approximate the TVaR for the transformed beta distribution.*

The transformed beta distribution (see Section 4.2) has pdf

$$f(x) = \frac{\Gamma(\alpha + \tau)}{\Gamma(\alpha)\Gamma(\tau)} \frac{\gamma(x/\theta)^{\gamma\tau}}{x[1 + (x/\theta)^{\gamma}]^{\alpha+\tau}}$$

Then, using L'Hôpital's rule,

$$
\begin{aligned}
\lim_{x \to \infty} \frac{\overline{F}(x)}{x^{-\alpha\gamma}} &= \lim_{x \to \infty} \frac{-f(x)}{-\alpha\gamma x^{-\alpha\gamma-1}} \\
&= \lim_{x \to \infty} \frac{1}{\alpha\gamma x^{-\alpha\gamma-1}} \frac{\Gamma(\alpha+\tau)}{\Gamma(\alpha)\Gamma(\tau)} \frac{\gamma(x/\theta)^{\gamma\tau}}{x[1 + (x/\theta)^{\gamma}]^{\alpha+\tau}} \\
&= \frac{\Gamma(\alpha+\tau)}{\alpha\Gamma(\alpha)\Gamma(\tau)} \theta^{\alpha\gamma} \lim_{x \to \infty} \left(\frac{x^{\gamma}}{\theta^{\gamma} + x^{\gamma}} \right)^{\alpha+\tau} \\
&= \frac{\Gamma(\alpha+\tau)}{\alpha\Gamma(\alpha)\Gamma(\tau)} \theta^{\alpha\gamma}
\end{aligned}
$$

Thus

$$\overline{F}(x) \sim \frac{\Gamma(\alpha+\tau)}{\alpha\Gamma(\alpha)\Gamma(\tau)} \left(\frac{x}{\theta}\right)^{-\alpha\gamma}, \quad x \to \infty$$

which satisfies (6.34). Then from Theorem 6.21

$$\overline{F}_S(x) \sim \mathrm{E}(N)\frac{\Gamma(\alpha+\tau)}{\alpha\Gamma(\alpha)\Gamma(\tau)}\left(\frac{x}{\theta}\right)^{-\alpha\gamma}, \quad x \to \infty.$$

Using L'Hôpital's rule, the resulting asymptotic shape of the conditional expected excess amount over a quantile can be found to be

$$
\begin{aligned}
\lim_{x_p \to \infty} \frac{\int_{x_p}^{\infty} \overline{F}_S(x)\,dx}{\overline{F}_S(x_p)} &= \lim_{x_p \to \infty} \frac{\int_{x_p}^{\infty} \overline{F}_S(x)\,dx}{\mathrm{E}(N)\dfrac{\Gamma(\alpha+\tau)}{\alpha\Gamma(\alpha)\Gamma(\tau)}\left(\frac{x_p}{\theta}\right)^{-\alpha\gamma}} \\[2mm]
&= \lim_{x_p \to \infty} \frac{\mathrm{E}(N)\dfrac{\Gamma(\alpha+\tau)}{\alpha\Gamma(\alpha)\Gamma(\tau)}\dfrac{1}{\alpha\gamma-1}\left(\frac{x_p}{\theta}\right)^{-\alpha\gamma+1}}{\mathrm{E}(N)\dfrac{\Gamma(\alpha+\tau)}{\alpha\Gamma(\alpha)\Gamma(\tau)}\left(\frac{x_p}{\theta}\right)^{-\alpha\gamma}} \\[2mm]
&= \frac{x_p}{\alpha\gamma-1}.
\end{aligned}
$$

Thus for large quantiles, the TVaR is approximately a multiple of the quantile

$$\mathrm{TVaR}_p(S) = \mathrm{E}(S \mid S > x_p)$$

$$\approx \frac{\alpha\gamma}{\alpha\gamma-1}x_p.$$

The mean of the transformed beta distribution exists only if $\alpha\gamma > 1$. The special cases of this distribution are the generalized Pareto ($\gamma = 1$), the Pareto ($\gamma = 1$, $\tau = 1$), the Burr ($\tau = 1$), and the loglogistic ($\alpha = 1$, $\tau = 1$). □

Example 6.23 *Approximate the TVaR for the lognormal distribution.*

Embrechts, Goldie, and Veraverbeke [29] show that the lognormal distribution is subexponential. The tail of the distribution satisfies

$$\overline{F}(x) \sim \frac{1}{\sqrt{2\pi}}\left(\frac{\sigma}{\ln x - \mu}\right)\exp\left[-\frac{1}{2}\left(\frac{\ln x - \mu}{\sigma}\right)^2\right], \quad x \to \infty.$$

Therefore the tail of the aggregate loss distribution satisfies

$$\overline{F}_S(x) \sim \mathrm{E}(N)\frac{1}{\sqrt{2\pi}}\left(\frac{\sigma}{\ln x - \mu}\right)\exp\left[-\frac{1}{2}\left(\frac{\ln x - \mu}{\sigma}\right)^2\right], \quad x \to \infty.$$

The expected loss in excess of a high quantile x_p is easily obtained as

$$\lim_{x_p \to \infty} \frac{\int_{x_p}^{\infty} \overline{F}_S(x)\,dx}{\overline{F}_S(x_p)} = \frac{x_p\sigma^2}{\ln x_p - \mu}.$$

Finally the TVaR for the asymptotic approximation for the lognormal distribution is then

$$\text{TVaR}_p(S) = \text{E}(S \mid S > x_p)$$

$$\approx x_p + \frac{x_p \sigma^2}{\ln x_p - \mu},$$

which increases at a rate slower than linear.   □

An intermediate class of distributions that can be used as severity distributions has been discussed by Embrechts and Goldie [28]. This class of medium-tailed distributions may or may not determine the tail of the aggregate loss distribution.

Definition 6.24 *A distribution is* **medium tailed** *if there exists a $\gamma > 0$ with*

$$\lim_{x \to \infty} \frac{1 - F^{*2}(x)}{1 - F(x)} = 2M(\gamma) < \infty$$

and

$$\lim_{x \to \infty} \frac{1 - F(x - y)}{1 - F(x)} = e^{\gamma y}$$

for any y.

If $\gamma = 0$, the subexponential class results. For the medium-tailed class, Teugels [115] shows that Theorem 6.21 generalizes to

$$\lim_{x \to \infty} \frac{1 - F_S(x)}{1 - F(x)} = P'[M(\gamma)] < \infty$$

if $P'[M(\gamma)] < \infty$.

Example 6.25 *Approximate TVaR of the inverse Gaussian distribution.*

The inverse Gaussian distribution with pdf

$$f(x) = \left(\frac{\theta}{2\pi x^3}\right)^{1/2} \exp\left(-\frac{\theta}{2x}\left(\frac{x - \mu}{\mu}\right)^2\right)$$

can be shown to be medium-tailed. The tail of the distribution satisfies

$$\overline{F}(x) \sim \left(\frac{2}{\pi\theta}\right)^{1/2} \mu^3 \exp\left(\frac{\theta}{\mu}\right) \cdot x^{-\frac{3}{2}} \exp\left(-\frac{\theta x}{2\mu^2}\right).$$

From this, $\gamma = \frac{\theta}{2\mu^2}$ and $M(\gamma) = \exp\left(\frac{\theta}{\mu}\right)$. Then for a particular choice of frequency distribution, if $P'[M(\gamma)] < \infty$, the tail of the aggregate loss distribution satisfies

$$\overline{F}(x) \sim P'\left[M\left(\frac{\theta}{2\mu^2}\right)\right]\left(\frac{2}{\pi\theta}\right)^{1/2} \mu^3 \exp\left(\frac{\theta}{\mu}\right) \cdot x^{-\frac{3}{2}} \exp\left(-\frac{\theta x}{2\mu^2}\right).$$

Finally, the conditional expected excess loss over quantile x_p can be shown to satisfy

$$\lim_{x_p \to \infty} \frac{\int_{x_p}^{\infty} \overline{F}_S(x)\,dx}{\overline{F}_S(x_p)} = \frac{2\mu^2}{\theta}.$$

So the approximate TVaR for the inverse Gaussian distribution is

$$\mathrm{TVaR}_p(S) = \mathrm{E}(S \mid S > x_p)$$

$$\approx x_p + \frac{2\mu^2}{\theta}.$$

$\square$

Embrechts [27] showed that the generalized inverse Gaussian (which includes the inverse Gaussian) distribution can be light- or medium-tailed depending on the choice of parameters.

6.10.4   Summary

Section 6.10 and related results suggest that the tail behavior of the aggregate loss distribution is essentially determined by the heavier of the frequency and severity distributions. If the frequency distribution is sufficiently heavy-tailed and the severity distribution is light-tailed, the tail of the aggregate loss distribution is determined by the frequency distribution through Theorem 6.20. If the severity distribution is sufficiently heavy-tailed and if the frequency distribution has a moment generating function, and is thus light-tailed, the tail of the aggregate loss distribution looks like a rescaled severity distribution. For medium-tailed distributions, such as the inverse Gaussian, the tail may or may not be determined by the severity distribution, depending on the parameter values of that severity distribution.

6.11   EXERCISES

6.1 For pgfs satisfying equation (6.2), show that the mean is proportional to α.

6.2 From equation (6.5), show that the relationships between the moments in formulas (6.6) hold.

6.3 Aggregate losses have been modeled by a compound negative binomial distribution with parameters $r = 15$ and $\beta = 5$. The loss amounts are uniformly distributed on the interval $(0, 10)$. Using the normal approximation, determine the amount such that the probability that losses will exceed that amount is 0.05.

EXERCISES   199

6.4 Assume X_1, X_2, and X_3 are mutually independent loss random variables with probability functions as given in Table 6.9. Determine the pf of $S = X_1 + X_2 + X_3$.

Table 6.9 Distributions for Exercise 6.4

x	$f_1(x)$	$f_2(x)$	$f_3(x)$
0	0.90	0.50	0.25
1	0.10	0.30	0.25
2	0.00	0.20	0.25
3	0.00	0.00	0.25

6.5 You have been asked by a risk manager to analyze office cigarette smoking patterns in order to assess health cost risks of employees. The risk manager has provided the information in Table 6.10 about the distribution of the number of cigarettes smoked during a workday. The number of male employees in a randomly selected office of n employees has a binomial distribution with parameters n and 0.4. Determine the mean and the standard deviation of the number of cigarettes smoked during a workday in a randomly selected office of eight employees.

Table 6.10 Data for Exercise 6.5

	Male	Female
Mean	6	3
Variance	64	31

6.6 A portfolio of risks produces N losses with the probabilities $\Pr(N = n)$ and loss amount distribution $f_X(x)$ according to the tables:

Table 6.11 Frequency Data for Exercise 6.6

n	$\Pr(N = n)$
0	0.5
1	0.4
3	0.1

Individual loss amounts and N are mutually independent. Calculate the probability that aggregate losses will exceed expected losses by a factor of 3 or more.

Table 6.12   Severity Data for Exercise 6.6

x	$f_X(x)$
1	0.9
10	0.1

6.7 The following questions concern closure under convolution.

(a) Show that the gamma and inverse Gaussian distributions are closed under convolution. Show that the gamma distribution has the additional property mentioned in Example 6.7.

(b) Discrete distributions can also be used as severity distributions. Which of the distributions in Chapter 5 are closed under convolution? How can this information be used in simplifying calculation of compound probabilities of the form (5.14)?

6.8 A compound negative binomial distribution has parameters $\beta = 1, r = 2$, and severity distribution $\{f_X(x); \ x = 0, 1, 2, \ldots\}$. How do the parameters of the distribution change if the severity distribution is $\{g_X(x) = f_X(x)/[1 - f_X(0)]; \ x = 1, 2, \ldots\}$ but the distribution of aggregate losses remains unchanged?

6.9 Consider the compound logarithmic distribution with exponential severity distribution.

(a) Show that the probability density function of aggregate losses may be expressed as

$$f_S(x) = \frac{1}{\ln(1+\beta)} \sum_{n=1}^{\infty} \frac{1}{n!} \left[\frac{\beta}{\theta(1+\beta)} \right]^n x^{n-1} e^{-x/\theta}.$$

(b) Reduce this to

$$f_S(x) = \frac{\exp\{-x/[\theta(1+\beta)]\} - \exp(-x/\theta)}{x \ln(1+\beta)}.$$

6.10 Consider a severity distribution that is a finite mixture of gamma distributions with integer shape parameters (such gamma distributions are called Erlang distributions), that is, one that may be expressed as

$$f_X(x) = \sum_{k=1}^{r} q_k \frac{\theta^{-k} x^{k-1} e^{-x/\theta}}{(k-1)!}, \quad x > 0.$$

(a) Show that the moment generating function may be written as

$$M_X(z) = Q\{(1 - \theta z)^{-1}\},$$

where

$$Q(z) = \sum_{k=1}^{r} q_k z^k$$

is the pgf of the distribution $\{q_1, q_2, \ldots, q_r\}$. Thus interpret $f_X(x)$ as the pf of a compound distribution.

(b) Show that the mgf of S is

$$M_S(z) = C\{(1 - \theta z)^{-1}\},$$

where

$$C(z) = \sum_{k=0}^{\infty} c_k z^k = P_N\{Q(z)\}.$$

(c) Describe how the distribution $\{c_k; \ k = 0, 1, 2, \ldots\}$ may be calculated recursively if the number of losses distribution is a member of the $(a, b, 1)$ class (Section 5.6).

(d) Show that the distribution function of S is given by

$$
\begin{aligned}
F_S(x) &= 1 - \sum_{n=1}^{\infty} c_n \sum_{j=0}^{n-1} \frac{(x/\theta)^j e^{-x/\theta}}{j!} \\
&= 1 - e^{-x/\theta} \sum_{j=0}^{\infty} \bar{C}_j \frac{(x/\theta)^j}{j!}, \qquad x \geq 0,
\end{aligned}
$$

where $\bar{C}_j = \sum_{n=j+1}^{\infty} c_n$.

6.11 Show that the method of local moment matching with $k = 1$ (matching total probability and the mean) using equations (6.20) and (6.21) results in

$$f_0 = 1 - \frac{\mathrm{E}[X \wedge h]}{h}$$

$$f_i = \frac{2\mathrm{E}[X \wedge ih] - \mathrm{E}[X \wedge (i-1)h] - \mathrm{E}[X \wedge (i+1)h]}{h}, \qquad i = 1, 2, \ldots,$$

and that $\{f_i; \ i = 0, 1, 2, \ldots\}$ forms a valid distribution with the same mean as the original severity distribution. Using the formula given here, verify the formula given in Example 6.13.

6.12 You are the agent for a baseball player who wants an incentive contract that will pay the amounts given in Table 6.13. The number of times at bat has a Poisson distribution with $k = 200$. The parameter x is determined so that the probability of the player earning at least $4,000,000 is at least 95%. Determine the player's expected compensation.

6.13 A weighted average of two Poisson distributions

$$p_k = w\frac{e^{-\lambda_1}\lambda_1^k}{k!} + (1 - w)\frac{e^{-\lambda_2}\lambda_2^k}{k!}$$

has been used by some authors,for example Tröbliger [118], to treat automobile drivers as either "good" or "bad" (see Example 5.26).

(a) Find the pgf $P_N(z)$ of the number of losses in terms of the two pgfs $P_1(z)$ and $P_2(z)$ of the number of losses of the two types of drivers.

(b) Let $f_X(x)$ denote a severity distribution defined on the nonnegative integers. How can formula (6.15) be used to compute the distribution of aggregate loss for the entire group?

(c) Can this be extended to other frequency distributions?

6.14 A compound Poisson aggregate loss model has five expected losses per year. The severity distribution is defined on positive multiples of $1,000. Given that $f_S(1) = e^{-5}$ and $f_S(2) = \frac{5}{2}e^{-5}$, determine $f_X(2)$.

6.15 For a compound Poisson distribution, $\lambda = 6$ and individual losses have pf $f_X(1) = f_X(2) = f_X(4) = \frac{1}{3}$. Some of the pf values for the aggregate distribution S are given in Table 6.14. Determine $f_S(6)$.

6.16 Consider the $(a, b, 0)$ class of frequency distributions and any severity distribution defined on the positive integers $\{1, 2, \ldots, M < \infty\}$, where M is the maximum possible single loss.

(a) Show that for the compound distribution the following backward recursion holds:

$$f_X(x) = \frac{f_S(x + M) - \sum_{y=1}^{M-1}\left(a + b\frac{M - y}{x + M}\right)f_X(M - y)f_S(x + y)}{\left(a + b\frac{M}{x + M}\right)f_X(M)}.$$

Table 6.13   Data for Exercise 6.12

Type of hit	Probability of hit per time at bat	Compensation per hit
Single	0.14	x
Double	0.05	$2x$
Triple	0.02	$3x$
Home run	0.03	$4x$

(b) For the binomial (m, q) frequency distribution, how can the above formula be used to obtain the distribution of aggregate losses? See Panjer and Wang [91].

6.17 On a given day, interruptions to activity of certain business processes are of two types labelled A and C. Let the number of such interruptions per month be N_A and N_C respectively. Assume N_A and N_C have Poisson distributions with parameters 3 and 2, respectively. The distributions of length of such interruptions are given in Table 6.15 It is reasonable to assume that N_A, N_C, and the lengths of interruption are independent. If losses are \$200 per hour while a machine is broken. Determine the probability that the loss in a given month is less than or equal to \$800.

6.18 You are given two independent compound Poisson random variables S_1 and S_2, where $f_j(x)$, $j = 1, 2$, are the two single-loss size distributions. You are given $\lambda_1 = \lambda_2 = 1$, $f_1(1) = 1$, and $f_2(1) = f_2(2) = 0.5$. Let $F_X(x)$ be the single-loss size distribution function associated with the compound distribution $S = S_1 + S_2$. Calculate $F_X^{*4}(6)$.

6.19 The variable S has a compound Poisson losses distribution with the following: a) Individual loss amounts are equal to 1, 2, or 3; b) $E(S) = 56$; c) $Var(S) = 126$; and, d) $\lambda = 29$. Determine the expected number of losses of size 2.

6.20 For a compound Poisson distribution with positive integer loss amounts, the probability function follows:

$$f_S(x) = \frac{1}{x}[0.16f_S(x - 1) + kf_S(x - 2) + 0.72f_S(x - 3)], \quad x = 1, 2, 3, \dots.$$

The expected value of aggregate losses is 1.68. Determine the expected number of losses.

6.21 A population has two classes of drivers. The number of accidents per individual driver has a geometric distribution. For a driver selected at random from Class I, the geometric distribution parameter has a uniform distribution

Table 6.14   Data for Exercise 6.15

x	$f_S(x)$
3	0.0132
4	0.0215
5	0.0271
6	$f_S(6)$
7	0.0410

Table 6.15   Data for Exercise 6.17

	Type A	Type C
1 hour	0.4	0.9
2 hour	0.6	0.1

over the interval $(0, 1)$. Twenty-five percent of the drivers are in Class I. All drivers in Class II have expected number of losses 0.25. For a driver selected at random from this population, determine the probability of exactly two accidents.

6.22 Demonstrate that if the exponential distribution is discretized by the method of rounding, the resulting discrete distribution is a ZM geometric distribution. Use a computer and compare the successive probabilities.

6.23 The physical damage incurred by the trucks in a company's fleet are self-insured by the company and treated as operational risk. The number of losses in a year has a Poisson distribution with $\lambda = 5$. The amount of a single loss has a gamma distribution with $\alpha = 0.5$ and $\theta = 2,500$ where θ is measure in dollars. The company is considering buying insurance to mitigate part of the risk. The proposed insurance contract covers aggregate losses in excess of \$20,000. Determine the probability that losses will reach the threshold of \$20,000. Use a span of \$100 and the method of rounding. This requires a computer.

7

Extreme value theory:
The study of jumbo losses

If there is a possibility of several things going wrong, the one that causes the most damage is the one to go wrong.
Corollary: If there is a worse time for something to go wrong, it will happen then.

— Murphy

7.1 INTRODUCTION

As discussed in Chapter 1, operational risks range from high-frequency-low-severity (HFLS) to low-frequency-high-severity (LFHS) types. Losses of the HFLS type lend themselves naturally to aggregate loss modeling as described in Chapter 6. The primary focus is on the impact of the sum of all the losses. While the same can be said of LFHS type, there also must be a focus on individual events that are increasingly rare but that have very large potential losses when a loss occurs. In the insurance field these are called "jumbo" risks or "jumbo" losses. In operational risk, jumbo losses are those that, with a single occurrence, can have a major impact on the organization, even putting its survival in jeopardy.

In practice, there are two major problems with managing jumbo risks. First, there are many risk types for which a loss has never occurred. Statistical analysis of historical data cannot in itself be very useful, except to indicate that the type of loss in question is very rare. The best statistical analysis is based on the study of very large losses over a period of time. The second problem with studying extreme outcomes, in particular the single largest loss each year, is that there can only be one observation per year. In practice, this means that the number of data points for analysis is inevitably small.

There are alternatives. One alternative is to study the largest loss each month rather than each year. This increases the number of data points by a factor of 12. However, if we are interested in understanding the annual maximum, it will be necessary to "translate" monthly results into annual results. Fortunately, this is easy to do in practice. Another alternative is to study several of the largest losses each year rather than the single largest. However, the statistical analysis of such high-order statistics becomes significantly more complex.

Another alternative is to study all the large losses, where "large" is defined by some threshold. All losses in excess of the threshold are considered large. Then one can study the impact of increasing the level of the threshold on the distribution, or some characteristics of the distribution) of the remaining large losses. In particular, we will examine the mean excess loss over the threshold as the threshold changes.

Extreme value theory (EVT) is a well-developed body of knowledge. It focuses on the asymptotic shape of the distribution of the largest observations and the excesses over thresholds. The use of EVT in the analysis of operational risk may be somewhat different from that in other fields. Consider the applications in the study of flood damage. Engineers designing dams for flood control are interested in knowing the probability of high water levels. These are typically described in terms like "the 100-year level" or the "one-year-in-a-hundred" event and are usually interpreted as the 99% percentile of the distribution of annual maxima. Building a dam at this level indicates a 1% annual probability of exceedence. This means that there is a 1% chance of loss as a result of flooding in a one-year period. In our operational risk environment, the focus is not only on the single largest event. Because we are interested in the impact of all operational risk losses, study of the extreme loss does not give complete insight in to the overall impact, unless that extreme loss is so much larger than other losses that it completely dominates them. If this is the case, understanding the potential impact of the largest losses provides opportunities for developing mitigation strategies for the occurrence of such extreme events. The study of all losses in excess of a threshold is useful in understanding the impact of those large losses and dealing with the consequences of those very large losses.

One of the key results in EVT is that the limiting distribution of the largest observation must be one of a very small number of distributions. Similarly, in a closely related result, the limiting distribution of the excess over a threshold must be one of a small number of distributions. The shape of the distribution from which the sample is drawn determines which one of the distributions is appropriate. This convenient theory allows us to rationally extrapolate to loss amounts that are well in excess of any historic loss and thus gives an idea of the magnitude of probabilities of jumbo losses, even when those losses have never before occurred.

7.2 EXTREME VALUE DISTRIBUTIONS

In this section, we introduce some distributions known as extreme value distributions. We do this here to provide background to the theoretical justification for the use of these distributions in later sections of this chapter. There are three related distributions, the Gumbel, Fréchet, and Weibull, in the family known as extreme value distributions. We also introduce some notation for convenient reference to these distributions used by Reiss and Thomas [98] in their comprehensive book dealing with extreme value theory and its applications.

Gumbel distribution

The standardized Gumbel distribution has df

$$F(x) = G_0(x) = \exp\left[-\exp\left(-x\right)\right], \ x > 0.$$

With location and scale parameters μ and θ included, it has df

$$F(x) = G_{0,\mu,\theta}(x) = \exp\left[-\exp\left(-\frac{x-\mu}{\theta}\right)\right], \ x > \mu, \ \theta > 0.$$

Fréchet distribution

The standardized Fréchet distribution has df

$$F(x) = G_{1,\alpha}(x) = \exp\left(-x^{-\alpha}\right), \ x \geq 0, \ \alpha > 0$$

where α is a shape parameter.

With location and scale parameters μ and θ included, it has df

$$F(x) = G_{1,\alpha,\mu,\theta}(x) = \exp\left[-\left(\frac{x-\mu}{\theta}\right)^{-\alpha}\right], \ x \geq \mu; \ \alpha, \theta > 0.$$

Note that the Fréchet distribution has support only for values of x greater than the location parameter μ. In the applications considered in this book, the location parameter will sometimes be set to zero, making the distribution a two-parameter distribution. The df of that two-parameter distribution will be denoted by $G_{1,\alpha,0,\theta}(x)$.

Weibull distribution

The standardized Weibull distribution has df

$$F(x) = G_{2,\alpha}(x) = \exp\left[-(-x)^{-\alpha}\right], \ x \leq 0, \ \alpha < 0.$$

With location and scale parameters μ and θ included, it has df

$$F(x) = G_{2,\alpha,\mu,\theta}(x) = \exp\left[-\left(-\frac{x-\mu}{\theta}\right)^{-\alpha}\right], \ x \leq \mu, \ \alpha < 0.$$

Note that this Weibull distribution has support only for values of x smaller than the location parameter μ. This distribution is often associated with the distribution of the minimum values of distributions and with distributions that have a finite right-hand endpoint of the support of the distribution. Because of this, it will not be considered in this book. It is referenced only for completeness of exposition of extreme value theory. It should be noted that because it has support only on values below a fixed maximum μ and because the parameter α is negative, this distribution is not the same as the Weibull distribution described in Chapter 4. However, that distribution can be obtained by a simple shifting and change of sign.

Generalized extreme value distribution

The generalized extreme value distribution is the family of distributions incorporating, in a single expression, the above three distributions as special cases. The general expression for the standardized df of the generalized extreme value distribution is

$$F(x) = \exp\left[-\left(1 + \frac{x}{\alpha}\right)^{-\alpha}\right].$$

For notational convenience, it is often written as

$$F(x) = G_\gamma(x) = \exp\left[-(1 + \gamma x)^{-1/\gamma}\right]. \tag{7.1}$$

Because the limiting value of $(1 + \gamma x)^{-1/\gamma}$ is $\exp(-x)$ as $\gamma \to 0$, it is clear that $G_0(x)$ is the standardized Gumbel distribution function. When γ is positive, the df $G_\gamma(x)$ has the form of a Fréchet distribution. When γ is negative, the df $G_\gamma(x)$ has the form of a Weibull distribution. With simple location and scale changes, these distributions can be written as standardized Fréchet and Weibull distributions.

7.3 DISTRIBUTION OF THE MAXIMUM

7.3.1 From a fixed number of losses

Consider a set of n observations of independent and identically distributed nonnegative random variables with common distribution function $F_X(x)$, where n is a fixed number. Let the maximum value of the n observations be denoted by M_n and let its distribution and density functions be denoted by $F_n(x)$ and $f_n(x)$. Then, because no observation can exceed the maximum, the df of the maximum is

$$F_n(x) = \Pr(M_n \leq x) = \Pr(X_1 \leq x, X_2 \leq x, ..., X_n \leq x).$$

Because of the independence of the observations, we can write

$$F_n(x) = \prod_{i=1}^{n} \Pr(X_i \le x) = [F_X(x)]^n . \tag{7.2}$$

This shows that the distribution function of the maximum is a simple function of the common distribution of the original random variables. As $n \to \infty$, the value of the right-hand side approaches either 0 or 1 depending on whether $F_X(x) < 1$ or $F_X(x) = 1$. Thus, the limiting distribution of the maximum is degenerate[1]. To avoid the effect of degeneracy in the limit, the study of the behavior of the maximum for large values of n requires appropriate normalization. This will be studied later in this chapter.

For nonnegative random variables, the mean (if it exists) of the maximum can be obtained as

$$E(M_n) = \int_0^\infty x f_n(x) dx$$
$$= \int_0^\infty [1 - F_n(x)] \, dx$$
$$= \int_0^\infty [1 - F_X(x)^n] \, dx.$$

It should be noted that for distributions with no upper limit of support, this maximum continues to increase without limit as $n \to \infty$. For distributions with a right-hand endpoint, the maximum approaches that right-hand endpoint as $n \to \infty$.

The second raw moment (if it exists) of the maximum can be obtained as

$$E(M_n^2) = \int_0^\infty x^2 f_n(x) dx$$
$$= 2 \int_0^\infty x [1 - F_n(x)] \, dx$$
$$= 2 \int_0^\infty x [1 - F_X(x)^n] \, dx.$$

Example 7.1 *From monthly to annual maxima.*

Suppose that we have carried out studies of the largest losses over many months and determined the distribution of the monthly maximum to be given by df $F(x)$. Then from equation (7.2), it follows that the distribution function of the annual maximum is given by $[F(x)]^{12}$.   □

---

[1] A degenerate distribution is a distribution that has all the probability at a single point.

Example 7.2 *Suppose that the monthly maximum in Example 7.1 follows a Gumbel distribution with df given by*

$$F(x) = G_{0,\mu,\theta}(x) = \exp\left[-\exp\left(-\frac{x-\mu}{\theta}\right)\right].$$

The annual maximum has distribution function given by

$$\begin{aligned}
[F(x)]^{12} &= \exp\left[-12\exp\left(-\frac{x-\mu}{\theta}\right)\right] \\
&= \exp\left[-\exp\left(-\frac{x-\mu^*}{\theta}\right)\right] \\
&= G_{0,\mu^*,\theta}(x)
\end{aligned}$$

where $\mu^* = \mu + \theta\ln 12$. □

This example shows that if the monthly maximum has a Gumbel distribution, the annual maximum also has a Gumbel distribution, but with a change in location.

Example 7.3 *Suppose instead that the monthly maximum in Example 7.1 follows a Fréchet distribution with df given by*

$$F(x) = G_{1,\alpha,\mu,\theta}(x) = \exp\left[-\left(\frac{x-\mu}{\theta}\right)^{-\alpha}\right].$$

Then the annual maximum has df given by

$$\begin{aligned}
[F(x)]^{12} &= \exp\left[-12\left(\frac{x-\mu}{\theta}\right)^{-\alpha}\right] \\
&= \exp\left[-\left(\frac{x-\mu}{\theta*}\right)^{-\alpha}\right] \\
&= G_{1,\alpha,\mu,\theta*}(x)
\end{aligned}$$

where $\theta^* = 12^{-1/\alpha}\theta$. □

This example shows that if the monthly maximum has a Fréchet distribution, the annual maximum also has a Fréchet distribution, but with a change in scale.

7.3.2   From a random number of losses

The distribution given by equation (7.2) assumes that the sample size each period is fixed. However, in operational risk modeling, because the number of losses is unknown in advance, we are generally interested in studying the behavior of a random number of losses. In this case, we can also get a very convenient expression for the largest of a random number of losses in a fixed time period.

Let N denote the random number of losses and its pgf by $P_N(z)$. We make the same independence assumptions as we did at the beginning of Chapter 6 where we studied the distribution of the sum of N losses. Here we consider the distribution of the maximum loss M_N where N is a random number:

$$
\begin{aligned}
F_{M_N}(x) &= \Pr(M_N \le x) \\
&= \sum_{n=0}^{\infty} \Pr(M_N \le x \mid N = n)\Pr(N = n) \\
&= \sum_{n=0}^{\infty} \Pr(N = n)\left[F_X(x)\right]^n. \\
&= P_N(F_X(x)).
\end{aligned}
\tag{7.3}
$$

Then, if we can specify the distribution of the frequency and severity of losses, we can easily have the exact distribution of the maximum loss. The distribution can be calculated for values for all nonnegative values of x. The distribution function (7.3) has value zero for negative values of x because only positive losses are considered. It has a jump at $x = 0$. The jump at $x = 0$ has value $P_N(F_X(0))$, the probability of no loss cost (either no loss event occurs, or all loss events have no cost). Further, if $F_X(0) = 0$ (all loss events have a positive loss), as is the case in most applications, the jump reduces to $P_N(0) = p_0$, the probability that no loss occurs, that is, that $N = 0$.

Example 7.4 *Consider a Poisson process that generates Poisson losses at a rate of λ losses per year.*

Then from (7.3), for a single year, the df of the maximum loss is given by

$$
F_{M_N}(x) = P_N(F_X(x)) = \exp\left[-\lambda\left(1 - F_X(x)\right)\right],
$$

and, for a period of k years, the df of the maximum loss is given by

$$
F_{M_N}(x) = \exp\left[-\lambda k\left(1 - F_X(x)\right)\right].
$$

$\square$

Example 7.5 (Example 7.4 continued) *Suppose, in addition, that the individual losses are exponentially distributed with*

$$
F_X(x) = 1 - \exp\left(-\frac{x}{\theta}\right), x > 0.
$$

Then the distribution of the maximum loss for a k-year period has df

$$F_{M_N}(x) = \exp\left[-k\lambda \exp\left(-\frac{x}{\theta}\right)\right]$$

which can be rewritten as

$$F_{M_N}(x) = \exp\left[-\exp\left(-\frac{x-\mu}{\theta}\right)\right], \quad x > 0$$

where $\mu = \theta \log(k\lambda)$. This is the df of an extreme value distribution, the Gumbel df $G_{0,\mu,\theta}(x)$.   □

Example 7.6 (Example 7.4 continued) *Suppose instead that the individual losses are Pareto distributed with df*

$$F(x) = 1 - \left(\frac{x+\beta}{\beta}\right)^{-\alpha}, \quad x \geq 0; \quad \alpha, \beta > 0.$$

Then the distribution of the maximum loss for a k-year period has df

$$F_{M_N}(x) = \exp\left[-k\lambda\left(\frac{x+\beta}{\beta}\right)^{-\alpha}\right], \quad x > 0.$$

which can be rewritten as

$$F_{M_N}(x) = \exp\left[-\left(\frac{x-\mu}{\theta}\right)^{-\alpha}\right]$$

where

$$\theta = \frac{\beta}{(k\lambda)^{1/\alpha}} \text{ and } \mu = -\beta.$$

This is the df of an extreme value distribution, the Fréchet df $G_{1,\alpha,\mu,\theta}(x)$. □

Examples 7.5 and 7.6 illustrate how the Gumbel and Fréchet distributions are distributions of extreme statistics, in this case maxima. We do not consider the Weibull, which plays the corresponding role for minima. Later, we will use some key theoretical results from the field of extreme value theory to show how extreme value distributions are the limiting distributions of extreme statistics for any distribution.

Example 7.7 *Suppose that the number of losses follows a negative binomial distribution with parameters r and β.*

Then from formula (7.3), the df of the maximum loss is given by

$$\begin{aligned} F_{M_N}(x) &= P_N(F_X(x)) \\ &= [1 - \beta\{F_X(x) - 1\}]^{-r} \\ &= [1 + \beta\{1 - F_X(x)\}]^{-r}. \end{aligned}$$

□

Example 7.8 (Example 7.7 continued) *Suppose, in addition, that the individual losses are exponentially distributed with*

$$F_X(x) = 1 - \exp\left(-\frac{x}{\theta}\right), \quad x > 0.$$

Then the distribution of the maximum loss for a k-year period has df

$$F_{M_N}(x) = \left[1 + \beta \exp\left(-\frac{x}{\theta}\right)\right]^{-r}, \quad x > 0.$$

□

Example 7.9 (Example 7.8 continued) *Suppose instead that the individual losses are Pareto distributed with df*

$$F(x) = 1 - \left(\frac{x+\theta}{\theta}\right)^{-\alpha}, \quad x \geq 0; \ \alpha, \theta > 0.$$

Then the distribution of the maximum loss for a k-year period has df

$$F_{M_N}(x) = [1 + \beta\{1 - F_X(x)\}]^{-r}$$
$$= \left[1 + \beta\left(\frac{x+\theta}{\theta}\right)^{-\alpha}\right]^{-r}, \quad x > 0.$$

□

7.4 STABILITY OF THE MAXIMUM OF THE EXTREME VALUE DISTRIBUTION

The Gumbel, Fréchet, and Weibull distributions have another property, called "stability of the maximum" or "max-stabilty" that is very useful in extreme value theory. This is already hinted at in Examples 7.1, 7.2, and 7.3.

First, for the standardized Gumbel distribution, we note that

$$[G_0(x + \ln n)]^n = \exp\left[-n \exp\left(-x - \ln n\right)\right]$$
$$= \exp\left[-\exp\left(-x\right)\right]$$
$$= G_0\left(x\right).$$

Equivalently,

$$[G_0\left(x\right)]^n = G_0\left(x - \ln n\right).$$

This shows that the distribution of the maximum of n observations from the standardized Gumbel distribution has itself a Gumbel distribution, after a shift of location of $\ln n$. Including location and scale parameters yields

$$[G_{0,\mu,\theta}(x)]^n = \left[G_0\left(\frac{x-\mu}{\theta}\right)\right]^n$$
$$= G_0\left(\frac{x-\mu}{\theta} - \ln n\right)$$
$$= G_0\left(\frac{x-\mu-\theta\ln n}{\theta}\right)$$
$$= G_0\left(\frac{x-\mu^*}{\theta}\right)$$
$$= G_{0,\mu^*,\theta}(x)$$

where $\mu^* = \mu + \theta\ln n$.

Similarly, for the standardized Fréchet distribution

$$\left[G_{1,\alpha}(n^{1/\alpha}x)\right]^n = \exp\left(-n\left(n^{1/\alpha}x\right)^{-\alpha}\right)$$
$$= \exp\left(-x^{-\alpha}\right)$$
$$= G_{1,\alpha}(x).$$

Equivalently,

$$[G_{1,\alpha}(x)]^n = G_{1,\alpha}\left(\frac{x}{n^{1/\alpha}}\right).$$

This shows that the distribution of the maximum of n observations from the standardized Fréchet distribution, after a scale change, has itself a Fréchet distribution. Including location and scale parameters yields

$$[G_{1,\alpha,\mu,\theta}(x)]^n = G_{1,\alpha}\left(\frac{x-\mu}{\theta n^{1/\alpha}}\right)$$
$$= G_{1,\alpha,\mu,\theta^*}(x)$$

where $\theta^* = \theta n^{1/\alpha}$.

The key idea of this section is that the distribution of the maximum, after a location or scale normalization, for each of the extreme value (EV) distributions also has the same EV distribution. Section 7.5 shows that these EV distributions are also approximate distributions of the maximum for (almost) any distribution.

7.5   THE FISHER-TIPPETT THEOREM

We now examine the distribution of the maximum value of a sample of fixed size n (as n becomes very large) when the sample is drawn from any distribution. As $n \to \infty$, the distribution of the maximum is degenerate. Therefore, in order to understand the shape of the distribution for large values of n, it will be necessary to normalize the random variable representing the maximum. We require linear transformations such that

$$\lim_{n \longrightarrow \infty} F_n \left(\frac{x - b_n}{a_n} \right) = G(x)$$

for all values of x, where $G(x)$ is a nondegenerate distribution. If such a linear transformation exists, Theorem [?] gives a very powerful result that forms a foundational element of extreme value theory.

Theorem 7.10 Fisher-Tippett Theorem

If $\left[F \left(\frac{x - b_n}{a_n} \right) \right]^n$ has a nondegenerate limiting distribution as $n \to \infty$, for some constants a_n and b_n that depend on n, then

$$\left[F \left(\frac{x - b_n}{a_n} \right) \right]^n \to G(x)$$

as $n \to \infty$, for all values of x, for some extreme value distribution G, which is one of G_0, $G_{1,\alpha}$ or $G_{2,\alpha}$ for some location and scale parameters.

The original theorem was given in a paper by Fisher and Tippett[37]. A detailed proof can be found in Resnick [99]. The Fisher-Tippett theorem proves that the appropriately normed maximum for any distribution (subject to the limiting nondegeneracy condition) converges in distribution to exactly one of the three extreme value distributions: Gumbel, Fréchet, and Weibull. This is an extremely important result. If we are interested in understanding how jumbo losses behave, we only need to look at three (actually two, because the Weibull has an upper limit) choices for a model for the extreme right-hand tail.

The Fisher-Tippett theorem requires normalization using appropriate norming constants a_n and b_n that depend on n. For specific distributions, these norming constants can be identified. We have already seen some of these for the distributions considered in the examples in Section 7.3.

The Fisher-Tippett theorem is a limiting result that can be applied any distribution $F(x)$. Because of this, it can be used as a general approximation to the true distribution of a maximum without having to completely specify the form of the underlying distribution $F(x)$. This is particularly useful when we only have data on extreme losses as a starting point, without specific knowledge of the form of the underlying distribution.

It now remains to describe which distributions have maxima converging to each of the three limiting distributions and to determine the norming constants a_n and b_n.

Example 7.11 (Maximum of exponentials) *Without any loss of generality, for notational convenience, we use the standardized version of the exponential distribution. Using the norming constants $a_n = 1$ and $b_n = -\ln n$, the* *distribution of the maximum is given by*

$$\Pr\left(\frac{M_n - b_n}{a_n} \leq x\right) = \Pr\left(M_n \leq a_n x + b_n\right)$$

$$= \left[\Pr\left(X \leq a_n x + b_n\right)\right]^n$$

$$= \left[\Pr\left(X \leq x - \ln n\right)\right]^n$$

$$= \left[1 - \exp(-x - \ln n)\right]^n$$

$$= \left[1 - \frac{\exp(-x)}{n}\right]^n$$

$$\rightarrow \exp\left(-\exp\left(-x\right)\right) \quad as\ n \rightarrow \infty.$$

Having chosen (somehow) the right norming constants, we see that the limiting distribution of the maximum of exponential random variables is the Gumbel distribution.   □

Example 7.12 (Maximum of Paretos) *Using the Pareto df*

$$\overline{F}(x) = \left(\frac{x+\theta}{\theta}\right)^{-\alpha}$$

$$= \left(1 + \frac{x}{\theta}\right)^{-\alpha}, \quad x \geq 0, \quad \alpha, \theta > 0.$$

and the norming constants $a_n = \theta n^{1/\alpha}/\alpha$ and $b_n = \theta n^{1/\alpha} - \theta$,

$$\Pr\left(\frac{M_n - b_n}{a_n} \leq x\right) = \Pr\left(M_n \leq a_n x + b_n\right)$$

$$= \left[\Pr\left(X \leq a_n x + b_n\right)\right]^n$$

$$= \left[\Pr\left(X \leq \frac{\theta n^{1/\alpha}}{\alpha} x + \theta n^{1/\alpha} - \theta\right)\right]^n$$

$$= \left[1 - \left(1 + \frac{\frac{\theta n^{1/\alpha}}{\alpha} x + \theta n^{1/\alpha} - \theta}{\theta}\right)^{-\alpha}\right]^n$$

$$= \left[1 - \frac{1}{n}\left(1 + \frac{x}{\alpha}\right)^{-\alpha}\right]^n$$

$$\rightarrow \exp\left(-\left(1 + \frac{x}{\alpha}\right)^{-\alpha}\right) \quad as\ n \rightarrow \infty.$$

This shows that the maximum of Pareto random variables has a Fréchet distribution with $\mu = -\alpha$ and $\theta = \alpha$.   □

7.6   MAXIMUM DOMAIN OF ATTRACTION

Definition 7.13 *The **maximum domain of attraction** (MDA) for any distribution G, is the set of all distributions that has G as the limiting distribution as $n \to \infty$ of the normalized maximum $(M_n - b_n)/a_n$ for some norming constants a_n and b_n.*

Essentially, distributions (with nondegenerate limits) can be divided into three classes according to their limiting distribution: Gumbel, Fréchet and Weibull. If we can identify the limiting distribution, and if we are only interested in modeling the extreme value, we no longer need to worry about trying to identify the exact form of the underlying distribution. We can simply treat the limiting distribution as an approximate representation of the distribution of the extreme value.

Because we are interested in the distribution of the maximum, it is natural that we only need to worry about the extreme right-hand tail of the underlying distribution. Furthermore, the MDA should depend on the shape of only the tail and not on the rest of the distribution. This is confirmed in Theorem 7.14.

Theorem 7.14 MDA characterization by tails
  A distribution F belongs to the maximum domain of attraction of an extreme value distribution G_i with norming constants a_n and b_n if and only if

$$\lim_{n \to \infty} n\overline{F}\left(a_n x + b_n\right) = -\ln G_i(x).$$

This result is illustrated in Examples 7.15 and 7.16.

Example 7.15 (Maximum of exponentials) *As in Example 7.11, we use the standardized version of the exponential distribution. Using the norming constants $a_n = 1$ and $b_n = -\ln n$, the distribution of the maximum is given by*

$$
\begin{aligned}
n\overline{F}\left(x + b_n\right) &= n \Pr\left(X > x + \ln n\right) \\
&= n \Pr\left(X > x + \ln n\right) \\
&= n \exp(-x - \ln n) \\
&= n\frac{\exp(-x)}{n} \\
&= \exp\left(-x\right) \\
&= -\ln G_0(x).
\end{aligned}
$$

Having chosen the right norming constants, we see that the limiting distribution of the maximum of exponential random variables is the Gumbel distribution.   □

It is also convenient, for mathematical purposes, to be able to treat distributions that have the same asymptotic tail shape in the same way. The above example suggest that if any distribution has a tail that is exponential, or close to exponential, or exponential asymptotically, then the limiting distribution of the maximum should be Gumbel. Therefore, we define two distributions F_X and F_Y as being *tail-equivalent* if

$$\lim_{x \to \infty} \frac{\overline{F}_X(x)}{\overline{F}_Y(x)} = c$$

where c is a constant. (Here the notation $x \to \infty$ should be interpreted as the x increasing to the right-hand endpoint if the distribution has a finite right-hand endpoint.) Clearly, if two distributions are tail-equivalent, they will be in the same maximum domain of attraction, because the constant c can be absorbed by the norming constants.

Then in order to determine the MDA for a distribution, it is only necessary to study any tail-equivalent distribution. this is illustrated through the Example 7.16.

Example 7.16 (Maximum of Paretos) *Using the Pareto df*

$$\overline{F}(x) = \left(\frac{x + \theta}{\theta} \right)^{-\alpha}, \quad x \geq 0, \quad \alpha, \theta > 0$$

and the norming constants $a_n = \theta n^{-1/\alpha}$ *and* $b_n = 0$, *and the tail-equivalence*

$$\overline{F}(x) \sim \left(\frac{x}{\theta} \right)^{-\alpha}$$

for large x, *we obtain*

$$\lim_{n \to \infty} n \overline{F}(a_n x + b_n) \sim \lim_{n \to \infty} n \left(\frac{\theta x}{\theta n^{1/\alpha}} \right)^{-\alpha}$$

$$= x^{-\alpha}$$

$$= -\ln G_1(x).$$

This shows that the maximum of Pareto random variables has a Fréchet distribution. □

Because tail-equivalent distributions have the same MDA, all distributions with tails of the asymptotic form $cx^{-\alpha}$ are in the Fréchet MDA and all distributions with tails of the asymptotic form $ke^{-x/\theta}$ are in the Gumbel MDA. Then, all other distributions (subject to the nondegenerate condition) with infinite right-hand limit of support must be in one of these classes; that is, some have tails that are closer, in some sense, to exponential tails. Similarly, some are closer to Pareto tails. There is a body of theory that deals with the issue of "closeness" for the Fréchet MDA. In fact, the constant c above can be replaced by a slowly varying function (see Definition 6.19). Slowly varying functions include positive functions converging to a constant and logarithms.

Theorem 7.17 *If a distribution has its right-tail characterized by $\overline{F}(x) \sim x^{-\alpha}C(x)$, where $C(x)$ is a slowly varying function, then it is in the Fréchet maximum domain of attraction.*

Example 7.16 illustrates this concept for the Pareto distribution that has $C(x) = 1$. Distributions that are in the Fréchet MDA of heavier-tailed distributions include all members of the transformed beta family and the inverse transformed gamma family that appear in Figures 4.1 and 4.2.

The distributions that are in the Gumbel MDA are not as easy to characterize. The Gumbel MDA includes distributions that are lighter-tailed than any power function. Distributions in the Gumbel MDA have moments of all orders. These include the exponential, gamma, Weibull, and lognormal distributions. In fact, all members of the transformed gamma family appearing in Figure 4.2 are in the Gumbel MDA, as is the inverse Gaussian distribution. The tails of the distributions in the Gumbel MDA are very different from each other, from the very light-tailed normal distribution to the much heavier-tailed inverse Gaussian distribution.

7.7 GENERALIZED PARETO DISTRIBUTIONS

In this section, we introduce some distributions known as generalized Pareto (GP) distributions[2] that are closely related to extreme value distributions. They are used in connection with the study of excesses over a threshold. In operational risk, this means losses that exceed some threshold in size. For these distribution functions, we use the general notation $W(x)$. Generalized Pareto distributions are related to the extreme value distributions by the simple relation

$$W(x) = 1 + \ln G(x) \tag{7.4}$$

with the added restriction that $W(x)$ must be nonnegative, that is, requiring that $G(x) \geq \exp(-1)$.

Paralleling the development of extreme value distributions, there are three related distributions in the family known as generalized Pareto distributions.

---

[2]The "generalized Pareto distribution" used in this chapter differs from the distribution with the same name used in Section 4.2. It is unfortunate that the term "generalized" is often used by different authors in connection with different generalizations of the same distribution. Since the usage in each chapter is standard usage (but in different fields), we leave it to the reader to be cautious about which definition is being used. The same comment applies to the used of the terms "beta distribution" and "Weibull distribution."

Exponential distribution

The standardized exponential distribution has df of the form

$$F(x) = W_0(x) = 1 - \exp(-x), \quad x > 0.$$

With location and scale parameters μ and θ included, it has df

$$F(x) = 1 - \exp\left(-\frac{x - \mu}{\theta}\right), \quad x > \mu.$$

Note that the exponential distribution has support only for values of x greater than μ. In the applications considered in this book, μ will generally be set to zero, making the distribution a one-parameter distribution with a left-hand endpoint of zero. The df of that one-parameter distribution will be denoted by

$$F(x) = W_{0,\theta}(x) = 1 - \exp\left(-\frac{x}{\theta}\right), \quad x > 0.$$

Pareto distribution

The standardized Pareto distribution has df of the form

$$F(x) = W_{1,\alpha}(x) = 1 - x^{-\alpha}; \quad x \geq 1, \quad \alpha > 0.$$

With location and scale parameters μ and θ included, it has df

$$F(x) = 1 - \left(\frac{x - \mu}{\theta}\right)^{-\alpha}; \quad x \geq \mu + \theta, \quad \alpha, \theta > 0.$$

Note that the Pareto distribution has support only for values of x greater than $\mu + \theta$. In the applications considered in this book, μ will generally be set to $-\theta$, making the distribution a two-parameter distribution with a zero left-hand endpoint. The df of the two-parameter Pareto distribution will be denoted by

$$F(x) = W_{1,\alpha,\theta}(x) = 1 - \left(\frac{\theta}{x + \theta}\right)^{\alpha}; \quad x \geq 0, \quad \alpha, \theta > 0.$$

Beta distribution

The standardized beta distribution has df of the form

$$F(x) = W_{2,\alpha}(x) = 1 - (-x)^{-\alpha}; \quad -1 \leq x \leq 0, \quad \alpha < 0.$$

With location and scale parameters μ and θ included, it has df

$$F(x) = 1 - \left(-\frac{x - \mu}{\theta}\right)^{-\alpha}; \quad \mu - \theta \leq x \leq \mu, \ \alpha < 0, \ \theta > 0.$$

Note that the beta distribution has support only for values of x on the interval $[\mu - \theta, \mu]$. As with the Weibull distribution, it will not be considered further in this book. It is included for completeness of exposition of extreme value theory. It should also be noted that the beta distribution is a (shifted) subclass of the usual beta distribution on the interval $(0, 1)$ interval which has an additional shape parameter, and where the shape parameters are positive.

Generalized Pareto distribution

The generalized Pareto distribution is the family of distributions incorporating, in a single expression, the above three distributions as special cases. The general expression for the df of the generalized Pareto distribution is

$$F(x) = 1 - \left(1 + \frac{x}{\alpha\theta}\right)^{-\alpha}.$$

For notational convenience, it is often written as

$$F(x) = W_{\gamma,\theta}(x) = 1 - \left(1 + \gamma\frac{x}{\theta}\right)^{-1/\gamma}.$$

Because the limiting value of $\left(1 + \gamma\frac{x}{\theta}\right)^{-1/\gamma}$ is $\exp(-\frac{x}{\theta})$ as $\gamma \to 0$, it is clear that $W_0(x)$ is the exponential distribution function. When γ (or equivalently α) is positive, the df $W_{\gamma,\theta}(x)$ has the form of a Pareto distribution.

7.8   THE FREQUENCY OF EXCEEDENCES

7.8.1   From a fixed number of losses

An important component in analyzing excesses (losses in excess of a threshold) is the change in the frequency distribution of the number of observations that exceed the threshold as the threshold is changed. When the threshold is increased, there will be fewer exceedences per time period; whereas if the threshold is lowered, there will be more exceedences.

Let X_j denote the severity random variable representing the "ground-up"[3] loss on the jth loss with common df $F(x)$. Let N^L denote the number of ground-up losses. We make the usual assumptions that the X_js are mutually independent and independent of N^L.

Now consider a threshold d such that $\overline{F}(d) = 1 - F(d) = \Pr(X > d)$, the survival function, is the probability that a loss will exceed the threshold. Next, define the indicator random variable I_j by $I_j = 1$ if the jth loss results in an exceedence and $I_j = 0$ otherwise. Then I_j has a Bernoulli distribution with parameter $\overline{F}(d)$ and the pgf of I_j is $P_{I_j}(z) = 1 - \overline{F}(d) + \overline{F}(d)z$.

---

[3]The term "ground-up" is a term that comes from insurance. Often there is a deductible amount so that the insurer pays less than the full loss to the insured. A ground-up loss is the full loss to the insured, not the (smaller) loss to the insurer. In the operational risk context, ground-up losses are measured from zero and are not the losses measured from the threshold.

If there are a fixed number n of ground-up losses, $N^E = I_1 + \cdots + I_n$ represents the number of exceedances. If $I_1, I_2, \ldots$ are mutually independent, then N^E has a binomial distribution with pgf

$$P_{NE}(z) = [P_{I_j}(z)]^n = [1 + \overline{F}(d)(z - 1)]^n.$$

Thus the binomial distribution with parameters n and $\overline{F}(d)$ represents the number of exceedances. This concept is similarly extended to the number of exceedances above some threshold d_2, when the number of exceedances above a lower threshold d_1 is known and denoted by n_1. In this case, the number of exceedances N_2^E has a binomial distribution with parameters n_1 and $\overline{F}(d_2)/\overline{F}(d_1)$.

It is often argued that the number of very rare events in a fixed time period follows a Poisson distribution. When the threshold is very high the probability of exceeding that threshold is very small. When also the number of ground-up losses is large the Poisson distribution serves as an approximation to the binomial distribution of the number of exceedances. This can be argued as follows:

$$P_{NE}(z) = [P_{I_j}(z)]^n = [1 + \overline{F}(d)(z - 1)]^n$$
$$\rightarrow \exp(\lambda(z - 1))$$

where $\lambda = n\overline{F}(d)$ as $n \rightarrow \infty$. Thus, asymptotically, the number of exceedances follows a Poisson distribution.

7.8.2 From a random number of losses

In practice, the number of losses is unknown in advance. In this case, the number of exceedances over the threshold d is random. If there is a random number of exceedances, $N^E = I_1 + \cdots + I_{N^L}$ represents the number of exceedances. If $I_1, I_2, \ldots$ are mutually independent and are also independent of N^L, then N^E has a compound distribution with N^L as the primary distribution and a Bernoulli secondary distribution. Thus

$$P_{NE}(z) = P_{N^L}[P_{I_j}(z)] = P_{N^L}[1 + \overline{F}(d)(z - 1)].$$

In the important special case in which the distribution of N^L depends on a parameter θ such that

$$P_{N^L}(z) = P_{N^L}(z; \theta) = B[\theta \cdot (z - 1)],$$

where $B(z)$ is functionally independent of θ (as in Theorem 5.11), then

$$P_{NE}(z) = B[\theta \cdot (1 - \overline{F}(d) + \overline{F}(d)z - 1)]$$
$$= B[\overline{F}(d) \cdot \theta \cdot (z - 1)]$$
$$= P_{N^L}(z; \overline{F}(d)\theta).$$

This implies that N^L and N^E are both from the same parametric family and only the parameter θ need be changed.

Example 7.18 *Demonstrate that the above result applies to the negative binomial distribution. Illustrate the effect when a threshold of $250 is applied to a Pareto distribution with $\alpha = 3$ and $\theta = \$1000$. Assume that N^L has a negative binomial distribution with parameters of $r = 2$ and $\beta = 3$.*

The negative binomial pgf is $P_{N^L}(z) = [1 - \beta(z - 1)]^{-r}$. Here β takes on the role of θ in the result and $B(z) = (1 - z)^{-r}$. Then N^E must have a negative binomial distribution with $r^* = r$ and $\beta^* = \beta \overline{F}(d)$. For the particular situation described,

$$\overline{F}(250) = 1 - F(250) = \left(\frac{1000}{1000 + 250}\right)^3 = 0.512$$

and so $r^* = 2$ and $\beta^* = 3(0.512) = 1.536$.   □

This result may be generalized for zero-modified and zero-truncated distributions. Suppose N^L depends on parameters θ and α such that

$$P_{N^L}(z) = P_{N^L}(z; \theta, \alpha) = \alpha + (1 - \alpha)\frac{B[\theta(z - 1)] - B(-\theta)}{1 - B(-\theta)}. \tag{7.5}$$

Note that $\alpha = P_{N^L}(0) = \Pr(N^L = 0)$ and so is the modified probability at zero. It is also the case that, if $B[\theta(z - 1)]$ is itself a pgf, then the pgf (7.5) is that for the corresponding zero-modified distribution. However, it is not necessary for $B[\theta(z - 1)]$ to be a pgf in order for $P_{N^L}(z)$ as given in formula (7.5) to be a pgf. In particular, $B(z) = 1 + \ln(1 - z)$ yields the zero-modified (ZM) logarithmic distribution, even though there is no distribution with $B(z)$ as its pgf. Similarly, $B(z) = (1 - z)^{-r}$ for $-1 < r < 0$ yields the ETNB distribution. A few algebraic steps reveal that for formula (7.5)

$$P_{N^E}(z) = P_{N^L}(z; \theta \overline{F}(x), \alpha^*),$$

where $\alpha^* = \Pr(N^E = 0) = P_{N^E}(0) = P_{N^L}(F(d); \theta, \alpha)$. It is expected that imposing a threshold will increase the value of α because periods with no exceedences will become more likely. In particular, if N^L is zero-truncated, N^E will be zero-modified.

Example 7.19 *Repeat the Example 7.18, only now let the frequency distribution be zero-modified negative binomial with $r = 2$, $\beta = 3$, and $p_0^M = 0.4$.*

The pgf is

$$P_{N^L}(z) = p_0^M + (1 - p_0^M)\frac{[1 - \beta(z - 1)]^{-r} - (1 + \beta)^{-r}}{1 - (1 + \beta)^{-r}}.$$

Then $\alpha = p_0^M$ and $B(z) = (1-z)^{-r}$. We then have $r^* = r$, $\beta^* = \beta \overline{F}(d)$, and

$$
\begin{aligned}
\alpha^* = p_0^{M*} &= p_0^M + (1 - p_0^M) \frac{(1+\beta^*)^{-r} - (1+\beta)^{-r}}{1 - (1+\beta)^{-r}} \\
&= \frac{p_0^M - (1+\beta)^{-r} + (1+\beta^*)^{-r} - p_0^M (1+\beta^*)^{-r}}{1 - (1+\beta)^{-r}}.
\end{aligned}
$$

For the particular distribution given, the new parameters are $r^* = 2$, $\beta^* = 3(0.512) = 1.536$, and

$$
p_0^{M*} = \frac{0.4 - 4^{-2} + 2.536^{-2} - 0.4(2.536)^{-2}}{1 - 4^{-2}} = 0.4595.
$$

$\square$

If we have values of the amounts of the excesses over a threshold, we may want to determine the distribution of N^L from that of N^E. That is, we may want to know the distribution of ground-up losses if the threshold is removed. Arguing as before,

$$
P_{N^L}(z) = P_{N^E}(1 - \overline{F}(d)^{-1} + z\overline{F}(d)^{-1}).
$$

This implies that the formulas derived previously hold with $\overline{F}(d)$ replaced by $\overline{F}(d)^{-1}$. However, it is possible that the resulting pgf for N^L is not valid. If this occurs, one of the modeling assumptions is invalid (for example, the assumption that changing the threshold does not change loss-related behavior).

Example 7.20 *Suppose that the number of exceedences with a threshold of $250 have the zero-modified negative binomial distribution with $r^* = 2$, $\beta^* = 1.536$, and $p_0^{M*} = 0.4595$. Suppose also that ground-up losses have the Pareto amount distribution with $\alpha = 3$ and $\theta = \$1000$. Determine the distribution of the number of losses when the threshold is removed. Repeat this calculation assuming $p_0^{M*} = 0.002$.*

In this case the formulas use $\overline{F}(d) = 1/0.512 = 1.953125$ and so $r = 2$ and $\beta = 1.953125(1.536) = 3$. Also,

$$
p_0^{M*} = \frac{0.4595 - 2.536^{-2} + 4^{-2} - 0.4595(4)^{-2}}{1 - 2.536^{-2}} = 0.4
$$

as expected. For the second case,

$$
p_0^{M*} = \frac{0.002 - 2.536^{-2} + 4^{-2} - 0.002(4)^{-2}}{1 - 2.536^{-2}} = -0.1079,
$$

which is not a legitimate probability.

$\square$

All members of the $(a, b, 0)$ and $(a, b, 1)$ classes meet the conditions of this section. Table 7.1 indicates how the parameters change when moving from

Table 7.1 Frequency adjustments

N^L	Parameters for N^E
Poisson	$\lambda^* = \bar{F}(d)\lambda$
ZM Poisson	$p_0^{M*} = \dfrac{p_0^M - e^{-\lambda} + e^{-\lambda^*} - p_0^M e^{-\lambda^*}}{1 - e^{-\lambda}}$
Binomial	$q^* = \bar{F}(d)q$
ZM binomial	$p_0^{M*} = \dfrac{p_0^M - (1-q)^m + (1-q^*)^m - p_0^M(1-q^*)^m}{1 - (1-q)^m}$
Negative binomial	$\beta^* = \bar{F}(d)\beta$
ZM negative binomial	$p_0^{M*} = \dfrac{p_0^M - (1+\beta)^{-r} + (1+\beta^*)^{-r} - p_0^M(1+\beta^*)^{-r}}{1 - (1+\beta)^{-r}}$
ZM logarithmic	$p_0^{M*} = 1 - (1 - p_0^M)\ln(1 + \beta^*)/\ln(1 + \beta)$

N^L to N^E. If N^L has a compound distribution, then we can write $P_{N^L}(z) = P_1[P_2(z)]$ and therefore

$$P_{N^E}(z) = P_{N^L}[1 + \bar{F}(d)(z - 1)] = P_1\{P_2[1 + \bar{F}(d)(z - 1)]\}.$$

Thus N^E will also have a compound distribution with the secondary distribution modified as indicated. If the secondary distribution has an $(a, b, 0)$ distribution, then it can modified as in Table 7.1. Example 7.21 indicates the adjustment to be made if the secondary distribution has an $(a, b, 1)$ distribution.

Example 7.21 *If N^L has a Poisson–ETNB distribution with $\lambda = 5$, $\beta = 0.3$, and $r = 4$. If $\bar{F}(d) = 0.5$, determine the distribution of N^E.*

From the discussion above, N^E is compound Poisson with $\lambda^* = 5$, but the secondary distribution is a zero-modified negative binomial with (from Table 7.1) $\beta^* = 0.5(0.3) = 0.15$,

$$p_0^{M*} = \frac{0 - 1.3^{-4} + 1.15^{-4} - 0(1.15)^{-4}}{1 - 1.3^{-4}} = 0.34103,$$

and $r^* = 4$. This would be sufficient, except we have acquired the habit of using the ETNB as the secondary distribution. From Theorem 5.11 a compound Poisson distribution with a zero-modified secondary distribution is equivalent to a compound Poisson distribution with a zero-truncated secondary distribution. The Poisson parameter must be changed to $(1 - p_0^{M*})\lambda^*$. Therefore, N^E has a Poisson–ETNB distribution with $\lambda^* = (1 - 0.34103)5 = 3.29485$, $\beta^* = 0.15$, and $r^* = 4$. $\square$

7.9   STABILITY OF EXCESSES OF THE GENERALIZED PARETO

The exponential, Pareto, and beta distributions have another property, called "stability of excesses," that is very useful in extreme value theory. Let $Y = X - d \mid X > d$ denote the conditional excess random random variable.

When X has an exponential distribution with zero left-hand endpoint

$$\Pr(X \le x) = W_{0,\theta}(x) = 1 - \exp\left(\frac{x}{\theta}\right), \quad x > 0.$$

Then

$$\Pr(Y \le y) = \Pr(X \le d + y \mid X > d)$$

$$= \frac{\exp\left(-\frac{d}{\theta}\right) - \exp\left(-\frac{d+y}{\theta}\right)}{\exp\left(-\frac{d}{\theta}\right)}$$

$$= 1 - \exp\left(\frac{y}{\theta}\right)$$

$$= W_{0,\theta}(y), \quad y > 0.$$

This shows that the distribution of the excess from the exponential distribution itself has an exponential distribution. The excess of the loss over the threshold has the same distribution as the original loss random variable X. This is known as the "memoryless property" of the exponential distribution.

Similarly, for the Pareto distribution beginning at zero,

$$\Pr(X \le x) = W_{1,\alpha,\theta}(x) = 1 - \left(\frac{x+\theta}{\theta}\right)^{-\alpha}, \quad x > 0; \ \alpha, \theta > 0,$$

we have

$$\Pr(Y \le y) = \Pr(X \le d + y \mid X > d)$$

$$= 1 - \frac{\overline{F}(d+y)}{\overline{F}(d)}$$

$$= 1 - \left(\frac{d+y+\theta}{d+\theta}\right)^{-\alpha}, \quad x > d$$

$$= 1 - \left(\frac{y+(d+\theta)}{d+\theta}\right)^{-\alpha}$$

$$= W_{1,\alpha,d+\theta}(y), \quad y > 0.$$

This shows that the excess over a threshold from the Pareto distribution, has itself a Pareto distribution. The excess over the threshold has a Pareto distribution that is the same as the original loss random variable, but with a change of scale from θ to $\theta + d$.

A similar result holds for the beta distribution, but will not be considered further. Thus, for the generalized Pareto distribution, the conditional distribution of the excess over a threshold is of the same form as the underlying distribution. The form for the distribution of conditional excesses of the generalized Pareto distribution can be written as

$$
\begin{aligned}
\Pr\left(Y \leq y\right) &= \Pr\left(X \leq d + y \mid X > d\right) \\
&= 1 - \frac{\overline{F}(d+y)}{\overline{F}(d)} \\
&= 1 - \left(\frac{1 + \gamma\left(\frac{d+y}{\theta}\right)}{1 + \gamma\left(\frac{d}{\theta}\right)}\right)^{-1/\gamma} \\
&= 1 - \left(\frac{\theta + \gamma\left(d + y\right)}{\theta + \gamma d}\right)^{-1/\gamma} \\
&= 1 - \left(1 + \gamma \frac{y}{\theta + \gamma d}\right)^{-1/\gamma} \\
&= W_{\gamma, \theta + \gamma d}\left(y\right), \quad y > 0.
\end{aligned}
$$

7.10 MEAN EXCESS FUNCTION

The mean of the distribution of the excess over d for a general distribution $F\left(x\right)$ can be written as

$$
e\left(d\right) = \int_d^\infty \frac{1 - F\left(x\right)}{1 - F\left(d\right)} dx = \int_d^\infty \frac{\overline{F}\left(x\right)}{\overline{F}\left(d\right)} dx.
$$

We use the "star" notation for the conditional distribution of the excess $Y = X - d \mid X > d$:

$$
\begin{aligned}
F^*\left(y\right) &= \Pr\left(Y \leq y\right) \\
&= \Pr\left(X \leq x \mid X > d\right) \\
&= \frac{F\left(x\right) - F\left(d\right)}{1 - F\left(d\right)}
\end{aligned}
$$

where $x = y + d$. In terms of this distribution the mean excess can be rewritten as

$$
e\left(d\right) = \mathrm{E}\left[Y\right] = \int_d^\infty \left[1 - F^*\left(y\right)\right] dy = \int_d^\infty \overline{F^*}\left(y\right) dy.
$$

Because of the memoryless property of the exponential distribution, the mean excess function is constant θ for all threshold levels. For the generalized Pareto distribution, the mean excess function is $\left(d + \theta\right) / \left(\alpha - 1\right) = \left(d + \theta\right) \gamma / \left(1 - \gamma\right)$ which increases linearly as a function of the threshold d.

When examining data, a very useful ad hoc procedure for identifying an appropriate distribution is to compute the empirical mean excess at each data point and examine its shape. This will be discussed in Chapter 13 dealing with fitting distributions for extreme value distributions.

7.11 LIMITING DISTRIBUTIONS OF EXCESSES

We now examine the distribution of excesses over some threshold d of a sample of size n for any distribution as n becomes very large. In particular, we are specifically interested in the limiting distribution as the threshold increases. As with the study of the maximum, in order to understand the shape of the distribution, it will be necessary to normalize the loss random variable in some way. This becomes clear in the following theorem.

We continue to use the "star" notation for the conditional distribution of the excess $Y = X - d \mid X > d$:

$$\begin{aligned} F^*(y) &= \Pr\left(Y \le y\right) \\ &= \Pr\left(X \le x \mid X > d\right) \\ &= \frac{F\left(x\right) - F\left(d\right)}{1 - F\left(d\right)} \end{aligned}$$

where $x = y + d$.

Theorem 7.22 is the analogue of the Fisher-Tippett theorem, but for excesses.

Theorem 7.22 Balkema-de Haan-Pickands Theorem

If, for some constants a_n and b_n that depend on n, the conditional distribution of excesses $F^*\left(a_n x + b_n\right)$ has a continuous limiting distribution as d approaches the right-hand endpoint of the support of X, then

$$F^*(x) \to W\left(x\right)$$

as $d \to \infty$, for all x, for some generalized Pareto distribution W that is one of W_{0,θ_d}, W_{1,α,θ_d} or W_{2,α,θ_d} for some scale parameter $\theta_d > 0$.

The Balkema-de Haan-Pickands Theorem (see [7] and [94]) shows that the right-hand tail of distribution of the excess converges in shape to exactly one of the three generalized Pareto distributions: exponential, Pareto and beta as the threshold becomes large. In practice, the limiting distribution serves as an approximating distribution for small sample sizes when the threshold is very high. Very high thresholds are of interest in studying the distribution of the size of jumbo losses.

It is also interesting to note that the upper tails of the standardized EV distribution and the standardized GP distribution converge asymptotically as $x \to \infty$. However, the left-hand end of the distributions are very different.

The similarity of the right-hand tails can be seen by examining the series expansion of the survival functions of each. From (formula 7.4),

$$\overline{W}(x) = -\ln\left(1 - \overline{G}(x)\right)$$

$$= \overline{G}(x) - \frac{\overline{G}(x)^2}{2} + \frac{\overline{G}(x)^3}{3} - \dots.$$

As x grows very large, the right-hand side is dominated by the first term and the remaining terms become insignificant.

7.12 TVaR FOR EXTREME VALUE DISTRIBUTIONS

The limiting distribution of the conditional excess over a threshold follows a generalized Pareto distribution. If the excess over a threshold d of a random variable X is assumed to follow a generalized Pareto distribution, then, for $x > d$, the tail of the (unconditional) distribution of X can be written as

$$\begin{aligned}
\overline{F}_X(x) &= \Pr\left(X > x\right) \\
&= \Pr\left(X > d\right)\Pr\left(X > x \mid X > d\right) \\
&= \overline{F}(d)\Pr\left(X - d > x - d \mid X > d\right) \\
&= \overline{F}_X(d)\overline{F_Y}^*(y),
\end{aligned}$$

where Y is the conditional random variable $X - d \mid X > d$, $y = x - d$ and $\overline{F_Y}^*(y)$ is the tail of the distribution of Y which is given by

$$\overline{F_Y}^*(y) = \left(1 + \gamma\frac{y}{\theta + \gamma d}\right)^{-1/\gamma}. \tag{7.6}$$

This distribution has mean

$$\begin{aligned}
\mathrm{E}(Y) &= \int_0^\infty \overline{F_Y}^*(y)\, dy = \int_0^\infty \left(1 + \gamma\frac{y}{\theta + \gamma d}\right)^{-1/\gamma} dy \\
&= (\theta + \gamma d)/(1 - \gamma) \\
&= \frac{\theta}{1 - \gamma} + \frac{\gamma}{1 - \gamma}d,
\end{aligned}$$

which is a linear function in d and exists only if $\gamma < 1$. When $\gamma = 0$, we have the exponential distribution and the memoryless property.

If the threshold d is the Value-at-Risk $x_p = \mathrm{VaR}_p(X)$, then we can write the Tail-Value-at-Risk as

$$\begin{aligned}
\mathrm{TVaR}_p(X) &= x_p + \frac{\theta}{1 - \gamma} + \frac{\gamma}{1 - \gamma}x_p \\
&= \frac{\mathrm{VaR}_p(X)}{1 - \gamma} + \frac{\theta}{1 - \gamma}.
\end{aligned}$$

If the threshold d is less than the Value-at-Risk, $x_p = \text{VaR}_p(X)$, then from formula (7.6), we can write the tail probability as

$$\overline{F}_X(x) = \overline{F}_X(d)\overline{F}_Y^*(y)$$

$$= \overline{F}_X(d)\left(1 + \gamma\frac{x-d}{\theta + \gamma d}\right)^{-1/\gamma}, \quad x_p > d.$$

From this the quantile, $x_p = \text{VaR}_p(X)$, can be obtained as

$$\text{VaR}_p(X) = d + \frac{\theta + \gamma d}{\gamma}\left[\left(\frac{1-p}{\overline{F}_X(d)}\right)^{-\gamma} - 1\right], \quad x_p > d,$$

and the Tail-Value-at-Risk follows as

$$\text{TVaR}_p(X) = \frac{\text{VaR}_p(X)}{1-\gamma} + \frac{\theta}{1-\gamma}.$$

7.13   FURTHER READING

The theory of extreme values was treated relatively informally in this chapter. Numerous recently published books are specially devoted to extreme value theory. The book by Embrechts et al. [30] was published in 1997 and remains one of the most comprehensive books. It provides a comprehensive treatment of relevant theory. Numerous papers by Embrechts and his collaborators, especially Alexander McNeil, (see for example McNeil [81] on various aspects of EVT are the leading papers and are frequently cited in the applied operational risk literature.

7.14   EXERCISES

7.1 Show that when γ is positive, the df $G_\gamma(x)$ (7.1) has the form of a Fréchet distribution. What is the left-hand endpoint of the support of the distribution? Express it as a function of γ.

7.2 Show that when γ is negative, the df $G_\gamma(x)$ (7.1) has the form of a Weibull distribution. What is the right-hand endpoint of the support of the distribution? Express it as a function of γ.

7.3 Consider a Poisson process in which 10 losses are expected each year. Further assume that losses are exponentially distributed with an average size of one million dollars. Calculate the 99%-Value-at-Risk, that is, the 99th percentile of the distribution.

7.4 Redo the calculation in Exercise 7.3 but using a Pareto loss distribution with the same average loss of one million dollars. Do the calculation for each of the shape parameters α equal to 20, 10, 5, 2, 1.5, and 1.1.

7.5 Suppose there is additional uncertainty about the expected number of loss. Suppose that the expected number of losses is given by a gamma prior distribution with mean 10 and standard deviation 5. Redo Exercise 7.3 incorporating this additional uncertainty.

7.6 Redo the calculations in Exercise 7.4 but incorporating the additional uncertainty described in Exercise 7.5.

7.7 Consider the standardized half-Cauchy distribution with pdf

$$f(x) = \frac{1}{2\pi (1 + x^2)}, \quad x > 0.$$

Prove that this has the Fréchet distribution as the limiting distribution of the maximum.

7.8 Show that when γ is positive, the df $W_\gamma(x)$ has the form of a Pareto distribution. What is the left-hand endpoint of the support of the distribution? Express it as a function of γ.

7.9 Show that when γ is negative, the df $W_\gamma(x)$ has the form of a beta distribution. What are the left-hand and right-hand endpoints of the support of the distribution? Express them as a function of γ.

7.10 Individual losses have a Pareto distribution with $\alpha = 2$ and $\theta = \$1000$. With a threshold of $\$500$ the frequency distribution for the number of exceedences is Poisson–inverse Gaussian with $\lambda = 3$ and $\beta = 2$. If the threshold is raised to $\$1000$, determine the distribution for the number of exceedences. Also, determine the pdf of the corresponding severity distribution (the excess amount per exceedence) for the new threshold.

7.11 Losses have a Pareto distribution with $\alpha = 2$ and $\theta = \$1000$. The frequency distribution for a threshold of $\$500$ is zero-truncated logarithmic with $\beta = 4$. Determine a model for the frequency when the threshold is reduced to 0.

7.12 Suppose that the number of losses N^L has the Sibuya distribution (see Exercises 5.8 and 5.20) with pgf $P_{N^L}(z) = 1 - (1 - z)^{-r}$, where $-1 < r < 0$. Demonstrate that the number of exceedences has a zero-modified Sibuya distribution.

8

Multivariate models

Everything goes wrong all at once.

—Murphy

8.1 INTRODUCTION

To this point, this book has focused on the modeling of specific risk types using univariate distributions. This chapter will focus on addressing the issue of possible dependencies between risks. The concern in building capital models for operational risk is that it may not be appropriate to assume that risks are mutually independent. In the case of independence the univariate probability (density) functions for each risk can be multiplied together to give the multivariate joint distribution of the set of risks. When risks are not independent, we say the risks are dependent.

There are a variety of sources for bivariate and multivariate models. Among them are the books by Hutchinson and Lai [58], Kotz, Balakrishnan, and Johnson [71], and Mardia [79]. Most distributions in these and other texts usually focus on multivariate distributions with marginal distributions of the same type. Of more interest and practical value are methods that construct bivariate or multivariate models from (possibly different) known marginal distributions and a dependence between risks.

There are many ways of describing this dependence or association between random variables. For example, the classical measure of dependence is the correlation coefficient. The correlation coefficient is a measure of the linearity between random variables. For two random variables X and Y, the correlation coefficient is exactly equal to 1 or -1 if there is a perfect linear relationship between X and Y, that is, if $Y = aX + b$. If a is positive, the correlation coefficient is equal to 1; if a is negative, the correlation coefficient is equal to -1. This explains why the correlation described here is often called linear correlation. Other measures of dependence between random variables are Kendall's tau, τ_K, and Spearman's rho, ρ_S, both of which will be discussed further in this chapter. Similar to the linear correlation coefficient, these measures of dependence take on values of 1 for perfect positive dependence and -1 for perfect negative dependence.

In developing capital models for operational risk, we will be especially interested in the behavior in the tails of the distributions, that is when very large losses occur. In particular, we will be interested in understanding dependencies between random variables in the tail. We would like to be able to address questions like "If one risk has a very large loss, is it more likely that another risk will also have a large loss?" and "What are the odds of having several large losses from different risk types?" The dependence in the tail is generally referred to, naturally, as tail dependence. This chapter will focus on modeling tail dependence.

Because all information about the relationship between random variables is captured in the multivariate distribution of those random variables, we begin our journey with the multivariate distribution, and a very important theorem that allows us to separate the dependence structure from the marginal distributions.

8.2   SKLAR'S THEOREM AND COPULAS

We shall define a d-variate copula C as the joint distribution function of d Uniform (0,1) random variables. If we label the d random variables as $U_1, U_2, ..., U_d$, then we can write the copula C as

$$C(u_1, ..., u_d) = \Pr(U_1 \leq u_1, ..., U_d \leq u_d).$$

Now consider any continuous random variables $X_1, X_2, ..., X_d$ with distributions functions $F_1, F_2, ..., F_d$ respectively and joint distribution function F. Because we also know from basic probability that the probability integral transforms $F_1(X_1), F_2(X_2), ..., F_d(X_d)$ are each distributed as Uniform (0,1) random variables, copulas can be seen to be joint distribution functions of Uniform (0,1) random variables. A copula evaluated at $F_1(x_1), F_2(x_2), ..., F_d(x_d)$ can be written as

$$C(F_1(x_1), ..., F_d(x_d)) = \Pr(U_1 \leq F_1(x_1), ..., U_d \leq F_d(x_d)).$$

Further defining the quantile function

$$F_j^{-1}(u) = \inf \{x : F_j(x) \geq u\},$$

the copula evaluated at $F_1(x_1), F_2(x_2), ..., F_d(x_d)$ can be rewritten as

$$\begin{aligned}
C(F_1(x_1), ..., F_d(x_d)) &= \Pr(F_1^{-1}(U_1) \leq x_1, ..., F_d^{-1}(U_d) \leq x_d) \\
&= \Pr(X_1 \leq x_1, ..., X_d \leq x_d) \\
&= F(x_1, ..., x_d).
\end{aligned}$$

Sklar's theorem [109] states this result in a more formal mathematical way (see Nelsen [85]). Essentially, Sklar's theorem states that for any joint distribution function F, there is a unique copula C that satisfies

$$F(x_1, ..., x_d) = C(F_1(x_1), ..., F_d(x_d)).$$

Conversely, for any copula C and any distribution functions $F_1(x_1), F_2(x_2),$ ..., $F_d(x_d)$, the function $C(F_1(x_1), ..., F_d(x_d))$ is a joint distribution function with marginals $F_1(x_1), F_2(x_2), ..., F_d(x_d)$.[1]

Sklar's theorem proves that in examining multivariate distributions, we can separate the dependence structure from the marginal distributions. Conversely, we can construct a multivariate joint distribution from (i) a set of marginal distributions, and (ii) a selected copula. The dependence structure is captured in the copula function and is independent of the form of the marginal distributions. This is especially useful in typical situations encountered in operational risk. Typically in practice, distributions of losses of various types are identified and modeled separately. There is often very little understanding of possible associations or dependencies among different risk type. However, there is a recognition of the fact that there may be linkages. Sklar's theorem allows us to experiment with different copulas while retaining identical marginal distributions.

In the rest of this chapter, we focus on bivariate copulas, or equivalently, on dependency structures between pairs of random variables. In the multivariate case, we will only be considering pairwise dependence between variables, reducing consideration to the bivariate case. It should be noted that in multivariate models, there could be higher-level dependencies based on interactions between three or more variables. From a practical point of view, this level of dependence is almost impossible to observe without vast amounts of data. Hence, we restrict consideration to the bivariate case.

In the bivariate case, it is interesting to note from basic probability arguments that

---

[1] For pedagogical reasons, we consider only distributions of the continuous type. It is possible to extend Sklar's theorem to distributions of all types. However, this requires more technical detail in the presentation. Furthermore, in operational risk modeling, it is generally sufficient to consider that the distributions of losses are of the continuous type.

$$\Pr\left(U_i > u_i, U_j > u_j\right) = 1 - u_i - u_j + C(u_i, u_j).$$

Then we have

$$C(u_i, u_j) = u_i + u_j - 1 + \Pr\left(U_i > u_i, U_j > u_j\right)$$
$$\geq u_i + u_j - 1. \tag{8.1}$$

From inequality (8.1) and the fact that $u_i + u_j - 1$ can be negative, we see that a lower bound on the copula cdf is

$$C(u_i, u_j) \geq \max\{0, u_i + u_j - 1\}. \tag{8.2}$$

The lower bound corresponds to the copula of the joint random variable $(U, 1 - U)$ the "countermonotonic" copula in which the random variables are perfectly negatively dependent. It is called the Fréchet lower bound. The copula density has no support in the lower left region of the unit square.

The corresponding Fréchet upper bound can be obtained from the simple fact that both

$$\Pr\left(U_i \leq u_i, U_j \leq u_j\right) \leq \Pr\left(U_i \leq u_i\right) = u_i$$

and

$$\Pr\left(U_i \leq u_i, U_j \leq u_j\right) \leq \Pr\left(U_j \leq u_j\right) = u_j$$

so that

$$\Pr\left(U_i \leq u_i, U_j \leq u_j\right) \leq \min\{u_i, u_j\}.$$

Thus we have Fréchet bounds

$$\max\{0, u_i + u_j - 1\} \leq C(u_i, u_j) \leq \min\{u_i, u_j\}.$$

It should also be noted that copulas are invariant under strictly increasing transformations of the underlying random variables. Because the copula links the ranks of random variables, transformations that preserve the ranks of random variable will also preserve the copula. For example, it makes no difference whether one models the random variables X_j or their logarithms $\ln(X_j)$. In financial fields, this is particularly important because the same copula applies to both prices as it does to (continuously compounded) returns. The resulting copulas for the multivariate distributions are identical.

Classical statistical analysis of multivariate distributions involved the multivariate distribution directly. One feature of these multivariate distributions is that all the marginals are of the same type, but with possible different parameter values. Hence, the distributions are typically described accordingly, for example, multivariate normal, multivariate t, etc. The multivariate distribution is usually analyzed directly without reference to the corresponding copula that exists in the multivariate distribution.

The copula approach allows us to separate the selection of the marginal distributions from the selection of the copula. The marginal distributions contain the information of the separate risks. The copula contains the information about the structure of dependency. The marginals contain information for the separate risk types and do not need to be of the same type. A good general introduction to copulas can be found in the article by Frees and Valdez [41].

8.3   MEASURES OF DEPENDENCY

It is well known that the linear correlation coefficient is a function of the marginal distributions. For example, changing the form of the marginals will necessarily change the value of the correlation coefficient. In describing dependency using copulas, it would be much more natural to have dependency measures that depend only on the copula and not on the marginals, because the copula does not depend on the form of the marginals and dependency is captured exclusively in the copula.

Fortunately, there are such measures of dependency available. The two most popular measures of association are Spearman's rho, and Kendall's tau which were originally developed in the field of non-parametric statistics.

8.3.0.1   Spearman's rho

Definition 8.1 *Consider a continuous bivariate random variable* (X_1, X_2) *with marginal distributions* $F_1(x_1)$ *and* $F_2(x_2)$. *The measure of association,* ***Spearman's rho***, $\rho_S(X_1, X_2)$, *is given by*

$$\rho_S(X_1, X_2) = \rho\left(F_1(X_1), F_2(X_2)\right)$$

where ρ *denotes (linear) correlation.*

Thus Spearman's rho represents the ordinary linear correlation between the variables U and V, where the U and V are the transformed random variables $U = F_1(X_1)$ and $V = F_2(X_2)$. Because U and V are both Uniform $(0,1)$ random variables with mean $1/2$ and variance $1/12$, we can rewrite Spearman's rho as

$$\rho_S(X_1, X_2) = \frac{\mathrm{E}\left[F_1(X_1)F_2(X_2)\right] - \mathrm{E}[F_1(X_1)]\mathrm{E}[F_2(X_2)]}{\sqrt{\mathrm{Var}(F_1(X_1))\mathrm{Var}(F_2(X_2))}}$$

$$= 12\mathrm{E}\left[F_1(X_1)F_2(X_2)\right] - 3.$$

In terms of copulas, Spearman's rho is then

$$\rho_S(X_1, X_2) = 12\mathrm{E}\left[UV\right] - 3$$

$$= 12 \int_0^1 \int_0^1 uv \, dC(u, v) - 3$$

$$= 12 \int_0^1 \int_0^1 C(u, v) \, du \, dv - 3.$$

Spearman's rho is the (linear) correlation coefficient between the integral transforms of the underlying random variables. This justifies the description of ρ_S as the Spearman's rank correlation coefficient. However, Kendall's tau has become more popular in connection with modeling using copulas. The will be seen later in connection with Archimedean copulas.

8.3.0.2   Kendall's tau

Definition 8.2 *Consider two independent and identically distributed continuous bivariate random variables (X_1, X_2) and (X_1^*, X_2^*) with marginal distribution $F_1(x_1)$ for X_1 and X_1^* and marginal distribution $F_2(x_2)$ for X_2 and X_2^*. The measure of association, **Kendall's tau**, $\tau_K(X_1, X_2)$, is given by*

$$\tau_K(X_1, X_2) = Pr\left[(X_1 - X_1^*)(X_2 - X_2^*) > 0\right] - Pr\left[(X_1 - X_1^*)(X_2 - X_2^*) < 0\right].$$

The first term measures concordance, in the sense that for each of the two dimensions, the differences between the random variables have the same sign. The second term then measures discordance. From the definition, it is easy to see that Kendall's tau can be rewritten as

$$\tau_K(X_1, X_2) = \mathrm{E}\left[\mathrm{sign}(X_1 - X_1^*)(X_2 - X_2^*)\right]. \qquad (8.3)$$

We now obtain an expression for Kendall's tau in terms of the copula function as follows:

$$\begin{aligned}
\tau_K(X_1, X_2) &= \Pr\left[(X_1 - X_1^*)(X_2 - X_2^*) > 0\right] - \Pr\left[(X_1 - X_1^*)(X_2 - X_2^*) < 0\right] \\
&= \Pr\left[(X_1 - X_1^*)(X_2 - X_2^*) > 0\right] \\
&\quad - \left\{1 - \Pr\left[(X_1 - X_1^*)(X_2 - X_2^*) > 0\right]\right\}
\end{aligned}$$

because the random variables are of the continuous type. From this

$$\begin{aligned}
\tau_K(X_1, X_2) &= \Pr\left[(X_1 - X_1^*)(X_2 - X_2^*) > 0\right] - \Pr\left[(X_1 - X_1^*)(X_2 - X_2^*) < 0\right] \\
&= 2\Pr\left[(X_1 - X_1^*)(X_2 - X_2^*) > 0\right] - 1.
\end{aligned}$$

Because the random variables are interchangeable,

$$\begin{aligned}
\tau_K(X_1, X_2) &= 4\Pr\left[(X_1 < X_1^*, \ X_2 < X_2^*\right] - 1 \\
&= 4\mathrm{E}\left\{\Pr\left[(X_1 < X_1^*, \ X_2 < X_2^* \mid X_1^*, X_2^*\right]\right\} - 1 \\
&= 4\int_{-\infty}^{\infty}\int_{-\infty}^{\infty} \Pr\left[(X_1 < x_1, \ X_2 < x_2\right] \, dF(x_1, x_2) - 1 \\
&= 4\int_{-\infty}^{\infty}\int_{-\infty}^{\infty} F(x_1, x_2) \, dF(x_1, x_2) - 1 \\
&= 4\int_{-\infty}^{\infty}\int_{-\infty}^{\infty} C\left(F(x_1), F(x_2)\right) \, dC\left(F(x_1), F(x_2)\right) - 1 \\
&= 4\int_0^1\int_0^1 C\left(u, v\right) \, dC\left(u, v\right) - 1.
\end{aligned}$$

Thus, in terms of the copula function for bivariate distributions $C(u, v)$ with Uniform (0,1) marginals, Kendall's tau is given by

$$\tau_K(X_1, X_2) = 4 \int_0^1 \int_0^1 C(u, v) \, dC(u, v) - 1$$
$$= 4E\left[C(U, V)\right] - 1.$$

If the copula is absolutely continuous, then this can be rewritten as

$$\tau_K(X_1, X_2) = 4 \int_0^1 \int_0^1 C(u, v) \frac{\partial^2 C(u, v)}{\partial u \partial v} \, du \, dv - 1.$$

8.4   TAIL DEPENDENCE

In recent years in the risk management field, there has been much focus not only on the question of the general behavior of random variables but specifically on behaviors in the tail of the distribution. This is because extreme outcomes are among the main concerns of those who have responsibility to manage risk and potential volatility. When there is dependence between loss random variables, there is also a need to understand the joint behavior when extreme outcomes occur. It has been observed that if extreme outcomes occur for one risk, there may be an increased chance of extreme outcomes for other risks. It has been suggested that, although in "normal times" there may be little correlation, in "bad times" there may be significant correlation between risks. ("Everything seems to go wrong at once.") Hence, this is especially important in risk management where the focus of attention is on the tail. The concept of tail dependence addresses this question. Measures of tail dependence have been developed to evaluate how strong the correlation is in the upper (or lower) tails.

Consider two continuous random variables X and Y with marginal distributions $F(x)$ and $G(y)$. The index of upper tail dependence λ_U is defined as

$$\lambda_U = \lim_{u \to 1} \Pr\left\{X > F^{-1}(u) \mid Y > G^{-1}(u)\right\}.$$

Roughly speaking, the index of upper tail dependence measures the chances that X is very large if it is known that Y is very large, where "very large" is measured in terms of equivalent quantiles. This can be seen simply by rewriting λ_U as

$$\lambda_U = \lim_{u \to 1} \Pr\left\{F(X) > u \mid G(Y) > u\right\}$$
$$= \lim_{u \to 1} \Pr\left\{U > u \mid V > u\right\}$$

where U and V are both Uniform (0,1) random variables.

This can be further rewritten as

$$\lambda_U = \lim_{u \to 1} \frac{1 - \Pr\{U \le u\} - \Pr\{V \le u\} + \Pr\{U \le u, V \le u\}}{1 - \Pr\{V \le u\}}$$

$$= \lim_{u \to 1} \frac{1 - 2u + C(u,u)}{1 - u}.$$

This formula demonstrates that tail dependency of X and Y as defined above can be measured by looking at the copula rather than the original distribution. The trick was to define tail dependence in terms of quantiles, which is completely natural in any case. Because λ_U was originally defined as a probability, it takes on values ranging from 0 to 1.

An index of lower dependence can be similarly defined. It is easily obtained by substituting $1 - u$ for u in the above, leading to

$$\lambda_L = \lim_{u \to 0} \Pr\{U \le u \mid V \le u\}$$

$$= \lim_{u \to 0} \frac{C(u,u)}{u}.$$

However, because our focus is on the right-tail of losses, we will not consider it further except occasionally to compare it with the index of upper tail dependence. The index of tail dependence is a very useful measure in describing a copula and in terms of comparing copulas.

8.5 ARCHIMEDEAN COPULAS

Archimedean copulas of dimension d are those of the form

$$C(u_1, ..., u_d) = \phi^{-1}[\phi(u_1) + ... + \phi(u_d)]$$

where $\phi(u)$ is called a **generator**. The generator is a strictly decreasing, convex, and continuous function that maps $[0,1]$ into $[0,\infty]$ with $\phi(1) = 0$. In addition, the inverse of the generator $\phi^{-1}(t)$ must be completely monotonic on $[0,\infty]$. A function $f(x)$ is completely monotonic on $[a,b]$ if it satisfies

$$(-1)^n \frac{d^n}{dx^n} f(x) \ge 0, \ n = 1, 2, 3, ...$$

From the definition of the bivariate Archimedean copula distribution $c(u,v)$, its support is the area in the unit square where $\phi(u) + \phi(v) \le \phi(0)$. Thus if $\phi(0) = \infty$, then the support is the entire unit square. Otherwise, it may be possible that a contiguous region in the lower left region of the unit square has $C(u,v) = 0$. The upper boundary of this region is the curve defined by $\phi(u) + \phi(v) = \phi(0)$.

The paper by Genest and McKay [45] introduced bivariate $(d = 2)$ Archimedean copulas and proved that it is also possible to characterize the measure of association, Kendall's tau, directly from the generator function of a copula as

$$\tau_K(X_1, X_2) = 1 + 4 \int_0^1 \frac{\phi(u)}{\phi'(u)} \, du.$$

This allows very easy comparisons of Archimedean copulas based solely on their generators.

The upper tail dependence of bivariate Archimedean copulas (or any two dimensions of a multivariate Archimedean copula) can be obtained from

$$\lambda_U = \lim_{u \to 1} \frac{1 - 2u + C(u, u)}{1 - u}$$

or from the copula generator because

$$\lambda_U = \lim_{u \to 1} \frac{1 - 2u + \phi^{-1}[2\phi(u)]}{1 - u}$$

$$= 2 - 2 \lim_{u \to 1} \frac{\frac{d}{du}\phi^{-1}[2\phi(u)]}{\frac{d}{du}\phi^{-1}[\phi(u)]} \quad \text{using L'Hôpital's rule}$$

$$= 2 - 2 \lim_{t \to 0} \frac{\frac{d}{dt}\phi^{-1}(2t)}{\frac{d}{dt}\phi^{-1}(t)}$$

provided that $\lim_{t \to 0} \frac{d}{dt}\phi^{-1}(t) = -\infty$. If $\lim_{t \to 0} \frac{d}{dt}\phi^{-1}(t) \neq -\infty$, then there is no upper tail dependence. It is also interesting to note that in similar fashion the corresponding index of lower tail dependence has the form

$$\lambda_L = 2 \lim_{t \to \infty} \frac{\frac{d}{dt}\phi^{-1}(2t)}{\frac{d}{dt}\phi^{-1}(t)}$$

provided that $\lim_{t \to \infty} \frac{d}{dt}\phi^{-1}(t) = 0$. Otherwise, there is no lower tail dependence.

Independence copula

For n independent random variables with common cumulative distribution function $F(x_j)$, $j = 1, 2, ..., d$, the joint cdf is given by $\prod_{j=1}^d F(x_j)$. The corresponding copula is called the independence (or product) copula and is given by

$$C(u_1, ..., u_d) = \prod_{j=1}^d u_j.$$

It is an Archimedean copula with generator $\phi(u) = -\ln u$. This trivial example is only included here to illustrate the fact that is Archimedean. The measure of association, Kendall's tau can be computed to be 0 as we should expect due to independence.

Note that in the bivariate case

$$\lambda_U = \lim_{u \to 1} \frac{1 - 2u + C(u,u)}{1 - u}$$

$$= \lim_{u \to 1} \frac{1 - 2u + u^2}{1 - u}$$

$$= \lim_{u \to 1} 1 - u$$

$$= 0,$$

demonstrating that independence does indeed result to no upper tail dependence as we would expect from the definition of independence. The corresponding index of lower tail dependence is also equal to 0. Note that

$$\lim_{t \to 0} \frac{d}{dt} \phi^{-1}(t) = \lim_{t \to 0} \frac{d}{dt} e^{-t} \neq -\infty.$$

Cook-Johnson copula

The Cook-Johnson copula [23] has generator $\phi(u) = u^{-\theta} - 1$, $\theta > 0$. Hence, the Cook-Johnson copula is the form

$$C(u_1, ..., u_d) = \left(u_1^{-\theta} + ... + u_d^{-\theta} - d + 1\right)^{-\frac{1}{\theta}}.$$

The Cook-Johnson copula is tuned through a single parameter θ which can be estimated from data using a statistical procedure, such as maximum likelihood. In a bivariate framework, the Cook-Johnson copula is also known as the **Clayton copula** [22].

The measure of association, Kendall's tau, is easily calculated to be

$$\tau_K(X_1, X_2) = \frac{\theta}{\theta + 2}.$$

The (pairwise) index of upper tail dependence is $\lambda_U = 0$ because

$$\lim_{t \to 0} \frac{d}{dt} \phi^{-1}(t) = \lim_{t \to 0} \frac{d}{dt} (t + 1)^{-\frac{1}{\theta}} = 1.$$

It does, however, have lower tail dependence of $\lambda_L = 2^{-1/\theta}$. The density of the Clayton copula is shown in Figure 8.1. The left panel shows the contours of the density function. The right panel shows a simulation of points from the Clayton copula. Note that there is a strong correlation in the lower left corner of each panel. This indicates the lower tail dependence. In contrast, in the upper right corner, there is no evidence of dependence. The corresponding Clayton copula pdf is shown in Figure 8.2.

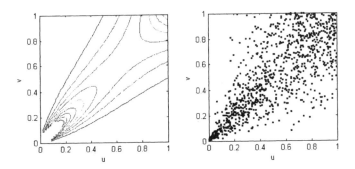

Fig. 8.1 Clayton copula density $(\theta = 3)$

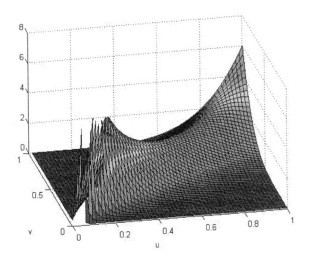

Fig. 8.2 Clayton copula pdf $(\theta = 3)$

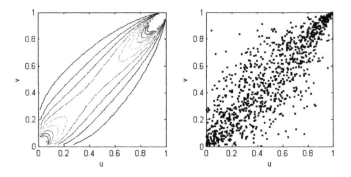

Fig. 8.3   Gumbel copula density ($\theta = 3$)

Gumbel-Hougaard copula
The Gumbel-Hougaard copula[49] has generator

$$\phi(u) = (-\ln u)^{\theta}, \quad \theta \geq 1.$$

Hence, the Gumbel-Hougaard copula is the form

$$C(u_1, ..., u_d) = \exp\left\{-\left[(-\ln u_1)^{\theta} + ... + (-\ln u_d)^{\theta}\right]\right\}^{\frac{1}{\theta}}.$$

The Gumbel-Hougaard copula is also tuned through a single parameter θ. In the bivariate case, it is known as the **Gumbel copula** [49].
The measure of association, Kendall's tau, is easily calculated to be

$$\tau_K(X_1, X_2) = 1 - 1/\theta.$$

The index of upper tail dependence is $\lambda_U = 2 - 2^{1/\theta}$. This upper tail dependence is evident in the upper right corner of each panel in Figure 8.3. The corresponding Gumbel copula pdf is shown in Figure 8.4. It is a bit difficult to see the tail dependence directly from this figure. The upper tail dependence is captured in the narrowness and steepness of the ridge in the upper right-hand corner. It should also be noted that there is no upper tail dependence when $\theta = 1$, and that tail dependence approaches 1 as θ becomes large.

Frank copula
The Frank copula [39] has generator

$$\phi(u) = -\ln\frac{e^{-\theta u} - 1}{e^{-\theta} - 1}, \quad -\infty < \theta < \infty, \theta \neq 0.$$

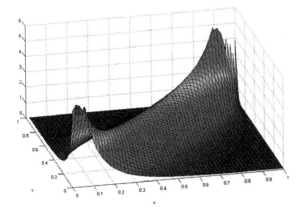

Fig. 8.4 Gumbel copula pdf ($\theta = 3$)

Hence, the Frank copula is the form

$$C\left(u_1, ..., u_d\right) = -\ln\left\{1 + \frac{\left(e^{-\theta u_1} - 1\right) ... \left(e^{-\theta u_d} - 1\right)}{e^{-\theta} - 1}\right\}^{\frac{1}{\theta}}.$$

The Frank copula is also tuned through a single parameter θ. The measure of association, Kendall's tau, for the Frank copula is

$$\tau_K\left(X_1, X_2\right) = 1 - \frac{4}{\theta}\left(\frac{1}{\theta}\int_0^\theta \frac{u}{e^u - 1}du + \frac{\theta}{2} - 1\right),$$

which is a rather complicated function.

The index of upper tail dependence is $\lambda_U = 0$, indicating that the Frank copula has no upper tail dependence. This can be seen from the fact that

$$\lim_{t \to 0} \frac{d}{dt}\phi^{-1}(t) = -\lim_{t \to 0}\frac{1}{\theta}\ln\left[1 - \left(1 - e^{-\theta}\right)e^{-t}\right] = \frac{1 - e^\theta}{\theta} \neq -\infty.$$

The lack of tail dependence can be seen from both Figures 8.5 and 8.6, where there is no concentration of points in the upper right and lower left corners. Frees, Carriere, and Valdez [40] use Frank's copula for a study of joint lifetimes.

Ali-Mikhail-Haq copula

The Ali-Mikhail-Haq (AMH) copula [4] has generator

$$\phi(u) = \ln\frac{1 - \theta(1 - u)}{u}, \quad -1 \leq \theta < 1.$$

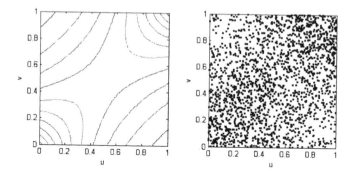

Fig. 8.5   Frank copula density $(\theta = 3)$

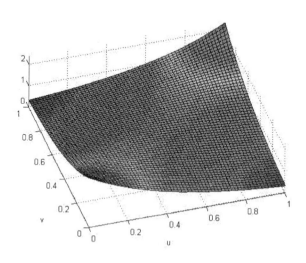

Fig. 8.6   Frank copula pdf $(\theta = 2)$

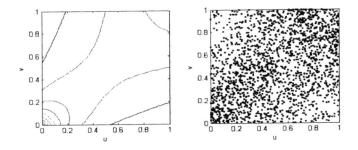

Fig. 8.7   Ali-Mikhail-Haq copula density ($\theta = 0.8$)

Hence, the AMH copula is the form

$$C\left(u_1, ..., u_d\right) = \frac{\prod_{j=1}^{d} u_j}{1 - \theta \prod_{j=1}^{d}\left(1 - u_j\right)}.$$

The AMH copula is also tuned through a single parameter θ. The measure of association, Kendall's tau, for the AMH copula can be calculated as

$$\tau_K\left(X_1, X_2\right) = 1 - 2\frac{\left(\theta - 1\right)^2 \ln\left(1 - \theta\right)}{3\theta^2} - \frac{1}{9\theta^3}.$$

The index of upper tail dependence is $\lambda_U = 0$ because

$$\lim_{t \to 0} \frac{d}{dt}\phi^{-1}(t) = \lim_{t \to 0}\frac{1 - \theta}{t - \theta} = -\frac{1 - \theta}{\theta^2} \neq -\infty.$$

This is also evident from Figures 8.7 and 8.8 by examining the upper right-hand corners.

Joe copula
The Joe copula [61] has generator

$$\phi(u) = -\ln\left[1 - \left(1 - u\right)^{\theta}\right], \ \theta \geq 1.$$

The Joe copula has the form

$$C\left(u_1, ..., u_d\right) = 1 - \left[\sum_{j=1}^{d}\left(1 - u_j\right)^{\theta} - \prod_{j=1}^{d}\left(1 - u_j\right)^{\theta}\right]^{1/\theta}.$$

Note that $\phi^{-1}(t) = 1 - \left(1 - e^{-t}\right)^{1/\theta}$, which has a slope of $-\infty$ as $t \to 0$. The measure of association, Kendall's tau, is very complicated, with no convenient closed form. With a bit of calculus, it can be shown that the index of upper

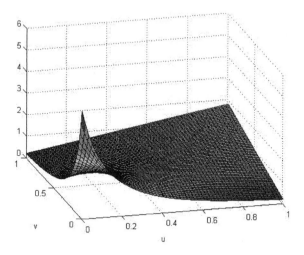

Fig. 8.8 Ali-Mikhail-Haq copula pdf ($\theta = 0.8$)

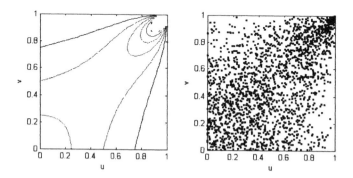

Fig. 8.9 Joe copula density ($\theta = 2$)

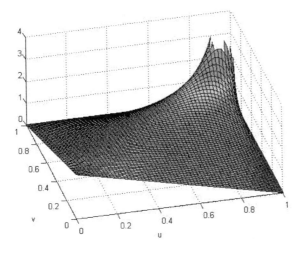

Fig. 8.10   Joe copula density ($\theta = 2$)

tail dependence is $2 - 2^{1/\theta}$. The concentration in the upper right-hand corner is seen in both Figures 8.9 and 8.10.

BB1 copula
The BB1 copula [62] is a two-parameter copula with generator

$$\phi(u) = (u^{-\delta} - 1)^{\theta}, \ \delta > 0, \ \theta \geq 1.$$

It has the form

$$C(u_1, ..., u_d) = \left\{ 1 + \left[\sum_{j=1}^{d} \left(u_j^{-\delta} - 1 \right)^{\theta} \right]^{1/\theta} \right\}^{-1/\delta}.$$

The upper tail dependence can be calculated to be $2 - 2^{1/\theta}$. Both upper and lower tail dependence can be seen in Figures 8.11 and 8.12.

BB3 copula
The BB3 copula [62] is a two-parameter copula with generator

$$\phi(u) = \exp \left[\delta \left(- \ln u \right)^{\theta} \right] - 1, \ \theta \geq 1, \ \delta > 0.$$

It has the form

$$C(u_1, ..., u_d) = \exp \left\{ - \frac{1}{\delta} \left[\ln \left(\sum_{j=1}^{d} \exp \left[\delta \left(- \ln u_j \right)^{\theta} \right] - 1 \right) \right] \right\}^{1/\theta}.$$

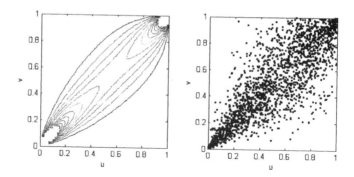

Fig. 8.11   BB1 copula density $(\theta = 2,\ \delta = 1.5)$

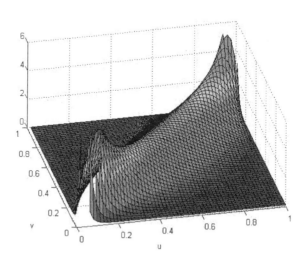

Fig. 8.12   BB1 copula pdf $(\theta = 2,\ \delta = 1.5)$

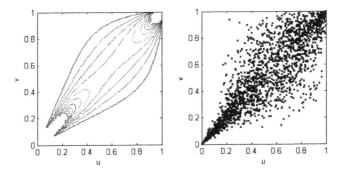

Fig. 8.13   BB3 copula density ($\theta = 2$, $\delta = 1.5$)

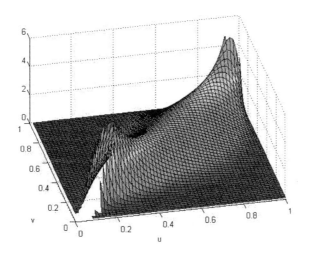

Fig. 8.14   BB3 copula pdf ($\theta = 2$, $\delta = 1.5$)

The BB3 copula has upper tail dependence of $\lambda_U = 2 - 2^{1-1/\theta}$. The upper tail dependence is evident in Figures 8.13 and 8.14.

BB6 copula

The BB6 copula [62] is a two-parameter copula with generator

$$\phi(u) = \left\{ -\ln\left[1 - (1-u)^\theta \right] \right\}^\delta, \; \theta \geq 1, \; \delta > 1.$$

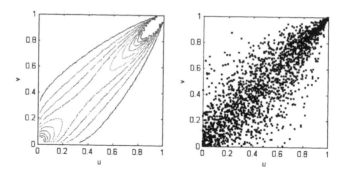

Fig. 8.15   BB6 copula density $(\theta = 2, \delta = 2)$

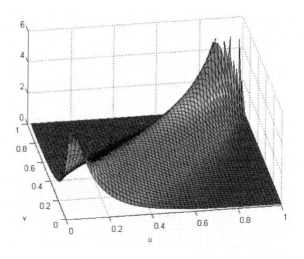

Fig. 8.16   BB6 copula pdf $(\theta = 2, \delta = 2)$

It has the form

$$C(u_1, ..., u_d) = 1 - \left\{ 1 - \exp\left[-\left(\ln \sum_{j=1}^{d} \left\{ -\ln\left[1 - (1 - u_j)^\theta \right] \right\}^\delta \right)^{1/\delta} \right] \right\}^{1/\theta}.$$

The BB6 copula has upper tail dependence of $\lambda_U = 2 - 2^{1/(\theta\delta)}$. See Figures 8.15 and 8.16 to confirm the tail dependence visually.

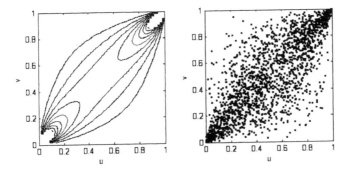

Fig. 8.17   BB7 copula density ($\theta = 2.7$, $\delta = 1.8$)

BB7 copula

The BB7 copula [62] is a two-parameter copula with generator

$$\phi(u) = \left\{ \left[1 - (1-u)^{\theta} \right] \right\}^{-\delta} - 1, \ \theta \geq 1, \ \delta > 0.$$

It has the form

$$C(u_1, ..., u_d) = 1 - \left\{ 1 - \left(\sum_{j=1}^{d} \left\{ \left[1 - (1-u_j)^{\theta} \right]^{-\delta} \right\} - 1 \right)^{-1/\delta} \right\}^{1/\theta}.$$

The BB7 copula has upper tail dependence of $2 - 2^{1/\theta}$. The tail dependence is evident from Figures 8.17 and 8.18.

8.6 ELLIPTICAL COPULAS

Elliptical copulas are those associated with elliptical distributions. The two main models are the Gaussian copula associated with the multivariate normal distribution and the (Student) t copula associated with the multivariate t distribution.

Gaussian copula

The Gaussian copula is given by

$$C(u_1, ..., u_d) = \Phi_{\mathbf{P}} \left(\Phi^{-1}(u_1), ..., \Phi^{-1}(u_d) \right)$$

where $\Phi(x)$ is the cdf of the standard univariate normal distribution and $\Phi_{\mathbf{P}}(x_1, ..., x_d)$ is the joint cdf of the standard multivariate normal distribution (with zero mean and variance of 1 for each component) and correlation matrix

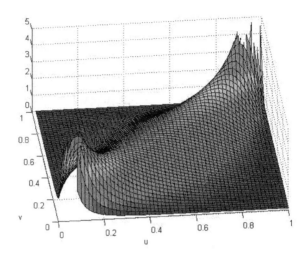

Fig. 8.18   BB7 copula pdf ($\theta = 2.7$, $\delta = 1.8$)

P. Because the correlation matrix contains $d(d - 1)/2$ pairwise correlations, this is the number of parameters in the copula. There is no simple closed form for the copula. In the two-dimensional case (with only one correlation element ρ), the Gaussian copula can be written as

$$C\left(u_1, u_2\right) = \int_{-\infty}^{\Phi^{-1}(u_1)} \int_{-\infty}^{\Phi^{-1}(u_2)} \frac{1}{2\pi\sqrt{1-\rho^2}} \exp\left\{-\frac{x^2 - 2\rho xy + y^2}{2\left(1-\rho^2\right)}\right\} dy\ dx.$$

It should be noted that if all the correlations in **P** are zero, then the Gaussian copula reduces to the independence copula.

The measure of association, Kendall's tau, has been shown to be

$$\tau_K\left(X_1, X_2\right) = \frac{2}{\pi} \arcsin\left(\rho\right)$$

by Fang and Fang [34] in the context of a much larger class. Then in the multivariate case, the pairwise Kendall's tau is

$$\tau_K\left(X_i, X_j\right) = \frac{2}{\pi} \arcsin\left(\rho_{ij}\right).$$

The Gaussian copula has no tail dependence ($\lambda_U = \lambda_L = 0$) except in the special case with $\rho = 1$, where there is perfect correlation resulting in indices of upper and lower tail dependence of 1. It is possible to construct copulas that are closely related by using finite mixtures of normal distributions rather than normal distributions. However, this approach does not introduce tail dependence.

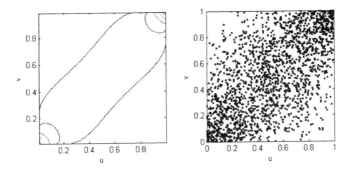

Fig. 8.19 Gaussian copula density ($\rho = 0.6$)

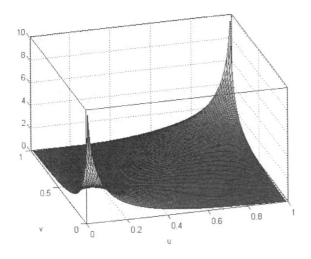

Fig. 8.20 Gaussian copula pdf ($\rho = 0.6$)

Figures 8.19 and 8.20 illustrate the Gaussian copula density function. It is interesting to note that it appears that there is some tail dependence, However, the definition of tail dependence is asymptotic in nature, that is, when it is a limiting function as the argument goes to either 0 or 1.

The t copula

The t copula is given by

$$C\left(u_1, ..., u_d\right) = \mathbf{t}_{\nu, \mathbf{P}}^{-1}\left(t_\nu^{-1}\left(u_1\right), ..., t_\nu^{-1}\left(u_d\right)\right)$$

where $t_\nu(x)$ is the cdf of the standard univariate t distribution with ν degrees of freedom and $\mathbf{t}_{v, \mathbf{P}}(x_1, ..., x_d)$ is the joint cdf of the standard multivariate t

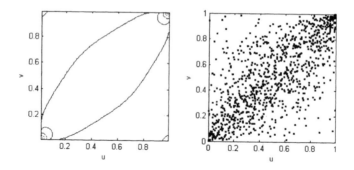

Fig. 8.21 t copula density ($\rho = 0.3$, $\nu = 4$)

distribution with ν degrees of freedom for each component and where $\mathbf{P}$ is a correlation matrix. In the two-dimensional case (with only one correlation element ρ), the t copula can be written as

$$C(u_1, u_2) = \int_{-\infty}^{t_\nu^{-1}(u_1)} \int_{-\infty}^{t_\nu^{-1}(u_2)} \frac{1}{2\pi\sqrt{1-\rho^2}} \left\{ 1 + \frac{x^2 - 2\rho xy + y^2}{\nu(1-\rho^2)} \right\}^{-1-\frac{\nu}{2}} dy \; dx.$$

The measure of association, Kendall's tau, has been shown by Lindskog et al. [77] to be

$$\tau_K(X_1, X_2) = \frac{2}{\pi} \arcsin \rho$$

identical to that of the Gaussian copula. It should be noted that, unlike the Gaussian copula, having the correlation ρ equal to zero does not result in the independence copula. The t copula has upper tail dependence of

$$\lambda_U = 2\, t_{\nu+1} \left(-\sqrt{\frac{1-\rho}{1+\rho}} (\nu + 1) \right).$$

Note that for $\rho = 0$, the upper tail dependence is not zero.

In the multivariate case, we can obtain pairwise Kendall's tau and the pairwise index of upper tail dependence for dimensions i and j as

$$\tau_K(X_i, X_j) = \frac{2}{\pi} \arcsin \rho_{ij}$$

$$\lambda_U = 2\, t_{\nu+1} \left(-\sqrt{\frac{1-\rho_{ij}}{1+\rho_{ij}}} (\nu + 1) \right).$$

Figures 8.21 and 8.22 illustrate the t copula density function. It is interesting to note that the density looks a lot like the Gaussian density but much more concentrated in the upper and lower corners. This feature has made the t

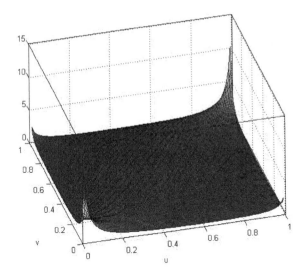

Fig. 8.22   t copula pdf ($\rho = 0.3$, $\nu = 4$)

copula the most popular alternative to the Gaussian copula. For a fixed correlation coefficient ρ, the degree of upper tail dependence can be tuned through
the single parameter ν, known as the "number of degrees of freedom," a term
that comes from the application of the t distribution in statistical sampling
theory.

8.7   EXTREME VALUE COPULAS

Another very important class of copulas is the extreme value class which is
associated with the extreme value distributions discussed in Chapter 7. This
class of copulas is defined in terms of the scaling property of extreme value
distributions.   A copula is an extreme value (EV) copula if it satisfies

$$C\left(u_1^n, ..., u_d^n\right) = C^n\left(u_1, ..., u_d\right)$$

for all $(u_1, ..., u_d)$ and for all $n > 0$.   This scaling property results in the EV
copula having the stability of the maximum (or max-stable) property. To see
this, we consider the bivariate case. Suppose that $(X_1, Y_1), (X_2, Y_2), ..., (X_n, Y_n)$
are n independent and identically distributed random pairs (bivariate random variables) drawn from joint distribution $F(x, y)$, with marginal distributions $F_X(x)$ and $F_Y(y)$ and copula $C(x, y)$. Let $M_X = \max(X_1, ..., X_n)$ and
$M_Y = \max(Y_1, ..., Y_n)$ denote the component-wise maxima. Then the distrib-

ution function of the random pair (M_X, M_Y) is

$$\Pr\left(M_X \le x,\ M_Y \le y\right) = \Pr\left(X_i \le x,\ Y_i \le y,\ \text{for all } i\right)$$
$$= F^n\left(x, y\right).$$

Similarly, the marginal distributions of M_X and M_Y are $F_X^n(x)$ and $F_Y^n(y)$. Then because

$$F(x, y) = C(F_X(x), F_Y(y)),$$

we can write the joint distribution of the maxima as

$$F^n\left(x, y\right) = C^n\left(F_X(x), F_Y(y)\right)$$
$$= C^n\left([F_X^n(x)]^{1/n}, [F_Y^n(y)]^{1/n}\right).$$

Therefore the copula of the maxima is given by

$$C_{\max}\left(u_1, u_2\right) = C^n(u_1^{1/n}, u_2^{1/n}),$$

or equivalently

$$C_{\max}\left(u_1^n, u_2^n\right) = C^n(u_1, u_2).$$

Thus if the copula for the maxima $C_{\max}$ is of the same form as the original copula C, then the copula has the max-stable property. Extreme value copulas are then defined as those copulas with the max-stable property. Max-stability means that the copula associated with the random pair (M_X, M_Y) is also $C(x, y)$. The result is illustrated for two dimensions above, but can be extended to the d-dimensional copula. The dependency of the random pair of maxima is very important in risk modeling. A positive dependency can be very dangerous because an extreme outcome of one risk means a greater chance of a simultaneous extreme outcome of the other. In operational risk, it is conceivable that there may be a common underlying cause driving both extremes.

In two dimensions, it can be shown [62] that the EV copula can be represented as

$$C\left(u_1, u_2\right) = \exp\left\{\ln\left(u_1 u_2\right)\ A\left(\frac{\ln u_1}{\ln\left(u_1 u_2\right)}\right)\right\}$$

where A is a dependence function satisfying

$$A(w) = \int_0^1 \max\left[x\left(1 - w\right), w\left(1 - x\right)\right]\ dH(x)$$

for any $w \in [0, 1]$ and H is a distribution function on $[0, 1]$. It turns out that $A(w)$ must be a convex function satisfying

$$\max(w, 1 - w) \le A\left(w\right) \le 1,\ \ 0 < w < 1$$

and that any differentiable, convex function $A(w)$ satisfying this inequality can be used to construct a copula. Note that the independence copula results from setting $A(w)$ to its upper bound $A(w) = 1$. At the other extreme, if $A(w) = \max(w, 1 - w)$, then there is perfect correlation, and hence perfect dependency with $C(u, u) = u$.

It is convenient to write the index of upper tail dependence in terms of the dependence function $A(w)$. The result is that

$$
\begin{aligned}
\lambda_U &= \lim_{u \to 1} \frac{1 - 2u + C(u, u)}{1 - u} \\
&= \lim_{u \to 1} \frac{1 - 2u + u^{2A(1/2)}}{1 - u} \\
&= \lim_{u \to 1} 2 - 2A(1/2)u^{2A(1/2)-1} \\
&= 2 - 2A(1/2).
\end{aligned}
$$

If a copula is specified through $A(w)$, then the index of upper tail dependency is easily calculated. There are several well-known copulas in this class.

Gumbel copula

The Gumbel copula was discussed previously as an example of an Archimedean copula. It is also an extreme value copula with dependence function

$$
A(w) = \left[w^\theta + (1 - w)^\theta \right]^{1/\theta}, \quad \theta \geq 0.
$$

From this, by setting $w = 1/2$, the Gumbel copula is seen to have index of upper tail dependence of $2 - 2^{1/\theta}$.

Galambos copula

The Galambos copula [42] has the dependence function

$$
A(w) = 1 - \left[w^{-\theta} + (1 - w)^{-\theta} \right]^{-1/\theta}, \quad \theta > 0.
$$

Unlike the Gumbel copula, it is not Archimedean. It has index of upper tail dependence of $2^{-1/\theta}$. The bivariate copula is of the form

$$
C(u_1, u_2) = u_1 u_2 \exp \left\{ \left[(-\ln u_1)^{-\theta} + (-\ln u_2)^{-\theta} \right]^{-\frac{1}{\theta}} \right\}.
$$

An asymmetric version of the Galambos copula with three parameters has dependence function

$$
A(w) = 1 - \left\{ (\alpha w)^{-\theta} + [\beta (1 - w)]^{-\theta} \right\}^{-1/\theta}, \quad 0 \leq \alpha, \beta \leq 1.
$$

It has index of upper tail dependence of $(\alpha^{-\theta} + \beta^{-\theta})^{-1/\theta}$. The one-parameter version is obtained by setting $\alpha = \beta = 1$. The bivariate asymmetric Galambos copula has the form

$$
C(u_1, u_2) = u_1 u_2 \exp \left\{ \left[(-\alpha \ln u_1)^{-\theta} + (-\beta \ln u_2)^{-\theta} \right]^{-1/\theta} \right\}.
$$

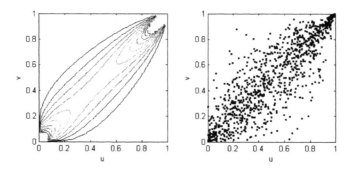

Fig. 8.23 Galambos copula density ($\theta = 2.5$)

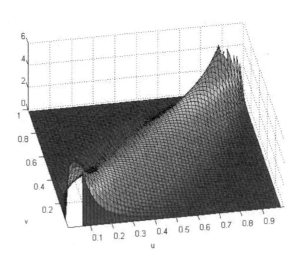

Fig. 8.24 Galambos copula pdf ($\theta = 2.5$)

Figures 8.23 and 8.24 demonstrate the clear upper tail dependence.

Hüsler and Reiss copula
The Hüsler and Reiss copula [57] has dependence function

$$A(w) = w\Phi\left[\frac{1}{\theta} + \frac{\theta}{2}\ln\left(\frac{w}{1-w}\right)\right] + (1-w)\Phi\left[\frac{1}{\theta} - \frac{\theta}{2}\ln\left(\frac{w}{1-w}\right)\right], \quad \theta > 0,$$

where $\Phi(x)$ is the cdf of the standard normal distribution. When $w = 1/2$, $A(1/2) = \Phi(1/\theta)$, resulting in an index of upper tail dependence of $2 - 2\Phi(1/\theta)$.

Tawn copula
The Gumbel copula can be extended to a three-parameter asymmetric version by introducing two additional parameters, α and β, into the dependence function [114]

$$A(w) = (1-\alpha)w + (1-\beta)(1-w) + \left\{(\alpha w)^\theta + [\beta(1-w)]^{1/\theta}\right\}, \quad 0 \le \alpha, \beta \le 1.$$

This is called the Tawn copula. Note that the one-parameter version of $A(w)$ is obtained by setting $\alpha = \beta = 1$. The bivariate asymmetric Gumbel copula has the form

$$C(u_1, u_2) = u_1^{1-\alpha} u_2^{1-\beta} \exp\left\{-\left[(-\alpha\ln u_1)^\theta + (-\beta\ln u_2)^\theta\right]^{1/\theta}\right\}.$$

BB5 copula
The BB5 copula [62] is another extension of the Gumbel copula but with only two parameters. Its dependence function is

$$A(w) = \left\{w^\theta + (1-w)^\theta - \left[w^{-\delta\theta} + (1-w)^{-\delta\theta}\right]^{-1/\delta}\right\}^{1/\theta}, \quad \delta > 0, \ \theta > 1.$$

The BB5 copula has the form

$$C(u_1, u_2) = \exp\left[-\left\{(-\ln u_1)^\theta + (-\ln u_2)^\theta - \left[(-\ln u_1)^{-\delta\theta} + (-\ln u_2)^{-\delta\theta}\right]^{-1/\delta}\right\}^{1/\theta}\right].$$

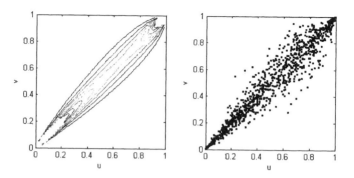

Fig. 8.25   BB4 copula density $(\theta = 3, \delta = 1.2)$

8.8   ARCHIMAX COPULAS

Archimedean and extreme value copulas can be combined into a single class of copulas called Archimax copulas. Archimax copulas are represented as

$$C(u_1, u_2) = \phi^{-1}\left[\{\phi(u_1) + \phi(u_2)\} A\left(\frac{\phi(u_1)}{\phi(u_1) + \phi(u_2)}\right)\right]$$

where $\phi(u)$ is a valid Archimedean generator and $A(w)$ is a valid dependence function. It can be shown [20] that that this is itself a valid copula. This general setup allows for a wide range of copulas and therefore shapes of distributions. The BB4 copula is one such example.

BB4 copula
The BB4 copula [62] is an Archimax copula with

$$\phi(u) = u^{-\theta} - 1, \ \theta \geq 0,$$

as with the Clayton copula and

$$A(w) = 1 - \left\{w^{-\delta} + (1 - w)^{-\delta}\right\}^{-1/\delta}, \ \theta > 0, \ \delta > 0,$$

leading to the copula of the form

$$C(u_1, u_2) = \left\{u_1^{-\theta} + u_2^{-\theta} - 1 - \left[\left(u_1^{-\theta} - 1\right)^{-\delta} + \left(u_2^{-\theta} - 1\right)^{-\delta}\right]^{-1/\delta}\right\}^{1/\theta}.$$

It is illustrated in Figures 8.25 and 8.26.

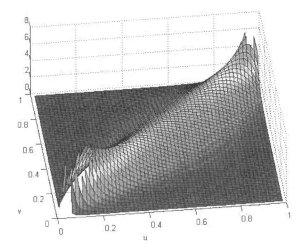

Fig. 8.26   BB4 copula pdf $(\theta = 2, \delta = 1.2)$

8.9   EXERCISES

8.1 Prove that the Clayton, Frank, and Ali-Mikhail-Haq copulas have no upper tail dependence.

8.2 Prove that the Gumbel copula has index of upper tail dependence equal to $2 - 2^{-1/\theta}$.

8.3 Prove that the Gaussian copula has no upper tail dependence. Hint: Begin by obtaining the conditional distribution of X given $Y = y$ from the bivariate normal distribution.

8.4 Prove that the t copula has index of upper tail dependence

$$\lambda_U = 2\, t_{\nu+1}\left(-\sqrt{\frac{1-\rho}{1+\rho}}\,(\nu+1)\right).$$

Hint: Begin by showing that if (X, Y) comes from a bivariate t distribution, each with ν degrees of freedom, conditional on $Y = y$, the random variable

$$\sqrt{\frac{\nu+1}{\nu+y^2}}\,\frac{X - \rho y}{\sqrt{1-\rho^2}}$$

has a t distribution with $\nu + 1$ degrees of freedom.

8.5 For the EV copula, show that if $A(w)=\max(w, 1-w)$, the copula is the straight line $C\,(u, u) = u$.

8.6 For the bivariate EV copula, show that $A\left(w\right) = -\ln C\left(e^{-w}, e^{-(1-w)}\right)$.

8.7 Prove that the index of upper tail dependence of the Gumbel copula is $2 - 2^{1/\theta}$.

Part III

Statistical methods for calibrating models of operational risk

9

Review of mathematical statistics

Nothing is as easy as it looks.

—Murphy

9.1 INTRODUCTION

In this chapter, we review some key concepts from mathematical statistics. Mathematical statistics is a broad subject that includes many topics not covered in this chapter. For those topics that are covered in this chapter, it is assumed that the reader has had at least some prior exposure. The topics of greatest importance for constructing models are estimation and hypothesis testing. Because the Bayesian approach to statistical inference is often either ignored or treated lightly in introductory mathematical statistics texts and courses, it receives a more in-depth coverage in this text in Section 10.5.

We begin by assuming that we have some data; that is, we have a sample. We also assume that we have a model (i.e., a distribution) that we wish to calibrate by estimating the "true" values of the parameters of the model. This data will be used to estimate the parameter values. The formula form of an estimate is called the **estimator**. The estimator is itself a random variable because it is a function of random variables, sometimes called a random function. The numerical value of the estimator based on data is called the **estimate**. The estimate is a single number.

Because the parameter estimates are based on a sample from the population and not the entire population, they will not be exactly the true values, but only estimates of the true values. In applications, it is important to have an idea of how good the estimates are by understanding the potential error of the estimates. One way to express this is with an interval estimate. Rather than focusing on a particular value, a range of plausible values can be presented.

9.2 POINT ESTIMATION

9.2.1 Introduction

Regardless of how a model is estimated, it is extremely unlikely that the estimated model will exactly match the true distribution. Ideally, we would like to be able to measure the error we will be making when using the estimated model. But this is clearly impossible! If we knew the amount of error we had made, we could adjust our estimate by that amount and then have no error at all. The best we can do is discover how much error is inherent in repeated use of the *procedure*, as opposed to how much error we actually make with our current estimate. Therefore, this section is about the quality of the answers produced from the procedure, not about the quality of a particular answer.

When constructing models, there are a number of types of error. Several will not be covered here. Among these are model error (choosing the wrong model) and sampling frame error (trying to draw inferences about a population that differs from the one sampled). An example of model error is selecting a Pareto distribution when the true distribution is Weibull. An example of sampling frame error is using sampled losses from one process to estimate those of another.

The type of error we can measure is the error that is due to the use of a sample from the population to make inferences about the entire population. Errors occur when the items sampled do not represent the population. As noted earlier, we cannot know whether the particular items sampled today do or do not represent the population. We can, however, estimate the extent to which estimators are affected by the possibility of a nonrepresentative sample.

The approach taken in this section is to consider all the samples that might be taken from the population. Each such sample leads to an estimated quantity (for example, a probability, a parameter value, or a moment). We do not expect the estimated quantities to always match the true value. For a sensible estimation procedure we do expect that for some samples the quantity will match the true value, for many it will be close, and for only a few it will be quite different. If we can construct a measure of how well the set of potential estimates matches the true value, we have a good idea of the quality of our estimation procedure. The approach outlined here is often called the **classical** or **frequentist** approach to estimation.

9.2.2 Measures of quality of estimators

9.2.2.1 Introduction There are a number of ways to measure the quality of an estimator. Three of them are discussed here. Two examples will be used throughout to illustrate them.

Example 9.1 *A population contains the values 1, 3, 5, and 9. We want to estimate the population mean by taking a sample of size 2 with replacement.*

Example 9.2 *A population has the exponential distribution with a mean of θ. We want to estimate the population mean by taking a sample of size 3 with replacement.*

Both examples are clearly artificial in that we know the answers prior to sampling (4.5 and θ). However, that knowledge will make apparent the error in the procedure we select. For practical applications, we will need to be able to estimate the error when we do not know the true value of the quantity being estimated.

9.2.2.2 Unbiasedness When constructing an estimator, it would be good if, on average, the errors we make cancel each other out. More formally, let θ be the quantity we want to estimate. Let $\hat{\theta}$ be the random variable that represents the estimator and let $\mathrm{E}(\hat{\theta}|\theta)$ be the expected value of the estimator $\hat{\theta}$ when θ is the true parameter value.

Definition 9.3 *An estimator, $\hat{\theta}$, is **unbiased** if $\mathrm{E}(\hat{\theta}|\theta) = \theta$ for all θ. The* **bias** *is* $\mathrm{bias}_{\hat{\theta}}(\theta) = \mathrm{E}(\hat{\theta}|\theta) - \theta$.

The bias depends on the estimator being used and may also depend on the particular value of θ.

Example 9.4 *For Example 9.1 determine the bias of the sample mean as an estimator of the population mean.*

The population mean is $\theta = 4.5$. The sample mean is the average of the two observations. It is also the estimator we would use when using the empirical approach. In all cases, we assume that sampling is random. In other words, every sample of size n has the same chance of being drawn. Such sampling also implies that any member of the population has the same chance of being observed as any other member. For this example, there are 16 equally likely ways the sample could have turned out. They are listed in Table 9.1.

This leads to the 16 equally likely values for the sample mean appearing in Table 9.2.

Combining the common values, the sample mean, usually denoted $\bar{X}$, has the probability distribution given in Table 9.3.

The expected value of the estimator is

$$\mathrm{E}(\bar{X}) = [1(1) + 2(2) + 3(3) + 4(2) + 5(3) + 6(2) + 7(2) + 9(1)]/16 = 4.5$$

Table 9.1   The 16 possible outcomes in Example 9.4

1,1	1,3	1,5	1,9	3,1	3,3	3,5	3,9
5,1	5,3	5,5	5,9	9,1	9,3	9,5	9,9

Table 9.2   The 16 possible sample means in Example 9.4

1	2	3	5	2	3	4	6
3	4	5	7	5	6	7	9

Table 9.3   Distribution of sample mean in Example 9.4

x	1	2	3	4	5	6	7	9
$p_{\bar{X}}(x)$	1/16	2/16	3/16	2/16	3/16	2/16	2/16	1/16

and so the sample mean is an unbiased estimator of the population mean for this example. □

Example 9.5 *For Example 9.2 determine the bias of the sample mean and the sample median as estimators of the population mean.*

The sample mean is $\bar{X} = (X_1 + X_2 + X_3)/3$, where each X_j represents one of the observations from the exponential population. Its expected value is

$$\mathrm{E}(\bar{X}) = \mathrm{E}\left(\frac{X_1 + X_2 + X_3}{3}\right) = \tfrac{1}{3}\left[\mathrm{E}(X_1) + \mathrm{E}(X_2) + \mathrm{E}(X_3)\right]$$
$$= \tfrac{1}{3}(\theta + \theta + \theta) = \theta$$

and therefore the sample mean is an unbiased estimator of the population mean.

Investigating the sample median is a bit more difficult. The distribution function of the middle of three observations can be found as follows, using Y as the random variable of interest and X as the random variable for an observation from the population:

$$F_Y(y) = \Pr(Y \le y) = \Pr(X_1, X_2, X_3 \le y) + \Pr(X_1, X_2 \le y, X_3 > y)$$
$$+ \Pr(X_1, X_3 \le y, X_2 > y) + \Pr(X_2, X_3 \le y, X_1 > y)$$
$$= F_X(y)^3 + 3F_X(y)^2[1 - F_X(y)]$$
$$= [1 - e^{-y/\theta}]^3 + 3[1 - e^{-y/\theta}]^2 e^{-y/\theta}.$$

The probability density function is

$$f_Y(y) = F_Y'(y) = \frac{6}{\theta}\left(e^{-2y/\theta} - e^{-3y/\theta}\right).$$

The expected value of this estimator is

$$E(Y|\theta) = \int_0^\infty y\frac{6}{\theta}\left(e^{-2y/\theta} - e^{-3y/\theta}\right)dy$$
$$= \frac{5\theta}{6}.$$

This estimator is clearly biased,[1] with $\text{bias}_Y(\theta) = 5\theta/6 - \theta = -\theta/6$. On average, this estimator underestimates the true value. It is also easy to see that the sample median can be turned into an unbiased estimator by multiplying it by 1.2. □

For the problem in Example 9.2, we have found two estimators (the sample mean and 1.2 times the sample median) that are both unbiased. We will need additional criteria to decide which one we prefer.

Some estimators exhibit a small amount of bias, which vanishes as the sample size goes to infinity.

Definition 9.6 *Let $\hat{\theta}_n$ be an estimator of θ based on a sample size of n. The estimator is **asymptotically unbiased** if*

$$\lim_{n\to\infty} E(\hat{\theta}_n|\theta) = \theta$$

for all θ.

Example 9.7 *Suppose a random variable has the uniform distribution on the interval $(0, \theta)$. Consider the estimator $\hat{\theta}_n = \max(X_1, \ldots, X_n)$. Show that this estimator is asymptotically unbiased.*

Let Y_n be the maximum from a sample of size n. Then

$$F_{Y_n}(y) = \Pr(Y_n \le y) = \Pr(X_1 \le y, \ldots, X_n \le y)$$
$$= [F_X(y)]^n$$
$$= (y/\theta)^n$$
$$f_{Y_n}(y) = \frac{ny^{n-1}}{\theta^n}, \quad 0 < y < \theta.$$

---

[1] The sample median is not likely to be a good estimator of the population mean. This example studies it for comparison purposes. Because the population median is $\theta \ln 2$, the sample median is biased for the population median.

The expected value is

$$E(Y_n|\theta) = \int_0^\theta ny^n\theta^{-n}dy = \frac{n}{n+1}y^{n+1}\theta^{-n}\Big|_0^\theta = \frac{n\theta}{n+1}.$$

As $n \to \infty$, the limit is θ, making this estimator asymptotically unbiased. □

9.2.2.3 Consistency

A second desirable property of an estimator is that it works well for extremely large samples. Slightly more formally, as the sample size goes to infinity, the probability that the estimator is in error by more than a small amount goes to zero. A formal definition follows.

Definition 9.8 *An estimator is* **consistent** *(often called, in this context,* **weakly consistent***) if, for all $\delta > 0$ and any θ,*

$$\lim_{n\to\infty} \Pr(|\hat{\theta}_n - \theta| > \delta) = 0.$$

A sufficient (although not necessary) condition for weak consistency is that the estimator be asymptotically unbiased and $\text{Var}(\hat{\theta}_n) \to 0$.

Example 9.9 *Prove that, if the variance of a random variable is finite, the sample mean is a consistent estimator of the population mean.*

From Exercise 9.2, the sample mean is unbiased. In addition,

$$\text{Var}(\bar{X}) = \text{Var}\left(\frac{1}{n}\sum_{j=1}^n X_j\right)$$

$$= \frac{1}{n^2}\sum_{j=1}^n \text{Var}(X_j)$$

$$= \frac{\text{Var}(X)}{n} \to 0.$$

The second step follows from assuming that the observations are independent.□

Example 9.10 *Show that the maximum observation from a uniform distribution on the interval $(0, \theta)$ is a consistent estimator of θ.*

From Example 9.7, the maximum is asymptotically unbiased. The second moment is

$$E(Y_n^2) = \int_0^\theta ny^{n+1}\theta^{-n}dy = \frac{n}{n+2}y^{n+2}\theta^{-n}\Big|_0^\theta = \frac{n\theta^2}{n+2}$$

and then

$$\text{Var}(Y_n) = \frac{n\theta^2}{n+2} - \left(\frac{n\theta}{n+1}\right)^2 = \frac{n\theta^2}{(n+2)(n+1)^2} \to 0.$$

□

9.2.2.4 Mean-squared error While consistency is nice, many estimators have this property. What would be truly impressive is an estimator that is not only correct on average but comes very close most of the time and, in particular, comes closer than rival estimators. One measure for a finite sample is motivated by the definition of consistency. The quality of an estimator could be measured by the probability that it gets within δ of the true value—that is, by measuring $\Pr(|\hat{\theta}_n - \theta| < \delta)$. But the choice of δ is arbitrary, and we prefer measures that cannot be altered to suit the investigator's whim. Then we might consider $E(|\hat{\theta}_n - \theta|)$, the average absolute error. But we know that working with absolute values often presents unpleasant mathematical challenges, and so the following has become widely accepted as a measure of accuracy.

Definition 9.11 *The **mean-squared error** (**MSE**) of an estimator is*

$$\mathrm{MSE}_{\hat{\theta}}(\theta) = E[(\hat{\theta} - \theta)^2 | \theta].$$

Note that the MSE is a function of the true value of the parameter. An estimator may perform extremely well for some values of the parameter but poorly for others.

Example 9.12 *Consider the estimator $\hat{\theta} = 5$ of an unknown parameter θ. The MSE is $(5 - \theta)^2$, which is very small when θ is near 5 but becomes poor for other values. Of course this estimate is both biased and inconsistent unless θ is exactly equal to 5.*

A result that follows directly from the various definitions is

$$\mathrm{MSE}_{\hat{\theta}}(\theta) = E\{[\hat{\theta} - E(\hat{\theta}|\theta) + E(\hat{\theta}|\theta) - \theta]^2 | \theta\} = \mathrm{Var}(\hat{\theta}|\theta) + [\mathrm{bias}_{\hat{\theta}}(\theta)]^2. \quad (9.1)$$

If we restrict attention to only unbiased estimators, the best such could be defined as follows. □

Definition 9.13 *An estimator, $\hat{\theta}$, is called a **uniformly minimum variance unbiased estimator** (**UMVUE**) if it is unbiased and for any true value of θ there is no other unbiased estimator that has a smaller variance.*

Because we are looking only at unbiased estimators, it would have been equally effective to make the definition in terms of MSE. We could also generalize the definition by looking for estimators that are uniformly best with regard to MSE, but the previous example indicates why that is not feasible. There are a few theorems that can assist with the determination of UMVUEs. However, such estimators are difficult to determine. On the other hand, MSE is still a useful criterion for comparing two alternative estimators.

Example 9.14 *For the problem described in Example 9.2 compare the MSEs of the sample mean and 1.2 times the sample median.*

The sample mean has variance

$$\frac{\text{Var}(X)}{3} = \frac{\theta^2}{3}.$$

When multiplied by 1.2, the sample median has second moment

$$E[(1.2Y)^2] = 1.44 \int_0^\infty y^2 \frac{6}{\theta} \left(e^{-2y/\theta} - e^{-3y/\theta} \right) dy$$

$$= 1.44 \frac{6}{\theta} \left[y^2 \left(\frac{-\theta}{2} e^{-2y/\theta} + \frac{\theta}{3} e^{-3y/\theta} \right) \right.$$

$$- 2y \left(\frac{\theta^2}{4} e^{-2y/\theta} - \frac{\theta^2}{9} e^{-3y/\theta} \right)$$

$$\left. + 2 \left(\frac{-\theta^3}{8} e^{-2y/\theta} + \frac{\theta^3}{27} e^{-3y/\theta} \right) \right]\Bigg|_0^\infty$$

$$= \frac{8.64}{\theta} \left(\frac{2\theta^3}{8} - \frac{2\theta^3}{27} \right) = \frac{38\theta^2}{25}$$

for a variance of

$$\frac{38\theta^2}{25} - \theta^2 = \frac{13\theta^2}{25} > \frac{\theta^2}{3}.$$

The sample mean has the smaller MSE regardless of the true value of θ. Therefore, for this problem, it is a superior estimator of θ.   □

Example 9.15 *For the uniform distribution on the interval $(0,\theta)$ compare the MSE of the estimators $2\bar{X}$ and $[(n+1)/n] \max(X_1, \ldots, X_n)$. Also evaluate the MSE of $\max(X_1, \ldots, X_n)$.*

The first two estimators are unbiased, so it is sufficient to compare their variances. For twice the sample mean,

$$\text{Var}(2\bar{X}) = \frac{4}{n} \text{Var}(X) = \frac{4\theta^2}{12n} = \frac{\theta^2}{3n}.$$

For the adjusted maximum, the second moment is

$$E\left[\left(\frac{n+1}{n} Y_n \right)^2 \right] = \frac{(n+1)^2}{n^2} \frac{n\theta^2}{n+2} = \frac{(n+1)^2\theta^2}{(n+2)n}$$

for a variance of

$$\frac{(n+1)^2\theta^2}{(n+2)n} - \theta^2 = \frac{\theta^2}{n(n+2)}.$$

Except for the case $n = 1$ (and then the two estimators are identical), the one based on the maximum has the smaller MSE. The third estimator is biased. For it, the MSE is

$$\frac{n\theta^2}{(n+2)(n+1)^2} + \left(\frac{n\theta}{n+1} - \theta \right)^2 = \frac{2\theta^2}{(n+1)(n+2)},$$

which is also larger than that for the adjusted maximum.   □

9.3 INTERVAL ESTIMATION

All of the estimators discussed to this point have been **point estimators**. That is, the estimation process produces a single value that represents our best attempt to determine the value of the unknown population quantity. While that value may be a good one, we do not expect it to exactly match the true value. A more useful statement is often provided by an **interval estimator**. Instead of a single value, the result of the estimation process is a range of possible numbers, any of which is likely to be the true value. A specific type of interval estimator is the confidence interval.

Definition 9.16 *A* $100(1-\alpha)\%$ ***confidence interval*** *for a parameter* θ *is a pair of random variables* L *and* U *computed from a random sample such that* $\Pr(L \leq \theta \leq U) \geq 1 - \alpha$ *for all* θ.

Note that this definition does not uniquely specify the interval. Because the definition is a probability statement and must hold for all θ, it says nothing about whether or not a particular interval encloses the true value of θ from a particular population. Instead, the **level of confidence**, $1-\alpha$, is a property of the method used to obtain L and U and not of the particular values obtained. The proper interpretation is that, if we use a particular interval estimator over and over on a variety of samples, at least $100(1 - \alpha)\%$ of the time our interval will enclose the true value.

Constructing confidence intervals is usually very difficult. For example, we know that, if a population has a normal distribution with unknown mean and variance, a $100(1 - \alpha)\%$ confidence interval for the mean uses

$$L = \bar{X} - t_{\alpha/2,n-1}s/\sqrt{n}, \quad U = \bar{X} + t_{\alpha/2,n-1}s/\sqrt{n}, \qquad (9.2)$$

where $s = \sqrt{\sum_{j=1}^{n}(X_j - \bar{X})^2/(n - 1)}$ and $t_{\alpha/2,b}$ is the $100(1 - \alpha/2)$th percentile of the t distribution with b degrees of freedom. But it takes a great deal of effort to verify that this is correct (see, for example, [52], p. 214).

However, there is a method for constructing approximate confidence intervals that is often accessible. Suppose we have a point estimator $\hat{\theta}$ of parameter θ such that $\mathrm{E}(\hat{\theta}) \doteq \theta$, $\mathrm{Var}(\hat{\theta}) \doteq v(\theta)$, and $\hat{\theta}$ has approximately a normal distribution. Theorem 10.13 shows that this is often the case. With all these approximations, we have that approximately

$$1 - \alpha \doteq \Pr\left(-z_{\alpha/2} \leq \frac{\hat{\theta} - \theta}{\sqrt{v(\theta)}} \leq z_{\alpha/2}\right), \qquad (9.3)$$

where $z_{\alpha/2}$ is the $100(1-\alpha/2)$th percentile of the standard normal distribution. Solving for θ produces the desired interval. Sometimes this is difficult to do (due to the appearance of θ in the denominator) and so, if necessary, replace $v(\theta)$ in (9.3) with $v(\hat{\theta})$ to obtain a further approximation,

$$1 - \alpha \doteq \Pr\left(\hat{\theta} - z_{\alpha/2}\sqrt{v(\hat{\theta})} \le \theta \le \hat{\theta} + z_{\alpha/2}\sqrt{v(\hat{\theta})}\right). \tag{9.4}$$

Example 9.17 *Use formula (9.4) to construct an approximate 95% confidence interval for the mean of a normal population with unknown variance.*

Use $\hat{\theta} = \bar{X}$ and then note that $\mathrm{E}(\hat{\theta}) = \theta$, $\mathrm{Var}(\hat{\theta}) = \sigma^2/n$, and $\hat{\theta}$ does have a normal distribution. The confidence interval is then $\bar{X} \pm 1.96s/\sqrt{n}$. Because $t_{.025,n-1} > 1.96$, this approximate interval must be narrower than the exact interval given by formulas (9.2). That means that our level of confidence is something less than 95%. □

Example 9.18 *Use formulas (9.3) and (9.4) to construct approximate 95% confidence intervals for the mean of a Poisson distribution. Obtain intervals for the particular case where $n = 25$ and $\bar{x} = 0.12$.*

Let $\hat{\theta} = \bar{X}$, the sample mean. For the Poisson distribution, $\mathrm{E}(\hat{\theta}) = \mathrm{E}(X) = \theta$ and $v(\theta) = \mathrm{Var}(\bar{X}) = \mathrm{Var}(X)/n = \theta/n$. For the first interval

$$0.95 \doteq \Pr\left(-1.96 \le \frac{\bar{X} - \theta}{\sqrt{\theta/n}} \le 1.96\right)$$

is true if and only if

$$|\bar{X} - \theta| \le 1.96\sqrt{\frac{\theta}{n}},$$

which is equivalent to

$$(\bar{X} - \theta)^2 \le \frac{3.8416\theta}{n}$$

or

$$\theta^2 - \theta\left(2\bar{X} + \frac{3.8416}{n}\right) + \bar{X}^2 \le 0.$$

Solving the quadratic produces the interval

$$\bar{X} + \frac{1.9208}{n} \pm \frac{1}{2}\sqrt{\frac{15.3664\bar{X} + 3.8416^2/n}{n}}$$

and for this problem the interval is 0.197 ± 0.156. For the second approximation the interval is $\bar{X} \pm 1.96\sqrt{\bar{X}/n}$, and for the example it is 0.12 ± 0.136. This interval extends below zero (which is not possible for the true value of θ). This is because formula (9.4) is too crude an approximation in this case. □

9.4   TESTS OF HYPOTHESES

Hypothesis testing is covered in detail in most mathematical statistics texts. This review will be fairly straightforward and will not address philosophical issues or consider alternative approaches. A hypothesis test begins with two hypotheses, one called the null and one called the alternative. The traditional notation is H_0 for the null hypothesis and H_1 for the alternative hypothesis. The two hypotheses are not treated symmetrically. Reversing them may alter the results. To illustrate this process, a simple example will be used.

Example 9.19 *Your bank has been assuming that, for a particular type of operational risk, the average loss is $1200. You wish to put this assumption to a rigorous test. The following data representing recent operational risk losses of the same type. What are the hypotheses for this problem?*

27	82	115	126	155	161	243	294	340	384
457	680	855	877	974	1193	1340	1884	2558	15,743

Let μ be the population mean. One possible hypothesis (the one you claim is true) is that $\mu > 1200$. The other hypothesis must be $\mu \leq 1200$. The only remaining task is to decide which of them is the null hypothesis. Whenever the universe of continuous possibilities is divided in two there is likely to be a boundary that needs to be assigned to one hypothesis or the other. The hypothesis that includes the boundary must be the null hypothesis. Therefore, the problem can be succinctly stated as:

$$H_0 : \mu \leq 1200$$
$$H_1 : \mu > 1200.$$

$\square$

The decision is made by calculating a quantity called a **test statistic**. It is a function of the observations and is treated as a random variable. That is, in designing the test procedure we are concerned with the samples that might have been obtained and not with the particular sample that was obtained. The test specification is completed by constructing a **rejection region**. It is a subset of the possible values of the test statistic. If the value of the test statistic for the observed sample is in the rejection region, the null hypothesis is rejected and the alternative hypothesis is announced as the result that is supported by the data. Otherwise, the null hypothesis is not rejected (more on this later). The boundaries of the rejection region (other than plus or minus infinity) are called the **critical values**.

Example 9.20 (Example 9.19 continued) *Complete the test using the test statistic and rejection region that are promoted in most statistics books. Assume that the population has a normal distribution with standard deviation 3435.*

The traditional test statistic for this problem is

$$z = \frac{\bar{x} - 1{,}200}{3435/\sqrt{20}} = 0.292$$

and the null hypothesis is rejected if $z > 1.645$. Because 0.292 is less than 1.645, the null hypothesis is not rejected. The data do not support the assertion that the average loss exceeds \$1200. □

The test in the previous example was constructed to meet certain objectives. The first objective is to control what is called the Type I error. It is the error made when the test rejects the null hypothesis in a situation where it happens to be true. In the example, the null hypothesis can be true in more than one way. This leads to the most common measure of the propensity of a test to make a Type I error.

Definition 9.21 *The **significance level** of a hypothesis test is the probability of making a Type I error given that the null hypothesis is true. If it can be true in more than one way, the level of significance is the maximum of such probabilities. The significance level is usually denoted by the letter α.*

This is a conservative definition in that it looks at the worst case. It is typically a case that is on the boundary between the two hypotheses.

Example 9.22 *Determine the level of significance for the test in Example 9.20.*

Begin by computing the probability of making a Type I error when the null hypothesis is true with $\mu = 1200$. Then,

$$\Pr(Z > 1.645 | \mu = 1200) = 0.05.$$

That is because the assumptions imply that Z has a standard normal distribution.

Now suppose μ has a value that is below \$1,200. Then

$$\Pr\left(\frac{\bar{X} - 1200}{3435/\sqrt{20}} > 1.645\right)$$
$$= \Pr\left(\frac{\bar{X} - \mu + \mu - 1200}{3435/\sqrt{20}} > 1.645\right)$$
$$= \Pr\left(\frac{\bar{X} - \mu}{3435/\sqrt{20}} > 1.645 - \frac{\mu - 1200}{3435/\sqrt{20}}\right).$$

Because μ is known to be less than \$1200, the right-hand side is always greater than 1.645. The left-hand side has a standard normal distribution and therefore the probability is less than 0.05. Therefore the significance level is 0.05.□

The significance level is usually set in advance and is often between 1% and 10%. The second objective is to keep the Type II error (not rejecting the null hypothesis when the alternative is true) probability small. Generally, attempts to reduce the probability of one type of error increase the probability of the other. The best we can do once the significance level has been set is to make the Type II error as small as possible, although there is no assurance that the probability will be a small number. The best test is one that meets the following requirement.

Definition 9.23 *A hypothesis test is **uniformly most powerful** if no other test exists that has the same or lower significance level and for a particular value within the alternative hypothesis has a smaller probability of making a Type II error.*

Example 9.24 (Example 9.22 continued) *Determine the probability of making a Type II error when the alternative hypothesis is true with $\mu = 2000$.*

$$
\begin{aligned}
&\Pr\left(\frac{\bar{X} - 1200}{3435/\sqrt{20}} < 1.645 \big| \mu = 2000\right) \\
&= \Pr(\bar{X} - 1200 < 1263.51 | \mu = 2000) \\
&= \Pr(\bar{X} < 2463.51 | \mu = 2000) \\
&= \Pr\left(\frac{\bar{X} - 2000}{3435/\sqrt{20}} < \frac{2463.51 - 2000}{3435/\sqrt{20}} = 0.6035\right) = 0.7269.
\end{aligned}
$$

For this value of μ, the test is not very powerful, having over a 70% chance of making a Type II error. Nevertheless (though this is not easy to prove), the test used is the most powerful test for this problem.   □

Because the Type II error probability can be high, it is customary to not make a strong statement when the null hypothesis is not rejected. Rather than say we choose to accept the null hypothesis, we say that we fail to reject it. That is, there was not enough evidence in the sample to make a strong argument in favor of the alternative hypothesis, so we take no stand at all.

A common criticism of this approach to hypothesis testing is that the choice of the significance level is arbitrary. In fact, by changing the significance level, any result can be obtained.

Example 9.25 (Example 9.24 continued) *Complete the test using a significance level of $\alpha = 0.45$. Then determine the range of significance levels for which the null hypothesis is rejected and for which it is not rejected.*

Because $\Pr(Z > 0.1257) = 0.45$, the null hypothesis is rejected when

$$\frac{\bar{X} - 1200}{3435/\sqrt{20}} > 0.1257.$$

In this example, the test statistic is 0.292, which is in the rejection region, and thus the null hypothesis is rejected. Of course, few people would place confidence in the results of a test that was designed to make errors 45% of the time. Because $\Pr(Z > 0.292) = 0.3851$, the null hypothesis is rejected for those who select a significance level that is greater than 38.51% and is not rejected by those who use a significance level that is less than 38.51%.   □

Few people are willing to make errors 38.51% of the time. Announcing this figure is more persuasive than the earlier conclusion based on a 5% significance level. When a significance level is used, readers are left to wonder what the outcome would have been with other significance levels. The value of 38.51% is called a p-value. A working definition is:

Definition 9.26 *For a hypothesis test, the **p-value** is the probability that the test statistic takes on a value that is less in agreement with the null hypothesis than the value obtained from the sample. Tests conducted at a significance level that is greater than the p-value will lead to a rejection of the null hypothesis, while tests conducted at a significance level that is smaller than the p-value will lead to a failure to reject the null hypothesis.*

Also, because the p-value must be between 0 and 1, it is on a scale that carries some meaning. The closer to zero the value is, the more support the data give to the alternative hypothesis. Common practice is that values above 10% indicate that the data provide no evidence in support of the alternative hypothesis, while values below 1% indicate strong support for the alternative hypothesis. Values in between indicate uncertainty as to the appropriate conclusion and may call for more data or a more careful look at the data or the experiment that produced it.

9.5 EXERCISES

9.1 For Example 9.1, show that the mean of three observations drawn without replacement is an unbiased estimator of the population mean while the median of three observations drawn without replacement is a biased estimator of the population mean.

9.2 Prove that for random samples the sample mean is always an unbiased estimator of the population mean.

9.3 Let X have the uniform distribution over the range $(\theta - 2, \theta + 2)$. That is, $f_X(x) = 0.25$, $\theta - 2 < x < \theta + 2$. Show that the median from a sample of size 3 is an unbiased estimator of θ.

9.4 Explain why the sample mean may not be a consistent estimator of the population mean for a Pareto distribution.

9.5 For the sample of size 3 in Exercise 9.3, compare the MSE of the sample mean and median as estimates of θ.

9.6 You are given two independent estimators of an unknown quantity θ. For estimator A, $E(\hat{\theta}_A) = 1000$ and $Var(\hat{\theta}_A) = 160,000$, while for estimator B, $E(\hat{\theta}_B) = 1{,}200$ and $Var(\hat{\theta}_B) = 40,000$. Estimator C is a weighted average, $\hat{\theta}_C = w\hat{\theta}_A + (1 - w)\hat{\theta}_B$. Determine the value of w that minimizes $Var(\hat{\theta}_C)$.

9.7 A population of losses has the Pareto distribution with $\theta = 6000$ and α unknown. Simulation of the results from maximum likelihood estimation based on samples of size 10 has indicated that $E(\hat{\alpha}) = 2.2$ and $MSE(\hat{\alpha}) = 1$. Determine $Var(\hat{\alpha})$ if it is known that $\alpha = 2$.

9.8 Two instruments are available for measuring a particular nonzero distance. The random variable X represents a measurement with the first instrument, and the random variable Y with the second instrument. Assume X and Y are independent with $E(X) = 0.8m$, $E(Y) = m$, $Var(X) = m^2$, and $Var(Y) = 1.5m^2$, where m is the true distance. Consider estimators of m that are of the form $Z = \alpha X + \beta Y$. Determine the values of α and β that make Z a UMVUE within the class of estimators of this form.

9.9 Two different estimators, $\hat{\theta}_1$ and $\hat{\theta}_2$, are being considered. To test their performance, 75 trials have been simulated, each with the true value set at $\theta = 2$. The following totals were obtained:

$$\sum_{j=1}^{75} \hat{\theta}_{1j} = 165, \quad \sum_{j=1}^{75} \hat{\theta}_{1j}^2 = 375, \quad \sum_{j=1}^{75} \hat{\theta}_{2j} = 147, \quad \sum_{j=1}^{75} \hat{\theta}_{2j}^2 = 312,$$

where $\hat{\theta}_{ij}$ is the estimate based on the jth simulation using estimator $\hat{\theta}_i$. Estimate the MSE for each estimator and determine the **relative efficiency** (the ratio of the MSEs).

9.10 Determine the method-of-moments estimate for an exponential model for Data Set B with observations censored at 250.

9.11 Let $x_1, \ldots, x_n$ be a random sample from a population with pdf $f(x) = \theta^{-1}e^{-x/\theta}$, $x > 0$. This exponential distribution has a mean of θ and a variance of θ^2. Consider the sample mean, $\bar{X}$, as an estimator of θ. It turns out that $\bar{X}/\theta$ has a gamma distribution with $\alpha = n$ and $\theta = 1/n$, where in the second expression the "θ" on the left is the parameter of the gamma distribution. For a sample of size 50 and a sample mean of 275, develop 95% confidence intervals by each of the following methods. In each case, if the formula requires the true value of θ, substitute the estimated value.

(a) Use the gamma distribution to determine an exact interval.

(b) Use a normal approximation, estimating the variance before solving the inequalities, as in equation (9.3).

(c) Use a normal approximation, estimating θ after solving the inequalities, as in Example ??.

9.12 (*Exercise 9.11 continued*) Test $H_0 : \theta \geq 325$ vs $H_1 : \theta < 325$ using a significance level of 5% and the sample mean as the test statistic. Also, compute the p-value. Do this using the exact distribution of the test statistic and a normal approximation.

10

Parameter estimation

Everything takes longer than you think.

—Murphy

10.1 INTRODUCTION

If a phenomenon is to be modeled using a parametric model, it is necessary to assign values to the parameters. This could be done arbitrarily based on educated guessing. However, a more reasonable is to base the assignment on any observations that are available from that phenomenon. In particular, we will assume that n independent observations have been collected. For some of the techniques it will be further assumed that all the observations are from the same random variable. For others, that restriction will be relaxed.

The methods introduced in Section 10.2 are relatively easy to implement but tend to give poor results. Section 10.3 covers maximum likelihood estimation. This method is more difficult to use but has superior statistical properties and is considerably more flexible.

Throughout this chapter, four examples will used repeatedly. Because they are simply data sets, they will be referred to as Data Sets A, B, C, and D.

Data Set A *This data set was first analyzed in the paper* [25] *by Dropkin in 1959. He collected data from* 1956–1958 *on the number of accidents per driver per year. The results for* 94,935 *drivers are in Table* 10.1.

Table 10.1   Data Set A

Number of accidents	Number of drivers
0	81,714
1	11,306
2	1,618
3	250
4	40
5 or more	7

Table 10.2   Data Set B

$27	$82	$115	$126	$155	$161	$243	$294	$340	$384
$457	$680	$855	$877	$974	$1193	$1340	$1884	$2558	$15,743

Table 10.3   Data Set C

Payment range	Number of losses
0–$7500	99
$7500–$17,500	42
$17,500–$32,500	29
$32,500–$67,500	28
$67,500–$125,000	17
$125,000–$300,000	9
Over $300,000	3

Data Set B *These numbers are artificial. They represent the full amount of the loss of a random sample of 20 losses (in units of $1000) as given in Table 10.2.*

Data Set C *These numbers are artificial. They represent losses on 227 losses. The data are in Table 10.3.*

Data Set D *These numbers are artificial. Forty machines are being studied for their reliability in providing accurate transactions. The period of study is the first 5 years of age of the machines. For each machine, one of three possible times is recorded. If the machine fails at some time before age 5, the age of first failure is recorded. If the machine is removed from the study (while operating without failure) for a reason unrelated to performance, the time of removal is recorded. If at age 5, the machine is still in the study and operating without failure, that time is recorded. Thirty machines are new at the beginning of the study. Ten machines (that are operating without past failure) enter the study at an advanced age.*

Table 10.4   Data Set D

Machine	First observed	Last observed	Event	Machine	First observed	Last observed	Event
1	0	0.1	w	16	0	4.8	f
2	0	0.5	w	17	0	4.8	w
3	0	0.8	w	18	0	4.8	w
4	0	0.8	f	19-30	0	5.0	e
5	0	1.8	w	31	0.3	5.0	e
6	0	1.8	w	32	0.7	5.0	e
7	0	2.1	w	33	1.0	4.1	f
8	0	2.5	w	34	1.8	3.1	f
9	0	2.8	w	35	2.1	3.9	w
10	0	2.9	f	36	2.9	5.0	e
11	0	2.9	f	37	2.9	4.8	w
12	0	3.9	w	38	3.2	4.0	f
13	0	4.0	f	39	3.4	5.0	e
14	0	4.0	w	40	3.9	5.0	e
15	0	4.1	w				

Table 10.4 *records the age of the first event (failure, removal, or expiration) for all* 40 *machines. The column headed "First observed" gives the age at which the policy was first observed in the study; the column headed "Last observed" gives the duration at which the policy was last observed; and the column headed "Event" is coded "f" for failure, "w" for withdrawal, and "e" for expiration of the study at age five without failure period.*

When observations are collected from a probability distribution, the ideal situation is to have the (essentially) exact[1] value of each observation. This is referred to as the case of "complete, individual data." This is the situation in Data Set B. There are two reasons why exact data may not be available. One is grouping, in which all that is recorded is the range of values in which the observation belongs. This is the case for Data Set C and for Data Set A for those with five or more accidents.

A second reason that exact values may not be available is the presence of censoring or truncation. When data are censored from below, observations below a given value are known to be below that value but the exact value is unknown. When data are censored from above, observations above a given value are known to be above that value but the exact value is unknown. Note that censoring effectively creates grouped data. For example, for the data in Data Set C, the censoring from above at $300,000 creates a group from $300,000 to infinity. In many settings, censoring from above is common. For

---

[1] Some measurements are never exact. Ages may be rounded to the nearest whole month, monetary amounts to the nearest dollar, car mileage to the nearest tenth of a mile, and so on. This text is not concerned with such rounding errors. Rounded values will be treated as if they are exact.

example, if a given loss is estimated to be above $300,000 but the actual amount is unknown, the loss is censored from above at $300,000.

In Data Set D, we also have censoring. Consider machine number 5. All that is known about the time of failure of the machine is that it will be after age 1.8 years. All of the policies are censored (from above) at 5 years of age by the nature of the study itself. Also, note that Data Set A has been censored from above at 5. In this case, it is more common to describe this as censoring than to say that Data Set A has some individual data and some grouped data.

When data are truncated from below, observations below a given value are not recorded. The existence of such losses is treated as unknown. Truncation from below is fairly common. If small losses, say less than $250, are never recorded, any losses below $250 will never come to the attention of the risk analyst and so will not appear in any data sets. Left truncation points may be different of different observations. For example, in Data Set D, observations 31–40 are truncated from below at varying values.

These four data sets will be used extensively to illustrate various concepts in the remainder of this chapter.

10.2   METHOD OF MOMENTS AND PERCENTILE MATCHING

For these methods we assume that all n observations are from the same parametric distribution. In particular, let the distribution function be given by

$$F(x) = F(x|\theta), \quad \theta^T = (\theta_1, \theta_2, \ldots, \theta_p)$$

where θ^T is the transpose of θ. That is, θ is a column vector containing the p parameters to be estimated. Furthermore, let $\mu'_k(\theta) = \mathrm{E}(X^k|\theta)$ be the kth raw moment and let $\pi_g(\theta)$ be the $100g$th percentile of the random variable. That is, $F[\pi_g(\theta)|\theta] = g$. If the distribution function is continuous, there will be at least one solution to that equation.

For a sample of n independent observations from this random variable, let $\hat{\mu}'_k = \frac{1}{n}\sum_{j=1}^{n} x_j^k$ be the empirical estimate of the kth moment and let $\hat{\pi}_g$ be the empirical estimate of the $100g$th percentile

Definition 10.1 *A **method-of-moments estimate** of θ is any solution of the p equations*

$$\mu'_k(\theta) = \hat{\mu}'_k, \ k = 1, 2, \ldots, p.$$

The motivation for this estimator is that it produces a model that has the same first p raw moments as the data (as represented by the empirical distribution). The traditional definition of the method of moments uses positive integers for the moments.

Example 10.2 *Use the method of moments to estimate parameters for the exponential, gamma, and Pareto distributions for Data Set B.*

The first two sample moments are

$$\hat{\mu}_1' = \tfrac{1}{20}(27 + \cdots + 15{,}743) = 1{,}424.4,$$
$$\hat{\mu}_2' = \tfrac{1}{20}(27^2 + \cdots + 15{,}743^2) = 13{,}238{,}441.9.$$

For the exponential distribution the equation is

$$\theta = 1424.4$$

with the obvious solution, $\hat{\theta} = 1{,}424.4$.

For the gamma distribution, the two equations are

$$E(X) = \alpha\theta = 1424.4,$$
$$E(X^2) = \alpha(\alpha + 1)\theta^2 = 13{,}238{,}441.9.$$

Dividing the second equation by the square of the first equation yields

$$\frac{\alpha + 1}{\alpha} = 6.52489, \quad 1 = 5.52489\alpha$$

and so $\hat{\alpha} = 1/5.52489 = 0.18100$ and $\hat{\theta} = 1424.4/0.18100 = 7869.61$.

For the Pareto distribution, the two equations are

$$E(X) = \frac{\theta}{\alpha - 1} = 1424.4,$$
$$E(X^2) = \frac{2\theta^2}{(\alpha - 1)(\alpha - 2)} = 13{,}238{,}441.9.$$

Dividing the second equation by the square of the first equation yields

$$\frac{2(\alpha - 1)}{(\alpha - 2)} = 6.52489$$

with a solution of $\hat{\alpha} = 2.442$ and then $\hat{\theta} = 1424.4(1.442) = 2053.985$.   □

There is no guarantee that the equations will have a solution or, if there is a solution, that it will be unique.

Definition 10.3 *A **percentile matching estimate** of θ is any solution of the p equations*

$$\pi_{g_k}(\theta) = \hat{\pi}_{g_k}, \quad k = 1, 2, \ldots, p,$$

where $g_1, g_2, \ldots, g_p$ are p arbitrarily chosen percentiles. From the definition of percentile, the equations can also be written

$$F(\hat{\pi}_{g_k}|\theta) = g_k, \quad k = 1, 2, \ldots, p.$$

The motivation for this estimator is that it produces a model with p percentiles that match the data (as represented by the empirical distribution).

As with the method of moments, there is no guarantee that the equations will have a solution or, if there is a solution, that it will be unique. One problem with this definition is that percentiles for discrete random variables (such as the empirical distribution) are not always well defined. For example, Data Set B has 20 observations. Any number between 384 and 457 has 10 observations below and 10 above and so could serve as the median. The convention is to use the midpoint. However, for other percentiles, there is no "official" interpolation scheme.[2] The following definition will be used here.

Definition 10.4 *The **smoothed empirical estimate** of a percentile is found by*

$$\hat{\pi}_g = (1 - h)x_{(j)} + hx_{(j+1)}, \text{ where}$$
$$j = \lfloor (n + 1)g \rfloor \text{ and } h = (n + 1)g - j.$$

Here $\lfloor \cdot \rfloor$ indicates the greatest integer function and $x_{(1)} \leq x_{(2)} \leq \cdots \leq x_{(n)}$ are the order statistics from the sample.

Unless there are two or more data points with the same value, no two percentiles will have the same value. One feature of this definition is that $\hat{\pi}_g$ cannot be obtained for $g < 1/(n+1)$ or $g > n/(n+1)$. This seems reasonable as we should not expect to be able to infer the value of large or small percentiles from small samples. We will use the smoothed version whenever an empirical percentile estimate is called for.

Example 10.5 *Use percentile matching to estimate parameters for the exponential and Pareto distributions for Data Set B.*

For the exponential distribution, select the 50th percentile. The empirical estimate is the traditional median of $\hat{\pi}_{0.5} = (384 + 457)/2 = 420.5$ and the equation to solve is

$$0.5 = F(420.5|\theta) = 1 - e^{-420.5/\theta},$$
$$\ln 0.5 = \frac{-420.5}{\theta},$$
$$\hat{\theta} = \frac{-420.5}{\ln 0.5} = 606.65.$$

For the Pareto distribution, select the 30th and 80th percentiles. The smoothed empirical estimates are found as follows:

30th: j $= \lfloor 21(0.3) \rfloor = \lfloor 6.3 \rfloor = 6, h = 6.3 - 6 = 0.3,$
      $\hat{\pi}_{0.3}$ $= 0.7(161) + 0.3(243) = 185.6,$
80th: j $= \lfloor 21(0.8) \rfloor = \lfloor 16.8 \rfloor = 16, h = 16.8 - 16 = 0.8,$
      $\hat{\pi}_{0.8}$ $= 0.2(1,193) + 0.8(1,340) = 1,310.6.$

---

[2]Hyndman and Fan [59] present nine different methods. They recommend a slight modification of the one presented here using $j = \lfloor g(n + \frac{1}{3}) + \frac{1}{3} \rfloor$ and $h = g(n + \frac{1}{3}) + \frac{1}{3} - j.$

The equations to solve are

$$0.3 = F(185.6) = 1 - \left(\frac{\theta}{185.6 + \theta} \right)^{\alpha},$$

$$0.8 = F(1{,}310.6) = 1 - \left(\frac{\theta}{1310.6 + \theta} \right)^{\alpha},$$

$$\ln 0.7 = -0.356675 = \alpha \ln \left(\frac{\theta}{185.6 + \theta} \right),$$

$$\ln 0.2 = -1.609438 = \alpha \ln \left(\frac{\theta}{1{,}310.6 + \theta} \right),$$

$$\frac{-1.609438}{-0.356675} = 4.512338 = \frac{\ln \left(\frac{\theta}{1{,}310.6+\theta} \right)}{\ln \left(\frac{\theta}{185.6+\theta} \right)}.$$

Numerical methods can be used to solve this equation for $\hat{\theta} = 715.03$. Then, from the first equation,

$$0.3 = 1 - \left(\frac{715.03}{185.6 + 715.03} \right)^{\alpha},$$

which yields $\hat{\alpha} = 1.54559$. □

The estimates are much different from those obtained in Example 10.2. This is one indication that these methods may not be particularly reliable.

10.3 MAXIMUM LIKELIHOOD ESTIMATION

10.3.1 Introduction

Estimation by the method of moments and percentile matching is often easy to do, but these estimators tend to perform poorly. The main reason for this is that they use a few features of the data, rather than the entire set of observations. It is particularly important to use as much information as possible when the population has a heavy right tail. For example, when estimating parameters for the normal distribution, the sample mean and variance are sufficient.[3] However, when estimating parameters for a Pareto distribution, it is important to know all the extreme observations in order to successfully estimate α. Another drawback of these methods is that they require that all the observations are from the same random variable. Otherwise, it is not clear

---

[3] This applies both in the formal statistical definition of sufficiency (not covered here) and in the conventional sense. If the population has a normal distribution, the sample mean and variance convey as much information as the original observations.

what to use for the population moments or percentiles. For example, if half the observations have a threshold (i.e., in insurance terms, a deductible) of 50 and half have a threshold of 100, it is not clear to what the sample mean should be equated. Finally, these methods allow the analyst to make arbitrary decisions regarding the moments or percentiles to use.

There are several estimation methods that use the individual data points. All of them are implemented by setting an objective function and then determining the parameter values that optimize that function. For example, we could estimate parameters by minimizing the maximum difference between the distribution function for the parametric model and the empirical distribution function. This is actually a very bad method! We will focus on the maximum likelihood method to produce estimates. The estimate is obtained by maximizing the likelihood function. The general form of this estimator is presented in this introduction. This is followed with useful special cases.

In order to keep the explanation simple, suppose that a data set consists of the outcomes of n events $A_1, \ldots, A_n$, where A_j represents whatever was observed for the jth observation. For example, A_j may consist of a single point or an interval. Observations that are intervals arise in connection with grouped data or when there is censoring. For example, when there is censoring at u, and an observation greater than u is observed (although its exact value remains unknown), the observed event is the interval from u to infinity. Further assume that the event A_j results from observing the random variable X_j. The random variables $X_1, \ldots, X_n$ need not have the same probability distribution, but their distributions must depend on the same parameter vector, θ. In addition, the random variables are assumed to be independent.

Definition 10.6 *The **likelihood function** is*

$$L(\theta) = \prod_{j=1}^{n} \Pr(X_j \in A_j | \theta)$$

*and the **maximum likelihood estimate** of θ is the value of θ that maximizes the likelihood function.*[4]

There is no guarantee that the function has a maximum at eligible parameter values. For example, if a parameter is required to be positive, it is still possible that the likelihood function "blows up" (becoming larger as the parameter approaches 0 from above or that the likelihood increases indefinitely as a parameter increases. Care must also be taken when maximizing this function because there may be local maxima in addition to the global maximum. Finally, it is not generally possible to maximize the likelihood function (by

---

[4]Some authors write the likelihood function as $L(\theta|\mathbf{x})$, where the vector $\mathbf{x}$ represents the observed data. Because observed data can take many forms, the dependence of the likelihood function on the data is suppressed in the notation.

setting partial derivatives equal to zero) analytically. Numerical approaches to maximization will usually be needed.

Because the observations are assumed to be independent, the product in the definition represents the joint probability $\Pr(X_1 \in A_1, \ldots, X_n \in A_n|\theta)$, that is, the likelihood function is the probability of obtaining the sample results that were obtained, given a particular parameter value. The estimate is then the parameter value that produces the model under which the actual observations are most likely to be observed. One of the major attractions of this estimator is that it is very general in principle and almost universally applicable.

Example 10.7 *Suppose the data in Data Set B were censored at $250. Determine the maximum likelihood estimate of θ for an exponential distribution.*

The first seven data points are uncensored. For them, the set A_j contains the single point equal to the observation x_j. When calculating the likelihood function for a single point for a continuous model, it is necessary to interpret $\Pr(X_j = x_j) = f(x_j)$. That is, the density function should be used. Thus the first seven terms of the product are

$$f(27)f(82)\cdots f(243) = \theta^{-1}e^{-27/\theta}\theta^{-1}e^{-82/\theta}\cdots\theta^{-1}e^{-243/\theta} = \theta^{-7}e^{-909/\theta}.$$

For the final 13 terms, the set A_j is the interval from 250 to infinity and therefore $\Pr(X_j \in A_j) = \Pr(X_j > 250) = e^{-250/\theta}$. There are 13 such factors making the likelihood function

$$L(\theta) = \theta^{-7}e^{-909/\theta}(e^{-250/\theta})^{13} = \theta^{-7}e^{-4159/\theta}.$$

It is easier to maximize the logarithm of the likelihood function. Because it occurs so often, we denote the **loglikelihood function** as $l(\theta) = \ln L(\theta)$. Then

$$l(\theta) = -7\ln\theta - 4159\,\theta^{-1},$$
$$l'(\theta) = -7\theta^{-1} + 4159\,\theta^{-2} = 0,$$
$$\hat{\theta} = \frac{4159}{7} = 594.14.$$

In this case, the calculus technique of setting the first derivative equal to zero is easy to do. Also, evaluating the second derivative at this solution produces a negative number, verifying that this solution is a maximum. $\square$

10.3.2 Complete, individual data

When there is no truncation and no censoring and the value of each observation is recorded, it is easy to write the loglikelihood function.

$$L(\theta) = \prod_{j=1}^{n} f_{X_j}(x_j|\theta), \quad l(\theta) = \sum_{j=1}^{n} \ln f_{X_j}(x_j|\theta).$$

The notation indicates that it is not necessary for each observation to come from the same distribution.

Example 10.8 *Using Data Set B determine the maximum likelihood estimates for an exponential distribution, for a gamma distribution where α is known to equal 2, and for a gamma distribution where both parameters are unknown.*

For the exponential distribution, the general solution is

$$l(\theta) = \sum_{j=1}^{n} \left(-\ln \theta - x_j \theta^{-1} \right) = -n \ln \theta - n\bar{x}\theta^{-1},$$

$$l'(\theta) = -n\theta^{-1} + n\bar{x}\theta^{-2} = 0,$$

$$n\theta = n\bar{x},$$

$$\hat{\theta} = \bar{x}.$$

For Data Set B, $\hat{\theta} = \bar{x} = 1424.4$. The value of the loglikelihood function is -165.23. For this situation the method-of-moments and maximum likelihood estimates are identical.

For the gamma distribution with $\alpha = 2$,

$$f(x|\theta) = \frac{x^{2-1}e^{-x/\theta}}{\Gamma(2)\theta^2} = x\theta^{-2}e^{-x/\theta},$$

$$\ln f(x|\theta) = \ln x - 2\ln \theta - x\theta^{-1},$$

$$l(\theta) = \sum_{j=1}^{n} \ln x_j - 2n \ln \theta - n\bar{x}\theta^{-1},$$

$$l'(\theta) = -2n\theta^{-1} + n\bar{x}\theta^{-2} = 0,$$

$$\hat{\theta} = \tfrac{1}{2}\bar{x}.$$

For Data Set B, $\hat{\theta} = 1424.4/2 = 712.2$ and the value of the loglikelihood function is -179.98. Again, this estimate is the same as the method of moments estimate.

For the gamma distribution with unknown parameters the equation is not as simple.

$$f(x|\alpha,\theta) = \frac{x^{\alpha-1}e^{-x/\theta}}{\Gamma(\alpha)\theta^\alpha},$$

$$\ln f(x|\alpha,\theta) = (\alpha - 1)\ln x - x\theta^{-1} - \ln \Gamma(\alpha) - \alpha \ln \theta.$$

The partial derivative with respect to α requires the derivative of the gamma function. The resulting equation cannot be solved analytically. Using numerical methods, the estimates are $\hat{\alpha} = 0.55616$ and $\hat{\theta} = 2561.1$ and the value of the loglikelihood function is -162.29. These do not match the method-of-moments estimates. □

10.3.3 Complete, grouped data

When data are complete and grouped, the observations may be summarized as follows. Begin with a set of numbers $c_0 < c_1 < \cdots < c_k$, where c_0 is the smallest possible observation (often zero) and c_k is the largest possible observation (often infinity). From the sample, let n_j be the number of observations in the interval $(c_{j-1}, c_j]$. For such data, the likelihood function is

$$L(\theta) = \prod_{j=1}^{k} [F(c_j|\theta) - F(c_{j-1}|\theta)]^{n_j}$$

and its logarithm is

$$l(\theta) = \sum_{j=1}^{k} n_j \ln[F(c_j|\theta) - F(c_{j-1}|\theta)].$$

Example 10.9 *From Data Set C, determine the maximum likelihood estimate for an exponential distribution.*

The loglikelihood function is

$$
\begin{aligned}
l(\theta) &= 99 \ln[F(7500) - F(0)] + 42 \ln[F(17{,}500) - F(7500)] + \cdots \\
&\quad + 3 \ln[1 - F(300{,}000)] \\
&= 99 \ln(1 - e^{-7500/\theta}) + 42 \ln(e^{-7500/\theta} - e^{-17{,}500/\theta}) + \cdots \\
&\quad + 3 \ln e^{-300{,}000/\theta}.
\end{aligned}
$$

A numerical routine is needed to produce $\hat{\theta} = 29{,}721$, and the value of the loglikelihood function is -406.03. □

10.3.4 Truncated or censored data

When data are censored, there is no additional complication. As noted in Example 10.7, right censoring simply creates an interval running from the censoring point to infinity. In that example, data below the censoring point were individual data, and so the likelihood function contains both density and distribution function terms.

Truncated data present more of a challenge. There are two ways to proceed. One is to shift the data by subtracting the truncation point from each observation. The other is to accept the fact that there is no information about values below the truncation point but then attempt to fit a model for the original population.

Example 10.10 *Assume that the values in Data Set B are truncated from below at $200 and that only that portion of losses above $200 are known. Using* *both methods, estimate the value of α for a Pareto distribution with $\theta = 800$ known. Then use the model to estimate the losses in excess of thresholds of 0, $200, and $400.*

Using the shifting approach, the data set has 14 points {$43, $94, $140, $184, $257, $480, $655, $677, $774, $993, $1140, $1684, $2358, and $15,543}. The likelihood function is

$$L(\alpha) = \prod_{j=1}^{14} \frac{\alpha(800^\alpha)}{(800 + x_j)^{\alpha+1}},$$

$$l(\alpha) = \sum_{j=1}^{14} [\ln \alpha + \alpha \ln 800 - (\alpha + 1) \ln(x_j + 800)]$$

$$= 14 \ln \alpha + 93.5846\alpha - 103.969(\alpha + 1)$$

$$= 14 \ln \alpha - 103.969 - 10.384\alpha,$$

$$l'(\alpha) = 14\alpha^{-1} - 10.384,$$

$$\hat{\alpha} = \frac{14}{10.384} = 1.3482.$$

Because the data are shifted, it is not possible to estimate the loss with threshold 0. With a threshold of $200, the expected cost is the expected value of the estimated Pareto distribution, $800/0.3482 = $2,298$. Raising the threshold to $400 is equivalent to imposing a threshold of $200 on the modeled distribution. From each loss, the expected loss over the $400 threshold is

$$\frac{E(X) - E(X \wedge 200)}{1 - F(200)} = \frac{\dfrac{800}{0.3482} \left(\dfrac{800}{200 + 800}\right)^{0.3482}}{\left(\dfrac{800}{200 + 800}\right)^{1.3482}} = \frac{1,000}{0.3482} = $2872.$$

For the unshifted approach we need to ask a key question required when constructing the likelihood function. What is the probability of observing each value knowing that values under 200 are omitted from the data set? This becomes a conditional probability and therefore the likelihood function is (where the x_j values are now the original values)

$$L(\alpha) = \prod_{j=1}^{14} \frac{f(x_j|\alpha)}{1 - F(200|\alpha)} = \prod_{j=1}^{14} \left[\frac{\alpha(800^\alpha)}{(800 + x_j)^{\alpha+1}} \middle/ \left(\frac{800}{800 + 200} \right)^\alpha \right]$$

$$= \prod_{j=1}^{14} \frac{\alpha(1,000^\alpha)}{(800 + x_j)^{\alpha+1}},$$

$$l(\alpha) = 14 \ln \alpha + 14\alpha \ln 1{,}000 - (\alpha + 1) \sum_{j=1}^{14} \ln(800 + x_j),$$

$$= 14 \ln \alpha + 96.709\alpha - (\alpha + 1)105.810,$$

$$l'(\alpha) = 14\alpha^{-1} - 9.101,$$

$$\hat{\alpha} = 1.5383.$$

This model is for losses with no threshold (i.e. deductible), and therefore the expected cost without a threshold is $800/0.5383 = \$1486$. Imposing thresholds of \$200 and \$400 produces the following results for excess losses:

$$\frac{E(X) - E(X \wedge 200)}{1 - F(200)} = \frac{1000}{0.5383} = \$1858,$$

$$\frac{E(X) - E(X \wedge 400)}{1 - F(400)} = \frac{1200}{0.5383} = \$2229.$$

$\square$

It should now be clear that the contribution to the likelihood function can be written for most any observation, whether exact or grouped, and for any truncation of censoring situation. The following two steps summarize the process of setting up the likelihood function:

1. For the numerator, use $f(x)$ if the exact value, x, of the observation is known. If it is only known that the observation is between y and z, use $F(z) - F(y)$.

2. For the denominator, let d be the threshold (use zero if there is no truncation). The denominator is then $1 - F(d)$.

Example 10.11 *Determine Pareto and gamma models for the time to failure for Data Set D.*

Table 10.5 shows how the likelihood function is constructed for these values. For failures, the time is known and so the exact value of x is available. For withdrawals or those reaching age 5, the observation is censored and therefore failure is known to be some time later; that is, in the interval from the withdrawal time, y, to infinity. In the table, $z = \infty$ is not noted because all interval observations end at infinity. The likelihood function must

Table 10.5 Likelihood function for Example 10.11

Obs.	x, y	d	L	Obs.	x, y	d	L
1	$y = 0.1$	0	$1 - F(0.1)$	16	$x = 4.8$	0	$f(4.8)$
2	$y = 0.5$	0	$1 - F(0.5)$	17	$y = 4.8$	0	$1 - F(4.8)$
3	$y = 0.8$	0	$1 - F(0.8)$	18	$y = 4.8$	0	$1 - F(4.8)$
4	$x = 0.8$	0	$f(0.8)$	19-30	$y = 5.0$	0	$1 - F(5.0)$
5	$y = 1.8$	0	$1 - F(1.8)$	31	$y = 5.0$	0.3	$\frac{1-F(5.0)}{1-F(0.3)}$
6	$y = 1.8$	0	$1 - F(1.8)$	32	$y = 5.0$	0.7	$\frac{1-F(5.0)}{1-F(0.7)}$
7	$y = 2.1$	0	$1 - F(2.1)$	33	$x = 4.1$	1.0	$\frac{f(4.1)}{1-F(1.0)}$
8	$y = 2.5$	0	$1 - F(2.5)$	34	$x = 3.1$	1.8	$\frac{f(3.1)}{1-F(1.8)}$
9	$y = 2.8$	0	$1 - F(2.8)$	35	$y = 3.9$	2.1	$\frac{1-F(3.9)}{1-F(2.1)}$
10	$x = 2.9$	0	$f(2.9)$	36	$y = 5.0$	2.9	$\frac{1-F(5.0)}{1-F(2.9)}$
11	$x = 2.9$	0	$f(2.9)$	37	$y = 4.8$	2.9	$\frac{1-F(4.8)}{1-F(2.9)}$
12	$y = 3.9$	0	$1 - F(3.9)$	38	$x = 4.0$	3.2	$\frac{f(4.0)}{1-F(3.2)}$
13	$x = 4.0$	0	$f(4.0)$	39	$y = 5.0$	3.4	$\frac{1-F(5.0)}{1-F(3.4)}$
14	$y = 4.0$	0	$1 - F(4.0)$	40	$y = 5.0$	3.9	$\frac{1-F(5.0)}{1-F(3.9)}$
15	$y = 4.1$	0	$1 - F(4.1)$				

be maximized numerically. For the Pareto distribution there is no solution. The likelihood function keeps getting larger as α and θ get larger.[5] For the gamma distribution the maximum is at $\hat{\alpha} = 2.617$ and $\hat{\theta} = 3.311$.   □

Discrete data present no additional problems.

Example 10.12 *For Data Set A, assume that the seven drivers with five or more accidents all had exactly five accidents. Determine the maximum likelihood estimate for a Poisson distribution and for a binomial distribution with $m = 8$.*

In general, for a discrete distribution with complete data, the likelihood function is

$$L(\theta) = \prod_{j=1}^{\infty} [p(x_j | \theta)]^{n_j},$$

---

[5] For a Pareto distribution, the limit as the parameters α and θ become infinite with the ratio being held constant is an exponential distribution. Thus, for this example, the exponential distribution is a better model (as measured by the likelihood function) than any Pareto model.

where x_j is one of the observed values, $p(x_j|\theta)$ is the probability of observing x_j, and n_x is the number of times x was observed in the sample. For the Poisson distribution

$$L(\lambda) = \prod_{x=0}^{\infty} \left(\frac{e^{-\lambda}\lambda^x}{x!} \right)^{n_x} = \prod_{x=0}^{\infty} \frac{e^{-n_x\lambda}\lambda^{xn_x}}{(x!)^{n_x}},$$

$$l(\lambda) = \sum_{x=0}^{\infty}(-n_x\lambda + xn_x \ln \lambda - n_x \ln x!) = -n\lambda + n\bar{x}\ln \lambda - \sum_{x=0}^{\infty} n_x \ln x!,$$

$$l'(\lambda) = -n + \frac{n\bar{x}}{\lambda} = 0,$$

$$\hat{\lambda} = \bar{x}.$$

For the binomial distribution

$$L(q) = \prod_{x=0}^{m}\left[\binom{m}{x} q^x(1-q)^{m-x} \right]^{n_x} = \prod_{x=0}^{m} \frac{m!^{n_x} q^{xn_x}(1-q)^{(m-x)n_x}}{(x!)^{n_x}[(m-x)!]^{n_x}},$$

$$l(q) = \sum_{x=0}^{m}[n_x \ln m! + xn_x \ln q + (m-x)n_x \ln(1-q)]$$

$$- \sum_{x=0}^{m}[n_x \ln x! + n_x \ln(m-x)!],$$

$$l'(q) = \sum_{x=0}^{m} \frac{xn_x}{q} - \frac{(m-x)n_x}{1-q} = \frac{n\bar{x}}{q} - \frac{mn - n\bar{x}}{1-q} = 0,$$

$$\hat{q} = \frac{\bar{x}}{m}.$$

For this problem, $\bar{x} = [81,714(0) + 11,306(1) + 1618(2) + 250(3) + 40(4) + 7(5)]/94,935 = 0.16313$. Therefore, for the Poisson distribution $\hat{\lambda} = 0.16313$, and for the binomial distribution $\hat{q} = 0.16313/8 = 0.02039$.   □

In Exercise 10.21 you are asked to estimate the Poisson parameter when the actual values for those with five or more accidents are not known.

10.4 VARIANCE AND INTERVAL ESTIMATION

In general, it is not easy to determine the variance of complicated estimators such as the maximum likelihood estimator. However, it is possible to approximate the variance. The key is a theorem that can be found in most mathematical statistics books. The particular version stated here and its multiparameter generalization are taken from reference [102] and stated without proof. Recall that $L(\theta)$ is the likelihood function and $l(\theta)$ its logarithm. All of the results assume that the population has a distribution that is a member of the chosen parametric family.

Theorem 10.13 *Assume that the pdf (pf in the discrete case) $f(x;\theta)$ satisfies the following for θ in an interval containing the true value (replace integrals by sums for discrete variables):*

(i) $\ln f(x;\theta)$ *is three times differentiable with respect to θ.*

(ii) $\int \frac{\partial}{\partial\theta} f(x;\theta)\, dx = 0$. *This implies that the derivative may be taken outside the integral and so we are just differentiating the constant 1.*[6]

(iii) $\int \frac{\partial^2}{\partial\theta^2} f(x;\theta)\, dx = 0$. *This is the same concept for the second derivative.*

(iv) $-\infty < \int f(x;\theta)\frac{\partial^2}{\partial\theta^2}\ln f(x;\theta)\, dx < 0$. *This establishes that the indicated integral exists and that the location where the derivative is zero is a maximum.*

(v) *There exists a function $H(x)$ such that $\int H(x)f(x;\theta)\, dx < \infty$ with $\left|\frac{\partial^3}{\partial\theta^3}\ln f(x;\theta)\right| < H(x)$. This makes sure that the population is not overpopulated with regard to extreme values.*

Then the following results hold:

(a) *As $n \to \infty$, the probability that the likelihood equation $[L'(\theta) = 0]$ has a solution goes to 1.*

(b) *As $n \to \infty$, the distribution of the maximum likelihood estimator $\hat{\theta}_n$ converges to a normal distribution with mean θ and variance such that $I(\theta)\,\mathrm{Var}(\hat{\theta}_n) \to 1$, where*

$$I(\theta) = -n\mathrm{E}\left[\frac{\partial^2}{\partial\theta^2}\ln f(X;\theta)\right] = -n\int f(x;\theta)\frac{\partial^2}{\partial\theta^2}\ln f(x;\theta)\, dx$$

$$= n\mathrm{E}\left[\left(\frac{\partial}{\partial\theta}\ln f(X;\theta)\right)^2\right] = n\int f(x;\theta)\left(\frac{\partial}{\partial\theta}\ln f(x;\theta)\right)^2 dx.$$

For any z, the last statement is to be interpreted as

$$\lim_{n\to\infty}\mathrm{Pr}\left(\frac{\hat{\theta}_n - \theta}{[I(\theta)]^{-1/2}} < z\right) = \Phi(z)$$

---

[6] The integrals in *(ii)* and *(iii)* are to be evaluated over the range of x values for which $f(x;\theta) > 0$.

and therefore $[I(\theta)]^{-1}$ is a useful approximation for $\mathrm{Var}(\hat{\theta}_n)$. The quantity $I(\theta)$ is called the **information** (sometimes more specifically, **Fisher's information**). It follows from this result that the maximum likelihood estimator is asymptotically unbiased and consistent. The conditions in statements *(i)–(v)* are often referred to as "mild regularity conditions." A skeptic would translate this statement as "conditions that are almost always true but are often difficult to establish, so we'll just assume they hold in our case." Their purpose is to ensure that the density function is fairly smooth with regard to changes in the parameter and that there is nothing unusual about the density itself.[7]

The results stated above assume that the sample consists of independent and identically distributed random observations. A more general version of the result uses the logarithm of the likelihood function:

$$I(\theta) = -\mathrm{E}\left[\frac{\partial^2}{\partial\theta^2}l(\theta)\right] = \mathrm{E}\left[\left(\frac{\partial}{\partial\theta}l(\theta)\right)^2\right].$$

The only requirement here is that the same parameter value apply to each observation.

If there is more than one parameter, the only change is that the vector of maximum likelihood estimates now has an asymptotic multivariate normal distribution. The covariance matrix[8] of this distribution is obtained from the inverse of the matrix with (r,s)th element,

$$\begin{aligned}\mathbf{I}(\theta)_{rs} &= -\mathrm{E}\left[\frac{\partial^2}{\partial\theta_s\,\partial\theta_r}l(\theta)\right] = -n\mathrm{E}\left[\frac{\partial^2}{\partial\theta_s\,\partial\theta_r}\ln f(X;\theta)\right]\\ &= \mathrm{E}\left[\frac{\partial}{\partial\theta_r}l(\theta)\frac{\partial}{\partial\theta_s}l(\theta)\right] = n\mathrm{E}\left[\frac{\partial}{\partial\theta_r}\ln f(X;\theta)\frac{\partial}{\partial\theta_s}\ln f(X;\theta)\right].\end{aligned}$$

The first expression on each line is always correct. The second expression assumes that the likelihood is the product of n identical densities. This matrix is often called the **information matrix**. The information matrix also forms the Cramér–Rao lower bound. That is, under the usual conditions, no unbiased estimator has a smaller variance than that given by the inverse of the information. Therefore, at least asymptotically, no unbiased estimator is more accurate than the maximum likelihood estimator.

Example 10.14 *Estimate the covariance matrix of the maximum likelihood estimator for the lognormal distribution. Then apply this result to Data Set B.*

[7] For an example of a situation where these conditions do not hold, see Exercise 10.42.
[8] For any multivariate random variable the covariance matrix has the variances of the individual random variables on the main diagonal and covariances in the off-diagonal positions.

The likelihood function and its logarithm are

$$L(\mu,\sigma) = \prod_{j=1}^{n} \frac{1}{x_j\sigma\sqrt{2\pi}} \exp\left[-\frac{(\ln x_j - \mu)^2}{2\sigma^2}\right],$$

$$l(\mu,\sigma) = \sum_{j=1}^{n}\left[-\ln x_j - \ln\sigma - \frac{1}{2}\ln(2\pi) - \frac{1}{2}\left(\frac{\ln x_j - \mu}{\sigma}\right)^2\right].$$

The first partial derivatives are

$$\frac{\partial l}{\partial\mu} = \sum_{j=1}^{n}\frac{\ln x_j - \mu}{\sigma^2} \quad\text{and}\quad \frac{\partial l}{\partial\sigma} = -\frac{n}{\sigma} + \sum_{j=1}^{n}\frac{(\ln x_j - \mu)^2}{\sigma^3}.$$

The second partial derivatives are

$$\frac{\partial^2 l}{\partial\mu^2} = -\frac{n}{\sigma^2},$$

$$\frac{\partial^2 l}{\partial\sigma\,\partial\mu} = -2\sum_{j=1}^{n}\frac{\ln x_j - \mu}{\sigma^3},$$

$$\frac{\partial^2 l}{\partial\sigma^2} = \frac{n}{\sigma^2} - 3\sum_{j=1}^{n}\frac{(\ln x_j - \mu)^2}{\sigma^4}.$$

The expected values are ($\ln X_j$ has a normal distribution distribution, nor-malwith mean μ and standard deviation σ)

$$E\left(\frac{\partial^2 l}{\partial\mu^2}\right) = -\frac{n}{\sigma^2},$$

$$E\left(\frac{\partial^2 l}{\partial\mu\,\partial\sigma}\right) = 0,$$

$$E\left(\frac{\partial^2 l}{\partial\sigma^2}\right) = -\frac{2n}{\sigma^2}.$$

Changing the signs and inverting produce an estimate of the covariance matrix (it is an estimate because Theorem 10.13 only provides the covariance matrix in the limit). It is

$$\begin{bmatrix} \frac{\sigma^2}{n} & 0 \\ 0 & \frac{\sigma^2}{2n} \end{bmatrix}.$$

For the lognormal distribution, the maximum likelihood estimates are the solutions to the two equations

$$\sum_{j=1}^{n}\frac{\ln x_j - \mu}{\sigma^2} = 0 \quad\text{and}\quad -\frac{n}{\sigma} + \sum_{j=1}^{n}\frac{(\ln x_j - \mu)^2}{\sigma^3} = 0.$$

From the first equation $\hat{\mu} = (1/n)\sum_{j=1}^{n} \ln x_j$, and from the second equation $\hat{\sigma}^2 = (1/n)\sum_{j=1}^{n}(\ln x_j - \hat{\mu})^2$. For Data Set B the values are $\hat{\mu} = 6.1379$ and $\hat{\sigma}^2 = 1.9305$ or $\hat{\sigma} = 1.3894$. With regard to the covariance matrix the true values are needed. The best we can do is substitute the estimated values to obtain

$$\widehat{\text{Var}}(\hat{\mu}, \hat{\sigma}) = \begin{bmatrix} 0.0965 & 0 \\ 0 & 0.0483 \end{bmatrix}. \tag{10.1}$$

The multiple "hats" in the expression indicate that this is an estimate of the variance of the estimators.   □

The zeros off the diagonal indicate that the two parameter estimates are asymptotically uncorrelated. For the particular case of the lognormal distribution, that is also true for any sample size. One thing we could do with this information is construct approximate 95% confidence intervals for the true parameter values. These would be 1.96 standard deviations on either side of the estimate:

$$\mu: \quad 6.1379 \pm 1.96(0.0965)^{1/2} = 6.1379 \pm 0.6089,$$

$$\sigma: \quad 1.3894 \pm 1.96(0.0483)^{1/2} = 1.3894 \pm 0.4308.$$

To obtain the information matrix, it is necessary to take both derivatives and expected values. This is not always easy to do. A way to avoid this problem is to simply not take the expected value. Rather than working with the number that results from the expectation, use the observed data points. The result is called the **observed information**.

Example 10.15 *Estimate the covariance in Example 10.14 using the observed information.*

Substituting the observations into the second derivatives produces

$$\frac{\partial^2 l}{\partial \mu^2} = -\frac{n}{\sigma^2} = -\frac{20}{\sigma^2},$$

$$\frac{\partial^2 l}{\partial \sigma \, \partial \mu} = -2\sum_{j=1}^{n} \frac{\ln x_j - \mu}{\sigma^3} = -2\frac{122.7576 - 20\mu}{\sigma^3},$$

$$\frac{\partial^2 l}{\partial \sigma^2} = \frac{n}{\sigma^2} - 3\sum_{j=1}^{n} \frac{(\ln x_j - \mu)^2}{\sigma^4} = \frac{20}{\sigma^2} - 3\frac{792.0801 - 245.5152\mu + 20\mu^2}{\sigma^4}.$$

Inserting the parameter estimates produces the negatives of the entries of the observed information,

$$\frac{\partial^2 l}{\partial \mu^2} = -10.3600, \quad \frac{\partial^2 l}{\partial \sigma \, \partial \mu} = 0, \quad \frac{\partial^2 l}{\partial \sigma^2} = -20.7190.$$

Changing the signs and inverting produce the same values as in equation (10.1). This is a feature of the lognormal distribution that needs not hold for other models. □

Sometimes it is not even possible to take the derivative. In that case an approximate second derivative can be used. A reasonable approximation is

$$\frac{\partial^2 f(\theta)}{\partial \theta_i \, \partial \theta_j} \doteq \frac{1}{h_i h_j} [f(\theta + \tfrac{1}{2}h_i \mathbf{e}_i + \tfrac{1}{2}h_j \mathbf{e}_j) - f(\theta + \tfrac{1}{2}h_i \mathbf{e}_i - \tfrac{1}{2}h_j \mathbf{e}_j)$$
$$- f(\theta - \tfrac{1}{2}h_i \mathbf{e}_i + \tfrac{1}{2}h_j \mathbf{e}_j) + f(\theta - \tfrac{1}{2}h_i \mathbf{e}_i - \tfrac{1}{2}h_j \mathbf{e}_j)],$$

where $\mathbf{e}_i$ is a vector with all zeros except for a 1 in the ith position and $h_i = \theta_i/10^v$, where v is one-third the number of significant digits used in calculations.

Example 10.16 *Repeat the Example 10.15 using approximate derivatives.*

Assume that there are 15 significant digits being used. Then $h_1 = 6.1379/10^5$ and $h_2 = 1.3894/10^5$. Reasonably close values are 0.00006 and 0.00001. The first approximation is

$$\frac{\partial^2 l}{\partial \mu^2} \doteq \frac{l(6.13796, 1.3894) - 2l(6.1379, 1.3894) + l(6.13784, 1.3894)}{(0.00006)^2}$$
$$= \frac{-157.71389308198 - 2(-157.71389304968) + (-157.71389305468)}{(0.00006)^2}$$
$$= -10.3604.$$

The other two approximations are

$$\frac{\partial^2 l}{\partial \sigma \, \partial \mu} \doteq 0.0003, \quad \frac{\partial^2 l}{\partial \sigma^2} \doteq -20.7208.$$

We see that here the approximation works very well. □

The information matrix provides a method for assessing the quality of the maximum likelihood estimators of a distribution's parameters. However, we are often more interested in a quantity that is a function of the parameters. For example, we might be interested in the lognormal mean as an estimate of the population mean. That is, we want to use $\exp(\hat{\mu} + \hat{\sigma}^2/2)$ as an estimate of the population mean, where the maximum likelihood estimates of the parameters are used. It is very difficult to evaluate the mean and variance of this random variable because it is a complex function of two variables that already have complex distributions. Theorem 10.17(from [97]) can help. The method is often called the **delta method**.

Theorem 10.17 *Let* $\mathbf{X}_n = (X_{1n}, \ldots, X_{kn})^T$ *be a multivariate random variable of dimension* k *based on a sample of size* n. *Assume that* $\mathbf{X}$ *is asymptotically normal with mean* θ *and covariance matrix* Σ/n, *where neither* θ *nor* Σ *depend on* n. *Let* g *be a function of* k *variables that is totally differentiable. Let* $G_n = g(X_{1n}, \ldots, X_{kn})$. *Then* G_n *is asymptotically normal with mean* $g(\theta)$ *and variance* $(\partial\mathbf{g})^T\Sigma(\partial\mathbf{g})/n$, *where* $\partial\mathbf{g}$ *is the vector of first derivatives, that is,* $\partial\mathbf{g} = (\partial g/\partial\theta_1, \ldots, \partial g/\partial\theta_k)^T$ *and it is to be evaluated at* θ, *the true parameters of the original random variable.*

The statement of the theorem is hard to decipher. The Xs are the estimators and g is the function of the parameters that are being estimated. For a model with one parameter, the theorem reduces to the following statement: Let $\hat{\theta}$ be an estimator of θ that has an asymptotic normal distribution with mean θ and variance σ^2/n. Then $g(\hat{\theta})$ has an asymptotic normal distribution with mean $g(\theta)$ and asymptotic variance $[g'(\theta)](\sigma^2/n)[g'(\theta)] = g'(\theta)^2\sigma^2/n$.

Example 10.18 *Use the delta method to approximate the variance of the maximum likelihood estimator of the probability that an observation from an exponential distribution exceeds* 200. *Apply this result to Data Set B.*

From Example 10.8 we know that the maximum likelihood estimate of the exponential parameter is the sample mean. We are asked to estimate $p = \Pr(X > 200) = \exp(-200/\theta)$. The maximum likelihood estimate is $\hat{p} = \exp(-200/\hat{\theta}) = \exp(-200/\bar{x})$. Determining the mean and variance of this quantity is not easy. But we do know that $\mathrm{Var}(\bar{X}) = \mathrm{Var}(X)/n = \theta^2/n$. Furthermore,

$$g(\theta) = e^{-200/\theta}, \quad g'(\theta) = 200\theta^{-2}e^{-200/\theta},$$

and therefore the delta method gives

$$\mathrm{Var}(\hat{p}) \doteq \frac{(200\theta^{-2}e^{-200/\theta})^2\theta^2}{n} = \frac{40{,}000\theta^{-2}e^{-400/\theta}}{n}.$$

For Data Set B,

$$\bar{x} = 1{,}424.4,$$

$$\hat{p} = \exp\left(-\frac{200}{1424.4}\right) = 0.86900$$

$$\widehat{\mathrm{Var}}(\hat{p}) = \frac{40{,}000(1424.4)^{-2}\exp(-400/1424.4)}{20} = 0.0007444.$$

A 95% confidence interval for p is $0.869 \pm 1.96\sqrt{0.0007444}$ or 0.869 ± 0.053. $\square$

Example 10.19 *Construct a 95% confidence interval for the mean of a lognormal population using Data Set B. Compare this to the more traditional confidence interval based on the sample mean.*

From Example 10.14 we have $\hat{\mu} = 6.1379$ and $\hat{\sigma} = 1.3894$ and an estimated covariance matrix of

$$\frac{\hat{\Sigma}}{n} = \begin{bmatrix} 0.0965 & 0 \\ 0 & 0.0483 \end{bmatrix}.$$

The function is $g(\mu, \sigma) = \exp(\mu + \sigma^2/2)$. The partial derivatives are

$$\frac{\partial g}{\partial \mu} = \exp\left(\mu + \tfrac{1}{2}\sigma^2\right)$$

$$\frac{\partial g}{\partial \sigma} = \sigma \exp\left(\mu + \tfrac{1}{2}\sigma^2\right)$$

and the estimates of these quantities are 1,215.75 and 1,689.16, respectively. The delta method produces the following approximation:

$$\widehat{\mathrm{Var}}[g(\hat{\mu}, \hat{\sigma})] = \begin{bmatrix} 1215.75 & 1689.16 \end{bmatrix} \begin{bmatrix} 0.0965 & 0 \\ 0 & 0.0483 \end{bmatrix} \begin{bmatrix} 1215.75 \\ 1689.16 \end{bmatrix}$$
$$= 280,444.$$

The confidence interval is $1215.75 \pm 1.96\sqrt{280,444}$ or $1,215.75 \pm 1037.96$.

The customary confidence interval for a population mean is $\bar{x} \pm 1.96 s/\sqrt{n}$ where is s^2 is the sample variance. For Data Set B the interval is $1424.4 \pm 1.96(3435.04)/\sqrt{20}$ or 1424.4 ± 1505.47. It is not surprising that this is a wider interval because we know that (for a lognormal population) the maximum likelihood estimator is asymptotically UMVUE. □

10.5 BAYESIAN ESTIMATION

All of the previous discussion on estimation has assumed a frequentist approach. That is, the population distribution is fixed but unknown, and our decisions are concerned not only with the sample we obtained from the population but also with the possibilities attached to other samples that might have been obtained. The Bayesian approach assumes that only the data actually observed are relevant and it is the population that is variable. For parameter estimation the following definitions describe the process and then Bayes' theorem provides the solution.

10.5.1 Definitions and Bayes' theorem

Definition 10.20 *The **prior distribution** is a probability distribution over the space of possible parameter values. It is denoted $\pi(\theta)$ and represents our opinion concerning the relative chances that various values of θ are the true value of the parameter.*

As before, the parameter θ may be scalar or vector valued. Determination of the prior distribution has always been one of the barriers to the widespread acceptance of Bayesian methods. It is almost certainly the case that your experience has provided some insights about possible parameter values before the first data point has been observed. (If you have no such opinions, perhaps the wisdom of the person who assigned this task to you should be questioned.) The difficulty is translating this knowledge into a probability distribution. An excellent discussion about prior distributions and the foundations of Bayesian analysis can be found in Lindley [76], and for a discussion about issues surrounding the choice of Bayesian versus frequentist methods, see Efron [26]. A good source for a thorough mathematical treatment of Bayesian methods is the text by Berger [15]. In recent years many advancements in Bayesian calculations have occurred. A good resource is [21]. The paper by Scollnik ?? addresses loss distribution modeling using Bayesian software tools.

Because of the difficulty of finding a prior distribution that is convincing (you will have to convince others that your prior opinions are valid) and the possibility that you may really have no prior opinion, the definition of prior distribution can be loosened.

Definition 10.21 *An **improper prior distribution** is one for which the probabilities (or pdf) are nonnegative but their sum (or integral) is infinite.*

A great deal of research has gone into the determination of a so-called **noninformative** or **vague** prior. Its purpose is to reflect minimal knowledge. Universal agreement on the best way to construct a vague prior does not exist. However, there is agreement that the appropriate noninformative prior for a scale parameter is $\pi(\theta) = 1/\theta, \theta > 0$. Note that this is an improper prior.

For a Bayesian analysis, the model is no different than before.

Definition 10.22 *The **model distribution** is the probability distribution for the data as collected given a particular value for the parameter. Its pdf is denoted $f_{\mathbf{X}|\Theta}(\mathbf{x}|\theta)$, where vector notation for $\mathbf{x}$ is used to remind us that all the data appear here. Also note that this is identical to the likelihood function and so that name may also be used at times.*

If the vector of observations $\mathbf{x} = (x_1, \ldots, x_n)^T$ consists of independent and identically distributed random variables, then

$$f_{\mathbf{X}|\Theta}(\mathbf{x}|\theta) = f_{X|\Theta}(x_1|\theta) \cdots f_{X|\Theta}(x_n|\theta).$$

We use concepts from multivariate statistics to obtain two more definitions. In both cases, as well as in the following, integrals should be replaced by sums if the distributions are discrete.

Definition 10.23 *The **joint distribution** has pdf*

$$f_{\mathbf{X},\Theta}(\mathbf{x}, \theta) = f_{\mathbf{X}|\Theta}(\mathbf{x}|\theta)\pi(\theta).$$

Definition 10.24 *The **marginal distribution** of* x *has pdf*

$$f_{\mathbf{X}}(\mathbf{x}) = \int f_{\mathbf{X}|\Theta}(\mathbf{x}|\theta)\pi(\theta)\,d\theta.$$

Compare this definition to that of a mixture distribution given by formula (4.5) on page 88. The final two quantities of interest are the following.

Definition 10.25 *The **posterior distribution** is the conditional probability distribution of the parameters given the observed data. It is denoted* $\pi_{\Theta|\mathbf{X}}(\theta|\mathbf{x})$.

Definition 10.26 *The **predictive distribution** is the conditional probability distribution of a new observation* y *given the data* x. *It is denoted* $f_{Y|\mathbf{X}}(y|\mathbf{x})$.[9]

These last two items are the key output of a Bayesian analysis. The posterior distribution tells us how our opinion about the parameter has changed once we have observed the data. The predictive distribution tells us what the next observation might look like given the information contained in the data (as well as, implicitly, our prior opinion). Bayes' theorem tells us how to compute the posterior distribution.

Theorem 10.27 *The posterior distribution can be computed as*

$$\pi_{\Theta|\mathbf{X}}(\theta|\mathbf{x}) = \frac{f_{\mathbf{X}|\Theta}(\mathbf{x}|\theta)\pi(\theta)}{\displaystyle\int f_{\mathbf{X}|\Theta}(\mathbf{x}|\theta)\pi(\theta)\,d\theta} \tag{10.2}$$

while the predictive distribution can be computed as

$$f_{Y|\mathbf{X}}(y|\mathbf{x}) = \int f_{Y|\Theta}(y|\theta)\pi_{\Theta|\mathbf{X}}(\theta|\mathbf{x})\,d\theta, \tag{10.3}$$

where $f_{Y|\Theta}(y|\theta)$ *is the pdf of the new observation, given the parameter value.*

The predictive distribution can be interpreted as a mixture distribution where the mixing is with respect to the posterior distribution. Example 10.28 illustrates the above definitions and results.

Example 10.28 *Consider the following losses:*

$$125 \quad 132 \quad 141 \quad 107 \quad 133 \quad 319 \quad 126 \quad 104 \quad 145 \quad 223$$

---

[9]In this section and in any subsequent Bayesian discussions, we reserve $f(\cdot)$ for distributions concerning observations (such as the model and predictive distributions) and $\pi(\cdot)$ for distributions concerning parameters (such as the prior and posterior distributions). The arguments will usually make it clear which particular distribution is being used. To make matters explicit, we also employ subscripts to enable us to keep track of the random variables.

The amount of a single loss has the single-parameter Pareto distribution with
$\theta = 100$ *and* α *unknown. The prior distribution has the gamma distribution*
with $\alpha = 2$ *and* $\theta = 1$. *Determine all of the relevant Bayesian quantities.*

The prior density has a gamma distribution and is

$$\pi(\alpha) = \alpha e^{-\alpha}, \quad \alpha > 0,$$

while the model is (evaluated at the data points)

$$f_{\mathbf{X}|A}(\mathbf{x}|\alpha) = \frac{\alpha^{10}(100)^{10\alpha}}{\left(\prod_{j=1}^{10} x_j^{\alpha+1}\right)} = \alpha^{10}e^{-3.801121\alpha - 49.852823}.$$

The joint density of $\mathbf{x}$ and A is (again evaluated at the data points)

$$f_{\mathbf{X},A}(\mathbf{x}, \alpha) = \alpha^{11}e^{-4.801121\alpha - 49.852823}.$$

The posterior distribution of α is

$$\pi_{A|\mathbf{X}}(\alpha|\mathbf{x}) = \frac{\alpha^{11}e^{-4.801121\alpha - 49.852823}}{\int_0^\infty \alpha^{11}e^{-4.801121\alpha - 49.852823}\, d\alpha} = \frac{\alpha^{11}e^{-4.801121\alpha}}{(11!)(1/4.801121)^{12}}. \quad (10.4)$$

There is no need to evaluate the integral in the denominator. Because we
know that the result must be a probability distribution, the denominator is
just the appropriate normalizing constant. A look at the numerator reveals
that we have a gamma distribution with $\alpha = 12$ and $\theta = 1/4.801121$.
    The predictive distribution is

$$f_{Y|\mathbf{X}}(y|\mathbf{x}) = \int_0^\infty \frac{\alpha 100^\alpha}{y^{\alpha+1}} \frac{\alpha^{11}e^{-4.801121\alpha}}{(11!)(1/4.801121)^{12}}\, d\alpha$$

$$= \frac{1}{y(11!)(1/4.801121)^{12}} \int_0^\infty \alpha^{12}e^{-(0.195951 + \ln y)\alpha}\, d\alpha$$

$$= \frac{1}{y(11!)(1/4.801121)^{12}} \frac{(12!)}{(0.195951 + \ln y)^{13}}$$

$$= \frac{12(4.801121)^{12}}{y(0.195951 + \ln y)^{13}}, \quad y > 100. \quad (10.5)$$

While this density function may not look familiar, you are asked to show in
Exercise 10.43 that $\ln Y - \ln 100$ has the Pareto distribution.   □

10.5.2   Inference and prediction

In one sense the analysis is complete. We begin with a distribution that
quantifies our knowledge about the parameter and/or the next observation
and we end with a revised distribution. However, you will likely want to

produce a single number, perhaps with a margin for error, is what is desired. The usual Bayesian solution is to pose a loss function.

Definition 10.29 *A **loss function** $l_j(\hat{\theta}_j, \theta_j)$ describes the penalty paid by the investigator when $\hat{\theta}_j$ is the estimate and θ_j is the true value of the jth parameter.*

It is also possible to have a multidimensional loss function $l(\widehat{\theta}, \theta)$ that allows the loss to depend simultaneously on the errors in the various parameter estimates.

Definition 10.30 *The **Bayes estimator** for a given loss function is the estimator that minimizes the expected loss given the posterior distribution of the parameter in question.*

The three most commonly used loss functions are defined as follows.

Definition 10.31 *For **squared-error loss** the loss function is (all subscripts are dropped for convenience) $l(\hat{\theta}, \theta) = (\hat{\theta} - \theta)^2$. For **absolute loss** it is $l(\hat{\theta}, \theta) = |\hat{\theta} - \theta|$. For **zero–one loss** it is $l(\hat{\theta}, \theta) = 0$ if $\hat{\theta} = \theta$ and is 1 otherwise.*

Theorem 10.32 indicates the Bayes estimates for these three common loss functions.

Theorem 10.32 *For squared-error loss, the Bayes estimator is the mean of the posterior distribution, for absolute loss it is a median, and for zero–one loss it is a mode.*

Note that there is no guarantee that the posterior mean exists or that the posterior median or mode will be unique. When not otherwise specified, the term **Bayes estimator** will refer to the posterior mean.

Example 10.33 (Example 10.28 continued) *Determine the three Bayes estimates of α.*

The mean of the posterior gamma distribution is $\alpha\theta = 12/4.801121 = 2.499416$. The median of 2.430342 must be determined numerically while the mode is $(\alpha - 1)\theta = 11/4.801121 = 2.291132$. Note that the α used here is the parameter of the posterior gamma distribution, not the α for the single-parameter Pareto distribution that we are trying to estimate.   □

For forecasting purposes, the expected value of the predictive distribution is often of interest. It can be thought of as providing a point estimate of the $(n+1)$th observation given the first n observations and the prior distribution.

It is

$$E(Y|\mathbf{x}) = \int y f_{Y|\mathbf{x}}(y|\mathbf{x})dy$$

$$= \int y \int f_{Y|\Theta}(y|\theta)\pi_{\Theta|\mathbf{x}}(\theta|\mathbf{x})d\theta dy$$

$$= \int \pi_{\Theta|\mathbf{x}}(\theta|\mathbf{x}) \int y f_{Y|\Theta}(y|\theta)dy d\theta$$

$$= \int E(Y|\theta)\pi_{\Theta|\mathbf{x}}(\theta|\mathbf{x})d\theta. \qquad (10.6)$$

Equation (10.6) can be interpreted as a weighted average using the posterior distribution as weights.

Example 10.34 (Example 10.28 continued) *Determine the expected value of the 11th observation, given the first 10.*

For the single-parameter Pareto distribution, $E(Y|\alpha) = 100\alpha/(\alpha - 1)$ for $\alpha > 1$. Because the posterior distribution assigns positive probability to values of $\alpha \leq 1$, the expected value of the predictive distribution is not defined. □

The Bayesian equivalent of a confidence interval is easy to construct. The following definition will suffice.

Definition 10.35 *The points $a < b$ define a $100(1-\alpha)\%$ **credibility interval** for θ_j provided that $\Pr(a \leq \Theta_j \leq b|\mathbf{x}) \geq 1 - \alpha$.*

The inequality is present for the case where the posterior distribution of θ_j is discrete. Then it may not be possible for the probability to be exactly $1 - \alpha$. This definition does not produce a unique solution. Theorem 10.36 indicates one way to produce a unique interval.

Theorem 10.36 *If the posterior random variable $\theta_j|\mathbf{x}$ is continuous and unimodal, then the $100(1 - \alpha)\%$ credibility interval with smallest width $b - a$ is the unique solution to*

$$\int_a^b \pi_{\Theta_j|\mathbf{x}}(\theta_j|\mathbf{x})\, d\theta_j = 1 - \alpha,$$

$$\pi_{\Theta|\mathbf{x}}(a|\mathbf{x}) = \pi_{\Theta|\mathbf{x}}(b|\mathbf{x}).$$

This interval is a special case of a highest posterior density (HPD) credibility set.

Example 10.37 may clarify the theorem.

Example 10.37 (Example 10.28 continued) *Determine the shortest 95% credibility interval for the parameter α. Also determine the interval that places 2.5% probability at each end.*

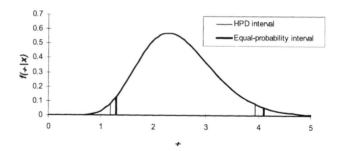

Fig. 10.1   Two Bayesian credibility intervals

The two equations from Theorem 10.36 are

$$\Pr(a \le A \le b | \mathbf{x}) = \Gamma(12; 4.801121b) - \Gamma(12; 4.801121a) = 0.95,$$
$$a^{11} e^{-4.801121a} = b^{11} e^{-4.801121b},$$

and numerical methods can be used to find the solution $a = 1.1832$ and $b = 3.9384$. The width of this interval is 2.7552.

Placing 2.5% probability at each end yields the two equations

$$\Gamma(12; 4.801121b) = 0.975, \quad \Gamma(12; 4.801121a) = 0.025.$$

This solution requires either access to the inverse of the incomplete gamma function or the use of root-finding techniques with the incomplete gamma function itself. The solution is $a = 1.2915$ and $b = 4.0995$. The width is 2.8080, wider than the first interval. Figure 10.1 shows the difference in the two intervals. The solid vertical bars represent the HPD interval. The total area to the left and right of these bars is 0.05. Any other 95% interval must also have this probability. To create the interval with 0.025 probability on each side, both bars must be moved to the right. To subtract the same probability on the right end that is added on the left end, the right limit must be moved a greater distance because the posterior density is lower over that interval than it is on the left end. This must lead to a wider interval. □

Definition 10.38 provides the equivalent result for any posterior distribution.

Definition 10.38 *For any posterior distribution the $100(1-\alpha)\%$ **HPD credibility set** is the set of parameter values C such that*

$$\Pr(\theta_j \in C) \ge 1 - \alpha \tag{10.7}$$

and

$$C = \{\theta_j : \pi_{\Theta_j | \mathbf{x}}(\theta_j | \mathbf{x}) \ge c\} \text{ for some } c,$$

where c is the largest value for which the inequality (10.7) holds.

This set may be the union of several intervals (which can happen with a multimodal posterior distribution). This definition produces the set of minimum total width that has the required posterior probability. Construction of the set is done by starting with a high value of c and then lowering it. As it decreases, the set C gets larger, as does the probability. The process continues until the probability reaches $1 - \alpha$. It should be obvious to see how the definition can be extended to the construction of a simultaneous credibility set for a vector of parameters, θ.

Sometimes it is the case that, while computing posterior probabilities is difficult, computing posterior moments may be easy. We can then use the Bayesian central limit theorem. The following theorem is paraphrased from Berger [15].

Theorem 10.39 *If $\pi(\theta)$ and $f_{X|\Theta}(x|\theta)$ are both twice differentiable in the elements of θ and other commonly satisfied assumptions hold, then the posterior distribution of Θ given $X = x$ is asymptotically normal.*

The "commonly satisfied assumptions" are like those in Theorem 10.13. As in that theorem, it is possible to do further approximations. In particular, the asymptotic normal distribution also results if the posterior mode is substituted for the posterior mean and/or if the posterior covariance matrix is estimated by inverting the matrix of second partial derivatives of the negative logarithm of the posterior density.

Example 10.40 (Example 10.28 continued) *Construct a 95% credibility interval for α using the Bayesian central limit theorem.*

The posterior distribution has a mean of 2.499416 and a variance of $\alpha\theta^2 = 0.520590$. Using the normal approximation, the credibility interval is $2.499416 \pm 1.96(0.520590)^{1/2}$, which produces $a = 1.0852$ and $b = 3.9136$. This interval (with regard to the normal approximation) is HPD because of the symmetry of the normal distribution.

The approximation is centered at the posterior mode of 2.291132 (see Example 10.33). The second derivative of the negative logarithm of the posterior density [from formula (10.4)] is

$$-\frac{d^2}{d\alpha^2} \ln\left[\frac{\alpha^{11} e^{-4.801121\alpha}}{(11!)(1/4.801121)^{12}}\right] = \frac{11}{\alpha^2}.$$

The variance estimate is the reciprocal. Evaluated at the modal estimate of α we get $(2.291132)^2/11 = 0.477208$ for a credibility interval of $2.29113 \pm 1.96(0.477208)^{1/2}$, which produces $a = 0.9372$ and $b = 3.6451$. $\square$

The same concepts can apply to the predictive distribution. However, the Bayesian central limit theorem does not help here because the predictive sample has only one member. The only potential use for it is that for a large original sample size we can replace the true posterior distribution in equation (10.3) with a multivariate normal distribution.

Example 10.41 (Example 10.28 continued) *Construct a 95% highest density prediction interval for the next observation.*

It is easy to see that the predictive density function (10.5) is strictly decreasing. Therefore the region with highest density runs from $a = 100$ to b. The value of b is determined from

$$0.95 = \int_{100}^{b} \frac{12(4.801121)^{12}}{y(0.195951 + \ln y)^{13}} \, dy$$

$$= \int_{0}^{\ln(b/100)} \frac{12(4.801121)^{12}}{(4.801121 + x)^{13}} \, dx$$

$$= 1 - \left[\frac{4.801121}{4.801121 + \ln(b/100)} \right]^{12}$$

and the solution is $b = 390.1840$. It is interesting to note that the mode of the predictive distribution is 100 (because the pdf is strictly decreasing) while the mean is infinite (with $b = \infty$ and an additional y in the integrand, after the transformation, the integrand is like $e^x x^{-13}$, which goes to infinity as x goes to infinity). □

Example 10.42 revisits a calculation done in Section 5.3. There the negative binomial distribution was derived as a gamma mixture of Poisson variables. Example 10.42 shows how the same calculations arise in a Bayesian context.

Example 10.42 *The number of losses in one year for a given type of transaction is known to have a Poisson distribution. The parameter is not known, but the prior distribution has a gamma distribution with parameters α and θ. Suppose in the past year there were x such losses. Use Bayesian methods to estimate the number of losses in the next year. Then repeat these calculations assuming loss counts for the past n years, $x_1, \ldots, x_n$.*

The key distributions are (where $x = 0, 1, \ldots,$ $\lambda, \alpha, \theta > 0$):

Prior: $\pi(\lambda) = \dfrac{\lambda^{\alpha-1} e^{-\lambda/\theta}}{\Gamma(\alpha)\theta^\alpha}$

Model: $p(x|\lambda) = \dfrac{\lambda^x e^{-\lambda}}{x!}$

Joint: $p(x, \lambda) = \dfrac{\lambda^{x+\alpha-1} e^{-(1+1/\theta)\lambda}}{x!\Gamma(\alpha)\theta^\alpha}$

Marginal: $p(x) = \displaystyle\int_0^\infty \dfrac{\lambda^{x+\alpha-1} e^{-(1+1/\theta)\lambda}}{x!\Gamma(\alpha)\theta^\alpha} d\lambda$

$\quad = \dfrac{\Gamma(x+\alpha)}{x!\Gamma(\alpha)\theta^\alpha (1+1/\theta)^{x+\alpha}}$

$\quad = \dbinom{x+\alpha-1}{x} \left(\dfrac{1}{1+\theta}\right)^\alpha \left(\dfrac{\theta}{1+\theta}\right)^x$

Posterior: $\pi(\lambda|x) = \dfrac{\lambda^{x+\alpha-1} e^{-(1+1/\theta)\lambda}}{x!\Gamma(\alpha)\theta^\alpha} \bigg/ \dfrac{\Gamma(x+\alpha)}{x!\Gamma(\alpha)\theta^\alpha (1+1/\theta)^{x+\alpha}}$

$\quad = \dfrac{\lambda^{x+\alpha-1} e^{-(1+1/\theta)\lambda}(1+1/\theta)^{x+\alpha}}{\Gamma(x+\alpha)}$

The marginal distribution is negative binomial with $r = \alpha$ and $\beta = \theta$. The posterior distribution is gamma with shape parameter "α" equal to $x+\alpha$ and scale parameter "θ" equal to $(1+1/\theta)^{-1} = \theta/(1+\theta)$. The Bayes estimate of the Poisson parameter is the posterior mean, $(x+\alpha)\theta/(1+\theta)$. For the predictive distribution, formula (10.3) gives

$$p(y|x) = \int_0^\infty \dfrac{\lambda^y e^{-\lambda}}{y!} \dfrac{\lambda^{x+\alpha-1} e^{-(1+1/\theta)\lambda}(1+1/\theta)^{x+\alpha}}{\Gamma(x+\alpha)} d\lambda$$

$$= \dfrac{(1+1/\theta)^{x+\alpha}}{y!\Gamma(x+\alpha)} \int_0^\infty \lambda^{y+x+\alpha-1} e^{-(2+1/\theta)\lambda} d\lambda$$

$$= \dfrac{(1+1/\theta)^{x+\alpha}\Gamma(y+x+\alpha)}{y!\Gamma(x+\alpha)(2+1/\theta)^{y+x+\alpha}}, \quad y = 0, 1, \ldots,$$

and some rearranging shows this to be a negative binomial distribution with $r = x+\alpha$ and $\beta = \theta/(1+\theta)$. The expected number of losses for the next year is $(x+\alpha)\theta/(1+\theta)$. Alternatively, from (10.6),

$$E(Y|x) = \int_0^\infty \lambda \dfrac{\lambda^{x+\alpha-1} e^{-(1+1/\theta)\lambda}(1+1/\theta)^{x+\alpha}}{\Gamma(x+\alpha)} d\lambda = \dfrac{(x+\alpha)\theta}{1+\theta}.$$

For a sample of size n, the key change is that the model distribution is now

$$p(\mathbf{x}|\lambda) = \dfrac{\lambda^{x_1+\cdots+x_n} e^{-n\lambda}}{x_1!\cdots x_n!}.$$

Following this through, the posterior distribution is still gamma, now with shape parameter $x_1 + \cdots + x_n + \alpha = n\bar{x} + \alpha$ and scale parameter $\theta/(1 + n\theta)$. The predictive distribution is still negative binomial, now with $r = n\bar{x} + \alpha$ and $\beta = \theta/(1 + n\theta)$. □

When only moments are needed, iterated expectation formulas can be very useful. Provided the moments exist, for any random variables X and Y,

$$E(Y) = E[E(Y|X)], \tag{10.8}$$
$$\text{Var}(Y) = E[\text{Var}(Y|X)] + \text{Var}[E(Y|X)]. \tag{10.9}$$

For the predictive distribution,

$$E(Y|\mathbf{x}) = E_{\Theta|\mathbf{x}}[E(Y|\Theta, \mathbf{x})]$$
$$= E_{\Theta|\mathbf{x}}[E(Y|\Theta)]$$

and

$$\text{Var}(Y|\mathbf{x}) = E_{\Theta|\mathbf{x}}[\text{Var}(Y|\Theta, \mathbf{x})] + \text{Var}_{\Theta|\mathbf{x}}[E(Y|\Theta, \mathbf{x})]$$
$$= E_{\Theta|\mathbf{x}}[\text{Var}(Y|\Theta)] + \text{Var}_{\Theta|\mathbf{x}}[E(Y|\Theta)].$$

The simplification on the inner expected value and variance results from the fact that, if Θ is known, the value of $\mathbf{x}$ provides no additional information about the distribution of Y. This is simply a restatement of formula (10.6).

Example 10.43 *Apply these formulas to obtain the predictive mean and variance for the previous example. .*

The predictive mean uses $E(Y|\lambda) = \lambda$. Then,

$$E(Y|\mathbf{x}) = E(\lambda|\mathbf{x}) = \frac{(n\bar{x} + \alpha)\theta}{1 + n\theta}.$$

The predictive variance uses $\text{Var}(Y|\lambda) = \lambda$, and then

$$\text{Var}(Y|\mathbf{x}) = E(\lambda|\mathbf{x}) + \text{Var}(\lambda|\mathbf{x})$$
$$= \frac{(n\bar{x} + \alpha)\theta}{1 + n\theta} + \frac{(n\bar{x} + \alpha)\theta^2}{(1 + n\theta)^2}$$
$$= (n\bar{x} + \alpha)\frac{\theta}{1 + n\theta}\left(1 + \frac{\theta}{1 + n\theta}\right).$$

These agree with the mean and variance of the known negative binomial distribution for y. However, these quantities were obtained from moments of the model (Poisson) and posterior (gamma) distributions. The predictive mean can be written as

$$\frac{n\theta}{1 + n\theta}\bar{x} + \frac{1}{1 + n\theta}\alpha\theta,$$

which is a weighted average of the mean of the data and the mean of the prior distribution. Note that as the sample size increases more weight is placed on the data and less on the prior opinion. The variance of the prior distribution can be increased by letting θ become large. As it should, this also increases the weight placed on the data. □

10.5.3   Computational issues

It should be obvious by now that all Bayesian analyses proceed by taking integrals or sums. So at least conceptually it is always possible to do a Bayesian analysis. However, only in rare cases are the integrals or sums easy to obtain analytically, and that means most Bayesian analyses will require numerical integration. While one-dimensional integrations are easy to do to a high degree of accuracy, multidimensional integrals are much more difficult to approximate. A great deal of effort has been expended with regard to solving this problem. A number of ingenious methods have been developed. Some of them are summarized in Klugman [68]. However, the one that is widely used today is called Markov chain Monte Carlo simulation. A good discussion of this method can be found in the article by Scollnik [105].

There is another way that completely avoids computational problems. This is illustrated using the example (in an abbreviated form) from Meyers [82], which also employed this technique. The example also shows how a Bayesian analysis is used to estimate a function of parameters.

Example 10.44 *Data were collected on* 100 *losses in excess of* $100,000. *The single-parameter Pareto distribution is to be used with* $\theta = \$100,000$ *and* α *unknown. The objective is to estimate the average severity for the portion of losses in excess of* $1,000,000 *but below* $5,000,000. *This is called the "layer average severity(LAS)"in insurance applications[10]. For the* 100 *losses, we have computed that* $\sum_{j=1}^{100} \ln x_j = 1{,}208.4354$.

The model density is

$$f_{\mathbf{X}|A}(\mathbf{x}|\alpha) = \prod_{j=1}^{100} \frac{\alpha(100{,}000)^\alpha}{x_j^{\alpha+1}}$$

$$= \exp\left[100\ln\alpha + 100\alpha\ln 100{,}000 - (\alpha+1)\sum_{j=1}^{100}\ln x_j \right]$$

$$= \exp\left(100\ln\alpha - \frac{100\alpha}{1.75} - 1{,}208.4354 \right).$$

---

[10]LAS can be used in operational risk modeling to estimate losses below a threshold when the company or bank obtains insurance to protect it against losses on a per occurrence basis.

The density appears in column 3 of Table 10.6. To prevent computer overflow, the value 1,208.4354 was not subtracted before exponentiation. This makes the entries proportional to the true density function. The prior density is given in the second column. It was chosen based on a belief that the true value is in the range 1–2.5 and is more likely to be near 1.5 than at the ends. The posterior density is then obtained using (10.2). The elements of the numerator are found in column 4. The denominator is no longer an integral but a sum. The sum is at the bottom of column 4 and then the scaled values are in column 5.

We can see from column 5 that the posterior mode is at $\alpha = 1.7$, as compared to the maximum likelihood estimate of 1.75 (see Exercise 10.45). The posterior mean of α could be found by adding the product of columns 1 and 5. Here we are interested in a layer average severity. For this problem it is

$$\text{LAS}(\alpha) = E(X \wedge 5{,}000{,}000) - E(X \wedge 1{,}000{,}000)$$
$$= \frac{100{,}000^\alpha}{\alpha - 1} \left(\frac{1}{1{,}000{,}000^{\alpha-1}} - \frac{1}{5{,}000{,}000^{\alpha-1}} \right), \quad \alpha \neq 1,$$
$$= 100{,}000 \left(\ln 5{,}000{,}000 - \ln 1{,}000{,}000 \right), \quad \alpha = 1.$$

Values of $\text{LAS}(\alpha)$ for the 16 possible values of α appear in column 6. The last two columns are then used to obtain the posterior expected values of the layer average severity. The point estimate is the posterior mean, 18,827. The posterior standard deviation is

$$\sqrt{445{,}198{,}597 - 18{,}827^2} = 9{,}526.$$

We can also use columns 5 and 6 to construct a credibility interval. Discarding the first five rows and the last four rows eliminates 0.0406 of posterior probability. That leaves (5,992, 34,961) as a 96% credibility interval for the layer average severity. In his paper [82], Meyers observed that even with a fairly large sample the accuracy of the estimate is poor.

The discrete approximation to the prior distribution could be refined by using many more than 16 values. This adds little to the spreadsheet effort. The number was kept small here only for display purposes. □

10.6 EXERCISES

10.1 Determine the method-of-moments estimate for a lognormal model for Data Set B.

10.2 The 20th and 80th percentiles from a sample are 5 and 12, respectively. Using the percentile matching method, estimate $\overline{F}(8)$ assuming the population has a Weibull distribution.

Table 10.6 Bayesian estimation of a layer average severity

α	$\pi(\alpha)$	$f(\mathbf{x}\mid\alpha)$	$\pi(\alpha)f(\mathbf{x}\mid\alpha)$	$\pi(\alpha\mid\mathbf{x})$	LAS(α)	$\pi\times L^*$	$\pi(\alpha\mid\mathbf{x})l(\alpha)^2$
1.0	0.0400	1.52×10^{-25}	6.10×10^{-27}	0.0000	160,944	0	6,433
1.1	0.0496	6.93×10^{-24}	3.44×10^{-25}	0.0000	118,085	2	195,201
1.2	0.0592	1.37×10^{-22}	8.13×10^{-24}	0.0003	86,826	29	2,496,935
1.3	0.0688	1.36×10^{-21}	9.33×10^{-23}	0.0038	63,979	243	15,558,906
1.4	0.0784	7.40×10^{-21}	5.80×10^{-22}	0.0236	47,245	1,116	52,737,840
1.5	0.0880	2.42×10^{-20}	2.13×10^{-21}	0.0867	34,961	3,033	106,021,739
1.6	0.0832	5.07×10^{-20}	4.22×10^{-21}	0.1718	25,926	4,454	115,480,050
1.7	0.0784	7.18×10^{-20}	5.63×10^{-21}	0.2293	19,265	4,418	85,110,453
1.8	0.0736	7.19×10^{-20}	5.29×10^{-21}	0.2156	14,344	3,093	44,366,353
1.9	0.0688	5.29×10^{-20}	3.64×10^{-21}	0.1482	10,702	1,586	16,972,802
2.0	0.0640	2.95×10^{-20}	1.89×10^{-21}	0.0768	8,000	614	4,915,383
2.1	0.0592	1.28×10^{-20}	7.57×10^{-22}	0.0308	5,992	185	1,106,259
2.2	0.0544	4.42×10^{-21}	2.40×10^{-22}	0.0098	4,496	44	197,840
2.3	0.0496	1.24×10^{-21}	6.16×10^{-23}	0.0025	3,380	8	28,650
2.4	0.0448	2.89×10^{-22}	1.29×10^{-23}	0.0005	2,545	1	3,413
2.5	0.0400	5.65×10^{-23}	2.26×10^{-24}	0.0001	1,920	0	339
	1.0000		2.46×10^{-20}	1.0000		18,827	445,198,597

$^*\pi(\alpha\mid\mathbf{x})$LAS($\alpha$)

10.3 From a sample you are given that the mean is 35,000, the standard deviation is 75,000, the median is 10,000, and the 90th percentile is 100,000. Using the percentile matching method, estimate the parameters of a Weibull distribution.

10.4 A sample of size 5 produced the values 4, 5, 21, 99, and 421. You fit a Pareto distribution using the method of moments. Determine the 95th percentile of the fitted distribution.

10.5 From a random sample the 20th percentile is 18.25 and the 80th percentile is 35.8. Estimate the parameters of a lognormal distribution using percentile matching and then use these estimates to estimate the probability of observing a value in excess of 30.

10.6 A loss process is a mixture of two random variables X and Y, where X has an exponential distribution with a mean of 1 and Y has an exponential distribution with a mean of 10. A weight of p is assigned to the distribution of X and $1-p$ to the distribution of Y. The standard deviation of the mixture is 2. Estimate p by the method of moments.

10.7 The following 20 losses (in millions of dollars) were recorded in one year:

$1 $1 $1 $1 $1 $2 $2 $3 $3 $4
$6 $6 $8 $10 $13 $14 $15 $18 $22 $25

Determine the sample 75th percentile using the smoothed empirical estimate.

10.8 The observations $1000, $850, $750, $1100, $1250, and $900 were obtained as a random sample from a gamma distribution with unknown parameters α and θ. Estimate these parameters by the method of moments.

10.9 A random sample of losses has been drawn from a loglogistic distribution. In the sample, 80% of the losses exceed 100 and 20% exceed 400. Estimate the loglogistic parameters by percentile matching.

10.10 Let $x_1, \ldots, x_n$ be a random sample from a population with cdf $F(x) = x^p$, $0 < x < 1$. Determine the method of moments estimate of p.

10.11 A random sample of 10 losses obtained from a gamma distribution is given below:

$$1500 \quad 6000 \quad 3500 \quad 3800 \quad 1800 \quad 5500 \quad 4800 \quad 4200 \quad 3900 \quad 3000.$$

Estimate α and θ by the method of moments.

10.12 A random sample of five losses from a lognormal distribution is given below:

$$\$500 \quad \$1000 \quad \$1500 \quad \$2500 \quad \$4500.$$

Estimate μ and σ by the method of moments. Estimate the probability that a loss will exceed $4500.

10.13 The random variable X has pdf $f(x) = \beta^{-2}x\exp(-0.5x^2/\beta^2)$, $x, \beta > 0$. For this random variable, $E(X) = (\beta/2)\sqrt{2\pi}$ and $\text{Var}(X) = 2\beta^2 - \pi\beta^2/2$. You are given the following five observations:

$$4.9 \quad 1.8 \quad 3.4 \quad 6.9 \quad 4.0.$$

Determine the method-of-moments and maximum likelihood estimates of β.

10.14 The random variable X has pdf $f(x) = \alpha\lambda^\alpha(\lambda + x)^{-\alpha-1}$, $x, \alpha, \lambda > 0$. It is known that $\lambda = 1,000$. You are given the following five observations:

$$43 \quad 145 \quad 233 \quad 396 \quad 775.$$

Determine the method-of-moments and maximum likelihood estimates of α.

10.15 Use the data in Table 10.7 to determine the method-of-moments estimate of the parameters of the negative binomial model.

10.16 Use the data in Table 10.8 to determine the method-of-moments estimate of the parameters of the negative binomial model.

Repeat Example 10.8 using the inverse exponential, inverse gamma with $\alpha = 2$, and inverse gamma distributions. Compare your estimates with the method-of-moments estimates.

Table 10.7   Data for Exercise 10.15

No. of losses	No. of observations
0	9,048
1	905
2	45
3	2
4+	0

Table 10.8   Data for Exercise 10.16

No. of losses	No. of observations
0	861
1	121
2	13
3	3
4	1
5	0
6	1
7+	0

10.17 From Data Set C, determine the maximum likelihood estimates for gamma, inverse exponential, and inverse gamma distributions.

10.18 Determine maximum likelihood estimates for Data Set B using the inverse exponential, gamma, and inverse gamma distributions. Assume the data have been censored at 250 and then compare your answers to those obtained in Example 10.8 and Exercise 10.16.

10.19 Repeat Example 10.10 using a Pareto distribution with both parameters unknown.

10.20 Repeat Example 10.11, this time finding the distribution of the time to withdrawal of the machine.

10.21 Repeat Example 10.12, but this time assume that the actual values for the seven drivers who have five or more accidents are unknown. Note that this is a case of censoring.

10.22 The model has hazard rate function $h(t) = \lambda_1$, $0 \leq t < 2$, and $h(t) = \lambda_2$, $t \geq 2$. Five items are observed from age zero, with the results in Table 10.9. Determine the maximum likelihood estimates of λ_1 and λ_2.

10.23 Five hundred losses are observed. Five of the losses are $1100, $3200, $3300, $3500, and $3900. All that is known about the other 495 losses is that

Table 10.9   Data for Exercise 10.22

Age last observed	Cause
1.7	Failure
1.5	Censoring
2.6	Censoring
3.3	Failure
3.5	Censoring

they exceed $4000. Determine the maximum likelihood estimate of the mean of an exponential model.

10.24 The survival function of the time to finally settle a loss (the time it takes to determine the final loss value) is $\overline{F}(t) = 1 - t/w$, $0 \le t \le w$. Five losses were studied in order to estimate the distribution of the time from the loss event to settlement. After five years, four of the losses were settled, the times being 1, 3, 4, and 4. Analyst X then estimates w using maximum likelihood. Analyst Y prefers to wait until all losses are settled. The fifth loss is settled after 6 years, at which time analyst Y estimates w by maximum likelihood. Determine the two estimates.

10.25 Four machines were first observed when they were 3 years old. They were then observed for r additional years. By that time, three of the machines had failed, with the failure ages being 4, 5, and 7. The fourth machine was still working at age $3+r$. The survival function has the uniform distribution on the interval 0 to w. The maximum likelihood estimate of w is 13.67. Determine r.

10.26 Ten losses were observed. The values of seven of them (in thousands) were $3, $7, $8, $12, $12, $13, and $14. The remaining three losses were all censored at $15. The proposed model has a hazard rate function given by

$$h(t) = \begin{cases} \lambda_1, & 0 < t < 5, \\ \lambda_2, & 5 \le t < 10, \\ \lambda_3, & t \ge 10. \end{cases}$$

Determine the maximum likelihood estimates of the three parameters.

10.27 You are given the five observations 521, 658, 702, 819, and 1217. Your model is the single-parameter Pareto distribution with distribution function

$$F(x) = 1 - \left(\frac{500}{x}\right)^{\alpha}, \quad x > 500, \alpha > 0.$$

Determine the maximum likelihood estimate of α.

10.28 You have observed the following five loss amounts: 11.0, 15.2, 18.0, 21.0, and 25.8. Determine the maximum likelihood estimate of μ for the following model:

$$f(x) = \frac{1}{\sqrt{2\pi x}} \exp\left[-\frac{1}{2x}(x-\mu)^2\right], \quad x, \mu > 0.$$

10.29 A random sample of size 5 is taken from a Weibull distribution with $\tau = 2$. Two of the sample observations are known to exceed 50 and the three remaining observations are 20, 30, and 45. Determine the maximum likelihood estimate of θ.

10.30 A sample of 100 losses revealed that 62 were below $1000 and 38 were above $1000. An exponential distribution with mean θ is considered. Using only the given information, determine the maximum likelihood estimate of θ. Now suppose you are also given that the 62 losses that were below $1000 totalled $28,140 while the total for the 38 above $1000 remains unknown. Using this additional information, determine the maximum likelihood estimate of θ.

10.31 The following values were calculated from a random sample of 10 losses:

$$\sum_{j=1}^{10} x_j^{-2} = 0.00033674, \quad \sum_{j=1}^{10} x_j^{-1} = 0.023999,$$

$$\sum_{j=1}^{10} x_j^{-0.5} = 0.34445, \quad \sum_{j=1}^{10} x_j^{0.5} = 488.97$$

$$\sum_{j=1}^{10} x_j = 31,939, \quad \sum_{j=1}^{10} x_j^2 = 211,498,983.$$

Losses come from a Weibull distribution with $\tau = 0.5$ so that $F(x) = 1 - e^{-(x/\theta)^{0.5}}$. Determine the maximum likelihood estimate of θ.

10.32 A sample of n independent observations $x_1, \ldots, x_n$ came from a distribution with a pdf of $f(x) = 2\theta x \exp(-\theta x^2)$, $x > 0$. Determine the maximum likelihood estimator of θ.

10.33 Let $x_1, \ldots, x_n$ be a random sample from a population with cdf $F(x) = x^p$, $0 < x < 1$.

(a) Determine the maximum likelihood estimate of p.

(b) Determine the asymptotic variance of the maximum likelihood estimator of p.

(c) Use your answer to obtain a general formula for a 95% confidence interval for p.

(d) Determine the maximum likelihood estimator of $E(X)$ and obtain its asymptotic variance and a formula for a 95% confidence interval.

10.34 A random sample of 10 losses obtained from a gamma distribution is given below:

  1500 6000 3500 3800 1800 5500 4800 4200 3900 3000

(a) Suppose it is known that $\alpha = 12$. Determine the maximum likelihood estimate of θ.

(b) Determine the maximum likelihood estimates of α and θ.

10.35 A random sample of five losses from a lognormal distribution is given below:

$$\$500 \quad \$1000 \quad \$1500 \quad \$2500 \quad \$4500$$

Estimate μ and σ by maximum likelihood. Estimate the probability that a loss will exceed $4500.

10.36 Let $x_1, \ldots, x_n$ be a random sample from a random variable with pdf $f(x) = \theta^{-1} e^{-x/\theta}$, $x > 0$.

(a) Determine the maximum likelihood estimator of θ. Determine the asymptotic variance of the maximum likelihood estimator of θ.

(b) Use your answer to obtain a general formula for a 95% confidence interval for θ.

(c) Determine the maximum likelihood estimator of $\text{Var}(X)$ and obtain its asymptotic variance and a formula for a 95% confidence interval.

10.37 Let $x_1, \ldots, x_n$ be a random sample from a random variable with cdf $F(x) = 1 - x^{-\alpha}$, $x > 1$, $\alpha > 0$.

(a) Determine the maximum likelihood estimator of α.

10.38 The following 20 observations were collected. It is desired to estimate $\Pr(X > 200)$. When a parametric model is called for, use the single-parameter Pareto distribution for which $F(x) = 1 - (100/x)^{\alpha}$, $x > 100$, $\alpha > 0$.

  $132 $149 $476 $147 $135 $110 $176 $107 $147 $165
  $135 $117 $110 $111 $226 $108 $102 $108 $227 $102

(a) Determine the empirical estimate of $\Pr(X > 200)$.

(b) Determine the method-of-moments estimate of the single-parameter Pareto parameter α and use it to estimate $\Pr(X > 200)$.

(c) Determine the maximum likelihood estimate of the single-parameter Pareto parameter α and use it to estimate $\Pr(X > 200)$.

Table 10.10   Data for Exercise 10.39

Loss	No. of observations	Loss	No. of observations
0–25	5	350–500	17
25–50	37	500–750	13
50–75	28	750–1000	12
75–100	31	1,000–1,500	3
100–125	23	1,500–2,500	5
125–150	9	2,500–5,000	5
150–200	22	5,000–10,000	3
200–250	17	10,000–25,000	3
250–350	15	25,000–	2

10.39 The data in Table 10.10 are the results of a sample of 250 losses. Consider the inverse exponential distribution with cdf $F(x) = e^{-\theta/x}$, $x > 0$, $\theta > 0$. Determine the maximum likelihood estimate of θ.

10.40 Consider the inverse Gaussian distribution with density given by $f_X(x) = \left(\frac{\theta}{2\pi x^3}\right)^{1/2} \exp\left[-\frac{\theta}{2x}\left(\frac{x-\mu}{\mu}\right)^2\right]$, $x > 0$.

(a) Show that

$$\sum_{j=1}^n \frac{(x_j - \mu)^2}{x_j} = \mu^2 \sum_{j=1}^n \left(\frac{1}{x_j} - \frac{1}{\bar{x}}\right) + \frac{n}{\bar{x}}(\bar{x} - \mu)^2,$$

where $\bar{x} = (1/n)\sum_{j=1}^n x_j$.

(b) For a sample $(x_1, \cdots, x_n)$, show that the maximum likelihood estimators of μ and θ are

$$\hat{\mu} = \bar{x}$$

and

$$\hat{\theta} = \frac{n}{\sum_{j=1}^n \left(\frac{1}{x_j} - \frac{1}{\bar{x}}\right)}.$$

10.41 Determine 95% confidence intervals for the parameters of exponential and gamma models for Data Set B. The likelihood function and maximum likelihood estimates were determined in Example 10.8.

10.42 Let X have a uniform distribution on the interval from 0 to θ. Show that the maximum likelihood estimator is $\hat{\theta} = \max(X_1, \ldots, X_n)$. Use Examples 9.7 and 9.10 to show that this estimator is asymptotically unbiased and to obtain its variance. Show that Theorem 10.13 yields a negative estimate of the variance and that item (ii) in the conditions does not hold.

10.43 Show that, if Y is the predictive distribution in Example 10.28, then $\ln Y - \ln 100$ has the Pareto distribution.

10.44 Determine the posterior distribution of α in Example 10.28 if the prior distribution is an arbitrary gamma distribution. To avoid confusion, denote the first parameter of this gamma distribution by γ. Next determine a particular combination of gamma parameters so that the posterior mean is the maximum likelihood estimate of α regardless of the specific values of $x_1, \ldots, x_n$. Is this prior improper?

10.45 For Example 10.44 demonstrate that the maximum likelihood estimate of α is 1.75.

10.46 Let $x_1, \ldots, x_n$ be a random sample from a lognormal distribution with unknown parameters μ and σ. Let the prior density be $\pi(\mu, \sigma) = \sigma^{-1}$.

   (a) Write the posterior pdf of μ and σ up to a constant of proportionality.

   (b) Determine Bayesian estimators of μ and σ by using the posterior mode.

   (c) Fix σ at the posterior mode as determined in (b) and then determine the exact (conditional) pdf of μ. Then use it to determine a 95% HPD credibility interval for μ.

10.47 A random sample of size 100 has been taken from a gamma distribution with α known to be 2, but θ unknown. For this sample, $\sum_{j=1}^{100} x_j = 30{,}000$. The prior distribution for θ is inverse gamma with β taking the role of α and λ taking the role of θ.

   (a) Determine the exact posterior distribution of θ. At this point the values of β and λ have yet to be specified.

   (b) The population mean is 2θ. Determine the posterior mean of 2θ using the prior distribution first with $\beta = \lambda = 0$ [this is equivalent to $\pi(\theta) = \theta^{-1}$] and then with $\beta = 2$ and $\lambda = 250$ (which is a prior mean of 250). Then, in each case, determine a 95% credibility interval with 2.5% probability on each side.

   (c) Determine the posterior variance of 2θ and use the Bayesian central limit theorem to construct a 95% credibility interval for 2θ using each of the two prior distributions given in (b).

   (d) Determine the maximum likelihood estimate of θ and then use the estimated variance to construct a 95% confidence interval for 2θ.

10.48 Suppose that given $\Theta = \theta$ the random variables $X_1, \ldots, X_n$ are independent and binomially distributed with pf

$$f_{X_j|\Theta}(x_j|\theta) = \binom{K_j}{x_j}\theta^{x_j}(1-\theta)^{K_j-x_j}, \quad x_j = 0, 1, \ldots, K_j,$$

and Θ itself is beta distributed with parameters a and b and pdf

$$\pi(\theta) = \frac{\Gamma(a+b)}{\Gamma(a)\Gamma(b)}\theta^{a-1}(1-\theta)^{b-1}, \quad 0 < \theta < 1.$$

(a) Verify that the marginal pf of X_j is

$$f_{X_j}(x_j) = \frac{\binom{-a}{x_j}\binom{-b}{K_j-x_j}}{\binom{-a-b}{K_j}}, \quad x_j = 0, 1, \ldots, K_j,$$

and $E(X_j) = aK_j/(a+b)$. This distribution is termed the binomial–beta or negative hypergeometric distribution.

(b) Determine the posterior pdf $\pi_{\Theta|\mathbf{X}}(\theta|\mathbf{x})$ and the posterior mean $E(\Theta|\mathbf{x})$.

10.49 Suppose that given $\Theta = \theta$ the random variables $X_1, \ldots, X_n$ are independent and identically exponentially distributed with pdf

$$f_{X_j|\Theta}(x_j|\theta) = \theta e^{-\theta x_j}, \quad x_j > 0,$$

and Θ is itself gamma distributed with parameters $\alpha > 1$ and $\beta > 0$,

$$\pi(\theta) = \frac{\theta^{\alpha-1}e^{-\theta/\beta}}{\Gamma(\alpha)\beta^\alpha}, \quad \theta > 0.$$

(a) Verify that the marginal pdf of X_j is

$$f_{X_j}(x_j) = \alpha\beta^{-\alpha}(\beta^{-1}+x_j)^{-\alpha-1}, \quad x_j > 0,$$

and that

$$E(X_j) = \frac{1}{\beta(\alpha-1)}.$$

This distribution is one form of the Pareto distribution.

(b) Determine the posterior pdf $\pi_{\Theta|\mathbf{X}}(\theta|\mathbf{x})$ and the posterior mean $E(\Theta|\mathbf{x})$.

10.50 Suppose that given $\Theta = \theta$ the random variables $X_1, \ldots, X_n$ are independent and identically negative binomially distributed with parameters r and θ with pf

$$f_{X_j|\Theta}(x_j|\theta) = \binom{r+x_j-1}{x_j}\theta^r(1-\theta)^{x_j}, \quad x_j = 0, 1, 2, \ldots,$$

and Θ itself is beta distributed with parameters a and b and pdf $\pi(\theta) = \frac{\Gamma(a+b)}{\Gamma(a)\Gamma(b)}\theta^{a-1}(1-\theta)^{b-1}$, $0 < \theta < 1$.

(a) Verify that the marginal pf of X_j is

$$f_{X_j}(x_j) = \frac{\Gamma(r+x_j)}{\Gamma(r)x_j!} \frac{\Gamma(a+b)}{\Gamma(a)\Gamma(b)} \frac{\Gamma(a+r)\Gamma(b+x_j)}{\Gamma(a+r+b+x_j)}, \quad x_j = 0,1,2,\dots,$$

and that

$$E(X_j) = \frac{rb}{a-1}.$$

This distribution is termed the **generalized Waring distribution**. The special case where $b = 1$ is the **Waring distribution** and the **Yule distribution** if $r = 1$ and $b = 1$.

(b) Determine the posterior pdf $f_{\Theta|\mathbf{X}}(\theta|\mathbf{x})$ and the posterior mean $E(\Theta|\mathbf{x})$.

10.51 Suppose that given $\Theta = \theta$ the random variables $X_1, \dots, X_n$ are independent and identically normally distributed with mean μ and variance θ^{-1} and Θ is gamma distributed with parameters α and (θ replaced by) $1/\beta$.

(a) Verify that the marginal pdf of X_j is

$$f_{X_j}(x_j) = \frac{\Gamma(\alpha + \frac{1}{2})}{\sqrt{2\pi\beta}\,\Gamma(\alpha)} \left[1 + \frac{1}{2\beta}(x_j - \mu)^2\right]^{-\alpha - 1/2}, \quad -\infty < x_j < \infty,$$

which is a form of the t-distribution.

(b) Determine the posterior pdf $f_{\Theta|\mathbf{X}}(\theta|\mathbf{x})$ and the posterior mean $E(\theta|\mathbf{x})$.

10.52 The number of losses in one year, Y, has the Poisson distribution with parameter θ. The parameter θ has the exponential distribution with pdf $\pi(\theta) = e^{-\theta}$. A particular risk had no losses in one year. Determine the posterior distribution of θ for this risk.

10.53 The number of losses in one year, Y, has the Poisson distribution with parameter θ. The prior distribution has the gamma distribution with pdf $\pi(\theta) = \theta e^{-\theta}$. There was one loss in one year. Determine the posterior pdf of θ.

10.54 Each machine's loss count has a Poisson distribution with parameter λ. All machines are identical and thus have the same parameter. The prior distribution is gamma with parameters $\alpha = 50$ and $\theta = 1/500$. Over a two-year period, the bank had 750 and 1100 such machines in years 1 and 2, respectively. There were 65 and 112 losses in years 1 and 2, respectively. Determine the coefficient of variation of the posterior gamma distribution.

10.55 The number of losses, r, made by an individual risk in one year has the binomial distribution with pf $f(r) = \binom{3}{r}\theta^r(1-\theta)^{3-r}$. The prior distribution for θ has pdf $\pi(\theta) = 6(\theta - \theta^2)$. There was one loss in a one-year period. Determine the posterior pdf of θ.

10.56 The number of losses of a certain type in one year has a Poisson distribution with parameter λ. The prior distribution for λ is exponential with an expected value of 2. There were three losses in the first year. Determine the posterior distribution of λ.

10.57 The number of losses in one year has the binomial distribution with $n = 3$ and θ unknown. The prior distribution for θ is beta with pdf $\pi(\theta) = 2800\theta^3(1-\theta)^4$, $0 < \theta < 1$. Two losses were observed. Determine each of the following:

(a) The posterior distribution of θ.

(b) The expected value of θ from the posterior distribution.

10.58 A risk has exactly zero or one loss each year. If a loss occurs, the amount of the loss has an exponential distribution with pdf $f(x) = te^{-tx}$, $x > 0$. The parameter t has a prior distribution with pdf $\pi(t) = te^{-t}$. A loss of 5 has been observed. Determine the posterior pdf of t.

11

Estimation for discrete distributions

Every solution breeds new problems.

—Murphy

11.1 INTRODUCTION

The principles of estimation of parameters of continuous models can be applied equally to frequency distributions. In this chapter we focus on the application of the maximum likelihood method for the classes of discrete distributions discussed in previous chapters. We illustrate the methods of estimation by first fitting a Poisson model.

11.2 POISSON DISTRIBUTION

Example 11.1 *The number of liability losses over a 10-year period are given in Table 11.1. Estimate the Poisson parameter using the method of moments and the method of maximum likelihood.*

These data can be summarized in a different way. We can count the number of years in which exactly zero losses occurred, one loss occurred, and so on, as in Table 11.2.

The total number of losses for the period 1985–1994 is 25. Hence, the average number of losses per year is 2.5. The average can also be computed

Table 11.1   Number of losses by year

Year	Number of losses
1985	6
1986	2
1987	3
1988	0
1989	2
1990	1
1991	2
1992	5
1993	1
1994	3

Table 11.2   Losses by frequency

Frequency (k)	Number of observations (n_k)
0	1
1	2
2	3
3	2
4	0
5	1
6	1
7+	0

from Table 11.2. Let n_k denote the number of years in which a frequency of exactly k losses occurred. The expected frequency (sample mean) is

$$\bar{x} = \frac{\sum_{k=0}^{\infty} k n_k}{\sum_{k=0}^{\infty} n_k},$$

where n_k represents the number of observed values at frequency k. Hence the method-of-moments estimate of the Poisson parameter is $\hat{\lambda} = 2.5$.

Maximum likelihood estimation can easily be carried out on these data. The likelihood contribution of an observation of k is p_k. Then the likelihood for the entire set of observations is

$$L = \prod_{k=0}^{\infty} p_k^{n_k}$$

and the loglikelihood is

$$l = \sum_{k=0}^{\infty} n_k \ln p_k.$$

The likelihood and loglikelihood functions are considered to be functions of the unknown parameters. In the case of the Poisson distribution, there is only one parameter, making the maximization easy.

For the Poisson distribution,

$$p_k = \frac{e^{-\lambda}\lambda^k}{k!}$$

and

$$\ln p_k = -\lambda + k \ln \lambda - \ln k!.$$

The loglikelihood is

$$l = \sum_{k=0}^{\infty} n_k(-\lambda + k \ln \lambda - \ln k!)$$

$$= -\lambda n + \sum_{k=0}^{\infty} k\, n_k \ln \lambda - \sum_{k=0}^{\infty} n_k \ln k!,$$

where $n = \sum_{k=0}^{\infty} n_k$ is the sample size. Differentiating the loglikelihood with respect to λ, we obtain

$$\frac{dl}{d\lambda} = -n + \sum_{k=0}^{\infty} k\, n_k \frac{1}{\lambda}.$$

By setting the derivative of the loglikelihood to zero, the maximum likelihood estimate is obtained as the solution of the resulting equation. The estimator is then

$$\hat{\lambda} = \frac{\sum_{k=0}^{\infty} k n_k}{n} = \bar{x}.$$

From this it can be seen that for the Poisson distribution the maximum likelihood and the method-of-moments estimators are identical.

If N has a Poisson distribution with mean λ, then

$$E(\hat{\lambda}) = E(N) = \lambda$$

and

$$\text{Var}(\hat{\lambda}) = \frac{\text{Var}(N)}{n} = \frac{\lambda}{n}.$$

Hence, $\hat{\lambda}$ is unbiased and consistent. From Theorem 10.13, the maximum likelihood estimator is asymptotically normally distributed with mean λ and variance

$$
\begin{aligned}
\mathrm{Var}(\hat{\lambda}) &= \left\{ -n\mathrm{E}\left[\frac{d^2}{d\lambda^2} \ln p_N \right] \right\}^{-1} \\
&= \left\{ -n\mathrm{E}\left[\frac{d^2}{d\lambda^2}(-\lambda + N\ln\lambda - \ln N!) \right] \right\}^{-1} \\
&= \left[n\mathrm{E}(N/\lambda^2) \right]^{-1} \\
&= \left(n\lambda^{-1} \right)^{-1} = \frac{\lambda}{n}.
\end{aligned}
$$

In this case the asymptotic approximation to the variance is equal to its true value. From this information, we can construct an approximate 95% confidence interval for the true value of the parameter. The interval is $\hat{\lambda} \pm 1.96(\hat{\lambda}/n)^{1/2}$. For this example, the interval becomes (1.52, 3.48). This confidence interval is only an approximation because it relies on large sample theory. The sample size is very small, and such a confidence interval should be used with caution.   □

The formulas presented so far have assumed that the counts at each observed frequency are known. Occasionally, data are collected so that this is not given. The most common example is to have a final entry given as $k+$, where the count is the number of times k or more losses were observed. If n_{k+} is the number of times this was observed, the contribution to the likelihood function is

$$
(p_k + p_{k+1} + \cdots)^{n_{k+}} = (1 - p_0 - \cdots - p_{k-1})^{n_{k+}}.
$$

The same adjustments apply to grouped frequency data of any kind. Suppose there were five observations at frequencies 3–5. The contribution to the likelihood function is

$$
(p_3 + p_4 + p_5)^5.
$$

Example 11.2 *For the data in Table 11.3[1] determine the maximum likelihood estimate for the Poisson distribution.*

The likelihood function is

$$
L = p_0^{47} p_1^{97} p_2^{109} p_3^{62} p_4^{25} p_5^{16}(1 - p_0 - p_1 - p_2 - p_3 - p_4 - p_5)^9,
$$

and when written as a function of λ, it becomes somewhat complicated. While the derivative can be taken, solving the equation when it is set equal to zero will require numerical methods. It may be just as easy to use a numerical

---

[1]This is the same data as will be analyzed in Example 12.14 except the observations at 6 or more have been combined.

Table 11.3 Data for Example 11.2

No. of losses/year	Observed no. of years
0	47
1	97
2	109
3	62
4	25
5	16
6+	9

method to directly maximize the function. A reasonable starting value can be obtained by assuming that all nine observations were exactly at 6 and then using the sample mean. Of course, this will understate the true maximum likelihood estimate, but should be a good place to start. For this particular example, the maximum likelihood estimate is $\hat{\lambda} = 2.0226$, which is very close to the value obtained when all the counts were recorded. □

11.3 NEGATIVE BINOMIAL DISTRIBUTION

The moment equations are

$$r\beta = \frac{\sum_{k=0}^{\infty} k n_k}{n} = \bar{x} \tag{11.1}$$

and

$$r\beta(1+\beta) = \frac{\sum_{k=0}^{\infty} k^2 n_k}{n} - \left(\frac{\sum_{k=0}^{\infty} k n_k}{n}\right)^2 = s^2 \tag{11.2}$$

with solutions $\hat{\beta} = (s^2/\bar{x}) - 1$ and $\hat{r} = \bar{x}/\hat{\beta}$. Note that this variance estimate is obtained by dividing by n, not $n-1$. This is a common, though not required, approach when using the method of moments. Also note that, if $s^2 < \bar{x}$, the estimate of β will be negative, an inadmissible value.

Example 11.3 (Example 11.1 continued) *Estimate the negative binomial parameters by the method of moments.*

The sample mean and the sample variance are 2.5 and 3.05 (verify this), respectively, and the estimates of the parameters are $\hat{r} = 11.364$ and $\hat{\beta} = 0.22$. □

When compared to the Poisson distribution with the same mean, it can be seen that β is a measure of "extra-Poisson" variation. A value of $\beta = 0$ means no extra-Poisson variation, while a value of $\beta = 0.22$ implies a 22% increase in the variance when compared to the Poisson distribution with the same mean.

We now examine maximum likelihood estimation. The loglikelihood for the negative binomial distribution is

$$
\begin{aligned}
l &= \sum_{k=0}^{\infty} n_k \ln p_k \\
&= \sum_{k=0}^{\infty} n_k \left[\ln \binom{r+k-1}{k} - r \ln(1+\beta) + k \ln \beta - k \ln(1+\beta) \right].
\end{aligned}
$$

The loglikelihood is a function of the two parameters β and r. In order to find the maximum of the loglikelihood, we differentiate with respect to each of the parameters, set the derivatives equal to zero, and solve for the parameters. The derivatives of the loglikelihood are

$$
\frac{\partial l}{\partial \beta} = \sum_{k=0}^{\infty} n_k \left(\frac{k}{\beta} - \frac{r+k}{1+\beta} \right) \tag{11.3}
$$

and

$$
\begin{aligned}
\frac{\partial l}{\partial r} &= -\sum_{k=0}^{\infty} n_k \ln(1+\beta) + \sum_{k=0}^{\infty} n_k \frac{\partial}{\partial r} \ln \frac{(r+k-1)\cdots r}{k!} \\
&= -n \ln(1+\beta) + \sum_{k=0}^{\infty} n_k \frac{\partial}{\partial r} \ln \prod_{m=0}^{k-1} (r+m) \\
&= -n \ln(1+\beta) + \sum_{k=0}^{\infty} n_k \frac{\partial}{\partial r} \sum_{m=0}^{k-1} \ln(r+m) \\
&= -n \ln(1+\beta) + \sum_{k=1}^{\infty} n_k \sum_{m=0}^{k-1} \frac{1}{r+m}.
\end{aligned} \tag{11.4}
$$

Setting these equations to zero yields

$$
\hat{\mu} = \hat{r}\hat{\beta} = \frac{\sum_{k=0}^{\infty} k n_k}{n} = \bar{x} \tag{11.5}
$$

and

$$
n \ln(1+\hat{\beta}) = \sum_{k=1}^{\infty} n_k \left(\sum_{m=0}^{k-1} \frac{1}{\hat{r}+m} \right). \tag{11.6}
$$

Note that the maximum likelihood estimator of the mean is the sample mean (as, by definition, in the method of moments). Equations (11.5) and (11.6) can be solved numerically. Replacing $\hat{\beta}$ in equation (11.6) by $\hat{\mu}/\hat{r}$ yields the equation

$$
H(\hat{r}) = n \ln \left(1 + \frac{\bar{x}}{\hat{r}} \right) - \sum_{k=1}^{\infty} n_k \left(\sum_{m=0}^{k-1} \frac{1}{\hat{r}+m} \right) = 0. \tag{11.7}
$$

If the right-hand side of equation (11.2) is greater than the right-hand side of equation (11.1), it can be shown that there is a unique solution of equation (11.7). If not, then the negative binomial model is probably not a good model to use because the sample variance does not exceed the sample mean.[2]

Equation (11.7) can be solved numerically for $\hat{r}$ using the Newton–Raphson method. The required equation for the kth iteration is

$$r_k = r_{k-1} - \frac{H(r_{k-1})}{H'(r_{k-1})}.$$

A useful starting value for r_0 is the moment-based estimator of r. Of course, any numerical root-finding method (e.g., bisection, secant) may be used.

The loglikelihood is a function of two variables that can be maximized numerically. For the case of the negative binomial distribution with complete data, because we know the estimator of the mean must be the sample mean, setting $\beta = \bar{x}/r$ reduces this to a one-dimensional problem.

Example 11.4 *Determine the maximum likelihood estimates of the negative binomial parameters for the data in Example 11.1.*

The maximum occurs at $\hat{r} = 10.9650$ and $\hat{\beta} = 0.227998$.   □

Example 11.5 *Tröbliger [118] studied the driving habits of 23,589 automobile drivers by counting the number of accidents per driver in a one-year time period. The data as well as fitted Poisson and negative binomial distributions are given in Table 11.4. Based on the information presented, which distribution appears to provide a better model?*   □

The expected counts are found by multiplying the sample size (23,589) by the probability assigned by the model. It is clear that the negative binomial probabilities produce expected counts that are much closer to those that were observed. In addition, the loglikelihood function is maximized at a significantly higher value. Formal procedures for model selection (including what it means to be *significantly higher*) are discussed in Chapter 12. However, in this case, the superiority of the negative binomial model is apparent.   □

---

[2] In other words, when the sample variance is less than or equal to the mean, the loglikelihood function will not have a maximum. The function will keep increasing as r goes to infinity and β goes to zero with the product remaining constant. This effectively says that the negative binomial distribution that best matches the data is the Poisson distribution that is a limiting case.

Table 11.4 Two models for automobile claims frequency

No. of claims/year	No. of drivers	Poisson expected	Negative binomial expected
0	20,592	20,420.9	20,596.8
1	2,651	2,945.1	2,631.0
2	297	212.4	318.4
3	41	10.2	37.8
4	7	0.4	4.4
5	0	0.0	0.5
6	1	0.0	0.1
7+	0	0.0	0.0
Parameters		$\lambda = 0.144220$	$r = 1.11790$ $\beta = 0.129010$
Loglikelihood		$-10{,}297.84$	$-10{,}223.42$

11.4 BINOMIAL DISTRIBUTION

The binomial distribution has two parameters, m and q. Frequently, the value of m is known and fixed. In this case, only one parameter, q, needs to be estimated. In many situations, q is interpreted as the probability of some event such as death or failure. In such cases the value of q is usually estimated as

$$\hat{q} = \frac{\text{number of observed events}}{\text{maximum number of possible events}},$$

which is the method-of-moments estimator when m is known.

In situations where frequency data are in the form of the previous examples in this chapter, the value of the parameter m, the largest possible observation, may be known and fixed or unknown. In any case, m must be no smaller than the largest observation. The loglikelihood is

$$l = \sum_{k=0}^{m} n_k \ln p_k$$

$$= \sum_{k=0}^{m} n_k \left[\ln \binom{m}{k} + k \ln q + (m - k) \ln(1 - q) \right].$$

When m is known and fixed, we need only to maximize l with respect to q.

$$\frac{\partial l}{\partial q} = \frac{1}{q} \sum_{k=0}^{m} k n_k - \frac{1}{1 - q} \sum_{k=0}^{m} (m - k) n_k.$$

Setting this equal to zero yields

$$\hat{q} = \frac{1}{m} \frac{\sum_{k=0}^{m} k n_k}{\sum_{k=0}^{m} n_k},$$

which is the sample proportion of observed events. For the method of moments, with m fixed, the estimator of q is the same as the maximum likelihood estimator because the moment equation is

$$mq = \frac{\sum_{k=0}^{m} k n_k}{\sum_{k=0}^{m} n_k}.$$

When m is unknown, the maximum likelihood estimator of q is

$$\hat{q} = \frac{1}{\hat{m}} \frac{\sum_{k=0}^{\infty} k n_k}{\sum_{k=0}^{\infty} n_k}, \tag{11.8}$$

where $\hat{m}$ is the maximum likelihood estimate of m. An easy way to approach the maximum likelihood estimation of m and q is to create a **likelihood profile** for various possible values of m as follows:

Step 1: Start with $\hat{m}$ equal to the largest observation.
Step 2: Obtain $\hat{q}$ using formula (11.8).
Step 3: Calculate the loglikelihood at these values.
Step 4: Increase $\hat{m}$ by 1.
Step 5: Repeat steps 2–4 until a maximum is found.

As with the negative binomial, there need not be a pair of parameters that maximizes the likelihood function. In particular, if the sample mean is less than or equal to the sample variance, the procedure above will lead to ever increasing loglikelihood values as the value of $\hat{m}$ is increased. Once again, the trend is toward a Poisson model. This can be checked out using the data from Example 11.1.

Example 11.6 *The number of losses per machine during a one-year period for a block of 15,160 machines are given in Table 11.5. Obtain moment-based and maximum likelihood estimators.*

The sample mean and variance are 0.985422 and 0.890355, respectively. The variance is smaller than the mean, suggesting the binomial as a reasonable distribution to try. The method of moments leads to

$$mq = 0.985422$$

and

$$mq(1 - q) = 0.890355.$$

Hence, $\hat{q} = 0.096474$ and $\hat{m} = 10.21440$. However, m can only take on integer values. We choose $\hat{m} = 10$ by rounding. Then we adjust the estimate of $\hat{q}$ to 0.0985422 from the first moment equation. Doing this will

Table 11.5   Number of losses per machine

No. of losses/machine	No. of machines
0	5,367
1	5,893
2	2,870
3	842
4	163
5	23
6	1
7	1
8+	0

Table 11.6   Binomial likelihood profile

$\hat{m}$	$\hat{q}$	$-$Loglikelihood
7	0.140775	19,273.56
8	0.123178	19,265.37
9	0.109491	19,262.02
10	0.098542	19,260.98
11	0.089584	19,261.11
12	0.082119	19,261.84

result in a model variance that differs from the sample variance because $10(0.0985422)(1 - 0.0985422) = 0.888316$. This shows one of the pitfalls of using the method of moments with integer-valued parameters.

We now turn to maximum likelihood estimation. From the data $m \geq 7$. If m is known, then only q needs to be estimated. If m is unknown, then we can produce a likelihood profile by maximizing the likelihood for fixed values of m starting at 7 and increasing until a maximum is found. The results are in Table 11.6.

The largest loglikelihood value occurs at $m = 10$. If, a priori, the value of m is unknown, then the maximum likelihood estimates of the parameters are $\hat{m} = 10$ and $\hat{q} = 0.0985422$. This is the same as the adjusted moment estimates. This is not necessarily the case for all data sets.   □

11.5   THE $(a, b, 1)$ CLASS

Estimation of the parameters for the $(a, b, 1)$ class follows the same general principles that were used in connection with the $(a, b, 0)$ class.

Assuming that the data are in the same form as the previous examples, the likelihood is, using formula (5.6),

$$L = \left(p_0^M\right)^{n_0} \prod_{k=1}^{\infty} \left(p_k^M\right)^{n_k} = \left(p_0^M\right)^{n_0} \prod_{k=1}^{\infty} \left[(1 - p_0^M)p_k^T\right]^{n_k}.$$

The loglikelihood is,

$$l = n_0 \ln p_0^M + \sum_{k=1}^{\infty} n_k [\ln(1 - p_0^M) + \ln p_k^T]$$

$$= n_0 \ln p_0^M + \sum_{k=1}^{\infty} n_k \ln(1 - p_0^M) + \sum_{k=1}^{\infty} n_k [\ln p_k - \ln(1 - p_0)],$$

where the last statement follows from $p_k^T = p_k/(1-p_0)$. The three parameters of the $(a, b, 1)$ class are p_0^M, a, and b, where a and b determine $p_1, p_2, \ldots$. Then it can be seen that

$$l = l_0 + l_1$$

with

$$l_0 = n_0 \ln p_0^M + \sum_{k=1}^{\infty} n_k \ln(1 - p_0^M),$$

$$l_1 = \sum_{k=1}^{\infty} n_k [\ln p_k - \ln(1 - p_0)],$$

where l_0 depends only on the parameter p_0^M and l_1 is independent of p_0^M, depending only on a and b. This simplifies the maximization because

$$\frac{\partial l}{\partial p_0^M} = \frac{\partial l_0}{\partial p_0^M} = \frac{n_0}{p_0^M} - \sum_{k=1}^{\infty} \frac{n_k}{1 - p_0^M} = \frac{n_0}{p_0^M} - \frac{n - n_0}{1 - p_0^M},$$

resulting in

$$\hat{p}_0^M = \frac{n_0}{n},$$

the proportion of observations at zero. This is the natural estimator because p_0^M represents the probability of an observation of zero.

Similarly, because the likelihood factors conveniently, the estimation of a and b is independent of p_0^M. Note that although a and b are parameters maximization should not be done with respect to them. That is because not all values of a and b produce admissible probability distributions.[3] For the

---

[3] Maximization can be done with respect to any parameterization because maximum likelihood estimation is invariant under parameter transformations. However, it is more difficult to maximize over bounded regions because numerical methods are difficult to constrain and analytic methods will fail because of the lack of differentiability. Therefore, estimation is usually done with respect to particular class members, such as the Poisson.

zero-modified Poisson distribution, the relevant part of the loglikelihood is

$$l_1 = \sum_{k=1}^{\infty} n_k \left[\ln \frac{e^{-\lambda} \lambda^k}{k!} - \ln(1 - e^{-\lambda}) \right]$$

$$= -(n - n_0)\lambda + \left(\sum_{k=1}^{\infty} k \, n_k \right) \ln \lambda - (n - n_0) \ln(1 - e^{-\lambda}) + c$$

$$= -(n - n_0)[\lambda + \ln(1 - e^{-\lambda})] + n\bar{x} \ln \lambda + c,$$

where $\bar{x} = \frac{1}{n} \sum_{k=0}^{\infty} k n_k$ is the sample mean, $n = \sum_{k=0}^{\infty} n_k$, and c is independent of λ. Hence,

$$\frac{\partial l_1}{\partial \lambda} = -(n - n_0) - (n - n_0) \frac{e^{-\lambda}}{1 - e^{-\lambda}} + n\frac{\bar{x}}{\lambda}$$

$$= -\frac{n - n_0}{1 - e^{-\lambda}} + \frac{n\bar{x}}{\lambda}.$$

Setting this to zero yields

$$\bar{x}(1 - e^{-\lambda}) = \frac{n - n_0}{n} \lambda. \tag{11.9}$$

By graphing each side as a function of λ, it is clear that, if $n_0 > 0$, there exist exactly two roots: one is $\lambda = 0$, the other is $\lambda > 0$. Equation (11.9) can be solved numerically to obtain $\hat{\lambda}$. Note that, because $\hat{p}_0^M = n_0/n$ and $p_0 = e^{-\lambda}$, (11.9) can be rewritten as

$$\bar{x} = \frac{1 - \hat{p}_0^M}{1 - p_0} \lambda. \tag{11.10}$$

Because the right-hand side of equation (11.10) is the theoretical mean of the zero-modified Poisson distribution (when $\hat{p}_0^M$ is replaced with p_0^M), equation (11.10) is a moment equation. Hence, an alternative estimation method yielding the same results as the maximum likelihood method is to equate p_0^M to the sample proportion at zero and the theoretical mean to the sample mean. This suggests that, by fixing the zero probability to the observed proportion at zero and equating the low-order moments, a modified moment method can be used to get starting values for numerical maximization of the likelihood function. Because the maximum likelihood method has better asymptotic properties, it is preferable to use the modified moment method only to obtain starting values.

For the purpose of obtaining estimates of the asymptotic variance of the maximum likelihood estimator of λ, it is easy to obtain

$$\frac{\partial^2 l_1}{\partial \lambda^2} = (n - n_0) \frac{e^{-\lambda}}{(1 - e^{-\lambda})^2} - \frac{n\bar{x}}{\lambda^2},$$

and the expected value is obtained by observing that

$$E(\bar{x}) = (1 - p_0^M)\lambda/(1 - e^{-\lambda})$$

. Finally, p_0^M may be replaced by its estimator, n_0/n. The variance of $\hat{p}_0^M$ is obtained by observing that the numerator, n_0, has a binomial distribution and therefore the variance is $p_0^M(1 - p_0^M)/n$.

For the zero-modified binomial distribution,

$$l_1 = \sum_{k=1}^{m} n_k \left\{ \ln\left[\binom{m}{k} q^k (1-q)^{m-k} \right] - \ln[1 - (1-q)^m] \right\}$$

$$= \left(\sum_{k=1}^{m} k n_k \right) \ln q + \sum_{k=1}^{m} (m-k) n_k \ln(1-q)$$

$$- \sum_{k=1}^{m} n_k \ln[1 - (1-q)^m] + c$$

$$= n\bar{x} \ln q + m(n - n_0) \ln(1-q) - n\bar{x} \ln(1-q)$$
$$- (n - n_0) \ln[1 - (1-q)^m] + c$$

where c does not depend on q and

$$\frac{\partial l_1}{\partial q} = \frac{n\bar{x}}{q} - \frac{m(n-n_0)}{1-q} + \frac{n\bar{x}}{1-q} - \frac{(n-n_0)m(1-q)^{m-1}}{1 - (1-q)^m}.$$

Setting this to zero yields

$$\bar{x} = \frac{1 - \hat{p}_0^M}{1 - p_0} mq, \tag{11.11}$$

where we recall that $p_0 = (1-q)^m$. This equation matches the theoretical mean with the sample mean.

If m is known and fixed, the maximum likelihood estimator of p_0^M is still

$$\hat{p}_0^M = \frac{n_0}{n}.$$

However, even with m known, (11.11) must be solved numerically for q. When m is unknown and also needs to be estimated, the above procedure can be followed for different values of m until the maximum of the likelihood function is obtained.

The zero-modified negative binomial (or extended truncated negative binomial) distribution is a bit more complicated because three parameters need to be estimated. Of course, the maximum likelihood estimator of p_0^M is $\hat{p}_0^M = n_0/n$ as before, reducing the problem to the estimation of r and β. The part of the loglikelihood relevant to r and β is

$$l_1 = \sum_{k=1}^{\infty} n_k \ln p_k - (n - n_0) \ln(1 - p_0). \tag{11.12}$$

Hence

$$
l_1 = \sum_{k=1}^{\infty} n_k \ln \left[\binom{k+r-1}{k} \left(\frac{1}{1+\beta} \right)^r \left(\frac{\beta}{1+\beta} \right)^k \right]
$$

$$
- (n - n_0) \ln \left[1 - \left(\frac{1}{1+\beta} \right)^r \right]. \tag{11.13}
$$

This function must be maximized over the (r, β) plane to obtain the maximum likelihood estimates. This can be done numerically using maximization procedures. Starting values can be obtained by the modified moment method by setting $\hat{p}_0^M = n_0/n$ and equating the first two moments of the distribution to the first two sample moments. It is generally easier to use raw moments (moments about the origin) than central moments for this purpose. In practice, it may be more convenient to maximize (11.12) rather than (11.13) because we can take advantage of the recursive scheme

$$
p_k = p_{k-1} \left(a + \frac{b}{k} \right)
$$

in evaluating (11.12). This makes computer programming a bit easier.

For zero-truncated distributions there is no need to estimate the probability at zero because it is known to be zero. The remaining parameters are estimated using the same formulas developed for the zero-modified distributions.

Example 11.7 *The data set in Table 11.7 comes from Beard et al. [13]. Determine a model that adequately describes the data.*

When a Poisson distribution is fitted to it, the resulting fit is very poor. There is too much probability for one accident and two little at subsequent values. The geometric distribution is tried as a one-parameter alternative. It has loglikelihood

$$
l = -n \ln(1 + \beta) + \sum_{k=1}^{\infty} n_k \ln \left(\frac{\beta}{1+\beta} \right)^k
$$

$$
= -n \ln(1 + \beta) + \sum_{k=1}^{\infty} k n_k [\ln \beta - \ln(1 + \beta)]
$$

$$
= -n \ln(1 + \beta) + n\bar{x} [\ln \beta - \ln(1 + \beta)]
$$

$$
= -(n + n\bar{x}) \ln(1 + \beta) + n\bar{x} \ln \beta,
$$

where $\bar{x} = \sum_{k=1}^{\infty} k \, n_k/n$ and $n = \sum_{k=0}^{\infty} n_k$.

Differentiation reveals that the loglikelihood has a maximum at

$$
\hat{\beta} = \bar{x}.
$$

Table 11.7 Fitted distributions to Beard data

Accidents	Observed	Poisson	Geometric	ZM Poisson	ZM geometric
0	370,412	369,246.9	372,206.5	370,412.0	370,412.0
1	46,545	48,643.6	43,325.8	46,432.1	46,555.2
2	3,935	3,204.1	5,043.2	4,138.6	3,913.6
3	317	140.7	587.0	245.9	329.0
4	28	4.6	68.3	11.0	27.7
5	3	0.1	8.0	0.4	2.3
6+	0	0.0	1.0	0.0	0.2
Parameters		λ: 0.13174	β: 0.13174	p_0^M: 0.87934 λ: 0.17827	p_0^M: 0.87934 β: 0.091780
Loglikelihood		−171,373	−171,479	−171,160	−171,133

A qualitative look at the numbers indicates that the zero-modified geometric distribution matches the data better than the other three models considered. A formal analysis is done in Example 12.15. □

11.6 COMPOUND MODELS

For the method of moments, the first few moments can be matched with the sample moments. The system of equations can be solved to obtain the moment based estimators. Note that the number of parameters in the compound model is the sum of the number of parameters in the primary and secondary distributions. The first two theoretical moments for compound distributions are

$$E(S) = E(N)E(M)$$
$$Var(S) = E(N)\,Var(M) + E(M)^2\,Var(N).$$

These results were developed in Chapter 6. The first three moments for the compound Poisson distribution are given in (5.20).

Maximum likelihood estimation is also carried out as before. The loglikelihood to be maximized is

$$l = \sum_{k=0}^{\infty} n_k \ln g_k.$$

When g_k is the probability of a compound distribution, the loglikelihood can be maximized numerically. The first and second derivatives of the loglikelihood can be obtained by using approximate differentiation methods as applied directly to the loglikelihood function at the maximum value.

Table 11.8 Automobile claims by year

Year	No. of machines	No. of losses
1996	2145	207
1997	2452	227
1998	3112	341
1999	3458	335
2000	3698	362
2001	3872	359

Example 12.16 provides a data set for which the Polya–Aeppli (Poisson-geometric) distribution is a good choice. Another useful compound Poisson distribution is the Poisson–extended truncated negative binomial (Poisson–ETNB) distribution. Although it does not matter whether the secondary distribution is modified or truncated, we prefer the truncated version here so that the parameter r may be extended.[4] Special cases are: $r = 1$, which is the Poisson–geometric (also called Polya–Aeppli); $r \to 0$, which is the Poisson–logarithmic (negative binomial); and $r = -0.5$, which is called the Poisson–inverse Gaussian. This name is not consistent with the others. Here the inverse Gaussian distribution is a mixing distribution (see Section 5.12). Example 12.17 provides a data set for which the Poisson–inverse Gaussian distribution is a good choice.

11.7 EFFECT OF EXPOSURE ON MAXIMUM LIKELIHOOD ESTIMATION

In Section 5.14 the effect of different exposures on discrete distributions was discussed. When aggregating data over several years, maximum likelihood estimation is still possible. The following example illustrates this for the Poisson distribution.

Example 11.8 *Determine the maximum likelihood estimate of the Poisson parameter for the data in Table 11.8.*

Let λ be the Poisson parameter for a single exposure. If year k has e_k exposures, then the number of losses has a Poisson distribution with parameter

---

[4]This does not contradict Theorem 5.11. When $-1 < r < 0$, it is still the case that changing the probability at zero will not produce new distributions. What is true is that there is no probability at zero that will lead to an ordinary $(a, b, 0)$ negative binomial secondary distribution.

λe_k. If n_k is the number of losses in year k, the likelihood function is

$$L = \prod_{k=1}^{6} \frac{e^{-\lambda e_k}(\lambda e_k)^{n_k}}{n_k!}.$$

The maximum likelihood estimate is found by

$$l = \ln L = \sum_{k=1}^{6}[-\lambda e_k + n_k \ln(\lambda e_k) - \ln(n_k!)],$$

$$\frac{\partial l}{\partial \lambda} = \sum_{k=1}^{6}\left(-e_k + n_k \lambda^{-1}\right) = 0,$$

$$\hat{\lambda} = \frac{\sum_{k=1}^{6} n_k}{\sum_{k=1}^{6} e_k} = \frac{1,831}{18,737} = 0.09772.$$

☐

In this example the answer is what we expected it to be, the average number of losses per exposure. This technique will work for any distribution in the $(a, b, 0)^5$ and compound classes.

11.8 EXERCISES

11.1 Assume that the binomial parameter m is known. Consider the maximum likelihood estimator of q.

(a) Show that the maximum likelihood estimator is unbiased.

(b) Determine the variance of the maximum likelihood estimator.

(c) Show that the asymptotic variance as given in Theorem 10.13 is the same as that developed in (b).

(d) Determine a simple formula for a confidence interval using formula (9.4) on page 276 that is based on replacing q with $\hat{q}$ in the variance term.

11.2 Use equation (11.5) to determine the maximum likelihood estimator of β for the geometric distribution. In addition, determine the variance of the maximum likelihood estimator and verify that it matches the asymptotic variance as given in Theorem 10.13.

11.3 A set of 10,000 risks produced the loss counts in Table 11.9.

---

[5] For the binomial distribution, the usual problem that m must be an integer remains.

Table 11.9 Data for Exercise 11.3

No. of claims	No. of risks
0	9,048
1	905
2	45
3	2
4+	0

Table 11.10 Data for Exercise 11.4

No. of claims	Underinsured	Uninsured
0	901	947
1	92	50
2	5	2
3	1	1
4	1	0
5+	0	0

(a) Determine the maximum likelihood estimate of λ for a Poisson model and then determine a 95% confidence interval for λ.

(b) Determine the maximum likelihood estimate of β for a geometric model and then determine a 95% confidence interval for β.

(c) Determine the maximum likelihood estimate of r and β for a negative binomial model.

(d) Assume that $m = 4$. Determine the maximum likelihood estimate of q of the binomial model.

(e) Construct 95% confidence intervals for q using the methods developed in (d) of Exercise 11.1.

(f) Determine the maximum likelihood estimate of m and q by constructing a likelihood profile.

11.4 (From insurance) An automobile insurance policy provides benefits for accidents caused by both underinsured and uninsured motorists. Data on 1,000 policies revealed the information in Table 11.10.

(a) Determine the maximum likelihood estimate of λ for a Poisson model for each of the variables N_1 = number of underinsured losses and N_2 = number of uninsured losses.

(b) Assume that N_1 and N_2 are independent. Use Theorem 5.1 on page 109 to determine a model for $N = N_1 + N_2$.

Table 11.11   Data for Exercise 11.5

No. of claims	No. of policies
0	861
1	121
2	13
3	3
4	1
5	0
6	1
7+	0

11.5 An alternative method of obtaining a model for N in Exercise 11.4 would be to record the total number of underinsured and uninsured losses for each of the 1,000 policies. Suppose this was done and the results were as in Table 11.11.

(a) Determine the maximum likelihood estimate of λ for a Poisson model.

(b) Determine the maximum likelihood estimate of β for a geometric model.

(c) Determine the maximum likelihood estimate of r and β for a negative binomial model.

(d) Assume that $m = 7$. Determine the maximum likelihood estimate of q of the binomial model.

(e) Determine the maximum likelihood estimates of m and q by constructing a likelihood profile.

12

Model selection

If you perceive that there are four possible ways in which a procedure can go wrong, and circumvent these, then a fifth way, unprepared for, will promptly develop.

—Murphy

12.1 INTRODUCTION

When using data to build a model, the process must end with the announcement of a "winner." While qualifications, limitations, caveats, and other attempts to escape full responsibility are appropriate, and often necessary, a commitment to a solution is often required. In this chapter we look at a variety of ways to evaluate a model and compare competing models. But we must also remember that whatever model we select it is only an approximation of reality. This is reflected in the following modeler's motto[1]:

> *All models are wrong, but some models are useful.*

Thus, our goal is to determine a model that is good enough to use to answer the question. The challenge here is that the definition of *good enough* will depend on the particular application. Another important modeling point is that a solid understanding of the question will guide you to the answer. The following quote from John Tukey [119] sums this up:

---

[1] It is usually attributed to George Box.

> *Far better an approximate answer to the right question, which is often vague, than an exact answer to the wrong question, which can always be made precise.*

In this chapter, a specific modeling strategy will be considered. Our preference is to have a single approach that can be used for any probabilistic modeling situation. A consequence is that for any particular modeling situation there may be a better (more reliable or more accurate) approach. For example, while maximum likelihood is a good estimation method for most settings, it may not be the best[2] for certain distributions. A literature search will turn up methods that have been optimized for specific distributions, but they will not be mentioned here. Similarly, many of the hypothesis tests used here give approximate results. For specific cases, better approximations, or maybe even exact results, are available. They will also be bypassed. The goal here is to outline a method that will give reasonable answers most of the time and be adaptable to a variety of situations.

This chapter assumes the reader has a basic understanding of statistical hypothesis testing as reviewed in Chapter 9. The remaining sections cover a variety of evaluation and selection tools. Each tool has its own strengths and weaknesses, and it is possible for different tools to lead to different models. This makes modeling as much art as science. At times, in real-world applications, the model's purpose may lead the analyst to favor one tool over another.

12.2   REPRESENTATIONS OF THE DATA AND MODEL

All the approaches to be presented attempt to compare the proposed model to the data or to another model. The proposed model is represented by either its density or distribution function or perhaps some functional of these quantities such as the limited expected value function or the mean excess loss function. The data can be represented by the empirical distribution function or a histogram. The graphs are easy to construct when there is individual, complete data. When there is grouping or observations have been truncated or censored, difficulties arise. Here, the only cases to be covered are those where all the data have been truncated at the same value (which could be zero) and are all censored at the same value (which could be infinity). Extensions to the case of multiple truncation or censoring points are detailed by Rioux and Klugman [100]. It should be noted that the need for such representations applies only to continuous models. For discrete data, issues of censoring,

---

[2] There are many definitions of "best." Combining the Cramér-Rao lower bound with Theorem 10.13 indicates that maximum likelihood estimators are asymptotically optimal using unbiasedness and minimum variance as the definition of best.

Table 12.1   Data Set B with highest value changed

$27	$82	$115	$126	$155	$161	$243
$294	$340	$384$457	$680	$855	$877	
$974	$1193	$1340	$1884	$2558	$3476	

truncation, and grouping rarely apply. The data can easily be represented by the relative or cumulative frequencies at each possible observation.

With regard to representing the data, the empirical distribution function will be used for individual data and the histogram will be used for grouped data.

In order to compare the model to truncated data, we begin by noting that the empirical distribution begins at the truncation point and represents conditional values (that is, they are the distribution and density function given that the observation exceeds the truncation point). In order to make a comparison to the empirical values, the model must also be truncated. Let the truncation point in the data set be t. The modified functions are

$$F^*(x) = \begin{cases} 0, & x < t, \\ \dfrac{F(x) - F(t)}{1 - F(t)}, & x \geq t, \end{cases}$$

$$f^*(x) = \begin{cases} 0, & x < t, \\ \dfrac{f(x)}{1 - F(t)}, & x \geq t. \end{cases}$$

12.3 GRAPHICAL COMPARISON OF THE DENSITY AND DISTRIBUTION FUNCTIONS

The most direct way to see how well the model and data match up is to plot the respective density and distribution functions.

Example 12.1 *Consider Data Sets B and C. However, for this example and all that follow, in Data Set B we replace the value at $15,743 by $3,476 (this is to allow the graphs to fit comfortably on a page). These data sets are reproduced here in Tables 12.1 and 12.2. Truncate Data Set B at $50 and Data Set C at $7,500. Estimate the parameter of an exponential model for each data set. Plot the appropriate functions and comment on the quality of the fit of the model. Repeat this for Data Set B censored at $1,000 (without any truncation).*

For Data Set B, there are 19 observations (the first observation is removed due to truncation). A typical contribution to the likelihood function is $f(82)/[1 - F(50)]$. The maximum likelihood estimate of the exponential

Table 12.2 Data Set C

Payment range	Number of payments
0–$7500	99
$7500–$17,500	42
$17,500–$32,500	29
$32,500–$67,500	28
$67,500–$125,000	17
$125,000–$300,000	9
Over $300,000	3

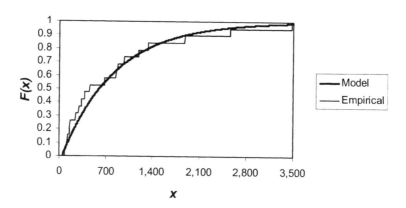

Fig. 12.1 Model vs. data cdf plot for Data Set B truncated at 50.

parameter is $\hat{\theta} = 802.32$. The empirical distribution function starts at 50 and jumps 1/19 at each data point. The distribution function, using a truncation point of 50, is

$$F^*(x) = \frac{1 - e^{-x/802.32} - \left(1 - e^{-50/802.32}\right)}{1 - \left(1 - e^{-50/802.32}\right)} = 1 - e^{-(x-50)/802.32}.$$

Figure 12.1 presents a plot of these two functions.

The fit is not as good as we might like because the model understates the distribution function at smaller values of x and overstates the distribution function at larger values of x. This is not good because it means that tail probabilities are understated.

Exponential fit

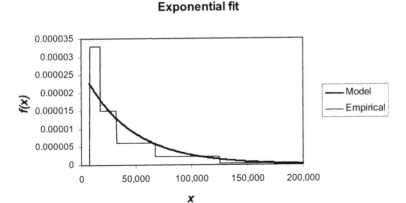

Fig. 12.2 Model vs. data density plot for Data Set C truncated at 7,500.

For Data Set C, the likelihood function uses the truncated values. For example, the contribution to the likelihood function for the first interval is

$$\left[\frac{F(17{,}500) - F(7500)}{1 - F(7500)} \right]^{42}.$$

The maximum likelihood estimate is $\hat{\theta} = 44{,}253$. The height of the first histogram bar is

$$\frac{42}{128(17{,}500 - 7500)} = 0.0000328$$

and the last bar is for the interval from \$125,000 to \$300,000 (a bar cannot be constructed for the interval from \$300,000 to infinity). The density function must be truncated at \$7,500 and becomes

$$f^*(x) = \frac{f(x)}{1 - F(7500)} = \frac{44{,}253^{-1} e^{-x/44{,}253}}{1 - (1 - e^{-7500/44{,}253})}$$

$$= \frac{e^{-(x-7500)/44{,}253}}{44{,}253}, \quad x > 7500.$$

The plot of the density function versus the histogram is given Figure 12.2.

The exponential model understates the early probabilities. It is hard to tell from the picture how the curves compare above \$125,000.

For Data Set B modified with a limit, the maximum likelihood estimate is $\hat{\theta} = 718.00$. When constructing the plot, the empirical distribution function must stop at \$1,000. The plot appears in Figure 12.3.

Once again, the exponential model does not fit well.   ☐

Exponential fit

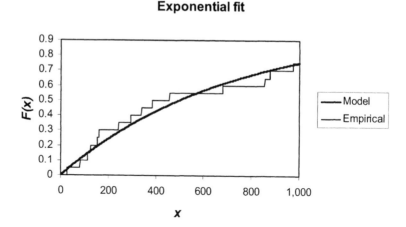

Fig. 12.3 Model vs. data cdf plot for Data Set B censored at 1,000.

When the model's distribution function is close to the empirical distribution function, it is difficult to make small distinctions. Among the many ways to amplify those distinctions, two will be presented here. The first is to simply plot the difference of the two functions. That is, if $F_n(x)$ is the empirical distribution function and $F^*(x)$ is the model distribution function, plot $D(x) = F_n(x) - F^*(x)$.

Example 12.2 *Plot $D(x)$ for Example 12.1.*

For Data Set B truncated at $50, the plot appears in Figure 12.4. The lack of fit for this model is magnified in this plot.

There is no corresponding plot for grouped data. For Data Set B censored at $1,000, the plot must again end at that value. It appears in Figure 12.5. The lack of fit continues to be apparent. □

Another way to highlight any differences is the p–p plot, which is also called a probability plot. The plot is created by ordering the observations as $x_1 \leq \cdots \leq x_n$. A point is then plotted corresponding to each value. The coordinates to plot are $(F_n(x_j), F^*(x_j))$. If the model fits well, the plotted points will be near the 45° line running from $(0,0)$ to $(1,1)$. However, for this to be the case, a different definition of the empirical distribution function is needed. It can be shown that the expected value of $F_n(x_j)$ is $j/(n+1)$ and therefore the empirical distribution should be that value and not the usual j/n. If two observations have the same value, either plot both points (they would have the same "y" value but different "x" values) or plot a single value by averaging the two "x" values.

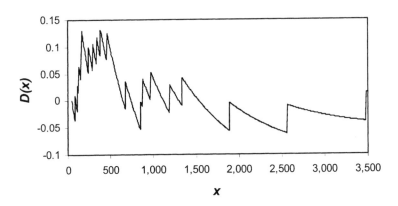

Fig. 12.4 Model vs. data $D(x)$ plot for Data Set B truncated at 50.

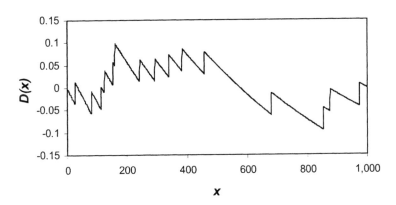

Fig. 12.5 Model vs. data $D(x)$ plot for Data Set B censored at 1,000.

Example 12.3 *Create a p–p plot for Example 12.1.*

For Data Set B truncated at $50, n = 19$ and one of the observed values is $x = 82$. The empirical value is $F_n(82) = \frac{1}{20} = 0.05$. The other coordinate is

$$F^*(82) = 1 - e^{-(82-50)/802.32} = 0.0391.$$

Exponential fit

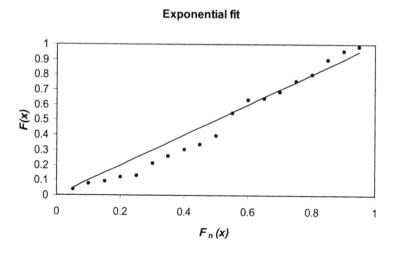

Fig. 12.6 p–p for Data Set B truncated at 50.

One of the plotted points will be $(0.05, 0.0391)$. The complete picture appears in Figure 12.6.

From the lower left part of the plot it is clear that the exponential model places less probability on small values than the data call for. A similar plot can be constructed for Data Set B censored at $1,000 and it appears in Figure 12.7.

This plot ends at about 0.75 because that is the highest probability observed prior to the censoring point at $1,000. There are no empirical values at higher probabilities. Again, the exponential model tends to underestimate the empirical values.   □

12.4 HYPOTHESIS TESTS

A picture may be worth many words, but sometimes it is best to replace the impressions conveyed by pictures with mathematical demonstrations. One such demonstration is a test of the hypotheses

H_0 : The data came from a population with the stated model.

H_1 : The data did not come from such a population.

The test statistic is usually a measure of how close the model distribution function is to the empirical distribution function. When the null hypothesis completely specifies the model (for example, an exponential distribution with

Exponential fit

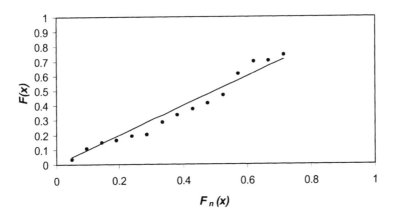

Fig. 12.7 p–p plot for Data Set B censored at 1,000.

mean $100), critical values are well known. However, it is more often the case that the null hypothesis states the name of the model but not its parameters. When the parameters are estimated from the data, the test statistic tends to be smaller than it would have been had the parameter values been prespecified. That is because the estimation method itself tries to choose parameters that produce a distribution that is close to the data. In that case, the tests become approximate. Because rejection of the null hypothesis occurs for large values of the test statistic, the approximation tends to increase the probability of a Type II error while lowering the probability of a Type I error.[3]

One method of avoiding the approximation is to randomly divide the sample in half. Use one half to estimate the parameters and then use the other half to conduct the hypothesis test. Once the model is selected, the full data set could be used to reestimate the parameters.

12.4.1 Kolmogorov-Smirnov test

Let t be the left truncation point ($t = 0$ if there is no truncation) and let u be the right censoring point ($u = \infty$ if there is no censoring). Then, the test

---

[3]Among the tests presented here, only the chi-square test has a built-in correction for this situation. Modifications for the other tests have been developed, but they will not be presented here.

Table 12.3 Calculation of D for Example 12.4

x	$F^*(x)$	$F_n(x-)$	$F_n(x)$	Maximum difference
82	0.0391	0.0000	0.0526	0.0391
115	0.0778	0.0526	0.1053	0.0275
126	0.0904	0.1053	0.1579	0.0675
155	0.1227	0.1579	0.2105	0.0878
161	0.1292	0.2105	0.2632	0.1340
243	0.2138	0.2632	0.3158	0.1020
294	0.2622	0.3158	0.3684	0.1062
340	0.3033	0.3684	0.4211	0.1178
384	0.3405	0.4211	0.4737	0.1332
457	0.3979	0.4737	0.5263	0.1284
680	0.5440	0.5263	0.5789	0.0349
855	0.6333	0.5789	0.6316	0.0544
877	0.6433	0.6316	0.6842	0.0409
974	0.6839	0.6842	0.7368	0.0529
1,193	0.7594	0.7368	0.7895	0.0301
1,340	0.7997	0.7895	0.8421	0.0424
1,884	0.8983	0.8421	0.8947	0.0562
2,558	0.9561	0.8947	0.9474	0.0614
3,476	0.9860	0.9474	1.0000	0.0386

statistic is

$$D = \max_{t \le x \le u} |F_n(x) - F^*(x)|.$$

This test should only be used on individual data. This is to ensure that the step function $F_n(x)$ is well defined. Also, the model distribution function $F^*(x)$ is assumed to be continuous over the relevant range.

Example 12.4 *Calculate D for Example* 12.1.

Table 12.3 provides the needed values. Because the empirical distribution function jumps at each data point, the model distribution function must be compared both before and after the jump. The values just before the jump are denoted $F_n(x-)$ in the table. The maximum is $D = 0.1340$.

For Data Set B censored at \$1,000, 15 of the 20 observations are uncensored. Table 12.4 illustrates the needed calculations. The maximum is $D = 0.0991$.□

All that remains is to determine the critical value. Commonly used critical values for this test are $1.22/\sqrt{n}$ for $\alpha = 0.10$, $1.36/\sqrt{n}$ for $\alpha = 0.05$, and $1.63/\sqrt{n}$ for $\alpha = 0.01$. When $u < \infty$, the critical value should be smaller because there is less opportunity for the difference to become large. Modifications for this phenomenon exist in the literature (see reference [111], for

Table 12.4 Calculation of D for Example 12.4 with censoring

x	$F^*(x)$	$F_n(x-)$	$F_n(x)$	Maximum difference
27	0.0369	0.00	0.05	0.0369
82	0.1079	0.05	0.10	0.0579
115	0.1480	0.10	0.15	0.0480
126	0.1610	0.15	0.20	0.0390
155	0.1942	0.20	0.25	0.0558
161	0.2009	0.25	0.30	0.0991
243	0.2871	0.30	0.35	0.0629
294	0.3360	0.35	0.40	0.0640
340	0.3772	0.40	0.45	0.0728
384	0.4142	0.45	0.50	0.0858
457	0.4709	0.50	0.55	0.0791
680	0.6121	0.55	0.60	0.0621
855	0.6960	0.60	0.65	0.0960
877	0.7052	0.65	0.70	0.0552
974	0.7425	0.70	0.75	0.0425
1000	0.7516	0.75	0.75	0.0016

example, which also includes tables of critical values for specific null distribution models), and one such modification is given in reference [100] but will not be introduced here.

Example 12.5 *Complete the Kolmogorov–Smirnov test for Example 12.4.*

For Data Set B truncated at $50 the sample size is 19. The critical value at a 5% significance level is $1.36/\sqrt{19} = 0.3120$. Because $0.1340 < 0.3120$, the null hypothesis is not rejected and the exponential distribution is a plausible model. While it is unlikely that the exponential model is appropriate for this population, the sample size is too small to lead to that conclusion. For Data Set B censored at 1,000 the sample size is 20 and so the critical value is $1.36/\sqrt{20} = 0.3041$ and the exponential model is again viewed as being plausible. □

For both this test and the Anderson–Darling test that follows, the critical values are correct only when the null hypothesis completely specifies the model. When the data set is used to estimate parameters for the null hypothesized distribution (as in the example), the correct critical value is smaller. For both tests, the change depends on the particular distribution that is hypothesized and maybe even on the particular true values of the parameters.

12.4.2   Anderson-Darling test

This test is similar to the Kolmogorov–Smirnov test, but uses a different measure of the difference between the two distribution functions. The test statistic is

$$A^2 = n \int_t^u \frac{[F_n(x) - F^*(x)]^2}{F^*(x)[1 - F^*(x)]} f^*(x) dx.$$

That is, it is a weighted average of the squared differences between the empirical and model distribution functions. Note that when x is close to t or to u the weights might be very large because of the small value of one of the factors in the denominator. This test statistic tends to place more emphasis on good fit in the tails than in the middle of the distribution. Calculating with this formula appears to be challenging. However, for individual data (so this is another test that does not work for grouped data), the integral simplifies to

$$A^2 = -nF^*(u) + n \sum_{j=0}^k [1 - F_n(y_j)]^2 \{\ln[1 - F^*(y_j)] - \ln[1 - F^*(y_{j+1})]\}$$

$$+ n \sum_{j=1}^k F_n(y_j)^2 [\ln F^*(y_{j+1}) - \ln F^*(y_j)],$$

where the unique noncensored data points are $t = y_0 < y_1 < \cdots < y_k < y_{k+1} = u$. Note that when $u = \infty$ the last term of the first sum is zero [evaluating the formula as written will ask for $\ln(0)$]. The critical values are 1.933, 2.492, and 3.857 for 10%, 5%, and 1% significance levels, respectively. As with the Kolmogorov–Smirnov test, the critical value should be smaller when $u < \infty$.

Example 12.6 *Perform the Anderson–Darling test for the continuing example.*

For Data Set B truncated at \$50, there are 19 data points. The calculation is in Table 12.5, where "summand" refers to the sum of the corresponding terms from the two sums. The total is 1.0226 and the test statistic is $-19(1) + 19(1.0226) = 0.4292$. Because the test statistic is less than the critical value of 2.492, the exponential model is viewed as plausible.

For Data Set B censored at \$1000, the results are in Table 12.6. The total is 0.7602 and the test statistic is $-20(0.7516) + 20(0.7602) = 0.1713$. Because the test statistic does not exceed the critical value of 2.492, the exponential model is viewed as plausible.   □

12.4.3   Chi-square goodness-of-fit test

Unlike the previous two tests, this test allows for some discretion. It begins with the selection of $k - 1$ arbitrary values, $t = c_0 < c_1 < \cdots < c_k = \infty$. Let

Table 12.5   Anderson–Darling test for Example 12.6

j	y_j	$F^*(x)$	$F_n(x)$	Summand
0	50	0.0000	0.0000	0.0399
1	82	0.0391	0.0526	0.0388
2	115	0.0778	0.1053	0.0126
3	126	0.0904	0.1579	0.0332
4	155	0.1227	0.2105	0.0070
5	161	0.1292	0.2632	0.0904
6	243	0.2138	0.3158	0.0501
7	294	0.2622	0.3684	0.0426
8	340	0.3033	0.4211	0.0389
9	384	0.3405	0.4737	0.0601
10	457	0.3979	0.5263	0.1490
11	680	0.5440	0.5789	0.0897
12	855	0.6333	0.6316	0.0099
13	877	0.6433	0.6842	0.0407
14	974	0.6839	0.7368	0.0758
15	1193	0.7594	0.7895	0.0403
16	1340	0.7997	0.8421	0.0994
17	1884	0.8983	0.8947	0.0592
18	2558	0.9561	0.9474	0.0308
19	3476	0.9860	1.0000	0.0141
20	∞	1.0000	1.0000	

$\hat{p}_j = F^*(c_j) - F^*(c_{j-1})$ be the probability that a truncated observation falls in the interval from c_{j-1} to c_j. Similarly, let $p_{nj} = F_n(c_j) - F_n(c_{j-1})$ be the same probability according to the empirical distribution. The test statistic is then

$$\chi^2 = \sum_{j=1}^{k} \frac{n(\hat{p}_j - p_{nj})^2}{\hat{p}_j},$$

where n is the sample size. Another way to write the formula is to let $E_j = n\hat{p}_j$ be the number of expected observations in the interval (assuming that the hypothesized model is true) and $O_j = np_{nj}$ be the number of observations in the interval. Then,

$$\chi^2 = \sum_{j=1}^{k} \frac{(E_j - O_j)^2}{E_j}.$$

The critical value for this test comes from the chi-square distribution with degrees of freedom equal to the number of terms in the sum (k) minus 1 minus the number of estimated parameters. There are a number of rules that have been proposed for deciding when the test is reasonably accurate. They center

Table 12.6 Anderson–Darling calculation for Example 12.6 with censored data

j	y_j	$F^*(x)$	$F_n^*(x)$	Summand
0	0	0.0000	0.00	0.0376
1	27	0.0369	0.05	0.0718
2	82	0.1079	0.10	0.0404
3	115	0.1480	0.15	0.0130
4	126	0.1610	0.20	0.0334
5	155	0.1942	0.25	0.0068
6	161	0.2009	0.30	0.0881
7	243	0.2871	0.35	0.0493
8	294	0.3360	0.40	0.0416
9	340	0.3772	0.45	0.0375
10	384	0.4142	0.50	0.0575
11	457	0.4709	0.55	0.1423
12	680	0.6121	0.60	0.0852
13	855	0.6960	0.65	0.0093
14	877	0.7052	0.70	0.0374
15	974	0.7425	0.75	0.0092
16	1000	0.7516	0.75	

around the values of $E_j = n\hat{p}_j$. The most conservative states that each must be at least 5. Some authors claim that values as low as 1 are acceptable. All agree the test works best when the values are about equal from term to term. If the data are grouped, there is little choice but to use the groups as given, although adjacent groups could be combined to increase E_j. For individual data, the data can be grouped for the purpose of performing this test.[4]

Example 12.7 *Perform the chi-square goodness-of-fit test for the exponential distribution for the continuing example.*

All three data sets can be evaluated with this test. For Data Set B truncated at \$50, establish boundaries at \$50, \$150, \$250, \$500, \$1000, \$2000, and infinity. The calculations appear in Table 12.7. The total is $\chi^2 = 1.4034$. With four degrees of freedom (6 rows minus 1 minus 1 estimated parameter) the critical value for a test at a 5% significance level is 9.4877. The exponential model is a good fit.

---

[4]Moore [83] cites a number of rules. Among them are (1) An expected frequency of at least 1 for all cells and and an expected frequency of at least 5 for 80% of the cells; (2) an average count per cell of at least 4 when testing at the 1% significance level and an average count of at least 2 when testing at the 5% significance level; and (3) a sample size of at least 10, at least 3 cells, and the ratio of the square of the sample size to the number of cells at least 10.

Table 12.7   Data Set B truncated at 50

Range	$\hat{p}$	Expected	Observed	χ^2
$50–$150	0.1172	2.227	3	0.2687
$150–$250	0.1035	1.966	3	0.5444
$250–$500	0.2087	3.964	4	0.0003
$500–$1000	0.2647	5.029	4	0.2105
$1000–$2000	0.2180	4.143	3	0.3152
$2,000–$\infty$	0.0880	1.672	2	0.0644
Total	1	19	19	1.4034

Table 12.8   Data Set B censored at 1,000

Range	$\hat{p}$	Expected	Observed	χ^2
0–$150	0.1885	3.771	4	0.0139
$150–$250	0.1055	2.110	3	0.3754
$250–$500	0.2076	4.152	4	0.0055
$500–$1000	0.2500	5.000	4	0.2000
$1000–$\infty$	0.2484	4.968	5	0.0002
Total	1	20	20	0.5951

For Data Set B censored at $1000, the first interval is from $0 to $150 and the last interval is from $1000 to ∞. Unlike the previous two tests, the censored observations can be used. The calculations are in Table 12.8. The total is $\chi^2 = 0.5951$. With three degrees of freedom (5 rows minus 1 minus 1 estimated parameter) the critical value for a test at a 5% significance level is 7.8147 and the p-value is 0.8976. The exponential model is a good fit.

For Data Set C the groups are already in place. The results are given Table 12.9. The test statistic is $\chi^2 = 61.913$. There are four degrees of freedom for a critical value of 9.488. The p-value is about 10^{-12}. There is clear evidence that the exponential model is not appropriate. A more accurate test would combine the last two groups (because the expected count in the last group is less than 1). The group from 125,000 to infinity has an expected count of 8.997 and an observed count of 12 for a contribution of 1.002. The test statistic is now 16.552 and with three degrees of freedom the p-value is 0.00087. The test continues to reject the exponential model.   □

Sometimes, the test can be modified to fit different situations. Example 12.8 illustrates this for aggregate frequency data.

Example 12.8 *Conduct an approximate goodness-of-fit test for the Poisson model determined in Example* 11.8. *The data are repeated in Table* 12.10.

Table 12.9 Data Set C

Range	$\hat{p}$	Expected	Observed	χ^2
$7500–$17,500	0.2023	25.889	42	10.026
$17,500–$32,500	0.2293	29.356	29	0.004
$32,500–$67,500	0.3107	39.765	28	3.481
$67,500–$125,000	0.1874	23.993	17	2.038
$125,000–$300,000	0.0689	8.824	9	0.003
$300,000–$\infty$	0.0013	0.172	3	46.360
Total	1	128	128	61.913

Table 12.10 Automobile claims by year

Year	Exposure	Claims
1986	2145	207
1987	2452	227
1988	3112	341
1989	3458	335
1990	3698	362
1991	3872	359

For each year we are assuming that the number of losses is the result of the sum of a number (given by the exposure) of independent and identical random variables. In that case the central limit theorem indicates that a normal approximation may be appropriate. The expected count (E_k) is the exposure times the estimated expected value for one exposure unit, and the variance (V_k) is the exposure times the estimated variance for one exposure unit. The test statistic is then

$$Q = \sum_k \frac{(n_k - E_k)^2}{V_k}$$

and has an approximate chi-square distribution with degrees of freedom equal to the number of data points less the number of estimated parameters. The expected count is $E_k = \lambda e_k$ and the variance is $V_k = \lambda e_k$ also. The test statistic is

$$Q = \frac{(207 - 209.61)^2}{209.61} + \frac{(227 - 239.61)^2}{239.61} + \frac{(341 - 304.11)^2}{304.11}$$
$$+ \frac{(335 - 337.92)^2}{337.92} + \frac{(362 - 361.37)^2}{361.37} + \frac{(359 - 378.38)^2}{378.38}$$
$$= 6.19.$$

With five degrees of freedom, the 5% critical value is 11.07 and the Poisson hypothesis is accepted. □

There is one important point to note about these tests. Suppose the sample size were to double but sampled values were not much different (imagine each number showing up twice instead of once). For the Kolmogorov–Smirnov test, the test statistic would be unchanged, but the critical value would be smaller. For the Anderson–Darling and chi-square tests, the test statistic would double while the critical value would be unchanged. As a result, for larger sample sizes, it is more likely that the null hypothesis (and thus the proposed model) will be rejected. This should not be surprising. We know that the null hypothesis is false (it is extremely unlikely that a simple distribution using a few parameters can explain the complex behavior that produced the observations), and with a large enough sample size we will have convincing evidence of that truth. When using these tests we must remember that although all our models are wrong, some may be useful.

12.4.4   Likelihood ratio test

An alternative question to "Could the population have distribution A?" is "Is the population more likely to have distribution B than distribution A?" More formally:

H_0 : The data came from a population with distribution A.

H_1 : The data came from a population with distribution B.

In order to perform a formal hypothesis test distribution A must be a special case of distribution B, for example, exponential versus gamma. An easy way to complete this test is given below.

Definition 12.9 *The **likelihood ratio test** is conducted as follows. First, let the likelihood function be written as $L(\theta)$. Let θ_0 be the value of the parameters that maximizes the likelihood function. However, only values of the parameters that are within the null hypothesis may be considered. Let $L_0 = L(\theta_0)$. Let θ_1 be the maximum likelihood estimator where the parameters can vary over all possible values from the alternative hypothesis and then let $L_1 = L(\theta_1)$. The test statistic is $T = 2\ln(L_1/L_0) = 2(\ln L_1 - \ln L_0)$. The null hypothesis is rejected if $T > c$, where c is calculated from $\alpha = \Pr(T > c)$, where T has a chi-square distribution with degrees of freedom equal to the number of free parameters in the model from the alternative hypothesis less the number of free parameters in the model from the null hypothesis.*

This test makes some sense. When the alternative hypothesis is true, forcing the parameter to be selected from the null hypothesis should produce a likelihood value that is significantly smaller.

Example 12.10 *You want to test the hypothesis that the population that produced Data Set B (using the original largest observation) has a mean that is other than $1200. Assume that the population has a gamma distribution and conduct the likelihood ratio test at a 5% significance level. Also, determine the p-value.*

The hypotheses are:

$$H_0 : \text{gamma with } \mu = 1200.$$
$$H_1 : \text{gamma with } \mu \neq 1200.$$

From earlier work the maximum likelihood estimates are $\hat{\alpha} = 0.55616$ and $\hat{\theta} = 2561.1$. The loglikelihood at the maximum is $\ln L_1 = -162.293$. Next, the likelihood must be maximized, but only over those values α and θ for which $\alpha\theta = 1200$. That means α can be free to range over all positive numbers but $\theta = 1200/\alpha$. Thus, under the null hypothesis, there is only one free parameter. The likelihood function is maximized at $\hat{\alpha} = 0.54955$ and $\hat{\theta} = 2183.6$. The loglikelihood at this maximum is $\ln L_0 = -162.466$. The test statistic is $T = 2(-162.293 + 162.466) = 0.346$. For a chi-square distribution with one degree of freedom, the critical value is 3.8415. Because $0.346 < 3.8415$, the null hypothesis is not rejected. The probability that a chi-square random variable with one degree of freedom exceeds 0.346 is 0.556, a p-value that indicates little support for the alternative hypothesis.   □

Example 12.11 (Example 5.4 continued) *Members of the $(a, b, 0)$ class were not sufficient to describe these data. Determine a suitable model.*

Thirteen different distributions were fit to the data. The results of that process revealed six models with p-values above 0.01 for the chi-square goodness-of-fit test. Information about those models is given in Table 12.11. The likelihood ratio test indicates that the three-parameter model with the smallest negative loglikelihood (Poisson–ETNB) is not significantly better than the two-parameter Poisson–inverse Gaussian model. The latter appears to be an excellent choice.   □

It is tempting to use this test when the alternative distribution simply has more parameters than the null distribution. In such cases the test is not appropriate. For example, it is possible for a two-parameter lognormal model to have a higher loglikelihood value than a three-parameter Burr model. This produces a negative test statistic, indicating that a chi-square distribution is not appropriate. When the null distribution is a limiting (rather than special) case of the alternative distribution, the test may still be used, but the test statistic's distribution is now a mixture of chi-square distributions (see [106]). Regardless, it is still reasonable to use the "test" to make decisions in these cases, provided it is clearly understood that a formal hypothesis test was not conducted. Further examples and exercises using this test to make decisions appear in Section ??.

Table 12.11 Six useful models for Example 12.11

Model	Number of parameters	Negative loglikelihood	χ^2	p-value
Negative binomial	2	5348.04	8.77	0.0125
ZM logarithmic	2	5343.79	4.92	0.1779
Poisson–inverse Gaussian	2	5343.51	4.54	0.2091
ZM negative binomial	3	5343.62	4.65	0.0979
Geometric–negative binomial	3	5342.70	1.96	0.3754
Poisson–ETNB	3	5342.51	2.75	0.2525

12.5 SELECTING A MODEL

SelectionSection

12.5.1 Introduction

Almost all of the tools are now in place for choosing a model. Before outlining a recommended approach, two important concepts must be introduced. The first is **parsimony**. The principle of parsimony states that unless there is considerable evidence to do otherwise a simpler model is preferred. The reason is that a complex model may do a great job of matching the data, but that is no guarantee that the model matches the population from which the observations were sampled. For example, given any set of 10 (x, y) pairs with unique x values, there will always be a polynomial of degree 9 or less that goes through all 10 points. But if these points were a random sample, it is highly unlikely that the population values all lie on that polynomial. However, there may be a straight line that comes close to the sampled points as well as the other points in the population. This matches the spirit of most hypothesis tests. That is, do not reject the null hypothesis (and thus claim a more complex description of the population holds) unless there is strong evidence to do so.

The second concept does not have a name. It states that, if you try enough models, one will look good, even if it is not. Suppose I have 900 models at my disposal. For most data sets, it is likely that one of them will fit well, but this does not help us learn about the population.

Thus, in selecting models, there are two things to keep in mind: (1) Use a simple model if at all possible; and, (2). Restrict the universe of potential models.

The methods outlined in the remainder of this section will help with the first point. The second one requires some experience. Certain models make more sense in certain situations, but only experience can enhance the modeler's senses so that only a short list of quality candidates is considered.

The section is split into two types of selection criteria. The first set is based on the modeler's judgment whereas the second set is more formal in the sense that most of the time all analysts will reach the same conclusions. That is because the decisions are made based on numerical measurements rather than charts or graphs.

12.5.2   Judgment-based approaches

Using one's own judgment to select models involves one or more of the three concepts outlined below. In all cases, the analyst's experience is critical.

First, the decision can be based on the various graphs (or tables based on the graphs) presented in this chapter.[5] This allows the analyst to focus on aspects of the model that are important for the proposed application. For example, it may be more important to fit the tail well or it may be more important to match the mode or modes. Even if a score-based approach is used, it may be appropriate to present a convincing picture to support the chosen model.

Second, the decision can be influenced by the success of particular models in similar situations or the value of a particular model for its intended use. If the Pareto distribution has frequently been used to model a particular set of losses, it may require more than the usual amount of evidence to change to an alternative distribution.

Finally, it should be noted that the more algorithmic approaches outlined below do not always agree. In that case judgment is most definitely required, if only to decide which algorithmic approach to use.

12.5.3   Score-based approaches

Some analysts might prefer an automated process for selecting a model. An easy way to do that would be to assign a score to each model and let the model with the best value win. The following scores are worth considering:

1. Lowest value of the Kolmogorov–Smirnov test statistic

2. Lowest value of the Anderson–Darling test statistic

3. Lowest value of the chi-square goodness-of-fit test statistic

4. Highest p-value for the chi-square goodness-of-fit test

5. Highest value of the likelihood function at its maximum

---

[5]Besides the ones discussed here, there are other plots/tables that could be used. Other choices are a q-q plot and a comparison of model and empirical limited expected values or mean residual life functions.

All but the chi-square p-value have a deficiency with respect to parsimony. First, consider the likelihood function. When comparing, say, an exponential to a Weibull model, the Weibull model must have a likelihood value that is at least as large as the exponential model. They would only be equal in the rare case that the maximum likelihood estimate of the Weibull parameter τ is equal to 1. Thus, the Weibull model would always win over the exponential model, a clear violation of the principle of parsimony. For the three test statistics, there is no assurance that the same relationship will hold, but it seems likely that, if a more complex model is selected, the fit measure is likely to be better. The only reason the p-value is immune from this problem is that with more complex models the test has fewer degrees of freedom. It is then possible that the more complex model will have a smaller p-value. There is no comparable adjustment for the first two test statistics listed.

With regard to the likelihood value, there are two ways to proceed. One is to perform the likelihood ratio test and the other is to extract a penalty for employing additional parameters. The likelihood ratio test is technically only available when one model is a special case of another (for example, Pareto vs. generalized Pareto). The concept can be turned into an algorithm by using the test at a 5% significance level. Begin with the best one-parameter model (the one with the highest loglikelihood value). Add a second parameter only if the two-parameter model with the highest loglikelihood value shows an increase of at least 1.92 (so twice the difference exceeds the critical value of 3.84). Then move to three-parameter models. If the comparison is to a two-parameter model, a 1.92 increase is again needed. If the early comparison led to keeping the one-parameter model, an increase of 3.00 is needed (because the test has two degrees of freedom). Adding three parameters requires a 3.91 increase, four parameters a 4.74 increase, and so on. In the spirit of this chapter, this algorithm can be used even for nonspecial cases. However, it would not be appropriate to claim that a likelihood ratio test was being conducted.

Aside from the issue of special cases, the likelihood ratio test has the same problem as the other hypothesis tests. Were the sample size to double, the loglikelihoods would also double, making it more likely that a model with a higher number of parameters will be selected. This tends to defeat the parsimony principle. On the other hand, it could be argued that, if we possess a lot of data, we have the right to consider and fit more complex models. A method that effects a compromise between these positions is the Schwarz Bayesian criterion (SBC) [107], which recommends that when ranking models a deduction of $(r/2)\ln n$ should be made from the loglikelihood value, where r is the number of estimated parameters and n is the sample size. Thus, adding a parameter requires an increase of $0.5\ln n$ in the loglikelihood. For larger sample sizes, a greater increase is needed, but it is not proportional to the sample size itself.

Table 12.12   Results for Example 12.12

Criterion	B truncated at $50		B censored at $1,000	
	Exponential	Weibull	Exponential	Weibull
K-S*	0.1340	0.0887	0.0991	0.0991
A-D*	0.4292	0.1631	0.1713	0.1712
χ^2	1.4034	0.3615	0.5951	0.5947
p-Value	0.8436	0.9481	0.8976	0.7428
Loglikelihood	-146.063	-145.683	-113.647	-113.647
SBC	-147.535	-148.628	-115.145	-116.643
C				
χ^2	61.913	0.3698		
p-Value	10^{-12}	0.9464		
Loglikelihood	-214.924	-202.077		
SBC	-217.350	-206.929		

*K-S and A-D refer to the Kolmogorov–Smirnov and Anderson–Darling
test statistics, respectively.

Example 12.12 *For the continuing example in this chapter, choose between the exponential and Weibull models for the data.*

Graphs were constructed in the various examples and exercises. Table 12.12 summarizes the numerical measures. For the truncated version of Data Set B, the SBC is calculated for a sample size of 19, while for the version censored at $1,000 there are 20 observations. For both versions of Data Set B, while the Weibull offers some improvement, it is not convincing. In particular, neither the likelihood ratio test nor the SBC indicates value in the second parameter. For Data Set C it is clear that the Weibull model is superior and provides an excellent fit.   □

Example 12.13 *In Example 5.19 an ad hoc method was used to demonstrate that the Poisson–ETNB distribution provided a good fit. Use the methods of this chapter to determine a good model.*

The data set is very large and, as a result, requires a very close correspondence of the model to the data. The results are given in Table 12.13.

From Table 12.13, it is seen that the negative binomial distribution does not fit well while the fit of the Poisson–inverse Gaussian is marginal at best ($p = 2.88\%$). The Poisson–inverse Gaussian is a special case ($r = -0.5$) of the Poisson–ETNB. Hence, a likelihood ratio test can be formally applied to determine whether the additional parameter r is justified. Because the loglikelihood increases by 5, which is more than 1.92, the three-parameter

Table 12.13 Results for Example 12.13

No. of claims	Observed frequency	Negative binomial	Poisson–inverse Gaussian	Poisson–ETNB
		Fitted distributions		
0	565,664	565,708.1	565,712.4	565,661.2
1	68,714	68,570.0	68,575.6	68,721.2
2	5,177	5,317.2	5,295.9	5,171.7
3	365	334.9	344.0	362.9
4	24	18.7	20.8	29.6
5	6	1.0	1.2	3.0
6+	0	0.0	0.1	0.4
Parameters		$\beta = 0.0350662$ $r = 3.57784$	$\lambda = 0.123304$ $\beta = 0.0712027$	$\lambda = 0.123395$ $\beta = 0.233862$ $r = -0.846872$
Chi square		12.13	7.09	0.29
Degrees of freedom		2	2	1
p-value		<1%	2.88%	58.9%
−Loglikelihood		251,117	251,114	251,109
SBC		−251,130	−251,127	−251,129

model is a significantly better fit. The chi-square test shows that the Poisson-ETNB provides an adequate fit. On the other hand, the SBC favors the Poisson-inverse Gaussian distribution. Given the improved fit in the tail for the three parameter model, it seems to be the best choice. □

Example 12.14 *The following example is taken from Douglas [24]. The number of accidents that cause loses per day are recorded. The data are in Table 12.14. Determine if a Poisson model is appropriate.*

A Poisson model is fitted to these data. The method of moments and the maximum likelihood method both lead to the estimate of the mean,

$$\hat{\lambda} = \frac{742}{365} = 2.0329.$$

The results of a chi-square goodness-of-fit test are in Table 12.15. Any time such a table is made, the expected count for the last group is

$$E_{k+} = n\hat{p}_{k+} = n(1 - \hat{p}_0 - \cdots - \hat{p}_{k-1}).$$

The last three groups were combined to ensure an expected count of at least one for each row. The test statistic is 9.93 with six degrees of freedom. The critical value at a 5% significance level is 12.59 and the p-value is

Table 12.14   Data for Example 12.14

No. of claims/day	Observed no. of days
0	47
1	97
2	109
3	62
4	25
5	16
6	4
7	3
8	2
9+	0

Table 12.15   Chi-square goodness-of-fit test for Example 12.14

Claims/day	Observed	Expected	Chi square
0	47	47.8	0.01
1	97	97.2	0.00
2	109	98.8	1.06
3	62	66.9	0.36
4	25	34.0	2.39
5	16	13.8	0.34
6	4	4.7	0.10
7+	5	1.8	5.66
Totals	365	365	9.93

0.1277. By this test the Poisson distribution is an acceptable model; however, it should be noted that the fit is poorest at the large values, and with the model understating the observed values, this may be a risky choice.   □

Example 12.15 *The data set in Table* 11.7 *come from Beard et al.* [13] *and were previously analyzed in Example* 11.7. *Determine a model that adequately describes the data.*

Parameter estimates from fitting four models are in Table 11.7. Various fit measures are given in Table 12.16. Only the zero-modified geometric distribution passes the goodness-of-fit test. It is also clearly superior according to the SBC. A likelihood ratio test against the geometric has a test statistic of $2(171{,}479 - 171{,}133) = 692$, which with one degree of freedom is clearly significant. This confirms the qualitative conclusion in Example 11.7.   □

Table 12.16 Test results for Example 12.15

	Poisson	Geometric	ZM Poisson	ZM geometric
Chi square	543.0	643.4	64.8	0.58
Degrees of freedom	2	4	2	2
p-value	$< 1\%$	$< 1\%$	$< 1\%$	74.9%
Loglikelihood	$-171,373$	$-171,479$	$-171,160$	$-171,133$
SBC	$-171,379.5$	$-171,485.5$	$-171,173$	$-171,146$

Example 12.16 *The data in Table* 12.17, *from Simon* [108], *represent the observed number of losses per insurance contract for* 298 *contracts. Determine an appropriate model.*

The Poisson, negative binomial, and Polya–Aeppli distributions are fitted to the data. The Polya–Aeppli and the negative binomial are both plausible distributions. The p-value of the chi-square statistic and the loglikelihood both indicate that the Polya–Aeppli is slightly better than the negative binomial. The SBC verifies that both models are superior to the Poisson distribution. The ultimate choice may depend on familiarity, prior use, and computational convenience of the negative binomial versus the Polya–Aeppli model. □

Example 12.17 *Consider the data in Table* 12.18 *on automobile accidents in Switzerland taken from Bühlmann* [19]. *Determine an appropriate model.*

Three models are considered in Table 12.18. The Poisson distribution is a very bad fit. Its tail is far too light compared with the actual experience. The negative binomial distribution appears to be much better but cannot be accepted because the p-value of the chi-square statistic is very small. The large sample size requires a better fit. The Poisson–inverse Gaussian distribution provides an almost perfect fit (p-value is large). Note that the Poisson–inverse Gaussian has two parameters, like the negative binomial. The SBC also favors this choice. This example shows that the Poisson–inverse Gaussian can have a much heavier right-hand tail than the negative binomial. □

Example 12.18 *(From insurance) Medical losses were studied by Bevan* [17] *in* 1963. *Male* (955) *and female* (1291) *losses were studied separately. The data appear in Table* 12.19, *where there was a deductible of* $25. *Can a common model be used?*

When using the combined data set the lognormal distribution is the best two-parameter model. Its negative loglikelihood (NLL) is 4580.20. This is 19.09 better than the one-parameter inverse exponential model and 0.13 worse than the three-parameter Burr model. Because none of these models is a

Table 12.17 Fit of Simon data

Number of losses/contract	Number of contracts	Fitted distributions		
		Poisson	Negative binomial	Polya–Aeppli
0	99	54.0	95.9	98.7
1	65	92.2	75.8	70.6
2	57	78.8	50.4	50.2
3	35	44.9	31.3	32.6
4	20	19.2	18.8	20.0
5	10	6.5	11.0	11.7
6	4	1.9	6.4	6.6
7	0	0.5	3.7	3.6
8	3	0.1	2.1	2.0
9	4	0.0	1.2	1.0
10	0	0.0	0.7	0.5
11	1	0.0	0.4	0.3
12+	0	0.0	0.5	0.3
Parameters		$\lambda = 1.70805$	$\beta = 1.15907$ $r = 1.47364$	$\lambda = 1.10551$ $\beta = 0.545039$
Chi square		72.64	4.06	2.84
Degrees of freedom		4	5	5
p-Value		<1%	54.05%	72.39%
Loglikelihood		−577.0	−528.8	−528.5
SBC		−579.8	−534.5	−534.2

special case of the other, the likelihood ratio test (LRT) cannot be used, but it is clear that when using the 1.92 difference as a standard, the lognormal is preferred. The SBC requires an improvement of $0.5 \ln(2246) = 3.86$ and again the lognormal is preferred. The parameters are $\mu = 4.5237$ and $\sigma = 1.4950$. When separate lognormal models are fit to males ($\mu = 3.9686$ and $\sigma = 1.8432$) and females ($\mu = 4.7713$ and $\sigma = 1.2848$), the respective NLLs are 1977.25 and 2583.82 for a total of 4561.07. This is an improvement of 19.13 over a common lognormal model, which is significant by both the LRT (3.00 needed) and SBC (7.72 needed). Sometimes it is useful to be able to use the same nonscale parameter in both models. When a common value of σ is used, the NLL is 4579.77, which is significantly worse than using separate models.☐

Table 12.18 Fit of Bhlmann data

No. of accidents	Observed frequency	Fitted distributions		
		Poisson	Negative binomial	P.–i.G.[a]
0	103,704	102,629.6	103,723.6	103,710.0
1	14,075	15,922.0	13,989.9	14,054.7
2	1,766	1,235.1	1,857.1	1,784.9
3	255	63.9	245.2	254.5
4	45	2.5	32.3	40.4
5	6	0.1	4.2	6.9
6	2	0.0	0.6	1.3
7+	0	0.0	0.1	0.3
Parameters		$\lambda = 0.155140$	$\beta = 0.150232$ $r = 1.03267$	$\lambda = 0.144667$ $\beta = 0.310536$
Chi square		1332.3	12.12	0.78
Degrees of freedom		2	2	3
p-Value		<1%	<1%	85.5%
Loglikelihood		−55,108.5	−54,615.3	−54,609.8
SBC		−55,114.3	−54,627.0	−54,621.5

[a]P.–i.G. stands for Poisson–inverse Gaussian.

12.6 EXERCISES

12.1 Repeat Example 12.1 using a Weibull model in place of the exponential model.

12.2 Repeat Example 12.2 for a Weibull model.

12.3 Repeat Example 12.3 for a Weibull model.

12.4 Use the Kolmogorov–Smirnov test to see whether a Weibull model is appropriate for the data used in Example 12.5.

12.5 Five observations are made from a random variable. They are 1, 2, 3, 5, and 13. Determine the value of the Kolmogorov–Smirnov test statistic for the null hypothesis that $f(x) = 2x^{-2}e^{-2/x}$, $x > 0$.

12.6 You are given the following five observations from a random sample: 0.1, 0.2, 0.5, 1.0, and 1.3. Calculate the Kolmogorov–Smirnov test statistic for the null hypothesis that the population density function is $f(x) = 2(1+x)^{-3}$, $x > 0$.

12.7 Perform the Anderson–Darling test of the Weibull distribution for Example 12.6.

Table 12.19   Medical losses for Example 12.18

Loss	Male	Female
$25–$50	184	199
$50–$100	270	310
$100–$200	160	262
$200–$300	88	163
$300–$400	63	103
$400–$500	47	69
$500–$1000	61	124
$1,000–$2,000	35	40
$2000–$3000	18	12
$3,000–$4,000	13	4
$4000–$5000	2	1
$5,000–$6,667	5	2
$6667–$7500	3	1
$7,500–$10,000	6	1

Table 12.20   Data for Exercise 12.10

No. of incidents	Days
0	209
1	111
2	33
3	7
4	3
5	2

12.8 Repeat Example 12.7 for the Weibull model.

12.9 Each day, for 365 days, the number of losses is recorded. The results were 50 days with no losses, 122 days with one loss, 101 days with two losses, 92 days with three losses, and no days with four or more losses. For a Poisson model determine the maximum likelihood estimate of λ and then perform the chi-square goodness-of-fit test at a 2.5% significance level.

12.10 During a one-year period, the number of incidents per day was distributed as given in Table 12.20. Test the hypothesis that the data are from a Poisson distribution with mean 0.6 using the maximum number of groups such that each group has at least five expected observations. Use a significance level of 5%.

12.11 Redo Example 12.8 assuming that each exposure unit has a geometric distribution. Conduct the approximate chi-square goodness-of-fit test. Is the geometric preferable to the Poisson model?

12.12 Using Data Set B (with the original largest value), determine whether a gamma model is more appropriate than an exponential model. Recall that an exponential model is a gamma model with $\alpha = 1$. Useful values were obtained in Example 10.8.

12.13 Use Data Set C to choose a model for the population that produced those numbers. Choose from the exponential, gamma, and transformed gamma models. Information for the first two distributions was obtained in Example 10.9 and Exercise 10.17, respectively.

12.14 Conduct the chi-square goodness-of-fit test for each of the models obtained in Exercise 11.3.

12.15 Conduct the chi-square goodness-of-fit test for each of the models obtained in Exercise 11.5 .

12.16 For the data in Table 12.18 determine the method-of-moments estimates of the parameters of the Poisson–Poisson distribution where the secondary distribution is the ordinary (not zero-truncated) Poisson distribution. Perform the chi-square goodness-of-fit test using this model.

12.17 You are given the data in Table 12.21 which represent results from 23,589 machines. The third column headed "fitted model" represents the expected number of losses for a fitted (by maximum likelihood) negative binomial distribution.

(a) Perform the chi-square goodness-of-fit test at a significance level of 5%.

(b) Determine the maximum likelihood estimates of the negative binomial parameters r and β. This can be done from the given numbers without actually maximizing the likelihood function.

12.18 The number of accidents for each of a sample of 1000 automobiles recorded. The results are in Table 12.22. Without doing any formal tests, determine which of the following five models is most appropriate: binomial, Poisson, negative binomial, normal, gamma.

12.19 For Example 12.1, determine whether a transformed gamma model is more appropriate than either the exponential model or the Weibull model for each of the three data sets.

Table 12.21   Data for Exercise 12.17

Number of losses, k	Number of machines, n_k	Fitted model
0	20,592	20,596.76
1	2651	2631.03
2	297	318.37
3	41	37.81
4	7	4.45
5	0	0.52
6	1	0.06
≥ 7	0	0.00

Table 12.22   Data for Exercise 12.18

No. of accidents	No. of automobiles
0	100
1	267
2	311
3	208
4	87
5	23
6	4
Total	1000

Table 12.23   Results for Exercise 12.21

Model	No. of parameters	Negative loglikelihood
Generalized Pareto	3	219.1
Burr	3	219.2
Pareto	2	221.2
Lognormal	2	221.4
Inverse exponential	1	224.3

12.20 From the data in Exercise 12.10 the maximum likelihood estimates are $\hat{\lambda} = 0.60$ for the Poisson distribution and $\hat{r} = 2.9$ and $\hat{\beta} = 0.21$ for the negative binomial distribution. Conduct the likelihood ratio test for choosing between these two models.

12.21 From a sample of size 100, five models are fit with the results given in Table 12.23. Use the Schwarz Bayesian criterion to select the best model.

Table 12.24   Data for Exercise 12.24

No. of medical losses	No. of accidents
0	529
1	146
2	169
3	137
4	99
5	87
6	41
7	25
8+	0

12.22 Using the results from Exercises 11.3 and 12.14, use the chi-square goodness-of-fit test, the likelihood ratio test, and the Schwarz Bayesian criterion to determine the best model from the members of the $(a, b, 0)$ class.

12.23 Using the results from Exercises 11.5 and 12.15, use the chi-square goodness-of-fit test, the likelihood ratio test, and the Schwarz Bayesian criterion to determine the best model from the members of the $(a, b, 0)$ class.

12.24 Table 12.24 gives the number of medical losses per reported automobile accident.

  (a) Construct a plot similar to Figure 5.1. Does it appear that a member of the $(a, b, 0)$ class will provide a good model? If so, which one?

  (b) Determine the maximum likelihood estimates of the parameters for each member of the $(a, b, 0)$ class.

  (c) Based on the chi-square goodness-of-fit test, the likelihood ratio test, and the Schwarz Bayesian criterion, which member of the $(a, b, 0)$ class provides the best fit? Is this model acceptable?

12.25 A frequency model that has not been mentioned to this point is the **zeta distribution**. It is a zero-truncated distribution with $p_k^T = k^{-(\rho+1)}/\zeta(\rho+1)$, $k = 1, 2, \ldots, \rho > 0$. The denominator is the zeta function, which must be evaluated numerically as $\zeta(\rho+1) = \sum_{k=1}^{\infty} k^{-(\rho+1)}$. The zero-modified zeta distribution can be formed in the usual way. More information can be found in Luong and Doray [78].

  (a) Determine the maximum likelihood estimates of the parameters of the zero-modified zeta distribution for the data in Example 11.7.

  (b) Is the zero-modified zeta distribution acceptable?

Table 12.25   Data for Exercise 12.26(a)

No. of losses	No. of automobiles
0	96,978
1	9240
2	704
3	43
4	9
5+	0

Table 12.26   Data for Exercise 12.26(b)

No. of deaths	No. of corps
0	109
1	65
2	22
3	3
4	1
5+	0

Table 12.27   Data for Exercise 12.26(c)

No. of wars	No. of years
0	223
1	142
2	48
3	15
4	4
5+	0

12.26 The five data sets presented in this problem are all taken from Lemaire [75]. For each data set compute the first three moments and then use the ideas in Section 5.11 to make a guess at an appropriate model from among the compound Poisson collection [Poisson, geometric, negative binomial, Poisson–binomial (with $m = 2$ and $m = 3$), Polya–Aeppli, Neyman Type A, Poisson–inverse Gaussian, and Poisson–ETNB]. From the selected model (if any) and members of the $(a, b, 0)$ and $(a, b, 1)$ classes, determine the best model.

(a) The data in Table 12.25 represent counts of losses from automobile accidents in Belgium.

Table 12.28 Data for Exercise 12.26(d)

No. of runs	No. of half-innings
0	1,023
1	222
2	87
3	32
4	18
5	11
6	6
7+	3

Table 12.29 Data for Exercise 12.26(e)

No. of goals	No. of games
0	29
1	71
2	82
3	89
4	65
5	45
6	24
7	7
8	4
9	1
10+	3

(b) The data in Table 12.26 represent the number of deaths due to horse kicks in the Prussian army between 1875 and 1894. The counts are the number of deaths in a corps (there were 10 of them) in a given year, and thus there are 200 observations. This data set is often cited as the inspiration for the Poisson distribution. For using any of our models, what additional assumption about the data must be made?

(c) The data in Table 12.27 represent the number of major international wars per year from 1500 through 1931.

(d) The data in Table 12.28 represent the number of runs scored in each half-inning of World Series baseball games played from 1947 through 1960.

(e) The data in Table 12.29 represent the number of goals per game per team in the 1966–1967 season of the National Hockey League.

12.27 Verify that the estimates presented in Example 5.26 are the maximum likelihood estimates. (Because only two decimals are presented, it is probably sufficient to observe that the likelihood function takes on smaller values at each of the nearby points.) The negative binomial distribution was fit to these data in Example 11.5. Which of these two models is preferable?

13

Fitting extreme value models

Nature always sides with the hidden flaw.

—Murphy

13.1   INTRODUCTION

The purpose of this chapter is to focus attention on specific issues for modeling jumbo losses. The probability theory aspects of extreme value theory were discussed in Chapter 7. In this chapter, we will discuss a number of techniques that are especially useful in the modeling of jumbo losses. The methods described in Chapters 9-12 can be used in building and selecting models involving extreme outcomes. However, if the primary interest is on studying extreme outcomes, there are a number of diagnostic and estimation procedures that are especially useful.

In this chapter, we begin with standard estimation procedures for distributions associated with extreme value theory. When we use extreme value models for only the tail of the distribution, we will also be interested in determining from data the point in the data at which we are able to rely on the extreme value model for the tail; that is, we want to answer the question *"Where does the right-hand tail begin?"*. This is an important question because we rely on asymptotic results from extreme value theory to capture the shape of the tail without reference to the underlying model of ground-up losses.

13.2 PARAMETER ESTIMATION

13.2.1 ML estimation from the extreme value distribution

We begin by assuming that we have a sample of size n of values of extreme outcomes. An example might be daily maximum errors in recording a certain type of transaction. For the purpose of this theory, we treat the observations as being outcomes of independent and identically distributed random variables[1]. As in earlier chapters, we denote the sample by $x_1, x_2, ..., x_n$. From Section 7.5, the distribution of extreme values for large samples is given by one of the three distributions that form the special cases of the generalized extreme value distribution. The standardized df of the generalized extreme value (GEVD) distribution is written as

$$G_\gamma(x) = \exp\left[-(1 + \gamma x)^{-1/\gamma}\right].$$

When γ is positive, the df $G_\gamma(x)$ has the form of a standardized Fréchet distribution. When γ is negative, the df $G_\gamma(x)$ has the form of a standardized Weibull distribution. When $\gamma = 0$, the df is the standardized Gumbel distribution function

$$G_0(x) = \exp\left[-\exp\left(-x\right)\right].$$

Inserting location and scale parameters results in the GEV distribution function

$$F(x) = G_{\gamma,\mu,\theta}(x) = \exp\left[-\left(1 + \gamma\frac{x - \mu}{\theta}\right)^{-1/\gamma}\right].$$

The corresponding GEV probability density function is

$$f(x) = g_{\gamma,\mu,\theta}(x) = \frac{1}{\theta}\left(1 + \gamma\frac{x - \mu}{\theta}\right)^{-(1+1/\gamma)}\exp\left[-\left(1 + \gamma\frac{x - \mu}{\theta}\right)^{-1/\gamma}\right].$$

When $\gamma = 0$, the density function is the Gumbel density

$$f(x) = g_{0,\mu,\theta}(x) = \frac{1}{\theta}\exp\left[-\frac{x - \mu}{\theta} - \exp\left(-\frac{x - \mu}{\theta}\right)\right].$$

The contribution of an observation x_i from the GEV to the log likelihood is

$$\ln f(x_i) = \ln g_{\gamma,\mu,\theta}(x_i)$$

$$= -\ln\theta - \left(1 + \frac{1}{\gamma}\right)\ln\left(1 + \gamma\frac{x_i - \mu}{\theta}\right) - \left(1 + \gamma\frac{x_i - \mu}{\theta}\right)^{-1/\gamma},$$

---

[1] The assumption of identical distributions may be violated, for example, if the maximum losses each period arise from different numbers of actual losses in each period.

which can be written as

$$\ln f\left(x_i\right) = \ln g_{\gamma,\mu,\theta}(x_i) = -\ln\theta - (1+\gamma)y_i - \exp(-y_i)$$

where

$$y_i = \frac{1}{\gamma}\ln\left(1 + \gamma\frac{x_i - \mu}{\theta}\right).$$

For a set of n observations, the negative loglikelihood function is then

$$-l(\gamma,\mu,\theta) = n\ln\theta + (1+\gamma)\sum_{i=1}^{n} y_i + \sum_{i=1}^{n}\exp(-y_i). \qquad (13.1)$$

Maximum likelihood estimates of the three parameters are obtained by minimizing the above negative loglikelihood (13.1). This can be done in several different ways. If the shape parameter γ is expected to be close to zero; that is, if the underlying distribution is close to Gumbel, then it would be wise to fit initially the Gumbel model which has only two parameters. This procedure provides initial estimates for fitting the full three-parameter GEV model. In the Gumbel case, the negative log likelihood function reduces to

$$-l(\mu,\theta) = n\ln\theta + \sum_{i=1}^{n}\frac{x_i - \mu}{\theta} + \sum_{i=1}^{n}\exp\left(-\frac{x_i - \mu}{\theta}\right). \qquad (13.2)$$

The loglikelihood (13.2) should be easily minimized by any standard optimization routine. Alternatively, we can obtain the estimates by differentiating (13.2), setting those derivatives to zero, and solving the resulting likelihood equations

$$\sum_{i=1}^{n}\exp\left(-\frac{x_i - \widehat{\mu}}{\widehat{\theta}}\right) = n,$$

$$\sum_{i=1}^{n}(x_i - \widehat{\mu})\left[1 - \exp\left(-\frac{x_i - \widehat{\mu}}{\widehat{\theta}}\right)\right] = n\widehat{\theta}.$$

which can be rewritten as

$$\widehat{\mu} = -\widehat{\theta}\ln\left[\frac{1}{n}\sum_{i=1}^{n}\exp\left(-\frac{x_i}{\widehat{\theta}}\right)\right], \qquad (13.3)$$

$$\widehat{\theta} = \sum_{i=1}^{n}\frac{x_i}{n} - \frac{\sum_{i=1}^{n} x_i\exp\left(-\frac{x_i}{\widehat{\theta}}\right)}{\sum_{i=1}^{n}\exp\left(-\frac{x_i}{\widehat{\theta}}\right)}. \qquad (13.4)$$

Because equation (13.4) does not involve $\widehat{\mu}$, it can be solved iteratively by starting with an initial guess of $\widehat{\theta}$ on the right-hand side. The result is then substituted into equation 13.3 to obtain $\widehat{\mu}$. The resulting parameter

FITTING EXTREME VALUE MODELS

estimates $\widehat{\mu}$ and $\widehat{\theta}$ (along with $\gamma = 0$) for this special case of the Gumbel distribution are useful starting values for minimizing the negative loglikelihood (13.1) numerically.

The hypothesis that $\gamma = 0$ can be formally tested using the likelihood ratio test. In order to justify adding the parameter γ, the difference between optimized values of (13.1) and (13.2) should be sufficiently large. Twice the difference follows a chi-square distribution with one degree of freedom. For example, at the 5% significance level, the chi-square distribution with one degree of freedom has a critical value of 3.84. In this case, we would expect the difference between the maximized loglikelihood functions to be at least 1.92 in order to include a nonzero value of γ in the model.

The precision of maximum likelihood estimators can be obtained approximately from asymptotic results. Theorem 10.13 shows that, if the regularity conditions are satisfied, the maximum likelihood estimates of the parameters are asymptotically unbiased and normally distributed with a covariance matrix that is the inverse of the Fisher information matrix $\mathbf{I}(\theta)$ whose (r, s)th element is

$$\mathbf{I}(\theta)_{rs} = -\mathrm{E}\left[\frac{\partial^2}{\partial\theta_s\,\partial\theta_r}l(\theta)\right] = \mathrm{E}\left[\frac{\partial}{\partial\theta_r}l(\theta)\frac{\partial}{\partial\theta_s}l(\theta)\right].$$

In the case of a sample of n independent and identically distributed random variables, this reduces to

$$\mathbf{I}(\theta)_{rs} = -n\mathrm{E}\left[\frac{\partial^2}{\partial\theta_s\,\partial\theta_r}\ln f(X;\theta)\right] = n\mathrm{E}\left[\frac{\partial}{\partial\theta_r}\ln f(X;\theta)\frac{\partial}{\partial\theta_s}\ln f(X;\theta)\right].$$

In the case of the generalized extreme value distribution with $\theta = (\mu, \theta, \gamma)$, the elements of the Fisher information matrix have been obtained by Prescott and Walden [95] as

$$\mathbf{I}(\theta)_{11} = \frac{n}{\theta^2}p$$

$$\mathbf{I}(\theta)_{22} = \frac{n}{\theta^2\gamma^2}\left[1 - 2\Gamma(2 + \gamma) + p\right]$$

$$\mathbf{I}(\theta)_{33} = \frac{n}{\gamma^2}\left[\frac{\pi^2}{6} + \left(1 - \xi + \frac{1}{\gamma}\right)^2 - \frac{2q}{\gamma} + \frac{p}{\gamma^2}\right] \qquad (13.5)$$

$$\mathbf{I}(\theta)_{12} = -\frac{n}{\theta^2\gamma}\left[p - \Gamma(2 + \gamma)\right]$$

$$\mathbf{I}(\theta)_{13} = -\frac{n}{\theta\gamma}\left[q - \frac{p}{\gamma}\right]$$

$$\mathbf{I}(\theta)_{23} = \frac{n}{\theta\gamma^2}\left[1 - \xi + \frac{1 - \Gamma(2 + \gamma)}{\gamma} - q + \frac{p}{\gamma}\right]$$

where $\Gamma(\cdot)$ is the gamma function (see Appendix A),

$$p = (1+\gamma)^2 \Gamma(1+2\gamma),$$

$$q = \Gamma(2+\gamma)\left[\Psi(1+\gamma) + \frac{1+\gamma}{\gamma}\right],$$

$$\Psi(x) = \frac{d}{dx}\log\Gamma(x)$$

is the digamma (psi) function, and $\xi = 0.5772157$ is Euler's constant. The digamma function can be evaluated in a number of ways. The simplest is to obtain the gamma function, take its logarithm, and evaluate the derivative numerically using a finite difference approximation to the derivative.

The regularity conditions are only satisfied if $\gamma > -0.5$. Note that this condition ensures that all the gamma functions in the Fisher information matrix have positive arguments. Because we are only interested in the Fréchet distribution (for which $\gamma > 0$) as the alternative to the Gumbel distribution, the regularity conditions are satisfied and the asymptotic results hold.

In the special case of the Gumbel distribution with $\theta = (\mu, \theta)$, the elements of the Fisher information matrix reduce to

$$\mathbf{I}(\theta)_{11} = \frac{n}{\theta^2}$$

$$\mathbf{I}(\theta)_{22} = \frac{n}{\theta^2}\left[\frac{\pi^2}{6} + (1-\xi)^2\right] \tag{13.6}$$

$$\mathbf{I}(\theta)_{12} = -\frac{n}{\theta^2}(1-\xi).$$

13.2.2 ML estimation from the generalized Pareto distribution

We begin by assuming the we have a sample of size n of values of excesses over a threshold d. An example might be daily maximum errors in recording a certain type of transaction. For the purpose of this theory, we treat the observations as being outcomes of independent and identically distributed random variables. We denote the sample by $x_1, x_2, ..., x_n$. (These are denoted as $y_1, y_2, ..., y_n$ in Section 7.9 where they are denoted as conditional excesses, conditional on the underlying random variable exceeding the threshold. In effect, this means that we ignore all observed losses that are less than the threshold, and consider only the exceedences). From Section 7.9, the distribution of excesses for large samples is given by one of the three distributions that are the special cases of the generalized Pareto distribution. The standardized df of the generalized extreme value distribution is written as

$$W_\gamma(x) = 1 - (1+\gamma x)^{-1/\gamma}.$$

When γ is positive, the df $W_\gamma(x)$ has the form of a standardized Pareto distribution. When γ is negative, the df $W_\gamma(x)$ has the form of a beta distribution. When $\gamma = 0$, the df is the standardized exponential distribution function

$$W_0(x) = 1 - \exp(-x).$$

Inserting location and scale parameters results in the generalized Pareto distribution function,

$$F(x) = W_{\gamma,\mu,\theta}(x) = 1 - \left(1 + \gamma \frac{x - \mu}{\theta}\right)^{-1/\gamma}.$$

When $\gamma = 0$ and $\mu = 0$, we have the exponential distribution

$$F(x) = W_{0,\theta}(x) = 1 - \exp\left(-\frac{x}{\theta}\right), \quad x > 0.$$

When $\gamma > 0$, and $\mu = -\theta$, we have, after writing α for $1/\gamma$, the Pareto distribution

$$F(x) = W_{1,\alpha,\theta}(x) = 1 - \left(1 + \frac{x}{\theta}\right)^{-\alpha}, \quad x > 0.$$

The contribution of an observation x_i from the generalized Pareto distribution to the log likelihood is

$$\ln f(x_i) = \ln w_{\gamma,\mu,\theta}(x_i) = -\ln\theta - \left(\left(1 + \frac{1}{\gamma}\right)\ln\left(1 + \gamma\frac{x_i - \mu}{\theta}\right),$$

which can be written as

$$\ln f(x_i) = \ln w_{\gamma,\mu,\theta}(x_i) = -\ln\theta - (1+\gamma)y_i$$

where

$$y_i = \frac{1}{\gamma}\ln\left(1 + \gamma\frac{x_i - \mu}{\theta}\right).$$

For a set of n observations, the negative log likelihood function is then

$$-l(\gamma, \mu, \theta) = n\ln\theta + (1+\gamma)\sum_{i=1}^{n} y_i. \tag{13.7}$$

When $\gamma = 0$ and $\mu = 0$, the model is the exponential distribution $W_{0,\theta}(x)$ and equation (13.7) reduces to

$$-l(\theta) = n\ln\theta + \frac{1}{\theta}\sum_{i=1}^{n} x_i, \tag{13.8}$$

resulting in the maximum likelihood estimate $\hat{\theta} = \bar{x}$, the sample mean.

Maximum likelihood estimates of the two parameters θ and γ (μ is normally fixed in advance) of the generalized Pareto distribution are obtained by minimizing the negative loglikelihood (13.7) with respect to θ and γ. This can be done in several different ways. If the shape parameter γ is expected to be close to zero; that is, if the underlying distribution is close to exponential, then the sample mean can serve as a useful initial estimate of θ. In the Pareto case starting at zero (with $\mu = -\theta$ and writing α for $1/\gamma$) , the negative loglikelihood function (13.7) is reduced to

$$-l(\alpha, \theta) = n \ln \theta + (1 + \alpha) \sum_{i=1}^{n} \ln \left(1 + \frac{x_i}{\theta} \right). \qquad (13.9)$$

The negative loglikelihood (13.9) is easily minimized numerically.

The hypothesis that $\gamma = 0$ can be formally tested using the likelihood ratio test. In order to justify choosing the generalized Pareto over the exponential, the difference between optimized values of the negative loglikelihoods (13.8) and (13.9) should be sufficiently large. Twice the difference follows a chi-square distribution with one degree of freedom. For example, at the 5% significance level, the chi-square distribution with one degree of freedom has a critical value of 3.84. In this case, we would expect the difference between the maximized loglikelihood functions to be at lease 1.92 in order to include a non-zero value of γ in the model.

The precision of maximum likelihood estimators can be obtained approximately from asymptotic results. For the Pareto distribution with $\theta = (\alpha, \theta)$, the elements of the Fisher information matrix are

$$\mathbf{I}(\theta)_{11} = \frac{n}{\alpha^2}$$

$$\mathbf{I}(\theta)_{22} = \frac{n\alpha}{\theta^2(\alpha + 2)} \qquad (13.10)$$

$$\mathbf{I}(\theta)_{12} = \mathbf{I}(\theta)_{21} = -\frac{n}{\theta(\alpha + 1)}$$

yielding an asymptotic covariance matrix

$$\frac{\alpha + 1}{n\alpha} \left(\begin{array}{cc} \alpha^3(\alpha + 1) & \alpha^2(\alpha + 2)\theta \\ \alpha^2(\alpha + 2)\theta & (\alpha + 1)(\alpha + 2)\theta^2 \end{array} \right). \qquad (13.11)$$

When $\gamma = 0$, the GPD reduces to the exponential distribution with asymptotic variance θ^2/n.

13.2.3 Estimating the Pareto shape parameter

One of the major issues in using extreme value methods is determining when such methods are appropriate. Because extreme value theory focuses only on the very large (or very small) outcomes, it is only necessary to consider the tail of the distribution that generates those extreme outcomes.

We consider any distribution with a tail that behaves like a Pareto distribution. From formula (7.16), the Pareto distribution is tail-equivalent to

$\left(\frac{x}{\theta}\right)^{-\alpha}$. To develop an estimator for α, we assume initially that we have some threshold d above which the tail is Pareto-equivalent. Consider a sample of n of independent and identically distributed random variables $X_1, X_2, ..., X_n$ coming from the distribution

$$\overline{F}_X(x) = \left(\frac{x}{d}\right)^{-\alpha}, \quad x > d.$$

It is easy to show that the maximum likelihood estimator of α from this distribution is of the form

$$\widehat{\alpha} = \left(\frac{1}{n} \sum_{i=1}^{n} \ln \frac{X_i}{d}\right)^{-1}.$$

We now allow the sample size to be random rather than fixed. The number of observations in excess of the threshold d is represented by the random variable N_d. The estimator, conditional on N_d, becomes

$$\widehat{\alpha} = \left(\frac{1}{N_d} \sum_{i=1}^{N_d} \ln \frac{X_i}{d}\right)^{-1}.$$

The Hill estimator [51] of α is based on the above ideas. We now complete the development of the Hill estimator. Consider a continuous distribution with a Pareto equivalent tail and with a unspecified form below the threshold:

$$F_X(x) = \text{unspecified}, \quad 0 < x \leq d$$

$$= 1 - p\left(\frac{x}{d}\right)^{-\alpha}, \quad x > d.$$

Note that p represents the expected proportion of observations in excess of d.

Suppose that the sample drawn from this distribution is of size n, and that the actual observations consist of the number of values in excess of d, the number of exceedences N_d, and the individual values of the N_d largest individual observations . The N_d largest observations are the values in excess of d. They can be relabeled $Y_1, Y_2, ..., Y_{N_d}$. Conditional on N_d, these values constitute an iid sample from a distribution of the form

$$\overline{F}_Y(y) = p\left(\frac{y}{d}\right)^{-\alpha}, \quad y > d.$$

The joint pdf of $(N_d, Y_1, Y_2, ..., Y_m)$ can then be written as the product of the pdf of N_d and the conditional pdf of $(Y_1, Y_2, ..., Y_m \mid N_d)$. The number of observations N_d in excess of d has a binomial distribution with parameters (n, p) and is independent of the parameter α . Thus the maximum likelihood estimator can be obtained by considering only the distribution of the Y_is and treating N_d as a fixed quantity. Consequently, the MLE of α is

$$\widehat{\alpha} = \left(\frac{1}{N_d} \sum_{i=1}^{N_d} \ln \frac{Y_i}{d}\right)^{-1}.$$

Because the N_d observations are the largest values of the sample of n observations drawn from the distribution $F_X(x)$, we label them from largest to smallest as the order statistics $X_{1,n} \geq X_{2,n}...X_{N_d,n}$. Thus, the above estimator can be rewritten as

$$\hat{\alpha} = \left(\frac{1}{N_d} \sum_{i=1}^{N_d} \ln \frac{X_{i,n}}{d} \right)^{-1}.$$

In practice the point at which the tail is Pareto-equivalent is not known in advance. The idea of the Hill estimator is to consider the above estimate to be a function of the number N_d and to use the high-order statistics as thresholds replacing d. The Hill estimator the above estimator based on the kth largest observations using the $(k+1)$st largest observation as the threshold

$$\hat{\alpha}(k) = \left(\frac{1}{k} \sum_{i=1}^{k} \ln \frac{X_{i,n}}{X_{k+1,n}} \right)^{-1}.$$

When considered as a function of k, the Hill estimator gives a profile of the shape parameter for all possible values of k. The Hill estimate is a consistent estimator when $n \to \infty$ and $k/n \to 0$ (see [80]).

In practice there is no precise way of choosing k. Most authors recommend choosing a value of k in a region where the Hill estimator is flat so that small changes in the choice of the threshold do not materially affect the result.

13.2.4   Estimating extreme probabilities

Fitting generalized Pareto distributions to excesses tells us about the shape of the tail of the distribution of losses but does not give us the probabilities because we have not used the information about losses below the threshold. We can obtain the extreme probabilities without imposing any model restrictions on the portion of the distribution below the selected threshold d. The tail of the unconditional distribution of X can be written as

$$\overline{F}_X(x) = \overline{F}_X(d)\overline{F}_Y^*(y), \quad x > d, \ y > 0$$

where Y is the conditional random variable $X - d \mid X > d$, $y = x - d$ and $\overline{F}_Y^*(y)$ is the tail of the distribution of Y which is given by

$$\overline{F}_Y^*(y) = \left(1 + \gamma \frac{y}{\theta + \gamma d} \right)^{-1/\gamma}, \quad y > 0.$$

We are interested in obtaining the estimate $\widehat{\overline{F}_X(x)}$ for large values of x. If we have obtained estimates of the parameters of the generalized Pareto distribution of the tail beyond threshold d using maximum likelihood or some other procedure, we have can obtain an estimate

$$\widehat{\overline{F_Y^*}(y)} = \left(1 + \hat{\gamma}\frac{y}{\hat{\theta} + \hat{\gamma}d}\right)^{-1/\hat{\gamma}}.$$

A simple nonparametric estimate of $\overline{F_X}(d)$ is the proportion of observed values in excess of d. This can be written as

$$\widehat{\overline{F_X}(d)} = \frac{\sum_{j=1}^{n} I_{\{x_j > d\}}}{n}.$$

The resulting estimate of the extreme tail probability is then

$$\widehat{\overline{F_X}(x)} = \frac{\sum_{j=1}^{n} I_{\{x_j > d\}}}{n}\left(1 + \hat{\gamma}\frac{y}{\hat{\theta} + \hat{\gamma}d}\right)^{-1/\hat{\gamma}}.$$

An advantage of using the nonparametric estimate is that the estimation of the tail is not complicated by estimation errors arising from model fitting to the left of the threshold, an area where we have much less interest in any case.

13.3   MODEL SELECTION

When confronted with real data, we need to decide on when to rely on the theoretical results on tail behavior and which of the possible models of the tail to choose. Graphical plots of the mean excess over various possible thresholds can be used to help answer these questions.

13.3.1   Mean excess plots

All information about a probability distribution is contained in the cumulative distribution function (cdf).   Similarly, the same information is contained in many other functions. These include the probability density function for continuous distributions, the probability function for discrete distributions, the moment generating function if it exists, the Laplace transform if it exists, or the characteristic function. Another interesting function is the mean excess function. A very useful graphical procedure in modeling the right-hand tail is to plot the mean excess against the threshold d. The observed mean excess at threshold d for a sample of size n is

$$\widehat{e(d)} = \frac{\sum_{j=1}^{n}(x_j - d)_+}{\sum_{j=1}^{n} I_{\{x_j > d\}}},$$

which is the total of all excesses divided by the number of excesses. This can be calculated easily using each of the observed values as threshold. The resulting plot should assist in choosing which of the GPD distributions should be selected as a model. From Chapter 7, for large thresholds, the graph should be approximately linearly increasing for the generalized Pareto with a positive shape parameter. If the plot looks rather flat, then the underlying distribution of the conditional tail is more like an exponential distribution. If it is decreasing, then a Weibull with a finite upper limit is the best choice, although we have generally ruled out this possibility in Chapter 7.

It is not advisable to use any numerical estimates (for example, the slope of a fitted mean excess line) of this exercise directly. The mean excess plot can by used to identify at what threshold value the plot becomes approximately linear. This provides guidance on the point at which the generalized Pareto distribution can be relied upon for the remainder of the distribution. Once the threshold is chosen, the estimates of the generalized Pareto distribution can be obtained using the maximum likelihood (or some other) method.

14

Fitting copula models

Mother nature is a b—- .

—Murphy

14.1 INTRODUCTION

Chapter 8 provided a large number of copulas. Each contained one or a small number of parameters. In practice, when one has data on operational losses, the data are usually from the marginal distributions of each risk type or from the corresponding joint multivariate distribution. If data are from each risk separately, there is usually no information about the joint distribution. In this case, the estimation and selection of a model for each of the risk types is done using the univariate methods described in previous chapters. The question of the impact of dependence is still important: *If things go really wrong for one type of risk, are they more likely to go wrong for other risk types? What impact does this have on the tail of the aggregate loss distribution?* These are important questions. In the absence of data on the joint behavior of losses, the risk analyst still has some choices. This chapter is devoted to the study of dependence models. With these tools, the risk analyst can experiment with different models and develop an understanding of the sensitivity of results to the choice of dependence model.

In this chapter, we first assume that multivariate data are available and that we will need to estimate the full multivariate distribution. As in other areas of statistical estimation, we can use parametric, nonparametric, or semi-

parametric methods. We begin by using fully parametric methods in which
we assume some distributions for the marginals and the copula and attempt
to fit the parameters simultaneously. Within the class of parametric methods,
as in earlier chapters dealing with univariate distributions, we prefer to use
maximum likelihood estimation, the advantages of which have been described
in earlier chapters.

14.2   MAXIMUM LIKELIHOOD ESTIMATION

Consider the joint distribution of a d-variate random variable $(X_1, X_2, ..., X_d)$
with continuous marginal distributions with pdfs $f_1(x_1)$, $f_2(x_2)$, ..., $f_d(x_d)$,
respectively, and continuous multivariate joint distribution with pdf $f(x_1,$
$x_2, ..., x_d)$.Using the usual convention of using upper case letters for the corresponding cdfs, we write the joint cdf as

$$F(x_1, ..., x_d) = C(F_1(x_1), ..., F_d(x_d))$$

where $C(u_1, ..., u_d)$ is the copula cdf evaluated at the point $(u_1, ..., u_d)$. By
differentiation, the corresponding pdf is given by

$$f(x_1, ..., x_d) = f_1(x_1) \cdot f_2(x_2) \cdot ... \cdot f_d(x_d) \cdot c(F_1(x_1), ..., F_d(x_d))$$

where $c(u_1, ..., u_d)$ is the copula pdf evaluated at the point $(u_1, ..., u_d)$.

From this it is clear that the estimation of the copula is dependent on the
estimation of the marginal distributions because the arguments of the copula
density are the cdfs of the marginal distributions $f_1(x_1)$, $f_2(x_2)$, ..., $f_d(x_d)$.
The number of parameters to be estimated is the sum of the parameters
in the marginals plus the number of parameters in the copula. This total
number can be quite large if the number of dimensions d is large. Typically
the marginals will have two or three parameters each. Similarly, the copula
can have at least one additional parameter. Thus if $d = 5$, then the number
of parameters is at least 11. With such large numbers of parameters, it is
necessary to have large amounts of data to model to get reasonably accurate
estimates of the parameters. Furthermore, maximization of a function in a
high number of dimensions can be quite challenging numerically. Maximum
likelihood estimates of the copula parameter(s) can be unstable because of
the additional uncertainty introduced by the estimation of the parameters of
the marginal distributions.

The logarithm of the pdf is

$$\ln f(x_1, ..., x_d) = \sum_{i=1}^{d} \ln f_i(x_i) + \ln c(F_1(x_1), ..., F_d(x_d)).$$

Now consider a sample of n iid observations in d dimensions. To index
the n observations, we add a second subscript. Thus $x_{i,j}$ represents the ith

dimension of the jth outcome. Then the loglikelihood function is

$$l = \sum_{j=1}^{n} \ln f(x_{1,j}, ..., x_{d,j})$$

$$= \sum_{j=1}^{n} \sum_{i=1}^{d} \ln f_i(x_{i,j}) + \sum_{j=1}^{n} \ln c(F_1(x_{1,j}), ..., F_d(x_{d,j})) \qquad (14.1)$$

$$= l_w + l_c. \qquad (14.2)$$

The maximum likelihood estimates are the values of the parameters that maximize the loglikelihood function. This form of the loglikelihood suggests obtaining approximate estimates of the parameters by first maximizing the first term (the. "marginals" term) and then maximizing the second term (the. "copula" term). Maximizing the marginals term involves maximizing the d different terms in l_w of the form

$$l_i = \sum_{j=1}^{n} \ln f_i(x_{i,j}), \quad i = 1, 2, ..., d \qquad (14.3)$$

where (14.3) is the loglikelihood function of the ith marginal distribution. Thus, we can first obtain all the parameter estimates for the marginal distributions using the univariate methods described earlier. It should be noted that these are not the ultimate maximum likelihood estimates because the ultimate estimates depend also on the estimates of the copula parameter(s) which have not yet been estimated. We shall refer to the estimates arising from the maximization of (14.3) as. "pseudo-MLEs." The efficiency of these estimates may be low because the information about the parameters contained in the second term of the loglikelihood (14.2) is ignored [110].

There are several approaches to maximizing the second term of loglikelihood (14.2). One way is to use the pseudo-MLEs. Let $\tilde{u}_{i,j} = \tilde{F}_i(x_{i,j})$ denote the pseudo-estimates of the cdf of the marginal distributions at each observed value. Then the pseudo-likelihood of the copula function is

$$\tilde{l}_c = \sum_{j=1}^{n} \ln c(\tilde{u}_{1,j}, ..., \tilde{u}_{dj}). \qquad (14.4)$$

This is then maximized with respect to the copula parameters to obtain the pseudo-MLEs of the copula parameters. This maximization can be done by any method, although we prefer the simplex method because it is very stable, especially with few parameters. We expect that in most cases in applications, where there are not large amounts of data, the principle of parsimony will dictate that very few parameters should be used for the copula. Most typically, this will be only one parameter. The second stage is to maximize the loglikelihood (14.2) overall. This can be done by using all the pseudo-MLEs as starting values for the maximization procedure. This will lead to the true

MLEs of all parameters as long as the necessary regularity conditions are satisfied.

Song et al. [110] suggest another algorithm for obtaining the MLEs. We denote the vector of parameters by θ.Denote the true value of the parameter by θ_0. They suggest first obtaining the pseudo-estimates θ_1 by maximizing l_w as we did above or, by solving the equations

$$\frac{\partial}{\partial\theta}l_w(\theta) = \mathbf{0}.$$

Because the true MLEs satisfy

$$\frac{\partial}{\partial\theta}l_w(\theta) = -\frac{\partial}{\partial\theta}l_c(\theta),$$

they recommend solving

$$\frac{\partial}{\partial\theta}l_w(\theta_k) = -\frac{\partial}{\partial\theta}l_c(\theta_{k-1})$$

for θ_k iteratively for $k = 2, 3, ...$, leading to the MLE $\widehat{\theta} = \theta_\infty$. They show that if the derivatives of the loglikelihoods are well-behaved, this iterative scheme will converge.

14.3   SEMIPARAMETRIC ESTIMATION OF THE COPULA

There are several semiparametric or nonparametric procedures that can be used for estimating the copula parameters directly from the data without reference to the form of the marginal distributions. The first way is to use a nonparametric estimate of the cdf terms $F_i(x_{i,j})$ using an empirical cdf estimator

$$\widetilde{u}_{i,j} = \widetilde{F}_i(x_{i,j}) = \frac{\text{rank}(x_{i,j})}{n+1} = \frac{\sum_{k=1}^{n}I_{\{x_{i,k}\leq x_{i,j}\}}}{n+1}$$

where $\text{rank}(x_{i,j})$ is the rank (from lowest to highest) of the observed values $x_{i,1}, x_{i,2}, ..., x_{i,n}$ from the ith marginal distribution.

The empirical cdf assigns the values $\frac{1}{n+1}, \frac{2}{n+1}, ..., \frac{n}{n+1}$ to the ordered values (from smallest to largest)[1]. The copula pseudo-MLEs are obtained by maximizing the pseudo-likelihood (14.4). This method for estimating the copula parameters does not depend on the values of the parameters of the marginal distributions (only the observed ranks) and the resulting uncertainty introduced by estimation process of the marginals.

---

[1] Using $n+1$ in the denominator provides a continuity correction and keeps the probilities away from 0 and 1.

Another approach to obtaining the copula parameter in the single-parameter case, is to obtain an estimate of the measure of association, Kendall's tau, directly from the data. From formula (8.3) in the bivariate case, Kendall's tau can be written as

$$\tau_K(X_1, X_2) = E\left[\text{sign}(X_1 - X_1^*)(X_2 - X_2^*)\right]$$

where (X_1, X_2) and (X_1^*, X_2^*) are iid random variables. Consider a sample (x_{1j}, x_{2j}), $j = 1, 2, ..., n$. for each dimension, there are $n(n-1)/2$ distinct pairs of points. Thus a natural estimator of Kendall's tau is

$$\widehat{\tau}_K(X_1, X_2) = \frac{2\sum_{j<k}\left[\text{sign}(X_{1j} - X_{1k})(X_{2j} - X_{2k})\right]}{n(n-1)}$$

which is easily calculated. Because there is a one-to-one correspondence between τ_K and the single copula parameter θ, we then can obtain the an estimate $\widehat{\theta}$.

Other techniques, or variations of the above techniques along with their properties have been discussed in detail by numerous authors including Genest and Rivest [46] and Genest, Ghoudri, and Rivest [44].

14.4   THE ROLE OF THRESHOLDS

In earlier chapters, we discussed thresholds below which losses are not recorded. As discussed in Chapter 1, the Basel II framework document suggests using a threshold of 10,000 Euros for operational losses. However, in practice it may be beneficial to use different thresholds for different risk types. For example, for high-frequency losses, recording lower amounts will give a better understanding of aggregate losses of this type. When thresholds are used, losses below this level are completely ignored. In any estimation exercise, if we want to build models incorporating different thresholds or to estimate ground-up losses, it will be necessary to recognize the distribution below the threshold(s). This complicates the likelihood function somewhat. We now consider the impact on the likelihood function of thresholds either when the data are individual observations or when the data are grouped.

Consider two ground-up loss random variable X_1 and X_2 with thresholds d_1 and d_2, respectively. The joint cdf is

$$F(x, y) = C\left(F_1(x_1), F_2(x_2)\right)$$

and the pdf is

$$f(x, y) = f_1(x_1) \cdot f_2(x_2) \cdot c\left(F_1(x_1), F_2(x_2)\right)$$

where $c(u_1, u_2)$ is the copula density function. We denote the derivatives of the copula function as

$$C_1(u_1, u_2) = \frac{\partial}{\partial u_1} C(u_1, u_2),$$

$$C_2(u_1, u_2) = \frac{\partial}{\partial u_2} C(u_1, u_2),$$

$$c(u_1, u_2) = C_{12}(u_1, u_2) = \frac{\partial}{\partial u_1} \frac{\partial}{\partial u_2} C(u_1, u_2).$$

For grouped (interval) data in setting up the likelihood function, we need to consider only the interval into which an observation falls. We denote the lower and upper limits of the interval for X_1 by v_1 and w_1 and for X_2 by v_2 and w_2.

We now consider the four possible cases and express the contribution to the likelihood function by a single bivariate observation expressed in terms of the distributions of X and Y and also expressed in terms of the copula distribution functions and derivatives. Writing down the likelihood contribution is a nontrivial. One needs to be careful about conditioning. If the outcome X_1 falls below its threshold d_1, then the outcome (X_1, X_2) is not observed. Hence observations need to be conditioned on $X_1 > d_1$ and also on $X_2 > d_2$.

Case 1. Individual observation for both X_1 and X_2

If the outcome X falls below its threshold d_1, then the outcome (X_1, X_2) is not observed. Hence observations need to be conditioned on $X_1 > d_1$; also on $X_2 > d_2$

$$\frac{f(x, y)}{1 - F_1(d_1) - F_2(d_2) + F(d_1, d_2)} \qquad (14.5)$$
$$= \frac{f_1(x_1) \cdot f_2(x_2) \cdot c\left(F_1(x_1), F_2(x_2)\right)}{1 - F_1(d_1) - F_2(d_2) + C(F_1(d_1), F_2(d_2))}.$$

Case 2. Individual observation for X_1 and grouped observation for X_2

$$\frac{\frac{\partial}{\partial x_1} F(x_1, w_2) - \frac{\partial}{\partial x_1} F(x_1, v_2)}{1 - F_1(d_1) - F_2(d_2) + F(d_1, d_2)}$$
$$= \frac{f_1(x_1) \cdot \left[C_1\left(F_1(x_1), F_2(w_2)\right) - C_1\left(F_1(x_1), F_2(v_2)\right)\right]}{1 - F_1(d_1) - F_2(d_2) + C(F_1(d_1), F_2(d_2))}. \qquad (14.6)$$

Case 3. Individual observation for X_2 and grouped observation for X_1

$$\frac{\frac{\partial}{\partial x_2} F(w_1, x_2) - \frac{\partial}{\partial x_2} F(v_1, x_2)}{1 - F_1(d_1) - F_2(d_2) + F(d_1, d_2)}$$
$$= \frac{f_2(x_2) \cdot [C_2(F_1(w_1), F_2(x_2)) - C_1(F_1(v_1), F_2(x_2))]}{1 - F_1(d_1) - F_1(d_2) + C(F_1(d_1), F_2(d_2))}. \qquad (14.7)$$

Case 4. Individual observation for X_1 and grouped observation for X_2

$$\frac{F(w_1, w_2) - F(v_1, w_2) - F(w_1, v_2) + F(v_1, v_2)}{1 - F_1(d_1) - F_2(d_2) + F(d_1, d_2)}$$
$$= \frac{\left[\begin{array}{l} C(F_1(w_1), F_2(w_2)) - C(F_1(v_1), F_2(w_2)) \\ -C(F_1(w_1), F_2(v_2)) + C(F_1(v_1), F_2(v_2)) \end{array} \right]}{1 - F_1(d_1) - F_2(d_2) + C(F_1(d_1), F_2(d_2))}. \qquad (14.8)$$

The likelihood function is the product of the contributions of all observations, in this case bivariate observations. The separation into two terms that allow a two-stage process (as in the previous section) to get approximate estimates of the parameters is not possible. In this case, it may be advisable to choose a representative point within each interval for each grouped observation, simplifying the problem considerably. This will lead to approximate estimates using the two-stage process. Then these estimates can be used as initial values for maximizing the likelihood function using the simplex method described in Appendix C.

14.5 GOODNESS-OF-FIT TESTING

Klugman and Parsa [70] address the issue of testing the fit of a bivariate copula. They point out that it is possible to use a standard chi-square test of fit. However, to do so requires that we group data into intervals, in this case rectangles over the unit square. Because the data may be concentrated in certain parts of the square, there are likely to be large areas where there are fewer than five expected observations falling into a rectangle. Following methods used in Chapter 11, it would seem logical to group adjacent intervals into larger areas until a minimum of five observations are expected. In two dimensions there is no obviously logical way of combining intervals. Thus we try a different strategy.

Consider two random variables X_1 and X_2 with cdfs $F_1(x)$ and $F_2(x)$ respectively. The random variables $U_1 = F_1(X_1)$ and $U_2 = F_2(X_2)$ are both uniform $(0,1)$ random variables. (This is key in simulation!) Now introduce the conditional random variables $V_1 = F_{12}(X_1 \mid X_2)$ and $V_2 = F_{21}(X_2 \mid X_1)$. Then the random variables V_1 and U_2 are mutually independent uniform $(0,$

1) random variables. This can be argued as follows. Consider the random variable $V_1 = F_{12}(X_1 \mid X_2 = x)$. Because it is a cdf, it must have a uniform $(0,1)$ distribution. This is true for any value of x. Therefore, the distribution of V_1 does not depend on the value of X_2 or the value of $U_2 = F_2(X_2)$. An identical argument shows that the random variables V_2 and U_1 are mutually independent uniform $(0, 1)$ random variables.

The observed value of distribution function of the conditional random variable X_2 given $X_1 = x_1$ is

$$F_{21}(x_2 \mid X_1 = x_1) = C_1\left(F_{X_1}(x_1),\ F_{X_2}(x_2)\right). \qquad (14.9)$$

The observed value v_2 of the random variable V_2 can be obtained from the observed values of the bivariate random variables (X_1, X_2) from

$$v_2 = \widehat{F}_{21}(x_2 \mid X_1 = x_1) = \widehat{C}_1\left(\widehat{F}_{X_1}(x_1),\ \widehat{F}_{X_2}(x_2)\right).$$

Thus, we can generate a univariate set of data that should look like a sample from a uniform $(0,1)$ distribution if the combination of marginal distributions and the copula fits the data well.

Klugman and Parsa [70] suggest the following procedure for testing the fit based entirely on univariate methods:

　　Step 1. Fit and select the marginal distributions using univariate methods

　　Step 2. Test the conditional distribution of V_1 for uniformity

　　Step 3. Test the conditional distribution of V_2 for uniformity

The tests for uniformity can be done using a formal goodness-of-fit test such as a Kolmogorov-Smirnov test. Alternatively, one can plot the cdf of the empirical distributions, which should be linear (or close to it). This is equivalent to doing a p-p plot for the uniform distribution.

In higher dimensions, the problems become more complicated. However, by following the above procedures for all pairs of random variables, one can be reasonably satisfied about the overall fit of the model (both marginals and copula). This requires a significant effort, but can be automated relatively easily.

14.6 AN EXAMPLE

We illustrate some of the concepts in this chapter using simulated data. The data consist of 100 pairs $\{(x_j, y_j),\ j = 1, 2, ..., 100\}$ that are simulated from the bivariate distribution with a Gumbel ($\theta = 3$) copula and marginal distributions loglogistic ($\theta = 1$, $\tau = 3$) and Weibull ($\theta = 1$, $\tau = 3$). This is a five-parameter model. We first use maximum likelihood to fit the same. "correct" five- parameter distribution but with all parameters treated as unknown. We then attempt to fit an "incorrect" distribution with marginals of the same form but a misspecified copula.

Given the 100 points, the 5-parameter joint distribution is easy to fit directly using maximum likelihood. The loglikelihood function is

$$l = \sum_{j=1}^{100} \ln f(x_{1,j}, x_{2,j})$$

$$= \sum_{j=1}^{100} \sum_{i=1}^{2} \ln f_i(x_{i,j}) + \sum_{j=1}^{100} \ln c(F_1(x_{1,j}), F_2(x_{2,j}))$$

where $f_1(x)$ and $f_2(x)$ are the marginal distributions and $c(x_1, u_2)$ is the copula density function. The first term was maximized with the following results

Distribution	θ	τ
Loglogistic	1.00035	3.27608
Weibull	0.74106	3.22952
Gumbel copula	-	-

These are the maximum likelihood estimates of the marginal distributions. The entire likelihood was then maximized. This resulted in the following estimates of the five parameters.

Distribution	θ	τ
Loglogistic	1.00031	3.25611
Weibull	0.75254	3.08480
Gumbel copula	2.84116	-

Note that the parameter estimates for the marginal distribution changed slightly as a result of simultaneously estimating the copula parameter. The overall negative loglikelihood was 10.06897. To illustrate the impact of estimation errors, we now simulate, using the same random numbers, 100 points from the fitted distribution. The results are illustrated in Figure 14.1, where both sets of simulated data are plotted.

The key observation from Figure 14.1 this plot is that the points from the fitted distribution are quite close to the original points. We repeat this exercise but using the Joe copula as an alternative. The results of the simultaneous maximum likelihood estimation of all five parameters gave the following estimates:

Distribution	θ	τ
Loglogistic	0.98330	3.12334
Weibull	0.74306	2.89547
Joe copula	3.85403	-

The overall negative loglikelihood increased to 15.68361. This is a quite large increase over that using the Gumbel copula. Note also that the estimates of the parameters of the marginal distributions are also changed. To illustrate

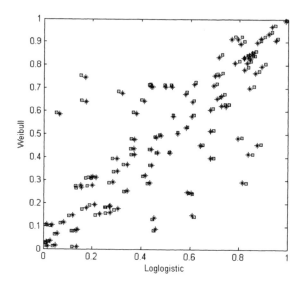

Fig. 14.1 MLE-fitted marginals and Gumbel copula

the impact of misspecification of the copula together with estimation errors, we simulated, using the same random numbers, 100 points from the fitted distribution. The results are illustrated in Figure 14.2, where both sets of simulated data are plotted. Note that the second set of points are further from the original set of simulated points.

For the same data, we also used the semiparametric approach. Rather than use the observed values of the marginal distribution to estimate the copula parameter, we used the ranks of those values. The ranks are independent of the choice of marginal distribution. Using these values, together with the "correct" specification of the copula, we also calculated the value of the negative loglikelihood with these estimates. Of course, the negative loglikelihood will be higher because the MLE method gave the lowest possible value. It is 13.67761 which is somewhat greater than the minimum of 10.06897. The new estimate of the Gumbel copula parameter is 2.69586. The corresponding simulated values are shown in Figure 14.3.

Finally, we also used the nonparametric approach with the misspecified copula function, the Joe copula. The estimate of the Joe copula parameter is 3.31770 with a corresponding likelihood of 21.58245, which is quite a lot greater than the other likelihood values. The corresponding simulated values are plotted in Figure ??.

It is quite interesting to note that a visual assessment of the scatterplots is not very helpful. It is impossible to distinguish the different plot in terms of the fit to the original data. All four plots look good. However, the values

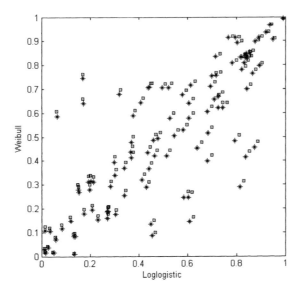

Fig. 14.2 MLE-fitted marinals and Joe copula

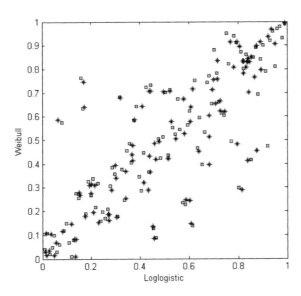

Fig. 14.3 Semiparametric-fitted Gumbel copula

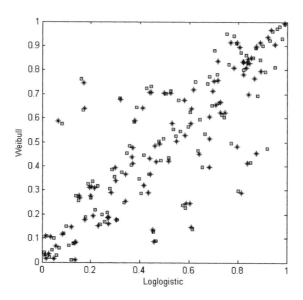

Fig. 14.4   Semiparametric-fitted Joe copula

of the likelihood function for the four cases are quite different. This suggest that it is important to carry out serious technical analysis of the data rather than relying on pure judgement based on observation.□

Appendix A
Gamma and related functions

The incomplete gamma function[1] is given by

$$\Gamma(\alpha; x) = \frac{1}{\Gamma(\alpha)} \int_0^x t^{\alpha-1} e^{-t}\, dt, \quad \alpha > 0,\ x > 0$$

$$\text{with } \Gamma(\alpha) = \int_0^\infty t^{\alpha-1} e^{-t}\, dt, \quad \alpha > 0.$$

Also, define

$$G(\alpha; x) = \int_x^\infty t^{\alpha-1} e^{-t}\, dt, \quad x > 0.$$

At times we will need this integral for nonpositive values of α. Integration by parts produces the relationship

$$G(\alpha; x) = -\frac{x^\alpha e^{-x}}{\alpha} + \frac{1}{\alpha} G(\alpha + 1; x).$$

---

[1] Some references, such as [2], denote this integral $P(\alpha, x)$ and define $\Gamma(\alpha, x) = \int_x^\infty t^{\alpha-1} e^{-t}\, dt$. Note that this definition does not normalize by dividing by $\Gamma(\alpha)$. When using software to evaluate the incomplete gamma function, be sure to note how it is defined.

This can be repeated until the first argument of G is $\alpha + k$, a positive number. Then it can be evaluated from

$$G(\alpha + k; x) = \Gamma(\alpha + k)[1 - \Gamma(\alpha + k; x)].$$

However, if α is a negative integer or zero, the value of $G(0; x)$ is needed. It is

$$G(0; x) = \int_x^\infty t^{-1} e^{-t}\, dt = E_1(x),$$

which is called the **exponential integral**. A series expansion for this integral is

$$E_1(x) = -0.57721566490153 - \ln x - \sum_{n=1}^\infty \frac{(-1)^n x^n}{n(n!)}.$$

When α is a positive integer, the incomplete gamma function can be evaluated exactly as given in Theorem A.1.

Theorem A.1 *For integer α,*

$$\Gamma(\alpha; x) = 1 - \sum_{j=0}^{\alpha-1} \frac{x^j e^{-x}}{j!}.$$

Proof: For $\alpha = 1$, $\Gamma(1; x) = \int_0^x e^{-t}\, dt = 1 - e^{-x}$, and so the theorem is true for this case. The proof is completed by induction. Assume it is true for $\alpha = 1, \ldots, n$. Then

$$\begin{aligned}
\Gamma(n+1; x) &= \frac{1}{n!} \int_0^x t^n e^{-t}\, dt \\
&= \frac{1}{n!} \left(-t^n e^{-t}\big|_0^x + \int_0^x n t^{n-1} e^{-t}\, dt \right) \\
&= \frac{1}{n!} \left(-x^n e^{-x} \right) + \Gamma(n; x) \\
&= -\frac{x^n e^{-x}}{n!} + 1 - \sum_{j=0}^{n-1} \frac{x^j e^{-x}}{j!} \\
&= 1 - \sum_{j=0}^{n} \frac{x^j e^{-x}}{j!}.
\end{aligned}$$

The incomplete beta function is given by

$$\beta(a, b; x) = \frac{\Gamma(a+b)}{\Gamma(a)\Gamma(b)} \int_0^x t^{a-1}(1-t)^{b-1}\, dt, \quad a > 0,\ b > 0,\ 0 < x < 1,$$

and when $b < 0$ (but $a > 1 + \lfloor -b \rfloor$), repeated integration by parts produces

$$\Gamma(a)\Gamma(b)\beta(a,b;x) = -\Gamma(a+b)\left[\frac{x^{a-1}(1-x)^b}{b}\right.$$
$$+\frac{(a-1)x^{a-2}(1-x)^{b+1}}{b(b+1)} + \cdots$$
$$\left.+\frac{(a-1)\cdots(a-r)x^{a-r-1}(1-x)^{b+r}}{b(b+1)\cdots(b+r)}\right]$$
$$+\frac{(a-1)\cdots(a-r-1)}{b(b+1)\cdots(b+r)}\Gamma(a-r-1)$$
$$\times \Gamma(b+r+1)\beta(a-r-1,b+r+1;x),$$

where r is the smallest integer such that $b + r + 1 > 0$. The first argument must be positive, that is $a - r - 1 > 0$.

Numerical approximations for both the incomplete gamma and the incomplete beta function are available in many statistical computing packages as well as in many spreadsheets because they are just the distribution functions of the gamma and beta distributions. The following approximations are taken from reference [2]. The suggestion regarding using different formulas for small and large x when evaluating the incomplete gamma function is from reference [96]. That reference also contains computer subroutines for evaluating these expressions. In particular, it provides an effective way of evaluating continued fractions.

For $x \leq \alpha + 1$, use the series expansion

$$\Gamma(\alpha;x) = \frac{x^\alpha e^{-x}}{\Gamma(\alpha)}\sum_{n=0}^{\infty}\frac{x^n}{\alpha(\alpha+1)\cdots(\alpha+n)},$$

whereas for $x > \alpha + 1$, use the continued-fraction expansion

$$1 - \Gamma(\alpha;x) = \frac{x^\alpha e^{-x}}{\Gamma(\alpha)}\cfrac{1}{x+\cfrac{1-\alpha}{1+\cfrac{1}{x+\cfrac{2-\alpha}{1+\cfrac{2}{x+\cdots}}}}}.$$

The incomplete gamma function can also be used to produce cumulative probabilities from the standard normal distribution. Let $\Phi(z) = \Pr(Z \leq z)$, where Z has the standard normal distribution. Then, for $z \geq 0$, $\Phi(z) = 0.5 + \Gamma(0.5; z^2/2)/2$ while, for $z < 0$, $\Phi(z) = 1 - \Phi(-z)$.

The incomplete beta function can be evaluated by the series expansion

$$\beta(a, b; x) = \frac{\Gamma(a + b)x^a(1 - x)^b}{a\Gamma(a)\Gamma(b)}$$
$$\times \left[1 + \sum_{n=0}^{\infty} \frac{(a + b)(a + b + 1) \cdots (a + b + n)}{(a + 1)(a + 2) \cdots (a + n + 1)} x^{n+1} \right].$$

The gamma function itself can be found from

$$\ln \Gamma(\alpha) \doteq (\alpha - \tfrac{1}{2}) \ln \alpha - \alpha + \frac{\ln(2\pi)}{2}$$
$$+ \frac{1}{12\alpha} - \frac{1}{360\alpha^3} + \frac{1}{1,260\alpha^5} - \frac{1}{1,680\alpha^7} + \frac{1}{1,188\alpha^9} - \frac{691}{360,360\alpha^{11}}$$
$$+ \frac{1}{156\alpha^{13}} - \frac{3,617}{122,400\alpha^{15}} + \frac{43,867}{244,188\alpha^{17}} - \frac{174,611}{125,400\alpha^{19}}.$$

For values of α above 10, the error is less than 10^{-19}. For values below 10, use the relationship

$$\ln \Gamma(\alpha) = \ln \Gamma(\alpha + 1) - \ln \alpha.$$

Appendix B
Discretization of the severity distribution

There are two relatively simple ways to discretize the severity distribution. One is the method of rounding, and the other is a mean-preserving method.

B.1 THE METHOD OF ROUNDING

This method has two features: All probabilities are positive, and the probabilities add to 1. Let h be the span and let Y be the discretized version of X. If there are no modifications, then

$$f_j = \Pr(Y = jh) = \Pr\left[\left(j - \tfrac{1}{2}\right)h \le X < \left(j + \tfrac{1}{2}\right)h\right]$$
$$= F_X\left[\left(j + \tfrac{1}{2}\right)h\right] - F_X\left[\left(j - \tfrac{1}{2}\right)h\right].$$

The recursive formula is then used with $f_X(j) = f_j$. Suppose a threshold of d and a limit of u are to be applied. If the modifications are to be applied before the discretization, then

$$g_0 = \frac{F_X(d + h/2) - F_X(d)}{1 - F_X(d)},$$

$$g_j = \frac{F_X[d + (j + 1/2)h] - F_X[d + (j - 1/2)h]}{1 - F_X(d)},$$

$$j = 1, \ldots, \frac{u - d}{h} - 1,$$

$$g_{(u-d)/h} = \frac{1 - F_X(u - h/2)}{1 - F_X(d)},$$

where $g_j = \Pr(Z = j\alpha h)$ and Z is the modified distribution. This method does not require that the limits be multiples of h but does require that $u - d$ be a multiple of h. Finally, if there is truncation from above at u, change all denominators to $F_X(u) - F_X(d)$ and also change the numerator of $g_{(u-d)/h}$ to $F_X(u) - F_X(u - h/2)$.

B.2 MEAN PRESERVING

This method ensures that the discretized distribution has the same mean as the original severity distribution. With no modifications the discretization is

$$f_0 = 1 - \frac{\mathrm{E}[X \wedge h]}{h},$$

$$f_j = \frac{2\mathrm{E}[X \wedge jh] - \mathrm{E}[X \wedge (j - 1)h] - \mathrm{E}[X \wedge (j + 1)h]}{h}, \quad j = 1, 2, \ldots.$$

For the modified distribution,

$$g_0 = 1 - \frac{\mathrm{E}[X \wedge d + h] - \mathrm{E}[X \wedge d]}{h[1 - F_X(d)]},$$

$$g_j = \frac{2\mathrm{E}[X \wedge d + jh] - \mathrm{E}[X \wedge d + (j - 1)h] - \mathrm{E}[X \wedge d + (j + 1)h]}{h[1 - F_X(d)]},$$

$$j = 1, \ldots, \frac{u - d}{h} - 1,$$

$$g_{(u-d)/h} = \frac{\mathrm{E}[X \wedge u] - \mathrm{E}[X \wedge u - h]}{h[1 - F_X(d)]}.$$

To incorporate truncation from above, change the denominators to

$$h[F_X(u) - F_X(d)]$$

and subtract $h[1 - F_X(u)]$ from the numerators of each of g_0 and $g_{(u-d)/h}$.

B.3 UNDISCRETIZATION OF A DISCRETIZED DISTRIBUTION

Assume we have $g_0 = \Pr(S = 0)$, the true probability that the random variable is zero. Let $p_j = \Pr(S^* = jh)$, where S^* is a discretized distribution and h is the span. The following are approximations for the cdf and LEV of S, the true distribution that was discretized as S^*. They are all based on the assumption that S has a uniform distribution over the interval from $(j-\frac{1}{2})h$ to $(j+\frac{1}{2})h$ for integral j. The first interval is from 0 to $h/2$, and the probability $p_0 - g_0$ is assumed to be uniformly distributed over it. Let S^{**} be the random variable with this approximate mixed distribution. (It is continuous, except for discrete probability g_0 at zero.) The approximate distribution function can be found by interpolation as follows. First, let

$$F_j = F_{S^{**}}\left[\left(j + \tfrac{1}{2}\right) h\right] = \sum_{i=0}^{j} p_i, \quad j = 0, 1, \ldots.$$

Then, for x in the interval $(j - \frac{1}{2})h$ to $(j + \frac{1}{2})h$,

$$F_{S^{**}}(x) = F_{j-1} + \int_{(j-1/2)h}^{x} h^{-1} p_j \, dt = F_{j-1} + \left[x - \left(j - \tfrac{1}{2}\right) h\right] h^{-1} p_j$$

$$= F_{j-1} + \left[x - \left(j - \tfrac{1}{2}\right) h\right] h^{-1}(F_j - F_{j-1})$$

$$= (1 - w)F_{j-1} + wF_j, \quad w = \frac{x}{h} - j + \tfrac{1}{2}.$$

Because the first interval is only half as wide, the formula for $0 \le x \le h/2$ is

$$F_{S^{**}}(x) = (1 - w)g_0 + wp_0, \quad w = \frac{2x}{h}.$$

It is also possible to express these formulas in terms of the discrete probabilities:

$$F_{S^{**}}(x) = \begin{cases} g_0 + \dfrac{2x}{h}[p_0 - g_0], & 0 < x \le \dfrac{h}{2}, \\ \displaystyle\sum_{i=0}^{j-1} p_i + \dfrac{x - (j - 1/2)h}{h} p_j, & (j - \tfrac{1}{2})h < x \le (j + \tfrac{1}{2})h. \end{cases}$$

With regard to the limited expected value, expressions for the first and kth LEVs are

$$E(S^{**} \wedge x) = \begin{cases} x(1 - g_0) - \dfrac{x^2}{h}(p_0 - g_0), & 0 < x \le \dfrac{h}{2}, \\ \dfrac{h}{4}(p_0 - g_0) + \displaystyle\sum_{i=1}^{j-1} ihp_i + \dfrac{x^2 - [(j - 1/2)h]^2}{2h} p_j & \\ \quad + x[1 - F_{S^{**}}(x)], & (j - \tfrac{1}{2})h < x \le (j + \tfrac{1}{2})h, \end{cases}$$

and, for $0 < x \le \dfrac{h}{2}$,

$$E[(S^{**} \wedge x)^k] = \frac{2x^{k+1}}{h(k+1)}(p_0 - g_0) + x^k[1 - F_{S^{**}}(x)],$$

while for $(j - \frac{1}{2})h < x \le (j + \frac{1}{2})h$,

$$E[(S^{**} \wedge x)^k] = \frac{(h/2)^k(p_0 - g_0)}{k+1} + \sum_{i=1}^{j-1} \frac{h^k[(i+\frac{1}{2})^{k+1} - (i-\frac{1}{2})^{k+1}]}{k+1} p_i$$
$$+ \frac{x^{k+1} - [(j-\frac{1}{2})h]^{k+1}}{h(k+1)} p_j + x^k[1 - F_{S^{**}}(x)].$$

Appendix C
Nelder-Mead simplex method

The Nelder-Mead simplex method (which is not related to the simplex method from operations research) was introduced for use with maximum likelihood estimation by Nelder and Mead in 1965 [84]. An excellent reference (and the source of the particular version presented here) is *Sequential Simplex Optimization* by Walters, Parker, Morgan, and Deming [121].

Let $\mathbf{x}$ be a $k \times 1$ vector and $f(\mathbf{x})$ be the function in question. The iterative step begins with $k+1$ vectors, $\mathbf{x}_1, \ldots, \mathbf{x}_{k+1}$, and the corresponding functional values, $f_1, \ldots, f_{k+1}$. At any iteration the points will be ordered so that $f_2 < \cdots < f_{k+1}$. When starting, also arrange for $f_1 < f_2$. Three of the points have names: $\mathbf{x}_1$ is called *worstpoint*, $\mathbf{x}_2$ is called *secondworstpoint*, and $\mathbf{x}_{k+1}$ is called *bestpoint*. It should be noted that after the first iteration these names may not perfectly describe the points. Now identify five new points. The first one, $\mathbf{y}_1$, is the center of $\mathbf{x}_2, \ldots, \mathbf{x}_{k+1}$, That is, $\mathbf{y}_1 = \sum_{j=2}^{k+1} \mathbf{x}_j / k$ and is called *midpoint*. The other four points are found as follows:

$$
\begin{aligned}
\mathbf{y}_2 &= 2\mathbf{y}_1 - \mathbf{x}_1, && \textit{refpoint}, \\
\mathbf{y}_3 &= 2\mathbf{y}_2 - \mathbf{x}_1, && \textit{doublepoint}, \\
\mathbf{y}_4 &= (\mathbf{y}_1 + \mathbf{y}_2)/2, && \textit{halfpoint}, \\
\mathbf{y}_5 &= (\mathbf{y}_1 + \mathbf{x}_1)/2, && \textit{centerpoint}.
\end{aligned}
$$

Then let $g_2, \ldots, g_5$ be the corresponding functional values, that is, $g_j = f(\mathbf{y}_j)$ (the value at $\mathbf{y}_1$ is never used). The key is to replace *worstpoint* $(\mathbf{x}_1)$ with one of these points. The decision process proceeds as follows:

1. If $f_2 < g_2 < f_{k+1}$, then replace it with *refpoint*.

2. If $g_2 \geq f_{k+1}$ and $g_3 > f_{k+1}$, then replace it with *doublepoint*.

3. If $g_2 \geq f_{k+1}$ and $g_3 \leq f_{k+1}$, then replace it with *refpoint*.

4. If $f_1 < g_2 \leq f_2$, then replace it with *halfpoint*.

5. If $g_2 \leq f_1$, then replace it with *centerpoint*.

After the replacement has been made, the old *secondworstpoint* becomes the new *worstpoint*. The remaining k points are then ordered. The one with the smallest functional value becomes the new *secondworstpoint*, and the one with the largest functional value becomes the new *bestpoint*. In practice, there is no need to compute $\mathbf{y}_3$ and g_3 until you have reached step 2. Also note that at most one of the pairs $(\mathbf{y}_4, g_4)$ and $(\mathbf{y}_5, g_5)$ needs to be obtained, depending on which (if any) of the conditions in steps 4 and 5 hold.

Iterations continue until the set of $k+1$ points becomes tightly packed. There are a variety of ways to measure that criterion. One example would be to calculate the standard deviations of each of the components and then average those values. Iterations can stop when a small enough value is obtained. Another option is to keep iterating until all $k+1$ vectors agree to a specified number of significant digits.

References

1. Abate, J., Choudhury, G., and Whitt, W. (2000) "An introduction to numerical transform inversion and its application to probability models," in W. Grassman, ed., *Computational Probability*, Boston: Kluwer.

2. Abramowitz, M. and Stegun, I. (1964) *Handbook of Mathematical Functions with Formulas, Graphs, and Mathematical Tables*, New York: Wiley.

3. Acerbi, C. and Tasche, D. (2002) "On the coherence of expected shortfall," *Journal of Banking and Finance*, **26**, 1487–1503.

4. Ali, M., Mikhail, N., and Haq, S. (1978) "A class of bivariate distributions including the bivariate logistics," *Journal of Multivariate Analysis*, **8**, 405-412.

5. Arnold, B. (1983) *Pareto Distributions (Statistical Distributions in Scientific Work)*, Vol. 5, Fairland, MD: International Co-operative Publishing House.

6. Artzner, P., Delbaen, F., Eber, J. and Heath, D. (1997) "Thinking coherently," *RISK*, **10**, 11, 68–71.

7. Balkema, A. and de Haan, L. (1974) "Residual life at great ages," *Annals of Probability*, **2**, 792-804.

8. Baker, C. (1977) *The Numerical Treatment of Integral Equations*, Oxford: Clarendon Press.

9. Basel Committee on Banking Supervision (1998) *Operational Risk Management*, Basel: Bank for International Settlements.

10. Basel Committee on Banking Supervision (1999) *A New Capital Adequacy Framework, Consultative Paper*, Basel: Bank for International Settlements.

11. Basel Committee on Banking Supervision (2001) *Operational Risk*, Basel: Bank for International Settlements.

12. Basel Committee on Banking Supervision (2005) *International Convergence of Capital Measurement and Capital Standards*, Basel: Bank for International Settlements.

13. Beard, R., Pentikainen, T., and Pesonen, E. (1984) *Risk Theory*, 3rd ed., London: Chapman & Hall.

14. Beirlant, J., Teugels, J., and Vynckier, P. (1996) *Practical Analysis of Extreme Values*, Leuven, Belgium: Leuven University Press.

15. Berger, J. (1985) *Bayesian Inference in Statistical Analysis*, 2nd ed., New York: Springer-Verlag.

16. Bertram, J. (1981) "Numerische berechnung von gesamtschadenverteilungen," *Blätter der Deutsche Gesellschaft für Versicherungsmathematik*, B, **15.2**, 175–194.

17. Bevan, J. (1963) "Comprehensive Medical Insurance - Statistical Analysis for Ratemaking," *Proceedings of the Casualty Actuarial Society*, **50**, 111–128.

18. British Bankers Association (1999) *Operational Risk Management Study*, London: BBA.

19. Bühlmann, H. (1970) *Mathematical Methods in Risk Theory*, New York: Springer-Varlag.

20. Capéraà, P., Fourgères, and Genest, C. (2000) "Bivariate distributions with given extreme value attractor," *Journal of Multivariate Analysis*, **72**, 30–49.

21. Carlin, B. and Louis, T. (2000) *Bayes and Empirical Bayes Methods for Data Analysis*, 2nd ed., Boca Raton, FL: CRC Press.

22. Clayton, D. (1978) "A model for association in bivariate life tables and its application in epidemiological studies of familial tendency in chronic disease incidence," *Biometrika*, **65**, 141–151.

23. Cook, R.D. and Johnson, M.E. (1981) "A family of distributions for modeling non-elliptically symmetric multivariate data," *Journal of the Royal Statistical Society*, Series B, **43**, 210–218.

24. Douglas, J. (1980) *Analysis with Standard Contagious Distributions*, Fairland, MD: International Co-operative Publishing House.

25. Dropkin, L. (1959) "Some considerations on automobile rating systems utilizing individual driving records," *Proceedings of the Casualty Actuarial Society*, **46**, 165–176.

26. Efron, B. (1986) "Why Isn't everyone a Bayesian?" *The American Statistician*, **40**, 1–11 (including comments and reply).

27. Embrechts, P., (1983) "A property of the generalized inverse Gaussian distribution with some applications," *Journal of Applied Probability*, **20**, 537–544.

28. Embrechts, P. and Goldie, C., (1982) "On convolution tails," *Stochastic Processes and their Applications*, **13**, 263–278.

29. Embrechts, P., Goldie, C. and Veraverbeke, N., (1979) "Subexponentiality and infinite divisibility," *Zeitschrift fur Wahrscheinlichkeitstheorie und Verwandte Gebiete*, **49**, 335–347.

30. Embrechts, P., Kluppelberg, C. and Mikosch, T. (1997) *Modelling Extremal Events for Insurance and Finance*, Berlin: Springer.

31. Embrechts, P., MacNeil, A. and Straumann, D. (2002) "Correlation and dependency in risk management: Properties and pitfalls," in *Risk Management: Value at Risk and Beyond*, M. Dempster (ed), Cambridge; Cambridge University Press.

32. Embrechts, P., Maejima, M. and Teugels, J. (1985) "Asymptotic behaviour of compound distributions," *ASTIN Bulletin*, **15**, 45–48.

33. Embrechts, P. and Veraverbeke, N. (1982) "Estimates for the probability of ruin with special emphasis on the possibility of large claims," *Insurance: Mathematics and Economics*, **1**, 55-72.

34. Fang, H and Fang, K. (2002) "The meta-elliptical distributions with given marginals," *Journal of Multivariate Analysis*, **82**, 1–16.

35. Feller, W. (1968) *An Introduction to Probability Theory and Its Applications*, Vol. 1, 3rd ed. rev., New York: Wiley.

36. Feller, W. (1971) *An Introduction to Probability Theory and Its Applications*, Vol. 2, 2nd ed., New York: Wiley.

37. , Fisher, R. and Tippett, L. (1928) "Limiting forms of the largest or smallest member of a sample," *Proceedings of the Cambridge Philosophical Society*, **24**, 180–190.

38. Fisz, M. (1963) *Probability Theory and Mathematical Statistics*, New York: Wiley.

39. Frank, M.J. (1979) "On the simultaneous associativity of *f(x)* and *x+y-f(x,y)* ," *Aequationes Mathematicae*, **19**, 194–226.

40. Frees, E., Carriere, J., and Valdez, E. (1996) "Annuity valuation with dependent mortality," *Journal of Risk and Insurance*, **63**, 229–261.

41. Frees, E. and Valdez, E. (1998) "Understanding relationships using copulas," *North American Actuarial Journal*, **2**, 1–25.

42. Galambos, J. (1975) "Order statistics of samples from multivariate distributions," *Journal of the American Statistical Association*, **70**, 674–680.

43. Genest, C. (1987) "Frank's family of bivariate distributions," *Biometrika*, **74**, 549–555.

44. Genest, C., Ghoudri, K. and Rivest, L-P. (1995) "A semi-parametric estimation procedure of dependent parameters in multivariate families of distributions," *Biometrika*, **82**, 543–552.

45. Genest, C. and McKay, J. (1986) "The joy of copulas: Bivariate distributions with uniform marginals," *The American Statistician*, **40**, 280–283.

46. Genest, C. and Rivest, L.-P. (1993) "Statistical inference procedures for bivariate Archimedean copulas," *Journal of the the American Statistical Association*, **88**, 1034–1043.

47. Gerber, H. (1982) "On the Numerical Evaluation of the Distribution of Aggregate Claims and Its Stop-Loss Premiums," *Insurance: Mathematics and Economics*, **1**, 13–18.

48. Gerber, H. and Jones, D. (1976) "Some Practical Considerations in Connection with the Calculation of Stop-Loss Premiums," *Transactions of the Society of Actuaries*, **28**, 215–231.

49. Gumbel, E.J. (1960) "Distributions des valeurs extrêmes en plusiers dimensions," *Publ. Inst. Statist. Univ. Paris*, **9**, 171-173.

50. Hayne, R. (1994), "Extended service contracts," *Proceedings of the Casualty Actuarial Society*, **81**, 243–302.

51. Hill, B. (1975) "A simple general approach to inference about the tail of a distribution," *Annals of Statistics*, **3**, 1163–1174.

52. Hogg, R. and Craig, A. (1978) *Introduction to Mathematical Statistics*, 4th ed., New York: Macmillan.

53. Hogg, R. and Klugman, S. (1984) *Loss Distributions*, New York: Wiley.

54. Holgate, P. (1970) "The modality of some compound Poisson distributions," *Biometrika*, **57**, 666–667.

55. Hossack, I., Pollard, J., and Zehnwirth, B. (1983) *Introductory Statistics with Applications in General Insurance*, Cambridge: Cambridge University Press.

56. Hougaard, P. (2000) *Analysis of Multivariate Survival Data*, New York: Springer-Verlag.

57. Hüsler, J. and Reiss, R.-D. (1989) "Maxima of normal random vectors:between independence and complete dependence," *Statistics and Probability Letters*, **7**, 283–286.

58. Hutchinson, T. and Lai, C. (1990) *Continuous Bivariate Distributions, Emphasizing Applications*, Adelaide: Rumsby.

59. Hyndman, R. and Fan, Y. (1996) "Sample quantiles in statistical packages," *The American Statistician*, **50**, 361–365.

60. International Actuarial Association, *A Global Framework for insurer Solvency Assessment* (2004) Ottawa: IAA

61. Joe, H. (1993) "Parametric families of multivariate distributions with given marginals," *Journal of Multivariate Analysis*, **46**, 262–282.

62. Joe, H. (1997) *Multivariate Models and Dependency Concepts*, London: Chapman and Hall.

63. Johnson, N., Kotz, S., and Balakrishnan, N. (1994) *Continuous Univariate Distributions*, Vol. 1, 2nd ed., New York: Wiley.

64. Johnson, N., Kotz, S., and Balakrishnan, N. (1995) *Continuous Univariate Distributions*, Vol. 2, 2nd ed., New York: Wiley.

65. Johnson, N., Kotz, S., and Kemp, A. (1993) *Univariate Discrete Distributions*, 2nd ed., New York: Wiley.

66. Karlin, S. and Taylor, H. (1981) *A Second Course in Stochastic Processes*, New York: Academic Press.

67. Kleiber, C. and Kotz, S. (2003) *Statistical Size Distributions in Economics and Actuarial Sciences*, New York: Wiley.

68. Klugman, S. (1992) *Bayesian Statistics in Actuarial Science with Emphasis on Credibility*, Boston: Kluwer.

69. Klugman, S., Panjer, H. and Willmot, G. (2004) *Loss Models: From Data to Decisions*, 2nd ed.,New York: Wiley.

70. Klugman, S. and Parsa, A. (1999) "Fitting bivariate distributions with copulas," *Insurance: Mathematics and Economics*, **24**, 139–148.

71. Kotz, S., Balakrishnan, N., and Johnson, N. (2000) *Continuous Multivariate Distributions*, Vol. 1, Models and Applications, New York: Wiley.

72. Lam, J. (2003) *Enterprise Risk Management:From Incentives to Controls*, New York: Wiley.

73. Landsman, Z. and Valdez E. (2003) "Tail conditional expectations for elliptical distributions," *North American Actuarial Journal*, **7**, 4, 55–71.

74. Landsman, Z. and Valdez E. (2005) "Tail conditional expectations for exponential dispersion models," *ASTIN Bulletin*, **35**, 1, 189–209.

75. Lemaire, J. (1995) *Automobile Insurance: Actuarial Models*, 2nd ed., Boston: Kluwer.

76. Lindley, D. (1987), "The probability approach to the treatment of uncertainty in artificial intelligence and expert systems," *Statistical Science*, **2**, 17–24 (also related articles in that issue).

77. Lindskog, F., McNeil, A. and Schmock, U. (2003) "Kendall's tau for elliptical distributions," in *Credit Risk: Measurement, Evaluation and Management*, G. Bol et al. (ed), Heidelberg: Physica.

78. Luong, A. and Doray, L. (1996) "Goodness of fit test statistics for the zeta family," *Insurance: Mathematics and Economics*, **10**, 45–53.

79. Mardia, K. (1970) *Families of Bivariate Distributions*, London: Griffin.

80. Mason, D. (1982), "Law of large numbers for sums of extreme values," *Annals of Probability*, **10**, 756–764.

81. McNeil, A. (1997) "Estimating the tails of loss severity distributions using extreme value theory," *ASTIN Bulletin*, **27**, 117–137.

82. Meyers, G. (1994) "Quantifying the uncertainty in claim severity estimates for an excess layer when using the single parameter Pareto," *Proceedings of the Casualty Actuarial Society*, **81**, 91–122 (including discussion).

83. Moore, D. (1986) "Tests of chi-squared type," in D'Agostino, R. and Stephens, M., eds., *Goodness-of-Fit Techniques*, New York: Dekker, 63–95.

84. Nelder, J. and Mead, U. (1965) "A Simplex method for function minimization," *The Computer Journal*, **7**, 308–313.

85. Nelsen, R., (1999) *An Introduction to Copulas*, New York: Springer.

86. Nelson, W. (1972) "Theory and applications of hazard plotting for censored failure data," *Technometrics*, **14**, 945–965.

87. Overbeck, L. (2000) "Allocation of economic capital in loan portfolios," in *Measuring Risk in Complex Systems*, Franke, J., Haerdle, W. and Stahl, G. (eds) Berlin: Springer.

88. Panjer, H. (1981) "Recursive evaluation of a family of compound distributions," *ASTIN Bulletin*, **12**, 22–26.

89. Panjer, H.H. (2002) "Measurement of risk, solvency requirements and allocation of capital within financial conglomerates," 2002 International Congess of Actuaries, Cancun, Mexico.

90. Panjer, H. and Lutek, B. (1983) "Practical aspects of stop-loss calculations," *Insurance: Mathematics and Economics*, **2**, 159–177.

91. Panjer, H. and Wang, S. (1993) "On the stability of recursive formulas," *ASTIN Bulletin*, **23**, 227–258.

92. Panjer, H. and Willmot, G. (1986) "Computational aspects of recursive evaluation of compound distributions," *Insurance: Mathematics and Economics*, **5**, 113–116.

93. Panjer, H. and Willmot, G. (1992) *Insurance Risk Models*, Chicago: Society of Actuaries.

94. Pickands, J. (1975) "Statistical inference using extreme order statistics," *Annals of Statistics*, **3**, 119–131.

95. Prescott, P. and Walden, A.T. (1980) "Maximum likelihood estimation of the parameters of the generalized extreme-value distribution," *Biometrika*, **67**, 723–724.

96. Press, W., Flannery, B., Teukolsky, S., and Vetterling, W. (1988) *Numerical Recipes in C*, Cambridge: Cambridge University Press.

97. Rao, C. (1965) *Linear Statistical Inference and Its Applications*, New York: Wiley.

98. Reiss, R. and Thomas, M. (1997) *Statistical Analysis of Extreme values*, Basel: Birkhauser.

99. Resnick, S. (1987) *Extreme Values, Regular Variation, and Point processes*, Berlin Springer.

100. Rioux, J. and Klugman S. (2006) "Toward a unified approach to fitting loss models," to appear in *North American Actuarial Journal*.

101. Robertson, J. (1992) "The computation of aggregate loss distributions," *Proceedings of the Casualty Actuarial Society*, **79**, 57–133.

102. Rohatgi, V. (1976) *An Introduction to Probability Theory and Mathematical Statistics*, New York: Wiley.

103. Ross, S. (1996) *Stochastic Processes*, 2nd ed., New York: Wiley.

104. Ross, S. (2003), *Introduction to Probability Models*, 8th ed., San Diego: Academic Press.

105. Scollnik, D. (2002) "Modeling size-of-loss distributions for exact data in WinBUGS," *Journal of Actuarial Practice*, **10**, 193–218.

106. Self, S. and Liang, K. (1987) "Asymptotic properties of maximum likelihood estimators and likelihood ratio tests under nonstandard conditions," *Journal of the American Statistical Association* **82**, 605–610.

107. Schwarz, G. (1978) "Estimating the dimension of a model," *Annals of Statistics*, **6**, 461–464.

108. Simon, L. (1961), "Fitting negative binomial distributions by the method of maximum likelihood," *Proceedings of the Casualty Actuarial Society*, **48**, 45–53.

109. Sklar, A. (1959) "Functions de réparation à n dimensions et leur marges," *Publications de l'Institut de Statistique de l'Université de Paris*, **8**, 229–231.

110. Song, P., Fan, Y. and Kalbfleisch, J. (2005) "Maximization by parts in likelihood inference," *Journal of the American Statistical Association*, **100**, 1145–1158.

111. Stephens, M. (1986), "Tests based on EDF statistics," in D'Agostino, R. and Stephens, M., eds., *Goodness-of-Fit Techniques*, New York: Dekker, 97–193.

112. Sundt, B. and Jewell, W. (1981) "Further results on recursive evaluation of compound distributions," *ASTIN Bulletin*, **12**, 27–39.

113. Tasche, D. (2002) "Expected shortfall and beyond," *Journal of Banking and Finance*, **26**, 1519-1533.

114. Tawn, J. (1988) "Bivariate extreme value theory: Models and estimation," *Biometrika* ,**75**, 397-415.

115. Teugels, J. (1985) "Approximation and estimation of some compound distributions," *Insurance: Mathematics and Economic*, **4**, 143-153.

116. Teugels, J. and Willmot, G. (1987) "Approximations for stop-loss premiums," *Insurance: Mathematics and Economic*, **6**, 195-202.

117. Thyrion, P. (1961) "Contribution a l'etude du bonus pour non sinstre en assurance automobile," *ASTIN Bulletin*, **1**, 142–162.

118. Tröbliger, A. (1961) "Mathematische Untersuchungen zur Beitragsruck-gewahr in der Kraftfahrversicherung," *Blatter der Deutsche Gesellschaft fur Versicherungsmathematik*, **5**, 327–348.

119. Tukey, J. (1962) "The future of data analysis," *Annals of Mathematical Statistics*, **33**, 1–67.

120. Venter, G. (1983) "Transformed beta and gamma distributions and aggregate losses," *Proceedings of the Casualty Actuarial Society*, **70**, 156–193. **20**, 217–243.

121. Walters, F., Parker, L., Morgan, S., and Deming, S. (1991) *Sequential Simplex Optimization*, Boca Raton, FL: CRC.

122. Wang, S. (1996) "Premium calculation by transforming the layer premium density," *ASTIN Bulletin* **26**, 71–92.

123. Wang, S. (1998) "Implementation of PH transforms in ratemaking," *Proceedings of the Casualty Actuarial Society* , **85**, 940–979 .

124. Wang, S. (2002) "A universal framework for pricing financial and insurance risks," *ASTIN Bulletin* **32**, 213–234.

125. Wang, S., Young , V. and Panjer, H. (1997) "Axiomatic characterization of insurance prices," *Insurance: Mathematics and Economics*, **21**, 173–183.

126. Willmot, G. (1989) "Limiting behaviour of some discrete compound distributions," *Insurance: Mathematics and Economics*, **8**, 175–185.

127. Willmot, G. (1990) "Asymptotic behaviour of Poisson mixtures with applications," *Advances in Applied Probability*, **22**, 147–159.

128. Wirch J. (1999) "Raising Value at Risk," *North American Actuarial Journal* **3**, 106–115.

129. Wirch, J., and Hardy, M. (1999) "A synthesis of risk measures for capital adequacy," *Insurance: Mathematics and Economics*, **25**, 337–348.

Index

E

WILEY SERIES IN PROBABILITY AND STATISTICS

ESTABLISHED BY WALTER A. SHEWHART AND SAMUEL S. WILKS

Editors: *David J. Balding, Noel A. C. Cressie, Nicholas I. Fisher,
Iain M. Johnstone, J. B. Kadane, Geert Molenberghs. Louise M. Ryan,
David W. Scott, Adrian F. M. Smith*
Editors Emeriti: *Vic Barnett, J. Stuart Hunter, David G. Kendall,
Jozef L. Teugels*

The *Wiley Series in Probability and Statistics* is well established and authoritative. It covers many topics of current research interest in both pure and applied statistics and probability theory. Written by leading statisticians and institutions, the titles span both state-of-the-art developments in the field and classical methods.

Reflecting the wide range of current research in statistics, the series encompasses applied, methodological and theoretical statistics, ranging from applications and new techniques made possible by advances in computerized practice to rigorous treatment of theoretical approaches.

This series provides essential and invaluable reading for all statisticians, whether in academia, industry, government, or research.

*Now available in a lower priced paperback edition in the Wiley Classics Library.
†Now available in a lower priced paperback edition in the Wiley–Interscience Paperback Series.

BECHHOFER, SANTNER, and GOLDSMAN · Design and Analysis of Experiments for
Statistical Selection, Screening, and Multiple Comparisons

BELSLEY · Conditioning Diagnostics: Collinearity and Weak Data in Regression

† BELSLEY, KUH, and WELSCH · Regression Diagnostics: Identifying Influential
Data and Sources of Collinearity

BENDAT and PIERSOL · Random Data: Analysis and Measurement Procedures,
Third Edition

BERRY, CHALONER, and GEWEKE · Bayesian Analysis in Statistics and
Econometrics: Essays in Honor of Arnold Zellner

BERNARDO and SMITH · Bayesian Theory

BHAT and MILLER · Elements of Applied Stochastic Processes, *Third Edition*

BHATTACHARYA and WAYMIRE · Stochastic Processes with Applications

† BIEMER, GROVES, LYBERG, MATHIOWETZ, and SUDMAN · Measurement Errors
in Surveys

BILLINGSLEY · Convergence of Probability Measures, *Second Edition*

BILLINGSLEY · Probability and Measure, *Third Edition*

BIRKES and DODGE · Alternative Methods of Regression

BLISCHKE AND MURTHY (editors) · Case Studies in Reliability and Maintenance

BLISCHKE AND MURTHY · Reliability: Modeling, Prediction, and Optimization

BLOOMFIELD · Fourier Analysis of Time Series: An Introduction, *Second Edition*

BOLLEN · Structural Equations with Latent Variables

BOLLEN and CURRAN · Latent Curve Models: A Structural Equation Perspective

BOROVKOV · Ergodicity and Stability of Stochastic Processes

BOULEAU · Numerical Methods for Stochastic Processes

BOX · Bayesian Inference in Statistical Analysis

BOX · R. A. Fisher, the Life of a Scientist

BOX and DRAPER · Empirical Model-Building and Response Surfaces

* BOX and DRAPER · Evolutionary Operation: A Statistical Method for Process
Improvement

BOX and FRIENDS · Improving Almost Anything, *Revised Edition*

BOX, HUNTER, and HUNTER · Statistics for Experimenters: Design, Innovation,
and Discovery, *Second Editon*

BOX and LUCEÑO · Statistical Control by Monitoring and Feedback Adjustment

BRANDIMARTE · Numerical Methods in Finance: A MATLAB-Based Introduction

BROWN and HOLLANDER · Statistics: A Biomedical Introduction

BRUNNER, DOMHOF, and LANGER · Nonparametric Analysis of Longitudinal Data in
Factorial Experiments

BUCKLEW · Large Deviation Techniques in Decision, Simulation, and Estimation

CAIROLI and DALANG · Sequential Stochastic Optimization

CASTILLO, HADI, BALAKRISHNAN, and SARABIA · Extreme Value and Related
Models with Applications in Engineering and Science

CHAN · Time Series: Applications to Finance

CHARALAMBIDES · Combinatorial Methods in Discrete Distributions

CHATTERJEE and HADI · Regression Analysis by Example, *Fourth Edition*

CHATTERJEE and HADI · Sensitivity Analysis in Linear Regression

CHERNICK · Bootstrap Methods: A Practitioner's Guide

CHERNICK and FRIIS · Introductory Biostatistics for the Health Sciences

CHILÈS and DELFINER · Geostatistics: Modeling Spatial Uncertainty

CHOW and LIU · Design and Analysis of Clinical Trials: Concepts and Methodologies,
Second Edition

CLARKE and DISNEY · Probability and Random Processes: A First Course with
Applications, *Second Edition*

* COCHRAN and COX · Experimental Designs, *Second Edition*

CONGDON · Applied Bayesian Modelling

*Now available in a lower priced paperback edition in the Wiley Classics Library.
†Now available in a lower priced paperback edition in the Wiley–Interscience Paperback Series.

---

*Now available in a lower priced paperback edition in the Wiley Classics Library.

†Now available in a lower priced paperback edition in the Wiley–Interscience Paperback Series.

FULLER · Introduction to Statistical Time Series, *Second Edition*
FULLER · Measurement Error Models
GALLANT · Nonlinear Statistical Models
GEISSER · Modes of Parametric Statistical Inference
GELMAN and MENG · Applied Bayesian Modeling and Causal Inference from
    Incomplete-Data Perspectives
GEWEKE · Contemporary Bayesian Econometrics and Statistics
GHOSH, MUKHOPADHYAY, and SEN · Sequential Estimation
GIESBRECHT and GUMPERTZ · Planning, Construction, and Statistical Analysis of
    Comparative Experiments
GIFI · Nonlinear Multivariate Analysis
GIVENS and HOETING · Computational Statistics
GLASSERMAN and YAO · Monotone Structure in Discrete-Event Systems
GNANADESIKAN · Methods for Statistical Data Analysis of Multivariate Observations,
    Second Edition
GOLDSTEIN and LEWIS · Assessment: Problems, Development, and Statistical Issues
GREENWOOD and NIKULIN · A Guide to Chi-Squared Testing
GROSS and HARRIS · Fundamentals of Queueing Theory, *Third Edition*
 * HAHN and SHAPIRO · Statistical Models in Engineering
HAHN and MEEKER · Statistical Intervals: A Guide for Practitioners
HALD · A History of Probability and Statistics and their Applications Before 1750
 † HALD · A History of Mathematical Statistics from 1750 to 1930
 † HAMPEL · Robust Statistics: The Approach Based on Influence Functions
HANNAN and DEISTLER · The Statistical Theory of Linear Systems
HEIBERGER · Computation for the Analysis of Designed Experiments
HEDAYAT and SINHA · Design and Inference in Finite Population Sampling
HEDEKER and GIBBONS · Longitudinal Data Analysis
HELLER · MACSYMA for Statisticians
HINKELMANN and KEMPTHORNE · Design and Analysis of Experiments, Volume 1:
    Introduction to Experimental Design
HINKELMANN and KEMPTHORNE · Design and Analysis of Experiments, Volume 2:
    Advanced Experimental Design
HOAGLIN, MOSTELLER, and TUKEY · Exploratory Approach to Analysis
    of Variance
 * HOAGLIN, MOSTELLER, and TUKEY · Exploring Data Tables, Trends and Shapes
 * HOAGLIN, MOSTELLER, and TUKEY · Understanding Robust and Exploratory
    Data Analysis
HOCHBERG and TAMHANE · Multiple Comparison Procedures
HOCKING · Methods and Applications of Linear Models: Regression and the Analysis
    of Variance, *Second Edition*
HOEL · Introduction to Mathematical Statistics, *Fifth Edition*
HOGG and KLUGMAN · Loss Distributions
HOLLANDER and WOLFE · Nonparametric Statistical Methods, *Second Edition*
HOSMER and LEMESHOW · Applied Logistic Regression, *Second Edition*
HOSMER and LEMESHOW · Applied Survival Analysis: Regression Modeling of
    Time to Event Data
 † HUBER · Robust Statistics
HUBERTY · Applied Discriminant Analysis
HUBERTY and OLEJNIK · Applied MANOVA and Discriminant Analysis,
    Second Edition
HUNT and KENNEDY · Financial Derivatives in Theory and Practice, *Revised Edition*
HUSKOVA, BERAN, and DUPAC · Collected Works of Jaroslav Hajek—
    with Commentary

*Now available in a lower priced paperback edition in the Wiley Classics Library.
†Now available in a lower priced paperback edition in the Wiley–Interscience Paperback Series.

HUZURBAZAR · Flowgraph Models for Multistate Time-to-Event Data

IMAN and CONOVER · A Modern Approach to Statistics

† JACKSON · A User's Guide to Principle Components

JOHN · Statistical Methods in Engineering and Quality Assurance

JOHNSON · Multivariate Statistical Simulation

JOHNSON and BALAKRISHNAN · Advances in the Theory and Practice of Statistics: A Volume in Honor of Samuel Kotz

JOHNSON and BHATTACHARYYA · Statistics: Principles and Methods, *Fifth Edition*

JOHNSON and KOTZ · Distributions in Statistics

JOHNSON and KOTZ (editors) · Leading Personalities in Statistical Sciences: From the Seventeenth Century to the Present

JOHNSON, KOTZ, and BALAKRISHNAN · Continuous Univariate Distributions, Volume 1, *Second Edition*

JOHNSON, KOTZ, and BALAKRISHNAN · Continuous Univariate Distributions, Volume 2, *Second Edition*

JOHNSON, KOTZ, and BALAKRISHNAN · Discrete Multivariate Distributions

JOHNSON, KEMP, and KOTZ · Univariate Discrete Distributions, *Third Edition*

JUDGE, GRIFFITHS, HILL, LÜTKEPOHL, and LEE · The Theory and Practice of Econometrics, *Second Edition*

JUREČKOVÁ and SEN · Robust Statistical Procedures: Aymptotics and Interrelations

JUREK and MASON · Operator-Limit Distributions in Probability Theory

KADANE · Bayesian Methods and Ethics in a Clinical Trial Design

KADANE AND SCHUM · A Probabilistic Analysis of the Sacco and Vanzetti Evidence

KALBFLEISCH and PRENTICE · The Statistical Analysis of Failure Time Data, *Second Edition*

KARIYA and KURATA · Generalized Least Squares

KASS and VOS · Geometrical Foundations of Asymptotic Inference

† KAUFMAN and ROUSSEEUW · Finding Groups in Data: An Introduction to Cluster Analysis

KEDEM and FOKIANOS · Regression Models for Time Series Analysis

KENDALL, BARDEN, CARNE, and LE · Shape and Shape Theory

KHURI · Advanced Calculus with Applications in Statistics, *Second Edition*

KHURI, MATHEW, and SINHA · Statistical Tests for Mixed Linear Models

* KISH · Statistical Design for Research

KLEIBER and KOTZ · Statistical Size Distributions in Economics and Actuarial Sciences

KLUGMAN, PANJER, and WILLMOT · Loss Models: From Data to Decisions, *Second Edition*

KLUGMAN, PANJER, and WILLMOT · Solutions Manual to Accompany Loss Models: From Data to Decisions, *Second Edition*

KOTZ, BALAKRISHNAN, and JOHNSON · Continuous Multivariate Distributions, Volume 1, *Second Edition*

KOTZ and JOHNSON (editors) · Encyclopedia of Statistical Sciences: Volumes 1 to 9 with Index

KOTZ and JOHNSON (editors) · Encyclopedia of Statistical Sciences: Supplement Volume

KOTZ, READ, and BANKS (editors) · Encyclopedia of Statistical Sciences: Update Volume 1

KOTZ, READ, and BANKS (editors) · Encyclopedia of Statistical Sciences: Update Volume 2

KOVALENKO, KUZNETZOV, and PEGG · Mathematical Theory of Reliability of Time-Dependent Systems with Practical Applications

LACHIN · Biostatistical Methods: The Assessment of Relative Risks

LAD · Operational Subjective Statistical Methods: A Mathematical, Philosophical, and Historical Introduction

*Now available in a lower priced paperback edition in the Wiley Classics Library.

†Now available in a lower priced paperback edition in the Wiley–Interscience Paperback Series.

LAMPERTI · Probability: A Survey of the Mathematical Theory, *Second Edition*
LANGE, RYAN, BILLARD, BRILLINGER, CONQUEST, and GREENHOUSE ·
  Case Studies in Biometry
LARSON · Introduction to Probability Theory and Statistical Inference, *Third Edition*
LAWLESS · Statistical Models and Methods for Lifetime Data, *Second Edition*
LAWSON · Statistical Methods in Spatial Epidemiology
LE · Applied Categorical Data Analysis
LE · Applied Survival Analysis
LEE and WANG · Statistical Methods for Survival Data Analysis, *Third Edition*
LePAGE and BILLARD · Exploring the Limits of Bootstrap
LEYLAND and GOLDSTEIN (editors) · Multilevel Modelling of Health Statistics
LIAO · Statistical Group Comparison
LINDVALL · Lectures on the Coupling Method
LIN · Introductory Stochastic Analysis for Finance and Insurance
LINHART and ZUCCHINI · Model Selection
LITTLE and RUBIN · Statistical Analysis with Missing Data, *Second Edition*
LLOYD · The Statistical Analysis of Categorical Data
LOWEN and TEICH · Fractal-Based Point Processes
MAGNUS and NEUDECKER · Matrix Differential Calculus with Applications in
  Statistics and Econometrics, *Revised Edition*
MALLER and ZHOU · Survival Analysis with Long Term Survivors
MALLOWS · Design, Data, and Analysis by Some Friends of Cuthbert Daniel
MANN, SCHAFER, and SINGPURWALLA · Methods for Statistical Analysis of
  Reliability and Life Data
MANTON, WOODBURY, and TOLLEY · Statistical Applications Using Fuzzy Sets
MARCHETTE · Random Graphs for Statistical Pattern Recognition
MARDIA and JUPP · Directional Statistics
MASON, GUNST, and HESS · Statistical Design and Analysis of Experiments with
  Applications to Engineering and Science, *Second Edition*
McCULLOCH and SEARLE · Generalized, Linear, and Mixed Models
McFADDEN · Management of Data in Clinical Trials
* McLACHLAN · Discriminant Analysis and Statistical Pattern Recognition
McLACHLAN, DO, and AMBROISE · Analyzing Microarray Gene Expression Data
McLACHLAN and KRISHNAN · The EM Algorithm and Extensions
McLACHLAN and PEEL · Finite Mixture Models
McNEIL · Epidemiological Research Methods
MEEKER and ESCOBAR · Statistical Methods for Reliability Data
MEERSCHAERT and SCHEFFLER · Limit Distributions for Sums of Independent
  Random Vectors: Heavy Tails in Theory and Practice
MICKEY, DUNN, and CLARK · Applied Statistics: Analysis of Variance and
  Regression, *Third Edition*
* MILLER · Survival Analysis, *Second Edition*
MONTGOMERY, PECK, and VINING · Introduction to Linear Regression Analysis,
  Fourth Edition
MORGENTHALER and TUKEY · Configural Polysampling: A Route to Practical
  Robustness
MUIRHEAD · Aspects of Multivariate Statistical Theory
MULLER and STOYAN · Comparison Methods for Stochastic Models and Risks
MURRAY · X-STAT 2.0 Statistical Experimentation, Design Data Analysis, and
  Nonlinear Optimization
MURTHY, XIE, and JIANG · Weibull Models
MYERS and MONTGOMERY · Response Surface Methodology: Process and Product
  Optimization Using Designed Experiments, *Second Edition*

*Now available in a lower priced paperback edition in the Wiley Classics Library.
†Now available in a lower priced paperback edition in the Wiley–Interscience Paperback Series.

MYERS, MONTGOMERY, and VINING · Generalized Linear Models. With Applications in Engineering and the Sciences
† NELSON · Accelerated Testing, Statistical Models, Test Plans, and Data Analyses
† NELSON · Applied Life Data Analysis
NEWMAN · Biostatistical Methods in Epidemiology
OCHI · Applied Probability and Stochastic Processes in Engineering and Physical Sciences
OKABE, BOOTS, SUGIHARA, and CHIU · Spatial Tesselations: Concepts and Applications of Voronoi Diagrams, *Second Edition*
OLIVER and SMITH · Influence Diagrams, Belief Nets and Decision Analysis
PALTA · Quantitative Methods in Population Health: Extensions of Ordinary Regressions
PANJER · Operational Risk: Modeling and Analysis
PANKRATZ · Forecasting with Dynamic Regression Models
PANKRATZ · Forecasting with Univariate Box-Jenkins Models: Concepts and Cases
* PARZEN · Modern Probability Theory and Its Applications
PEÑA, TIAO, and TSAY · A Course in Time Series Analysis
PIANTADOSI · Clinical Trials: A Methodologic Perspective
PORT · Theoretical Probability for Applications
POURAHMADI · Foundations of Time Series Analysis and Prediction Theory
PRESS · Bayesian Statistics: Principles, Models, and Applications
PRESS · Subjective and Objective Bayesian Statistics, *Second Edition*
PRESS and TANUR · The Subjectivity of Scientists and the Bayesian Approach
PUKELSHEIM · Optimal Experimental Design
PURI, VILAPLANA, and WERTZ · New Perspectives in Theoretical and Applied Statistics
† PUTERMAN · Markov Decision Processes: Discrete Stochastic Dynamic Programming
QIU · Image Processing and Jump Regression Analysis
* RAO · Linear Statistical Inference and Its Applications, *Second Edition*
RAUSAND and HØYLAND · System Reliability Theory: Models, Statistical Methods, and Applications, *Second Edition*
RENCHER · Linear Models in Statistics
RENCHER · Methods of Multivariate Analysis, *Second Edition*
RENCHER · Multivariate Statistical Inference with Applications
* RIPLEY · Spatial Statistics
* RIPLEY · Stochastic Simulation
ROBINSON · Practical Strategies for Experimenting
ROHATGI and SALEH · An Introduction to Probability and Statistics, *Second Edition*
ROLSKI, SCHMIDLI, SCHMIDT, and TEUGELS · Stochastic Processes for Insurance and Finance
ROSENBERGER and LACHIN · Randomization in Clinical Trials: Theory and Practice
ROSS · Introduction to Probability and Statistics for Engineers and Scientists
ROSSI, ALLENBY, and McCULLOCH · Bayesian Statistics and Marketing
† ROUSSEEUW and LEROY · Robust Regression and Outlier Detection
* RUBIN · Multiple Imputation for Nonresponse in Surveys
RUBINSTEIN · Simulation and the Monte Carlo Method
RUBINSTEIN and MELAMED · Modern Simulation and Modeling
RYAN · Modern Regression Methods
RYAN · Statistical Methods for Quality Improvement, *Second Edition*
SALEH · Theory of Preliminary Test and Stein-Type Estimation with Applications
* SCHEFFE · The Analysis of Variance
SCHIMEK · Smoothing and Regression: Approaches, Computation, and Application
SCHOTT · Matrix Analysis for Statistics, *Second Edition*
SCHOUTENS · Levy Processes in Finance: Pricing Financial Derivatives
SCHUSS · Theory and Applications of Stochastic Differential Equations

---

*Now available in a lower priced paperback edition in the Wiley Classics Library.
†Now available in a lower priced paperback edition in the Wiley–Interscience Paperback Series.

*Now available in a lower priced paperback edition in the Wiley Classics Library.

†Now available in a lower priced paperback edition in the Wiley–Interscience Paperback Series.

WINKER · Optimization Heuristics in Economics: Applications of Threshold Accepting

WONNACOTT and WONNACOTT · Econometrics, *Second Edition*

WOODING · Planning Pharmaceutical Clinical Trials: Basic Statistical Principles

WOODWORTH · Biostatistics: A Bayesian Introduction

WOOLSON and CLARKE · Statistical Methods for the Analysis of Biomedical Data, *Second Edition*

WU and HAMADA · Experiments: Planning, Analysis, and Parameter Design Optimization

WU and ZHANG · Nonparametric Regression Methods for Longitudinal Data Analysis

YANG · The Construction Theory of Denumerable Markov Processes

ZELTERMAN · Discrete Distributions—Applications in the Health Sciences

* ZELLNER · An Introduction to Bayesian Inference in Econometrics

ZHOU, OBUCHOWSKI, and McCLISH · Statistical Methods in Diagnostic Medicine